THE NEW MIDDLE AGES

BONNIE WHEELER, *Series Editor*

The New Middle Ages is a series dedicated to transdisciplinary studies of medieval cultures, with particular emphasis on recuperating women's history and on feminist and gender analyses. This peer-reviewed series includes both scholarly monographs and essay collections.

PUBLISHED BY PALGRAVE:

Women in the Medieval Islamic World
    edited by Gavin R. G. Hambly

The Ethics of Nature in the Middle Ages: On Boccaccio's Poetaphysics
    by Gregory B. Stone

Presence and Presentation: Women in the Chinese Literati Tradition
    by Sherry J. Mou

The Lost Letters of Heloise and Abelard: Perceptions of Dialogue in Twelfth-Century France
    by Constant J. Mews

Understanding Scholastic Thought with Foucault
    by Philipp W. Rosemann

For Her Good Estate: The Life of Elizabeth de Burgh
    by Frances A. Underhill

Constructions of Widowhood and Virginity in the Middle Ages
    edited by Cindy L. Carlson and Angela Jane Weisl

Motherhood and Mothering in Anglo-Saxon England
    by Mary Dockray-Miller

Listening to Heloise: The Voice of a Twelfth-Century Woman
    edited by Bonnie Wheeler

The Postcolonial Middle Ages
    edited by Jeffrey Jerome Cohen

Chaucer's Pardoner and Gender Theory: Bodies of Discourse
    by Robert S. Sturges

Crossing the Bridge: Comparative Essays on Medieval European and Heian Japanese Women Writers
    edited by Barbara Stevenson and Cynthia Ho

Engaging Words: The Culture of Reading in the Later Middle Ages
    by Laurel Amtower

Robes and Honor: The Medieval World of Investiture
    edited by Stewart Gordon

Representing Rape in Medieval and Early Modern Literature
    edited by Elizabeth Robertson and Christine M. Rose

Same Sex Love and Desire among Women in the Middle Ages
    edited by Francesca Canadé Sautman and Pamela Sheingorn

Sight and Embodiment in the Middle Ages: Ocular Desires
    by Suzannah Biernoff

Listen, Daughter: The Speculum Virginum *and the Formation of Religious Women in the Middle Ages*
    edited by Constant J. Mews

Science, the Singular, and the Question of Theology
    by Richard A. Lee, Jr.

Gender in Debate from the Early Middle Ages to the Renaissance
    edited by Thelma S. Fenster and Clare A. Lees

Malory's Morte Darthur: *Remaking Arthurian Tradition*
by Catherine Batt

The Vernacular Spirit: Essays on Medieval Religious Literature
edited by Renate Blumenfeld-Kosinski, Duncan Robertson, and Nancy Warren

Popular Piety and Art in the Late Middle Ages: Image Worship and Idolatry in England 1350–1500
by Kathleen Kamerick

Absent Narratives, Manuscript Textuality, and Literary Structure in Late Medieval England
by Elizabeth Scala

Creating Community with Food and Drink in Merovingian Gaul
by Bonnie Effros

Representations of Early Byzantine Empresses: Image and Empire
by Anne McClanan

Encountering Medieval Textiles and Dress: Objects, Texts, Images
edited by Désirée G. Koslin and Janet Snyder

Eleanor of Aquitaine: Lord and Lady
edited by Bonnie Wheeler and John Carmi Parsons

Isabel La Católica, Queen of Castile: Critical Essays
edited by David A. Boruchoff

Homoeroticism and Chivalry: Discourses of Male Same-Sex Desire in the Fourteenth Century
by Richard E. Zeikowitz

Portraits of Medieval Women: Family, Marriage, and Politics in England 1225–1350
by Linda E. Mitchell

Eloquent Virgins: From Thecla to Joan of Arc
by Maud Burnett McInerney

The Persistence of Medievalism: Narrative Adventures in Contemporary Culture
by Angela Jane Weisl

Capetian Women
edited by Kathleen D. Nolan

Joan of Arc and Spirituality
edited by Ann W. Astell and Bonnie Wheeler

The Texture of Society: Medieval Women in the Southern Low Countries
edited by Ellen E. Kittell and Mary A. Suydam

Charlemagne's Mustache: And Other Cultural Clusters of a Dark Age
by Paul Edward Dutton

Troubled Vision: Gender, Sexuality, and Sight in Medieval Text and Image
edited by Emma Campbell and Robert Mills

Queering Medieval Genres
by Tison Pugh

Sacred Place in Early Medieval Neoplatonism
by L. Michael Harrington

The Middle Ages at Work
edited by Kellie Robertson and Michael Uebel

Chaucer's Jobs
by David R. Carlson

Medievalism and Orientalism
by John M. Ganim

Queer Love in the Middle Ages
by Anna Klosowska

Performing Women: Sex, Gender and the Iberian Lyric
by Denise K. Filios

Necessary Conjunctions: The Social Self in Medieval England
by David Gary Shaw

Visual Culture in the German Middle Ages
edited by Kathryn Starkey and
Horst Wenzel

*Medieval Paradigms: Essays in
Honor of Jeremy duQuesnay Adams,
Volumes 1 and 2*
edited by Stephanie Hayes-Healy

*False Fables and Exemplary Truth in Later
Middle English Literature*
by Elizabeth Allen

*Ecstatic Transformation: On the Uses of Alterity
in the Middle Ages*
by Michael Uebel

*Sacred and Secular in Medieval and Early
Modern Cultures: New Essays*
edited by Lawrence Besserman

Tolkien's Modern Middle Ages
edited by Jane Chance and Alfred K.
Siewers

*Representing Righteous Heathens in Late
Medieval England*
by Frank Grady

*Byzantine Dress: Representations
of Secular Dress in Eighth-to-Twelfth
Century Painting*
by Jennifer L. Ball

*The Laborer's Two Bodies: Labor and the
"Work" of the Text in Medieval Britain,
1350–1500*
by Kellie Robertson

*The Dogaressa of Venice, 1250–1500: Wife
and Icon*
by Holly S. Hurlburt

*Logic, Theology, and Poetry in Boethius,
Abelard, and Alan of Lille: Words in the
Absence of Things*
by Eileen Sweeney

*The Theology of Work: Peter Damian and the
Medieval Religious Movement*
by Patricia Ranft

*On the Purification of Women: Churching in
Northern France, 1100–1500*
by Paula Rieder

*Writers of the Reign of Henry II:
Twelve Essays*
edited by Ruth Kennedy and Simon
Meecham-Jones

*Lonesome Words: The Vocal Poetic
of the Old English Lament and the African
American Blues Songs*
by M.G. McGeachy

*Performing Piety: Musical Culture in Medieval
English Nunneries*
by Anne Bagnell Yardley

*The Flight from Desire: Augustine and Ovid to
Chaucer*
by Robert R. Edwards

*Mindful Spirit in Late Medieval
Literature: Essays in Honor
of Elizabeth D. Kirk*
edited by Bonnie Wheeler

*Medieval Fabrications: Dress, Textiles,
Clothwork, and Other Cultural Imaginings*
edited by E. Jane Burns

*Was the Bayeux Tapestry Made in France?:
The Case for St. Florent of Saumur*
by George Beech

*Women, Power, and Religious Patronage in the
Middle Ages*
by Erin L. Jordan

*Hybridity, Identity, and Monstrosity
in Medieval Britain: On Difficult
Middles*
by Jeremy Jerome Cohen

*Medieval Go-Betweens and Chaucer's
Pandarus*
by Gretchen Mieszkowski

*The Surgeon in Medieval
English Literature*
by Jeremy J. Citrome

Temporal Circumstances: Form and History in the Canterbury Tales
  by Lee Patterson

Erotic Discourse and Early English Religious Writing
  by Lara Farina

Odd Bodies and Visible Ends in Medieval Literature
  by Sachi Shimomura

On Farting: Language and Laughter in the Middle Ages
  by Valerie Allen

Women and Medieval Epic: Gender, Genre, and the Limits of Epic Masculinity
  edited by Sara S. Poor and Jana K. Schulman

Race, Class, and Gender in "Medieval" Cinema
  edited by Lynn T. Ramey and Tison Pugh

Allegory and Sexual Ethics in the High Middle Ages
  By Noah D. Guynn

England and Iberia in the Middle Ages, 12th–15th Century: Cultural, Literary, and Political Exchanges
  edited by María Bullón-Fernández

ENGLAND AND IBERIA IN THE MIDDLE AGES, 12TH – 15TH CENTURY

CULTURAL, LITERARY, AND POLITICAL EXCHANGES

Edited by María Bullón-Fernández

ENGLAND AND IBERIA IN THE MIDDLE AGES, 12TH–15TH CENTURY
© María Bullón-Fernández, 2007.

All rights reserved. No part of this book may be used or reproduced in any manner whatsoever without written permission except in the case of brief quotations embodied in critical articles or reviews.

First published in 2007 by
PALGRAVE MACMILLAN™
175 Fifth Avenue, New York, N.Y. 10010 and
Houndmills, Basingstoke, Hampshire, England RG21 6XS
Companies and representatives throughout the world.

PALGRAVE MACMILLAN is the global academic imprint of the Palgrave Macmillan division of St. Martin's Press, LLC and of Palgrave Macmillan Ltd. Macmillan® is a registered trademark in the United States, United Kingdom and other countries. Palgrave is a registered trademark in the European Union and other countries.

ISBN-13: 978–1–4039–7224–8
ISBN-10: 1–4039–7224–9

Library of Congress Cataloging-in-Publication Data
    England and Iberia in the Middle Ages, 12th–15th century : cultural, literary, and political exchanges / ed. María Bullón-Fernández.
      p. cm.—(New Middle Ages)
    Includes bibliographical references and index.
    ISBN 1–4039–7224–9 (alk. paper)
      1. Great Britain—Foreign relations—Spain. 2. Great Britain—Foreign relations—Portugal. 3. Spain—Foreign relations—Great Britain. 4. Portugal—Foreign relations—Great Britain. 5. Middle Ages—Intellectual life. 6. Great Britain—Intellectual life—1066–1485. 7. Spain—Intellectual life—711–1516. 8. Portugal—Intellectual life.
    I. Bullón-Fernández, María, 1965– II. Series: New Middle Ages (Palgrave Macmillan (Firm))

DA47.9.I2E54 2007
303.48′2420460902—dc22   2006044638

A catalogue record for this book is available from the British Library.

Design by Newgen Imaging Systems (P) Ltd., Chennai, India.

First edition: April 2007
10 9 8 7 6 5 4 3 2 1

Printed in the United States of America.

A mi padre Modesto Bullón Ramírez
(1919–2006)
In Memoriam

CONTENTS

List of Figures xi

Acknowledgments xiii

Introduction: Not All Roads Lead to Rome: Anglo-Iberian
Exchanges in the Middle Ages 1
María Bullón-Fernández

1 Medieval England and Iberia: A Chivalric Relationship 11
 Jennifer Goodman Wollock

2 British Influence in Medieval Catalan Writing: An Overview 29
 Lluís Cabré

3 The Shrine as Mediator: England, Castile,
 and the Pilgrimage to Compostela 47
 Ana Echevarría Arsuaga

4 Leonor of England and Eleanor of Castile: Anglo-Iberian
 Marriage and Cultural Exchange in the Twelfth and
 Thirteenth Centuries 67
 Rose Walker

5 A Castilian in King Edward's Court:
 The Career of Giles Despagne, 1313–27 89
 Cynthia L. Chamberlin

6 Anglo-Portuguese Trade during the Reign of João I
 of Portugal, 1385–1433 119
 Jennifer C. Geouge

7 Philippa of Lancaster, Queen of Portugal—and
 Patron of the Gower Translations? 135
 Joyce Coleman

8   "Os Doze de Inglaterra": A Romance of Anglo-Portuguese
    Relations in the Later Middle Ages?   167
    Amélia P. Hutchinson

9   Chaucer Translates the Matter of Spain   189
    R.F. Yeager

Contributors   215

Bibliography   217

Index   243

LIST OF FIGURES

4.1	Westminster Abbey, tomb of Eleanor of Castile	77
4.2	Las Huelgas, tombs of Alfonso VIII and Leonor of England (west)	78
4.3	Las Huelgas, tombs of Alfonso VIII and Leonor of England (east)	79
4.4	Burgos Cathedral, tomb of Díaz Peñafiel, figure of Mary from an Annunciation	81
7.1	Lancastrian and Anglo-Iberian alliances	138
7.2	Hypothetical reconstruction of Robert Payn's genealogy	153

ACKNOWLEDGMENTS

The idea for this collection of essays came from conversations I had with Antonio Cortijo Ocaña several years ago at the International Medieval Congress at Kalamazoo. My own work on John Gower, whose *Confessio Amantis* is probably the first major English literary work to be translated into another medieval vernacular, first Portuguese and then Castilian, made me acutely aware of the lack of research on Anglo-Iberian relations. Cortijo's own interest in late-medieval Spanish literature in an international context also made him aware of these gaps. I am indebted to him for his role in helping me envision this book. I am also grateful to the writers who have contributed their essays. As experts in their respective fields, they have read and commented on each others' essays, establishing a dialogue that has greatly strengthened the book. This has indeed been a collaborative project.

Several of the essays herein have been presented as earlier versions at a session on England and Iberia at the International Medieval Congress in 2003 as well as at two other sessions on the same topic at the International Medieval Congress in 2005. My colleague Theresa Earenfight was a co-organizer of the 2005 sessions; I wish to thank her for being an invaluable colleague and for her thoughtful suggestions and insights regarding Anglo-Iberian relations in the Middle Ages. I am also grateful to Bonnie Wheeler for believing in the importance of this project from the outset. For their generous editorial assistance I am thankful to Julia Cohen, Kristy Lilas, and Maran Elancheran. I have been fortunate to serve as Seattle University's Pigott-McCone Endowed Chair between 2004 and 2006. This opportunity has given me the time to devote myself to the book and I am thankful for it. Finally, I thank Angela for giving me perspective throughout this process and, especially, for her love and support.

I dedicate this book to my father, Modesto Bullón Ramírez, who passed away during the last stages of production. My academic vocation owes a great deal to him, as I learned from him the love and joy of reading literature and history.

INTRODUCTION

NOT ALL ROADS LEAD TO ROME:
ANGLO-IBERIAN EXCHANGES IN
THE MIDDLE AGES

María Bullón-Fernández

The Introduction explores some of the reasons for the dearth of research on Anglo-Iberian relations in the Middle Ages and introduces the essays in the volume.

From a geographical point of view, England (together with Ireland) and the Iberian Peninsula constituted, respectively, the Western and Southern borders, the geographical margins, of medieval Christendom and Europe. Beyond those borders was the dangerous "other" or the unknown for the Christian. Being on the edges of the Christian world, England and Iberia did not seem as important as Rome, the religious, although not exactly geographical, center, and, France, which was arguably a fundamental cultural and political center in the high and later Middle Ages. While Muslim Iberia played a vital cultural and intellectual role in the high Middle Ages, from the twelfth and thirteenth centuries on, partly due to the gradual defeat of the Muslims, intellectual activity became more important in other countries. Moreover, even if some medieval thinkers may have recognized the intellectual importance of Muslim Iberia, for most Europeans Iberia was a liminal area, the border where crusading activity took place; it was the margin of Europe that separated Christians and Muslims. Medieval England also seemed marginal. Englishmen themselves, as Nigel Saul has noted, did not see themselves as central: "[f]or most Englishmen of the day the places that gave meaning to their lives [Rome, Paris and Jerusalem] lay far from their shores."[1] It may be in part because of this "marginal" position that England and the Iberian kingdoms often, albeit not always, looked to the centers of Europe—France, the Church in Rome, and the Holy Roman Empire—for their alliances as well as for their rivalries. Partly for this reason too, medievalists themselves have focused primarily on the English and Iberian kingdoms' connections with these "centers" rather than on their attempts to connect with each other. However, the political and cultural traffic in the Middle Ages never used exclusively simple one-way roads between margins and centers. As the various pilgrimage routes themselves make it clear, the traffic proceeded along a much more complex system of roads which connected different kingdoms and peoples. Not all roads led to Rome. Sometimes the roads led from England to Iberia and vice versa.

Recognition of these more complex cultural and political traffic patterns, particularly regarding England and Iberia, has been slow to emerge among medievalists. At the beginning of the twentieth century, even as he recognized some Anglo-Iberian interactions in the Middle Ages, James Fitzmaurice-Kelly still argued that at that time there was an "almost complete insulation of [Spain and England] with regard to one another."[2] At the beginning of the twenty-first century few would agree with Fitzmaurice-Kelly. And yet work on England and Spain, or, more broadly, Iberia in the Middle Ages has been scant. In the first half of the twentieth century one monograph focused on medieval Spain and England, William J. Entwistle's *The Arthurian Legend in the Literatures of the Spanish Peninsula*.[3] Two other books, one looking at Anglo-Spanish and the second one at Anglo-Portuguese relations included some chapters on the medieval period, Martin Hume's *Spanish Influence on English Literature*, and a book of essays edited by Edgar Prestage, *Chapters in Anglo-Portuguese Relations*.[4] The most important works were written in the second half of the twentieth century: P.E. Russell's 1955 study, *The English Intervention in Spain and Portugal in the Time of Edward III and Richard II*, a comprehensive and detailed historical study of the political relations between Iberia and England in the second half of the fourteenth century; Alice E. Lasater's *Spain to England: A Comparative Study of Arabic, European, and English Literature of the Middle Ages*, a book that focuses on the influence of Hispano-Arabic culture on Middle English literature and was published in 1974; Wendy Childs's history monograph, *Anglo-Castilian Trade in the Middle Ages*, which centers on England and the kingdom of Castile; and Derek W. Lomax and R.J. Oakley's *The English in Portugal 1367–87*.[5] In addition, although he has not published a monograph on the topic, we need to make special mention of Anthony Goodman, one of the few scholars who have published several articles on English and Iberian relationships in the Middle Ages.[6] One can also find articles on specific aspects of Anglo-Iberian relationships—for instance, there are important essays on Geoffrey Chaucer's mission to Spain as well as on Juan Ruiz and Chaucer.[7] But such articles are few and far apart and, while providing us with important details on specific events, they do not allow us to consider those events in the broader context of Anglo-Iberian interactions.

The small number of studies on Anglo-Iberian relations in the Middle Ages contrasts with the relative abundance of studies on Spain, and to a lesser extent, Portugal, on the one hand, and England, on the other, in the Early Modern period. This is a topic that scholars have been more likely to turn to, partly for obvious reasons—at that time Spain, together with Portugal, was at the center of Western politics and expansion, and there was a more pronounced rivalry between the established and powerful Portuguese and Spanish empires, on the one hand, and the emergent English power, on the other. Thus, for instance, there are numerous history books and articles that examine various aspects of their military and political relations, especially of their naval rivalry.[8] Literary comparisons between England and Iberia also abound and there is also a monograph on artistic relations between Britain and Spain.[9] Whether literary, artistic, or historical, though, those works which examine Anglo-Iberian relationships in the Early Modern period do not usually turn to its immediate past, even though studies of the relationship between these powers *before* the Early Modern period can provide great insights into the Early Modern period itself.

Whatever the complex reasons for the relative dearth of research on England and Iberian relations in the Middle Ages, the present book aims to finally turn the tide. The essays that follow delve deeply into Anglo-Iberian relations in the Middle Ages in order to provide readers with a complex understanding of the relationship between England and Iberia in the Middle Ages, on the one hand, and the relationship between them and the rest of Europe, on the other. They also suggest further avenues of research in the area of Anglo-Iberian relations. This book also hopes to help put Anglo-Iberian relations in the Early Modern period in greater historical perspective. In the following pages I will outline the relationships between England and the Iberian kingdoms from the twelfth through the fifteenth centuries in order to provide a useful background to the essays that follow and will also introduce the essays themselves.

This collection of essays is interdisciplinary. It analyzes the relations between England and Iberia through the lenses of history, literature, and art history. It is also transnational in two senses. First, to the extent that one can speak about nations in the twelfth through the fifteenth centuries, it studies relationships between nations. Second, it puts in dialogue contemporary scholars from England, the United States, and Iberia. While Anglo-Iberian relationships in the Middle Ages is a broad topic, three restrictions will give the book particular coherence. First, rather than considering Britain as a whole, the essays generally concentrate on England's relationship with the Iberian kingdoms, leaving more detailed analyses of Scottish and Welsh connections for future studies. Second, while some of the essays draw our attention to Muslim Iberia, they focus on Christian Iberia, with the hope that others in the future will turn their attention to the connections between Muslim Iberia and England, an area of study that has great potential and which few scholars currently work on.[10] The disadvantage of this method is, of course, that important considerations have to be bracketed at this point. The advantage is that, despite the breadth of the topic, readers will be able both to see greater connections between the essays than would be possible if they covered a wider range of issues and will also be able to consider some specific issues or events from more than one perspective.

Finally, the third restriction is chronological. The essays cover a span from the twelfth to the fifteenth centuries. This chronological demarcation allows us to focus on the English and Iberian kingdoms at a time when they began more insistently to look outward to other countries in Europe, and thus to each other, in order to build alliances and exert influence beyond their own borders. In the words of Anthony Goodman, "[i]n the twelfth century, convergent Iberian and northern European interests created the first significant and enduring links between the Peninsula and England."[11] Before 1066 the various Anglo-Saxon kingdoms were primarily interested in defending and expanding their territories within the British Isles, while between the first Muslim invasions and the twelfth century the Iberian Christian kingdoms devoted themselves to fighting the Muslims in Iberia. Starting in the twelfth century, once England was dominated initially by the Norman aristocracy and later by Anglo-Norman rulers, and once the Iberian kingdoms had made very significant inroads against the Muslims, they became more interested in each other. Thus it is between the twelfth and fifteenth centuries that one can see an intensification of the relations between Medieval England and Iberia.

The first three essays in the collection are general overviews spanning the twelfth through the fifteenth centuries thus setting the stage for the more detailed studies that follow. The first essay, "Medieval England and Iberia: A Chivalric Relationship" by Jennifer Goodman Wollock, provides us with a general examination of the circulation of chivalric poems and narratives between England and Iberia as well as of exchanges among historical knights and royal family members. The second essay, "British Influence in Medieval Catalan Writing: An Overview" by Lluís Cabré, examines the circulation of writings focusing, more specifically, on British and Catalan writings. The third essay, Ana Echevarría Arsuaga's "The Shrine as Mediator: England, Castile, and the Pilgrimage to Compostela," analyzes the English pilgrimage to Santiago de Compostela, which became especially popular from the twelfth century on and was second only to Canterbury as a major destination for medieval English pilgrims. From the twelfth through the fifteenth centuries the "camino de Santiago" provided a major venue for interactions and exchanges between England and Iberia.

The essays that follow these three opening studies are arranged chronologically, starting with the twelfth century. As noted, from the point of view of royal alliances and politics, the twelfth century saw an increasing Anglo-Norman interest in Iberia and, particularly, Castile. A main reason for this interest, Anthony Goodman notes, was the Angevin rule over Aquitaine, a duchy which bordered with Navarre and Aragon and which was a major source of tension between France and England.[12] As part of the increasing collaboration between England and Castile, Henry II married his daughter Leonor to Alfonso VIII in 1176.[13] This marriage had a wide range of implications. Chapter 4 in this book, Rose Walker's "Leonor of England and Leonor of Castile: Anglo-Iberian Marriage and Cultural Exchange in the Twelfth and Thirteenth Centuries," examines the importance of their marriage and its influence on Anglo-Iberian exchanges from a cultural and art historical perspective—for instance, the convent of Las Huelgas was founded by Eleanor and Alfonso VIII. Walker also examines a later Anglo-Iberian royal marriage which was similarly connected with Las Huelgas: Henry III's son, the future Edward I, married Alfonso X's sister, Eleanor, probably at the convent in 1254. As Anthony Goodman notes, particularly this latter marriage shows that England was starting to see that "[t]he *Reconquista* by Castile and Aragon, gathering pace from the 1230s, made them undisputedly the great powers of the Iberian Peninsula."[14] In 1254, moreover, Henry III and Alfonso X signed the crucial Treaty of Toledo, which put an end to Alfonso's claims over Aquitaine, and which, as Goodman explains, "[bound] them and their successors in a close family alliance."[15] These contacts between Henry III, Alfonso X, Edward I and Eleanor, also resulted in major cultural and diplomatic exchanges between England and Castile that need to be explored further. Although Goodman argues that Edward II did not show great interest in Iberia until his dispute with France over Gascony, chapter 5 in this collection, Cynthia L. Chamberlin's "A Castilian in King Edward's Court: The Career of Giles Despagne, 1313–1327," demonstrates, through an analysis of the career of a Castilian courtier in Edward II's court, that this king did use his important Castilian connections before the dispute with France.[16]

The last four essays study different aspects of Anglo-Iberian relations during the reign of his son Edward III and his grandson Richard II. Whereas Edward II used his Castilian connections, his son Edward III promoted a more direct involvement and interventionist policy in Castilian and, generally, in Iberian affairs as he also sought alliances with Portugal, Navarre, and Aragon. During Edward III's reign and later during the reign of his grandson, Richard II, we see perhaps the most intense period in Anglo-Iberian relationships in the Late Middle Ages. Edward III's son, the Black Prince, intervened in the dynastic dispute between Pedro I and Enrique of Trastámara, taking sides with Pedro. After defeating Enrique, Pedro and the Black Prince's alliance faltered. The Black Prince considered himself betrayed by Pedro I and ultimately the latter was killed in 1369 by his brother Enrique who went on to found the Trastámara dynasty and rule as Enrique II. Two years later, in 1371, the English continued their interventionist policy through the marriage of John of Gaunt, also son of Edward III, to Constance, the daughter of Pedro I, with a view to enabling Gaunt to claim the throne of Castile. Gaunt subsequently did so and made war against Castile with the help of Portugal. He had ensured the help of Portugal by first marrying his daughter Philippa to King João I. When Gaunt failed in his attempt to become king of Castile, he changed his tactic in order to continue to have an influence on Iberian politics: he married his daughter Catherine to Enrique, the heir of Juan I, king of Castile, who had succeeded Enrique II. Enrique subsequently became Enrique III of Castile and Catherine became a powerful Castilian queen.[17] Probably due to the intensification of the relationship between the English and the Portuguese and Castilian courts which resulted from these royal marriages, a major Middle English work, John Gower's *Confessio Amantis*, was translated in the first few decades of the fifteenth century first into Portuguese by an Englishman who lived in the Portuguese court, Robert Payn, and then from Portuguese into Castilian by a Castilian author, Juan de Cuenca. These translations, the first known of a major English literary work into any Continental language, suggest the richness of the relationship that was developing between the English and the Iberian kingdoms at the end of the fourteenth century.

Three of the last four essays in this book focus on Portugal and the last one on Castile during this particularly crucial period for Anglo-Iberian relations. In "Anglo-Portuguese Trade during the Reign of João I of Portugal (1385–1433)," Jennifer C. Geouge studies a significant aspect of the Anglo-Portuguese alliance, the intensification of trade between the two countries at the end of the fourteenth and beginning of the fifteenth centuries. The following essay, Joyce Coleman's "Philippa of Lancaster, Queen of Portugal—and Patron of the Gower Translations?" explores the role of Philippa of Lancaster as queen of Portugal, her relationship with her brother Henry IV, and her role as patron of cultural and literary productions, including possibly the Gower translations. Amélia P. Hutchinson's

" 'Os Doze de Inglaterra': A Romance of Anglo-Portuguese Relations in the Later Middle Ages?" examines Anglo-Portuguese relations through a supposedly historical incident which gave rise to the legend of "Os Doze de Inglaterra." This legend was recounted in different romance versions and became very popular in the Late Middle Ages and in the Early Modern period, particularly in Portugal. Finally, the collection ends with R.F. Yeager's essay, "Chaucer Translates the Matter of Spain." Chaucer lived during the reigns of Edward III and Richard II. He seems to have participated actively in the Black Prince's campaign, even traveling to Spain on, probably, a diplomatic mission. Chaucer's trip to Spain and his involvement with some of the Anglo-Castilian political issues of his time explain to an extent his interest on what the essay calls the "Matter of Spain." But, as Yeager argues, we also need to understand his interest more broadly and both compare Chaucer's work with works by Spanish authors such as the Archpriest of Hita's *Libro de Buen Amor*, as some scholars have done, as well as study the likely influence of other Spanish works such as Petrus Alfonsi's *Disciplina clericalis* or Don Juan Manuel's *El Conde Lucanor*.

The exchanges between England and Iberia had much to do with royal policies and with royal alliances through marriages. However, as the essays in this book show, the exchanges did not happen solely at the level of the royal court and did not solely affect royal members and royal policies. English and Iberian people who may or may not have had significant political power also engaged with each other for religious, economic, intellectual, and literary reasons. Whether the relationships and exchanges happened at higher or at lower levels of society, England and Iberia were, thus, far from insulated from each other. As medievalists as well as scholars of other periods increasingly question notions of national and geographic boundaries and pay greater attention to the mixing of peoples, it is particularly timely to turn to this area of study. Recent work on globalization and postcolonial criticism, which does not often enough consider the time before the nineteenth century, is having an increasingly strong impact on the work of medievalists.[18] This book is inspired by such work and hopes to contribute to considering European interactions in the Middle Ages from a more multidimensional viewpoint than traditionally employed. Work on nation-building has shown that nations emerge out of complex processes of formation that are never "pure." No one homogeneous group of people ever was the only one to constitute a nation. Peoples and cultures from different backgrounds have always mixed in these processes. Although nations have often constructed their identity on the basis of a discourse that excludes others and tries to define the nation against those others, this does not mean that such exclusions did actually take place, at least to the extent that the rhetoric suggests. And it is incumbent upon us to ask questions about such rhetoric and to examine the different ways in which peoples and nations interacted and influenced each other, even when it seems that they did not.

England and Iberia in the Middle Ages, 12th–15th Century examines then the "mixing" between the English and Iberian kingdoms. As mentioned above, two of its aims are to expand our knowledge of Anglo-Iberian relationships and to encourage further study by suggesting new avenues of research. More broadly, this book hopes to encourage medievalists to begin to connect cultures and nations, like those of England and Iberia, which, until now, have been but sketchily associated at best. For it is fundamental to understand the myriad ways in which cultures came in contact in the past, not only in order to understand the past but in order to understand our present as well. This book will hopefully foster dialogue between the English world and the various cultures and nations of the Iberian Peninsula. Particularly in the United States, as Spanish becomes the second national language, one expects that an interest in the historical connections between the English and the Spanish worlds will increase significantly. In Europe the gradually more profound integration among nations fostered by the European Union also calls on us to pay renewed attention to the historical relations among them.[19] The essays' authors, coming from the English, American, and Iberian worlds, showcase the wide scope and diverse issues that concerned the relationships between England and Iberia and also suggest the great potential of this interdisciplinary and dynamic area of research in the field of Medieval Studies.

Notes

1. Nigel Saul, "England and Europe: Problems and Possibilities," in *England in Europe, 1066–1453*, ed. Nigel Saul (New York: St. Martin's Press, 1994), pp. 10–11 [9–20].
2. James Fitzmaurice-Kelly, "Some Correlations of Spanish Literature," *Revue Hispanique* 15 (1906): 73 [58–85].
3. William J. Entwistle, *The Arthurian Legend in the Literatures of the Spanish Peninsula* (London: J.M. Dent, 1925; repr., New York: Phaeton Press, 1975).
4. Martin A.S. Hume, *Spanish Influence on English Literature* (London: Nash, 1905; repr., New York: Haskell House, 1964); Edgar Prestage, ed., *Chapters in Anglo-Portuguese Relations* (Watford: Voss and Michael, 1935; repr., Westport, CT: Greenwood Press, 1971).
5. P.E. Russell, *The English Intervention in Spain and Portugal in the Time of Edward III and Richard II* (Oxford: Clarendon Press, 1955); Alice E. Lasater, *Spain to England: A Comparative Study of Arabic, European, and English Literature of the Middle Ages* (Jackson: University Press of Mississippi, 1974); Wendy R. Childs, *Anglo-Castilian Trade in the later Middle Ages* (Manchester: Manchester

University Press, 1978); Derek W. Lomax and R.J. Oakley, *The English in Portugal 1367–87* (Warminster: Aris & Phillips, 1988). See also by Wendy R. Childs, "Anglo-Portuguese Trade in the Fifteenth Century," *Transactions of the Royal Historical Society*, 6th ser., 2 (1992): 195–219.
6. See Anthony Goodman, "Before the Armada: Iberia and England in the Middle Ages," in Saul, *England in Europe*, pp. 108–20; "England and Iberia in the Middle Ages," in *England and Her Neighbours, 1066–1453: Essays in Honour of Pierre Chaplais*, ed. Michael Jones and Malcolm Vale (London: Hambledon Press, 1989), pp. 73–96; and "Sentiment and Policy: English Attitudes toward Spain in the Later Middle Ages," in *Estudios sobre Málaga y el reino de Granada en el V Centenario de la Conquista*, ed. J.E. López de Coca (Málaga: Diputación Provincial, 1987), pp. 73–81.
7. See, for instance, Albert C. Baugh, "The Background of Chaucer's Mission to Spain," in *Chaucer und seine Zeit: Symposion für Walter F. Schirmer*, ed. Arno Esch (Tübingen: Max Niemeyer Verlag, 1968), pp. 55–69; Haldeen Braddy, "The Two Petros in the 'Monkes Tale,' " *PMLA* 50 (1935): 69–80, and "Chaucer's Don Pedro and the Purpose of the 'Monk's Tale,' " *Modern Language Quarterly* 13 (1952): 3–5; Thomas Jay Garbáty, "Chaucer in Spain, 1366: Soldier of Fortune or Agent of the Crown?" *English Language Notes* 5 (1967): 81–87; and Benjamin F. Taggie, "John of Gaunt, Geoffrey Chaucer and 'O Noble, O Worthy Petro, Glorie of Spayne,' " *Fifteenth-Century Studies* 10 (1984): 195–228. See also chapter 9 in this volume, "Chaucer Translates the Matter of Spain." For a recent survey of works comparing Chaucer and Juan Ruiz, see Eugenio M. Olivares Merino, "Juan Ruiz's Influence on Chaucer Revisited: A Survey," *Neophilologus* 88 (2004): 145–61.
8. Among some of the more relatively recent books on England and the Spanish and Portuguese naval powers, see, for instance, Carlos Gómez Centurión, *La Invencible y la empresa de Inglaterra* (Madrid: Nerea, 1988); James McDermott, *A Necessary Quarrel: England and the Spanish Armada* (New Haven: Yale University Press, 2005); Víctor Morales Lezcano, *Relaciones entre Inglaterra y los archipiélagos del Atlántico Ibérico* (La Laguna: Instituto de Estudios Canarios, 1970); R.B. Wernham, *Expedition of Sir John Norris and Sir Francis Drake to Spain and Portugal, 1589* (Aldershot, Hants: Temple Smith, 1988), and also by Wernham, *The Return of the Armadas: The Last Years of the Elizabethan War Against Spain, 1595–1603* (Oxford: Oxford University Press, 1994). Books that center on other aspects of Anglo-Iberian political relations are, for instance, Manuel Fernández Alvarez, *Tres embajadores de Felipe II en Inglaterra* (Madrid: Instituto Jerónimo Zurita, 1951); William S. Maltby, *La leyenda negra en Inglaterra: Desarrollo del sentimiento anti-hispánico, 1558–1660* (México: Fondo de Cultura Económica, 1982); Glyn Redworth, *The Prince and the Infanta: The Cultural Politics of the Spanish Match* (New Haven: Yale University Press, 2003).
9. Some relatively recent studies on Anglo-Iberian literary relations include Jonathan Brown and John Elliott, eds., *The Sale of the Century: Artistic Relations between Spain and Great Britain (1604–1655)* (New Haven: Yale University Press, 2002); Walter Cohen, *Drama of a Nation: Public Theater in*

Renaissance England and Spain (Ithaca: Cornell University Press, 1985); Hillaire Kallendorf, ed., *Exorcism and Its Texts: Subjectivity in Early Modern Literature of England and Spain* (Toronto: University of Toronto Press, 2003); John Loftis, *Renaissance Drama in England and Spain: Topical Allusions and History Plays* (Princeton: Princeton University Press, 1987). For an earlier comparative study, see Hilda Urén Stubbings, *Renaissance Spain in Its Literary Relations with England: A Critical Bibliography* (Nashville: Vanderbilt University Press, 1969).

10. Lasater's *Spain to England* is one of the exceptions, as is Thomas E. Burnam, "*Tafsīr* and Translation: Traditional Arabic Qur'ān Exegesis and the Latin Qur'āns of Robert of Ketto and Mark of Toledo," *Speculum* 73 (1998): 703–32.
11. Goodman, "Before the Armada," p. 108.
12. See Goodman, "Before the Armada," p. 109, and "England and Iberia in the Middle Ages," p. 75.
13. Historians differ on whether to refer to Leonor of England and Eleanor of Castile by the native form of their first names or by the form used in the conuntries over which they reigned. In this book we are following the latter convention since we are writing about them primarily as queens of their adoptive countries rather than as princesses in their countries of origin. Thus throughout this book Leonor of England is the daughter of Henry II of England and wife of Alfonso VIII of Castile, and Eleanor of Castile is the daughter of Fernando III of Leon and Castile and wife of Edward I of England.
14. Goodman, "Before the Armada," p. 109.
15. Goodman, "Before the Armada," p. 110.
16. Goodman, "Before the Armada," p. 113 and "England and Iberia," pp. 83–84.
17. For an analysis of Catherine's important role in Castilian politics, see Ana Echevarría, "Catalina of Lancaster, the Castilian Monarchy and Coexistence," in *Medieval Spain: Culture, Conflict and Coexistence: Studies in Honour of Angus MacKay*, ed. Roger Collins and Anthony Goodman (Houndsmills: Palgrave, 2002), pp. 79–122.
18. See, for instance, Jeffrey Jerome Cohen, ed., *The Postcolonial Middle Ages* (New York: Palgrave, 2001). First published in 2000 by St. Martin's Press.
19. In his "Preface" to *England in Europe* Saul makes a similar point (pp. 7–8).

CHAPTER 1

MEDIEVAL ENGLAND AND IBERIA:
A CHIVALRIC RELATIONSHIP

Jennifer Goodman Wollock

This essay surveys the history of Anglo-Iberian chivalric encounters from the early Middle Ages through the sixteenth century.

In the course of the later Middle Ages, England and the Iberian Peninsula developed a lively chivalric relationship that has left its mark on world history and culture. Through crusades, dynastic marriages, tournaments, romances, and visual artifacts, knights and aristocrats of the British Isles and Iberia built up a tradition of chivalric collaboration and rivalry. In *Chivalry and Exploration, 1298–1630*, I sketch the connection from the fourteenth through the sixteenth centuries.[1] This essay explores the dimensions of this dynamic Anglo-Iberian chivalric relationship in more detail in the context of European cultural geography within and beyond the medieval period.

Crusades

The earliest Iberian military connection with Britain involves Roman legions in the province of Britannia, among them the ill-fated Ninth Hispana, an object of historical speculation since its disappearance in 117 CE while quelling a tribal revolt in Scotland.[2]

Anglo-Iberian military contact entered a new phase in 1112, when English and Scottish crusaders bound for Jerusalem stopped off in Spain and Portugal to assist the Reconquista. Clerical arguments (from 1123 to 1124 on) equated the reconquest of Spain with the voyage to Jerusalem.[3] One valuable eyewitness account, *De expugnatione Lynxbonensi*, describes the British role in the expedition against Lisbon of October 1147, the one major success of the Second Crusade. The attack is justified in speeches by the authorities on the scene. The bishop of Oporto tells the English and Scottish crusaders "The praiseworthy thing is not to have been to Jerusalem, but to have lived a good life while on the way." He then promises them an earthly reward in the form of plunder. One of the English leaders, the East Anglian Hervey of Glanvill, appeals to their sense of honor and unity, and an unidentified priest (possibly the author himself, in all probability Hervey of Glanvill's chaplain) leads them in a renewal of their crusading vows and urges confession, repentance, and the confidence that anyone who died "signed with this cross" would go to heaven. The English went on to Jerusalem afterward, to be on the safe side.[4]

From this point on, English and Scottish crusaders can be found fighting Islamic opponents alongside Castilians and Portuguese. As late as 1578, the swashbuckling English recusant sea-captain Sir Thomas Stukeley (ca. 1525–78) died alongside King Sebastian of Portugal at the Battle of Alcazar-Quivir. Earlier he had commanded three galleys at the battle of Lepanto under Don Juan of Austria, and hatched various schemes against Elizabeth I in collaboration with Philip II of Spain. Stukeley became the hero of two English plays, George Peele's *The Battel of Alcazar. . .with the Death of Captain Stukely* (London: E. Allde, 1594), which dramatizes his final expedition, and the more comprehensive anonymous play *The Famous History of the Life and Death of Captain Thomas Stukeley* (London: printed for Thomas Panyer, 1605), as well as numerous ballads. For his English contemporaries Stukeley was a heroic figure in the mold of "Mohamet, Tamburlaine, and Charlemagne."[5]

The best-remembered British chivalric event in Iberia may be the death of Sir James Douglas (1286–1330), Robert Bruce's friend, fighting alongside the forces of Alfonso XI "the Righteous" (or, elsewhere, alternatively, "the Implacable") of Castile (1311–50) against Mohammed IV of Granada's Nazari troops at Teba in Málaga, as Douglas was carrying Bruce's heart to the Holy Land. The incident is recorded in John Barbour's *Bruce* of 1375.[6] Bruce had specified on his deathbed that since he was unable to undertake a crusade as penance for the deaths of the innocent in the course of his military career, his heart should be carried into battle against "the enemies of God." Barbour describes Douglas's reception by King Alfonso:

> The King Alfons him eftre send
> And hym rycht weill ressavyt he
> And perofferyt him in gret plente
> Gold and tresour hors and armyng,
> Bot he wald tak tharoff na thing

> For he said he tuk that vaiage
> To pas intill pilgramage
> On Goddis fayis, that his travaill
> Mycht till his saule hele avail.
> . . . .
> The king him thankyt curtasly
> And betaucht him gud men that war
> Weill knawyn of that landis wer. . . . .[7]

Barbour describes Douglas's friendly relations with Spaniards and knights of other nations in Spanish service, especially the English. When word arrives that the "high king of Belmeryne" has invaded with intent to conquer the entire country, King Alfonso gives Douglas charge of the vanguard. Douglas's speech to his troops is reported: he tells them "To do weill and na deid to dred, / For hevynnys blys suld be thar mede / Gyff that thai deyt in Goddis service."[8] After a successful advance, Douglas finds himself cut off from the main army. When he sees his friend Sir William Sinclair surrounded by Saracens he charges to the rescue. Both Douglas and Sinclair are killed, leaving the remaining Scots to mourn their loss.[9] Barbour records the sympathy expressed by King Alfonso as he gives them leave to return home.[10] In later works Douglas is represented as hurling Bruce's heart in its silver casket into the midst of the Moorish ranks and riding after it, supplied with a variety of stirring war cries ("After you, Brave Heart!").

The English offered their own high-ranking delegation to Alfonso XI. In May 1343, Edward III sent Henry of Grosmont, earl of Derby (later first duke of Lancaster) and William Montague, earl of Salisbury, to negotiate a naval treaty with Castile. The English ambassadors fought under Alfonso's banner at the siege of Algeciras—an expedition described as fighting "the enemies of God and the Christian." According to the Castilian chronicler, the English had come "for the salvation of their souls, as well as to get to know the king."[11] In Granada they would have encountered Alfonso's Order of the Band (la Banda) of 1330, the earliest known secular monarchical order of chivalry. This innovative organization seems to have been designed to enlist the younger sons of nobles into the king's service. Richard Barber suggests that their accounts of this new Castilian fellowship of knights, with its striking emblem—the black or (later) gold strip of cloth the selected knights wore as a badge—may have inspired Edward III's attempts to found an order of his own, leading eventually to the establishment of the Order of the Garter.[12] Lancaster and Salisbury were the first English knights to take the Garter oath in 1344. Henry of Lancaster, who also took part in one of the Teutonic Knights' expeditions against the still pagan Lithuanians in Prussia, and who wrote an Anglo-Norman spiritual autobiography, *Le Livre de Seyntz Medicines*, was one of the patterns of fourteenth-century English chivalry. (He was also the father-in-law of John of Gaunt, Chaucer's patron.) Algeciras is included on the itinerary of Chaucer's knight in the *Canterbury Tales*: "In Gernade at the seege eek hadde he be / Of Algezir."[13]

Englishmen, particularly seamen, participated in the 1415 Portuguese expedition of João I and his sons against Ceuta in North Africa, and in later-fifteenth-century combats against the Moors in Spain. (As noted in chapter 8 in this collection, English archers had also aided the Portuguese against the Castilians at Aljubarrota in 1385.) When the printer William Caxton's patron Anthony Woodville, Earl Rivers, requested permission from his brother-in-law Edward IV to go on an Iberian crusade, he was rebuffed with the comment that this was a cowardly attempt to avoid responsibilities in the king's service closer to home. Rivers went on pilgrimage to Compostela anyway. The preface to his translation of *The Dicts and Sayengs of the Philosophres* published by Caxton describes his shipboard conversation with a French knight in his entourage. In his *Conquest of Granada*, Washington Irving claimed to be translating one Fray Antonio Agapida's description of an English contingent led by a second Woodville brother, Richard Woodville, Lord Scales and Earl Rivers, the only brother of Henry VII's queen Elizabeth of York to survive the Wars of the Roses, at the siege of Granada in 1492. Agapida, it emerges, is a character of Irving's own invention, somewhat along the lines of the same author's better-known fictional historian Diedrich Knickerbocker of *The History of New York*.[14] Irving explained twenty years later that "Agapida was intended as a personification of the monkish zealots, who hovered about the sovereigns in their campaigns, marring the chivalry of the camp by the bigotry of the cloister, and chronicling in rapturous strains every act of intolerance towards the Moors." Nevertheless Irving's historical research is solid. Much of the material ascribed to Agapida is translated from reputable historians of the fifteenth and sixteenth centuries—in this case from Andres Bernaldez (cited in Irving as Cura de los Palacios), Pulgar, and Peter Martyr.[15] Irving's description of Lord Scales and his entourage is notable for its detail and for its remarks on the Spanish view of their fifteenth-century English counterparts—which may upon further research turn out to be Irving's own nineteenth-century contribution:

> This cavalier was from the far island of England, and brought with him a train of his vassals: men who had been hardened in certain civil wars which raged in their country. They were a comely race of men but too fair and fresh for warriors, not having the sun-burnt warlike hue of our old Castilian

soldiery. They were huge feeders also, and deep carousers, and could not accommodate themselves to the sober diet of our troops, but must fain eat and drink after the manner of their own country. They were often noisy and unruly, also, in their wassail, and their quarter of the camp was prone to be a scene of loud revel and sudden brawl. They were, withal, of great pride, yet it was not like our inflammable Spanish pride; they stood not much upon the *pundonor*, the high punctilio, and rarely drew the stiletto in their disputes; but their pride was silent and contumelious. Though from a remote and somewhat barbarous island, they believed themselves the most perfect men upon earth, and magnified their chieftain, the lord Scales, beyond the greatest of their grandees. With all this, it must be said of them that they were marvellous good men in the field, dexterous archers, and powerful with the battle-axe...Withal they were much esteemed yet little liked by our soldiery, who considered them staunch companions in the field, but coveted little fellowship with them in the camp.

Their commander, the lord Scales, was an accomplished cavalier, of gracious and noble presence and fair speech: it was a marvel to see so much courtesy in a knight brought up so far from our Castilian court. He was much honored by the king and queen, and found great favor with the fair dames about the court, who indeed are rather prone to be pleased with foreign cavaliers.[16]

Irving cites Bernaldez on the martial exploits of Lord Scales, who leads the charge that captures a suburb at Loxa, losing two front teeth in the process, and who later appears in procession directly behind King Ferdinand.[17] Until Irving's sources can be further traced it will remain difficult to disentangle the history from the satire in this fascinating and historically exasperating work, which is itself a notable artifact in the history of Anglo-Iberian chivalric relations and their extension to the Americas.

The traffic was not all one way. In the fifteenth century, Spanish ships raided the English coast. Don Pero Niño, "the Unconquered Knight," as his chivalric biography *El Victorial* describes him, led one such expedition to Cornwall in 1405, sacking Plymouth, Portland, and Poole in support of Castile's French allies, represented on this occasion by Messire Charles de Savoisy, a somewhat disgraced former cupbearer of Charles VI. During their descent on the island of Portland the Castilians express some chivalrous qualms, awakened by the obvious poverty of the English villagers. Diego de Games, Don Pero Niño's retainer and biographer, ruminates in this context on "why the English are different from all other nations."[18]

> The English are folk very diverse in character and different from all other nations...They have no wish to live in peace with any other nation, for peace suits them not, seeing they are so numerous that they cannot keep within their country and in time of peace many cannot find subsistence

there...They have a liking for no other nation, and if it happen that some valiant knight visits them...the English try to seek some way of dishonouring them or of offering them an affront.[19]

Don Pero Niño, fresh from pursuing Barbary corsairs in the Mediterranean, should be seen as a transitional figure linking crusade and armada. Though Diego Games agrees with the French in characterizing the English as "this evil nation," he does not portray his lord's depredations against the English as a crusade, but his words and actions show a decided tilt in this direction.

The English also complained about the Spaniards. Richard Barber cites Jean Froissart on the earl of Pembroke's captivity in Spain in 1372: "They conducted their prisoners to a strong castle and fastened them with iron chains according to their usual custom: for the Spaniards know not how to show courtesy to their prisoners."[20] Whether this observation represents English or French opinion is unclear. (As Barber notes, the Germans receive similar criticism in Froissart.) It may reflect the nature of Reconquest as frontier warfare at a time of increasing religious polarization. Fighting against opponents of another faith may have influenced certain commanders' practices, contravening the established rules of chivalrous warfare elsewhere.

Perkin Warbeck, one of the pretenders to the English throne who vexed Henry VII in the 1490s, first surfaces in the service of a Sir Edward Brampton (Duarte Brandão), a Portuguese Jewish convert knighted by Richard III. (Brampton's first name suggests that Edward IV must have stood godfather when he was baptized.) Warbeck, who according to his confession served as a page to the eminent and somewhat notorious one-eyed knight Pero Vaz de Cunha at the Portuguese court between 1487 and 1491, claimed to be Edward IV's younger son Richard, and applied for Iberian military support in a letter to Queen Isabella in 1493.[21] But Warbeck's attempt to reconquer England for the house of York was a crusade that Iberia would ignore.

The idea of the crusade remained powerful in both England and Iberia to the end of the sixteenth century and beyond. Henry VIII was much involved in projecting crusades against the Turks in the company of his nephew, Charles V, and as we have seen, Sir Thomas Stukeley joined more than one celebrated expedition against Islamic opponents in the later sixteenth century.

After their return to Protestantism with the accession of Elizabeth I the English themselves became the object of Spanish crusading enterprises. In 1588 Sixtus V's bull equated Philip II's projected invasion of England with an expedition against the Turks or to the Holy Land. On April 25 the

Banner of the Armada was blessed in the cathedral of Lisbon.[22] At the same time, English volunteers set out to fight Spain in support of the rebellious Netherlands in much the same spirit of crusading chivalry. The history of the influence of the crusades is in fact much larger than their official history would indicate. For the chivalric relationship between England and Iberia the crusade remains the central paradigm, though by no means the only pattern of chivalric interaction available.

Dynastic Warfare

In the late 1300s the sons of Edward III of England became entangled in a connected series of Iberian dynastic conflicts. Pedro the Cruel was restored to the throne of Castile by his ally Edward the Black Prince after his illegitimate brother Henry of Trastamara and his French allies had driven him into exile. Among the treasures Pedro may have promised (and failed to deliver to) his English allies was an artifact straight out of romance: "a gold table with hinges of fine gold, bordered with many stones of the Orient. On azure and blood-red enamel, Roland and Oliver fought the Moors. In the center glittered a carbuncle of such great virtue that it shone at midnight as the sun does at noon. Its fire had guided the fugitive king by night through the forests and sierras. Lastly, this magic stone also had the property of becoming as black as coal if any evil-working poison was served on the table."[23]

This conflict became an extension of the Hundred Years' War, with the French constable Bertrand du Guesclin opposing the Black Prince in Spain as in France. It also figures as an Iberian crusade of sorts: Bertrand du Guesclin and his men (including a number of English knights and soldiers of fortune, members of the notorious Great Company) wore white crosses when they set off on their expedition of 1366 in support of Henry of Trastamara, and applied for permission to enter Spain as crusaders on their way to fight the Moors of Granada.[24] They had in fact obtained papal sanction at Avignon for their project of deposing Pedro: Pope Urban V was anxious to see these rapacious mercenaries depart on any foreign mission he could persuade them to undertake. Henry of Trastamara and his allies encouraged the rumor that Pedro was a Jewish changeling allied with the Moslems, and the pope classified him as an infidel:

> And besyde all this, ther ran a brute of hym among his owne men, howe that he was amyably alyed with the kynge of Grenade, and with the kyng of Tresbell Maryne (Belmarin—Morocco), and the kyng of Tresmesaries (Tlemcen), who wer all Goddes enemyes and infydeles. . . . Than advyse and counsell was taken by the Pope, and by the coledge, what waye they might

correct hym, and ther it was determyned, that he was nat worthy to bere the name of a kynge, nor to holde any realme. And there in playne consistory in Avygnon, in the chambre of excommunycacion, he was openly declared an infidell.[25]

Pedro fled to his English allies who returned him to power the following year, defeating Henry at the battle of Nájera on April 3, 1367. It was while waiting in vain for payment that the Black Prince contracted the dysentery that plagued him until his death in 1376. Two years later Henry returned with some of the same French allies, and this time he succeeded in capturing and killing Pedro. Froissart reports that on March 23, 1369, when Henry of Trastamara burst into the room where his captive half-brother was being held, he was shouting "Where's that Jewish son of a whore who calls himself king of Castile?"[26]

In Chaucer's *Monk's Tale* Pedro of Castile figures as a tragic hero, and the French knights who captured him as despicable traitors, in the tradition not of the Peers of Charlemagne but of the arch-traitor Ganelon who sold Roland to the Moslems:

> O noble, O worthy Petro, glorie of Spayne,
> Whom fortune heeld so hye in magestee,
> Wel oghten men thy pitous deeth complaye!
> Out of thy land thy brother made thee flee,
> And after, at a seege, by subtiltee,
> Thou were bitraysed and lad unto his tente,
> Where as he with his owene hand slow thee,
> Succedynge in thy regne and in thy rente.

> The feeld of snow, with th'egle of blak therinne,
> Caught with the lymrod coloured as the gleede,
> He brew this cursednesse and al this synne.
> The wikkked nest was werker of this nede.
> Noght Charles Olyver, that took ay heede
> Of trouthe and honour, but of Armorike
> Genylon-Olyver, corrupt for meede,
> Broghte this worthy kyng in swich a brike.[27]

The white coat of arms with the black eagle is that of du Guesclin himself. The "wikked nest" is the Breton knight Oliver de Manny. As Walter Skeat pointed out, Chaucer is punning on his name in French ("mau ni"—"mal nid") and remarking on the chivalric distance that separates Charles the Great's noble peer Oliver from his fourteenth-century namesake. As in the case of Don Pero Niño, Anglo-French conflict sparks Anglo-Iberian conflict.

England and Spain serve as stages for new scenes in the escalating Hundred Years' War, with Spanish knights (and kings) fighting on both sides.

Royal Marriages

The subject of dynastic conflict is inextricable from that of royal marriage alliances, with one continually causing the other. Edward III's son John of Gaunt's marriage to Pedro's daughter Constance of Castile gave him a claim to her father's throne, which he exploited in 1386 when he brought an English army to the Iberian Peninsula in pursuit of the crown. (His brother Edmund, duke of York, had married Constance's sister Isabella at the same time.) The conflict was settled by another marriage treaty in 1388, with John of Gaunt marrying his daughter by Constance, Catherine (Catalina), to the future Enrique III of Castile. His daughter by his first wife Blanche of Lancaster (Henry of Lancaster's daughter), Philippa, had already married João I of Portugal. Both of these queens were to play striking roles in the history of the Iberian Peninsula. Philippa, in particular, is celebrated as the mother of five energetic and chivalrous Portuguese princes, Henry the Navigator being the best known of the five outside of Portugal, and an influential duchess of Burgundy, Isabel of Portugal. The Dominican monastery at Batalha, near the site of João's great victory at Aljubarrota in 1385, contains the tomb of D. João and Queen Philippa, the earliest built for a married couple in Portugal, surrounded by the tombs of their four younger sons. The effigies of the king and queen are holding hands. D. João is depicted wearing the Order of the Garter, and the arms of Avis and Lancaster appear on the monument. The chapel, completed in 1434, shows signs of English architectural influence. It remains a moving and emphatic visual expression of the chivalric and marital alliance of Lancaster and Aviz.[28]

This was by no means the first marriage alliance between England and Iberia. Edward I of England had married as his first wife Eleanor (1244–90), daughter of Ferdinand III of Castile, and sister of Alfonso X el Sabio. Through this alliance, Alfonso hoped to gain England's support for his election as Holy Roman emperor. After their wedding in 1254, possibly at Las Huelgas in Burgos, Eleanor was sent to England. This was another successful marriage. Eleanor accompanied Edward on many military expeditions, including his crusade of 1270–72, where she is reported to have saved his life. Two of her sixteen children were born in Palestine. Like Philippa of Lancaster, she merits study as one of the chivalrous queens who are important in later medieval English and Iberian history. When Eleanor died at Nottingham in 1290, Edward marked the stages where her body rested while en route to London with a famous series of monumental stone crosses, the twelve "Eleanor Crosses" of which three survive.

Other matches were projected but not carried out. Edward I had arranged to wed his eldest daughter, also named Eleanor, to Alfonso III of Aragon, but the marriage was delayed by the pope's objections and then frustrated by Alfonso's sudden death in 1291. In the next century Edward III's daughter Joan was betrothed to Alfonso XI of Castile but died before the ceremony could take place.

The best-known royal marriage alliance between England and Spain occurred at the end of the fifteenth century, when Ferdinand and Isabella's youngest daughter Catherine of Aragon wed two English princes in succession—Henry VII's eldest son Arthur in 1501 and, after his death, Arthur's younger brother Henry VIII in 1509. (In the sixteenth century, Catherine's daughter Mary Tudor married Philip II of Spain.) The festivities always included chivalric contests and brought English and Iberian knights together.

Chivalric Exchanges

In its early days the order of the Sash (or Band) did not admit any members who were not vassals of the king of Castile. However, foreign kings and knights were elected to the Order of the Garter. Among the first group admitted were Henry IV's brother-in-law João I of Portugal (1400), Duarte I of Portugal (1436) and his brothers Pedro (1428) and Enrique (1443). Afonso V of Portugal, Alfons V of Aragon and the Two Sicilies, Ferran II of Aragon and Castile, João II of Portugal and the emperor Charles V were all members of the English monarchical order at one time or another. After the Spanish and Burgundian dynasties were united under Charles V, the monarch could offer his foreign allies like Henry VIII the Burgundian Order of the Golden Fleece.

The story of "the twelve of England" in Camões's *Lusiads*, discussed later in this collection, is not supported by any surviving English historical record.[29] Camões's Portuguese epic and several earlier chronicles relate the tradition that twelve Portuguese knights visited England at the suggestion of John of Gaunt to defend the honor of a group of twelve ladies who had been insulted by English knights. The ladies, perhaps members of his wife Constance of Castile's entourage, appeal to John of Gaunt, who recommends that they petition the Portuguese court for twelve champions. The Portuguese knights then vindicate the ladies in a tournament.[30]

In 1438–39 the Valencian knight Joannot Martorell, the future author of the great fifteenth-century Catalan chivalric romance *Tirant lo Blanc*, toured England, whence he bombarded his cousin Joan de Montpalau with challenges to avenge the honor of his sister, this duel to be umpired by that mentally challenged monarch Henry VI.[31]

English records do describe one encounter: in 1441 the Aragonese knight Felip Boïl challenged the English squire John Astley (d. 1486) to joust at Smithfield. Boïl's challenge survives, with an illustration depicting their foot combat with battleaxes on January 30, 1441–42. Henry VI appears in a judge's stand in the background. He knighted Astley after the event. Having made his reputation in this way, Astley would be called upon to advise participants in judicial duels in 1446 and 1453. In 1461 he was elected Knight of the Garter. In the mid-1460s he seems to have been captured by the Scots. He took part in Edward IV's funeral procession, carrying a blue and gold canopy.

Chivalric exchanges continued into the sixteenth century without a break. In the winter of 1506, Philip of Burgundy and his wife Joanna, the daughter of Ferdinand and Isabella later known as Juana la Loca, were shipwrecked in England. Henry VII welcomed them; their tour included a visit to Winchester to see King Arthur's Round Table. The largest surviving piece of medieval furniture in Europe, it is now known to have been constructed around 1290, probably for one of Edward I's Round Table tournaments at which he planned to announce marriage alliances for several of his children.[32] Already accepted as an authentic relic of the historical King Arthur by William Caxton in his 1485 preface to Sir Thomas Malory's *Morte Darthur*, it can be seen here becoming a mandatory stop on the chivalrous tourist's itinerary.

Henry VIII and his nephew by marriage Charles V exchanged visits that combined English and Spanish or imperial chivalric motifs in 1520 at the time of Henry VIII's meetings with Francis I at the Field of the Cloth of Gold, where the emperor effectively trumped the French diplomatic effort. On Charles V's visit to England in 1522 he was entertained with jousts in which both monarchs participated, and an elaborate royal entry where the merchants of London mounted pageants alluding to Charles V's Order of the Golden Fleece, his descent from Charlemagne, the linked ancestry of the English and Spanish royal lines (going back to John of Gaunt and Alfonso el Sabio respectively), and a scene of King Arthur entertaining visiting monarchs—in which Henry VIII presented himself as the descendant of Arthur.[33] On this occasion the two rulers rode through London in identical costumes, except that Henry wore the emblems of the Order of the Golden Fleece and Charles wore those of the Order of the Garter. One account includes a visit by the Spanish contingent to King Arthur's Round Table at Winchester, which Henry VIII in 1516 had ordered newly painted with Tudor colors and the dynastic emblem of the Tudor rose in the center.[34] Biddle suggests that this assertion of England's glorious Arthurian past was part of Henry VIII's unsuccessful bid for election as emperor, the title that Charles V received in the same year.

From his marriage to Mary I in1554 on, Philip II tried to use tournaments to encourage friendships between the "white, pink, and quarrelsome" English and his Spanish knights. Henry Kamen observes that for at least some Spanish courtiers the trip to England was a kind of chivalric pilgrimage (or sightseeing trip) to "the meadows of Amadís." Like earlier sixteenth-century Spanish visitors they traveled to Winchester to view the Round Table. One of the first major chivalric events of the visit was Philip's investiture as a Knight of the Order of the Garter in St. George's Chapel at Windsor. On a later visit in 1557 he presided over a Garter ceremony for St. George's Day. Alan Young documents eight tournaments of different types instigated by Philip II between December 1554 and December 1557. At Easter in 1555 in the great yard at Westminster, Philip and his team of Spanish knights in blue challenged a group of English knights to joust. Sydney Anglo's analysis suggests that rather than promoting "male bonding" between the English and the Spaniards, their encounters in the tiltyard only intensified growing feelings of resentment and religious and ethnic difference.[35] A chivalric alliance was fast becoming a chivalric rivalry, which burst into flame after Mary's death, with the reign of her Protestant sister Elizabeth I. Philip II pronounced a chivalric vow to recover England for Catholicism, and English and Spanish competition found a global stage. Chivalric elements of this later sixteenth-century competition are diverse and important, but beyond the scope of this article.[36] It is fair to see them as a direct continuation of the medieval chivalric relationship outlined here.

Chivalric Fiction

The Anglo-Iberian chivalry of real life was diverse and fascinating: but there was also an Anglo-Iberian chivalry of the imagination, and the imaginary remained in constant interaction with the factual. Here, too, Iberia is associated with crusading warfare and opportunities for combat against Moslem opponents—as in *Fierabras*, also known as *Charles the Grete* or *La Historia de Carlo Magno*, the most popular version of the Charlemagne cycle in England and Spain. England is associated with Arthur—in the many Arthurian romances translated into Castilian, Catalan, and Portuguese in the course of the later Middle Ages, as well as in English tradition. These basic chivalric associations underlie a variety of new European romances of chivalry that exploited the possibilities of English and Iberian knightly contacts.

Romances of Anglo-Iberian interest were produced in France as well as in England, Spain, and Portugal. *Le Roi Ponthus et la Belle Sidoine* (originally the Middle English romance of *King Horn*) was relocated to reflect a later medieval chivalric geography about 1290 by Geoffroy de la Tour Landry. This version's hero Ponthus (Horn) is a Galician knight who is exiled to

England and marries a Breton princess.[37] This work inspired the later French author of *Cleriadus et Meliadice*, which also survives in a fifteenth-century Middle Scots translation. Its hero Cleriadus is the son of the count of Esture (Asturias), regent of England. (The title "prince of Asturias" was adopted by the heir to the throne of Castile, the future Enrique III, on his marriage with John of Gaunt's daughter Catherine, September 14, 1388.) Cleriadus, the Spanish prince, wins the love of the English princess Meliadice after adventures in Portugal and Spain. (He also liberates Cyprus from the Saracens and becomes king of Ireland.) Gaston Zink notes that the otherwise skillful author of this attractive romance seems to have only a cloudy sense of Iberian geography.[38]

The first continuation of the Charlemagne cycle romance *Huon de Bordeaux* tells of the winning of Huon's daughter Clariet by Florent, prince of Aragon, and the surprising adventures of their daughter Ide, who becomes constable of Rome. The fifteenth-century French prose version was translated into English early in the sixteenth century by that eminent Early Tudor translator John Bourchier, Lord Berners, who is remembered as the translator of Froissart's chronicles and the first English writer to emulate the stylistic innovations of Spanish humanistic literature.[39]

Oliveros de Castille et Artus d'Algarbe is a romance of friendship. Its anonymous French author sends two runaway princes from Castille and Portugal to the wilds of England and Ireland—and in this romance England and Ireland are truly wild. Oliver of Castile is held up by highway robbers, apparently a frequent experience of real-life Spanish courtiers in England. The Portuguese knight Artus talks in sign language to the savage Irish and encounters monsters in forests. This French romance also survives in English and Spanish translations.[40]

Meanwhile by the fifteenth century Iberian romances betray a preference for English heroes. *Tirant lo Blanc* was written between 1460 and 1464. Joannot Martorell, its author, a knight from Valencia who is known to have visited England, includes the earliest version of the legend of the founding of the Order of the Garter in his romance, and includes the English chivalric hero Guy of Warwick as one of his characters. In this Catalan romance Tirant goes on to reconquer North Africa and Byzantium, but at the beginning of the story his father William repels an invasion of England by a fictional Saracen king of the Canary Islands.[41] In fact, the Canary Islands had been invaded in 1402 by three French chivalric adventurers, who attempted to hunt down, convert, and enslave the (perhaps needless to say, non-Muslim) indigenous inhabitants. At the time *Tirant lo Blanc* was written, the islands were still resisting Castilian control, and would continue to do so through 1496. Here as elsewhere, then, Martorell's story is an imaginative reworking of recent historical events.

The Arthurian foundations of *Amadís de Gaula* are now well established. As in *Tirant* its heroes begin their adventures in the British Isles and later fight Islamic opponents in the eastern Mediterranean. Both works try to ground the knightly hero in the glorious past of English chivalric legend, whether Arthurian or not, and then to bring him up to date by dispatching him against the most feared contemporary opponents of Christendom, the North African and Turkish Muslims. These Iberian authors portray Britain as a kind of nursery or training ground for knights. Unlike *Tirant*, *Amadís* and his continuations would find an English readership, but not until around 1580.[42]

Middle English romances in turn describe the adventures of exotic Hispanic knights errant. *Sir Triamour*, a late-fourteenth-century North Midlands romance, introduces an Aragonese king, Ardus, his wife Margaret (one of a number of falsely accused queens who figure in medieval romances), and their son Triamour, with Hungarian and German episodes and the tale of a faithful dog. *Sir Torrent of Portyngale*, a late-fourteenth or early-fifteenth-century East Midland romance, tells of the adventures of a Portuguese knight and his family in Portugal, Norway, and the Holy Land. His main rival is Aragonese.

One exception to this pattern, the Child ballad of *King Estmere* involves a King Estmere of England and his brother Adler Young in combat with a pagan king of Spain, for the hand of the daughter of King Adland.[43] It employs the prince's disguise as a harper in the hall at a wedding feast, paralleling the famous English romances *King Horn* and *Bevis of Hampton*.

But the most influential Iberian chivalric work of the Middle Ages in England was not a work of fiction (except for its prologue). The text of Ramon Llull's celebrated chivalric manual *El Libre del orde de cavayleria* (*The Boke of the Ordre of Chyualry*), originally written in Catalan and translated into French with the anonymous translator's augmentations in the fourteenth century, appeared in English in a 1456 Middle Scots translation by Sir Gilbert Hay and in William Caxton's translation and edition of ca. 1483, which was itself put into Middle Scots by Adam Loutfut in 1495.[44] Around the same time, it was also used by Joannot Martorell in *Tirant lo Blanc* as a textbook for the young knight. Here we see English and Iberian knights without question on the same page.

Conclusions

The Anglo-Iberian chivalric relationship as it develops in the high Middle Ages may reflect both regions' status as frontiers, albeit frontiers of different kinds—Iberia as an historic boundary region where Christendom meets Islam, England as a magical Arthurian island at the edge of the known world. Both geographic areas functioned in life, literature, and the imaginations of contemporaries as stages for heroic adventures where the marvelous can be expected to manifest itself on a regular basis. Both countries developed variants of what might be called chivalric tourism that enabled late medieval and Early Modern knights to perform military exploits in the tiltyard or even on the battlefield. These border knights continue to be drawn to combat on the margins, on a geographic edge which keeps expanding outward. They see themselves as heirs to a chivalric tradition that involves defending their frontier and expanding the boundaries of their control.

Anglo-Iberian chivalry developed within a larger European chivalric geography. Even the present sketch, focused on Britain and Iberia, cannot ignore France, the Holy Roman Empire, North Africa, and other countries. Yet over three centuries an elaborate interplay linked the chivalries of Britain and Iberia, moving toward a chivalric rivalry to be played out on a global stage in the building of the rival empires of England, Spain, and Portugal.

Notes

1. Jennifer R. Goodman, *Chivalry and Exploration, 1298–1630* (Rochester, NY: Boydell, 1998), pp. 169–72.
2. See Rosemary Sutcliff's historical novel, *The Eagle of the Ninth* (London: Oxford University Press, 1954; repr. 1973).
3. Christopher Tyerman, *England and the Crusades, 1095–1588* (Chicago: University of Chicago Press, 1988), pp. 33, 43.
4. Tyerman, *England and the Crusades.*
5. George Peele, *The Battle of Alcazar,* repr. in *Dramatic and Political Works of Robert Greene and George Peele,* ed. Alexander Dyce (London: George Routledge, 1861); *The Famous History of the Life and Death of Captain Thomas Stukeley* (London: Printed for Thomas Panyer, 1605); repr. in Richard Simpson, *The School of Shakespeare,* Vol. 1 (New York: J.W. Bouton, 1878). Simpson includes the ballads and a biography of Stukeley.
6. John Barbour, *The Bruce,* ed. A.A.M. Duncan (Edinburgh: Canongate Books, 1997), Book 20; see also Matthew P. McDiarmaid, ed., *The Bruce,* 3 vols. (Edinburgh: Scottish Text Society, 1985); Alan McQuarrie, *Scotland and the Crusades, 1095–1560* (Edinburgh: John Donald, 1985).
7. Barbour, *Bruce,* Book 20, lines 338–51. "The King Alfonso sent after him and received him very well. He offered him much gold, treasure, horses and armor, but Douglas would take none of it because he said he took that journey on the way to a pilgrimage against God's enemies, so that his labor might profit his soul's health, and since he knew [the king] had war with the Saracens he would stay there and serve him loyally to the best of his power." The translations from Barbour are my own.

8. Barbour, *Bruce*, Book 20, lines 413–15. "To do well and to fear no death, for joy in heaven would be their reward if they should die in God's service."
9. Barbour, *Bruce*, Book 20, lines 441–90.
10. Barbour, *Bruce*, Book 20, lines 577–78. The crowned heart on the Douglas family coat of arms refers to this exploit.
11. Tyerman, *England and the Crusades*, pp. 277–78, cites the *Crónica del Rey Don Alfonso el Onceno, Crónicas de los Reyes de Castilla*, ed. C. Rosell, Biblioteca de Autores Españoles, vols. 66, 68 (Madrid, 1875, 1877), 1:360.
12. For Alfonso's Order of the Band and Edward III's later Round Table order, the precursor of his Order of the Garter, see Richard W. Barber and Juliet R.V. Barker, *Tournaments: Jousts, Chivalry and Pageants in the Middle Ages* (Woodbridge: Boydell, 1989), and D'Arcy J. Boulton, *The Knights of the Crown: The Monarchical Orders of Knighthood in Later Medieval England, 1325–1520* (New York: St. Martin's Press, 1987), pp. 46–95, 109.
13. Geoffrey Chaucer, "General Prologue," *The Canterbury Tales, The Riverside Chaucer*, ed. Larry D. Benson (Boston: Houghton Mifflin, 1987), p. 24, lines 56–57.
14. Washington Irving, *A History of New York*, ed. Edwin T. Bowden (New Haven: College and University Press; and Boston: Twayne, 1964). The editor remarks in his introduction that "Irving made fun of his scholarship—the first books are aimed at ridiculing pedanticism, learned and cryptic footnotes, citation of odd sources, all the paraphernalia of the weighty historical scholarship of his day—and yet the hidden joke is that his knowledge is real" (p. 14).
15. On Washington Irving's methodology and sources, see his note to the Revised Edition of 1850, in *A Chronicle of the Conquest of Granada by Fray Antonio Agapida*, intro. Earl N. Harbert, ed. Miriam J. Shillingsburg (Boston: Twayne, 1988), pp. 411–13; William H. Prescott, "Irving's Conquest of Granada" in *Prescott's Works: Biographical and Critical Miscellanies* (New York: The Kelmscott Society, 1845), pp. 64–87; Louise M. Hoffman, "Irving's Use of Spanish Sources in the Conquest of Granada," *Hispania* 28.4 (1945): 483–98; Richard V. McLamore, "Postcolonial Columbus: Washington Irving and *The Conquest of Granada*," *Nineteenth-Century Literature* 48.1 (1993): 26–43. For Washington Irving's translator, George Washington Montgomery, and his attempt to expunge Agapida from his "carefully condensed" Spanish version of *The Conquest of Granada*, see Stanley T. Williams, "The first version of the Writings of Washington Irving in Spanish," *Modern Philology* 28.2 (1930): 185–201.
16. Irving, *A Chronicle*, pp. 125–26. One of Irving's sources here seems to be Peter Martyr de Anghiera, *Opus Epistolarum* lib. 1, ep. 62. For the later adventures of Lord Scales and his death in France while fighting for the duke of Brittany, see William H. Prescott, *Ferdinand and Isabella* (New York: The Kelmscott Society, 1845), 1:370.
17. Irving, *A Chronicle*, p. 141. Compare Bernaldez, *Don Fernando è Doña Isabel*, in *Crónicas de los reyes de Castilla*, ed. Cayetano Rosell y López, Biblioteca de Autores Españoles 3 (Madrid: Ediciones Atlas, 1953), 3:623: "Allegó el Conde de Inglaterra luego en pos del Rey á hacer recibimiento á la Reyna

y a la Infanta, muy pomposo en estraña manera, á la postre de todos, armado en blanco á la guisa, encima de un caballo castaño con los paramentos fasta el suelo de seda azul, y las orladuras tan anchas como una mano de seda rasa blanca, y todos los paramentos estrellados de oro en forrados en ceptí morado; y él traia sobre las armas una ropeta francesa da brocado negro raso, un sombrero blanco francés con un plumaje, é traia en su brazo izquierdo un broquelete redondo é varas de oro, é una cimera muy pomposa, fecha de tan nueva manera que á todos parecia bien; é traia consigo cinco caballos encobertados con sus pajes encima todos vestidos de seda y brocado; y venian con él ciertos gentiles hombres de los suyos muy ataviados, é ansi llegó á facer reverencia y recibimiento á la Reyna y á la Infanta, é despues fizo reverencia al Rey, y anduvo un rato festajando ante todos encima de su caballo, é saltando á un cabo é á otro muy concertadamente, mirándolo todos los grandes é toda la jente, é á todos pareció bien de esto."

18. Gutierrez Díez de Gámez, *El Victorial: Crónica de don Pero Niño*, ed. Rafael Beltrán Llavador (Salamanca: Universidad de Salamanca, 1997); Gutierrez Diaz de Gamez, *The Unconquered Knight: A Chronicle of the Deeds of Don Pero Niño, Count of Buelna*, trans. Joan Evans (selection only) (London: George Routledge and Sons, Ltd., 1928), pp. 42–75; see also Richard Barber, *The Knight and Chivalry* (Woodbridge: Boydell, 1995), p. 151.
19. Diaz de Gamez, *The Unconquered Knight*, p. 42.
20. Barber, *The Knight and Chivalry*, p. 206.
21. Perkin Warbeck's career is detailed at length in Anne Wroe, *The Perfect Prince* (New York: Random House, 2003), pp. 17–49. See also Cecil Roth, "Perkin Warbeck and His Jewish Master," *Transactions of the Jewish Historical Society of England* 9 (1922): 143–62. Pero Vaz da Cunha became infamous for his murder of the exiled Jalof king Bemoy, discussed by Wroe, *The Perfect Prince*, pp. 38–39, and in Peter E. Russell, "White Kings on Black Kings: Rui de Piña and the Problem of Black African Sovereignty," in *Medieval and Renaissance Studies in Honour of Robert Brian Tate*, ed. Ian Michael and Richard A. Cardwell (Oxford: Dolphin Book, 1986), pp. 151–64.
22. Graham Winston, *The Spanish Armadas* (New York: Doubleday, 1972.)
23. Roger Vercel, *Bertrand of Brittany. A Biography of Messire du Guesclin*, trans. Marion Saunders (New Haven: Yale University Press, 1934), p. 157.
24. Jean Froissart, *Chronicles*, trans. John Bourchier, Lord Berners, 6 vols. (London: Tudor Translation Series, 1901–03).
25. Froissart, *Chronicles*, trans. John Bourchier, Lord Berners.
26. Jean Froissart, *Chronicles*, trans. and ed. Geoffrey Brereton (Harmondsworth: Penguin, 1968), p. 173.
27. Geoffrey Chaucer, "The Monk's Tale," in *The Canterbury Tales, The Riverside Chaucer*, pp. 246–47, lines 2375–90.
28. For more on Philippa of Lancaster see chapter 7 in this volume; see also my essay, "The Lady with the Sword: Philippa of Lancaster and the Chivalry of Henry the Navigator," in *Chivalry and Exploration* (Rochester, NY: Boydell, 1998), pp. 134–48.

29. Chapter 8 in this volume discusses other Portuguese sources for this event and their historicity.
30. Luis de Camões, *The Lusiads*, trans. Leonard Bacon (New York: Hispanic Society of America, 1950; repr. 1966). Faria y Sousa lists the Portuguese knights who participated as: Antão Vaz (or Vasques) de Almada, who commanded the left at the battle of Aljubarrota (in Ford's list, Rui Mendes Cerveira; Alvaro Vaz de Almada, later count of Avranches, Antão Vaz's nephew, confused with his uncle by Camões).
31. For details see David H. Rosenthal's historical introduction to his translation of Joanot Martorell and Martí Joan de Galba, *Tirant lo Blanch*, trans. David H. Rosenthal (New York: Warner, 1984).
32. See Martin Biddle, ed., *King Arthur's Round Table: An Archaeological Investigation* (Woodbridge, UK: Boydell, 2000), pp. 387–90.
33. These pageants are discussed in Sydney Anglo, *Spectacle, Pageantry, and Early Tudor Policy*, 2nd ed. (Oxford: Clarendon Press, 1997), pp. 158–63, 168–206.
34. See Biddle, *King Arthur's Round Table*.
35. Anglo, *Spectacle, Pageantry, and Early Tudor Policy*, pp. 318–43.
36. See Goodman, *Chivalry and Exploration*.
37. Marie-Claude de Crécy, ed., *Le Roman de Ponthus et Sidoine* (Geneva: Droz, 1997).
38. Gaston Zink, ed., *Cleriadus et Meliadice* (Geneva: Droz, 1984). For Enrique III, see Fernão Lopes, Extracts from the *Chronicles of Dom Fernando and Dom João de boa memoria*, in *The English in Portugal, 1367–87*, ed. and trans. Derek W. Lomax and R.J. Oakley (Warminster, UK: Aris & Phillips, 1988), pp. 302–03, 56, note 1 to chapter CXX.
39. Michel J. Raby, ed., *Huon de Bordeaux, roman en prose du XVème siècle*, Studies in the Humanities, Vol. 27 (New York: P. Lang, 1998).
40. Gail Orgelfinger, ed., *The Hystorye of Olyuer of Castylle*, trans. Henry Watson (New York: Garland, 1988) has a detailed bibliography.
41. Martorell and Galba, *Tirant lo Blanch*. See Goodman, *Chivalry and Exploration*, pp. 131–33, where I discuss further this imaginary king of the Canary Islands as depicted in *Tirant lo Blanc*. Lluís Cabré's essay in this book (chapter 2) discusses *Tirant* in full; I am grateful for Cabré's suggestions and comments.
42. See Goodman, *Chivalry and Exploration*, p. 32.
43. Child ballad no. 60: from Percy's *Reliques*, edition of 1794, 1:64.
44. See Jennifer R. Goodman, *Malory and William Caxton's Prose Romances of 1485* (New York: Garland, 1985).

CHAPTER 2

BRITISH INFLUENCE IN MEDIEVAL CATALAN WRITING: AN OVERVIEW

Lluís Cabré

Highlighting Continental mediation, this chapter examines the nature of British influence in Catalan writing and reassesses the established English connection of Tirant lo Blanc.

The direct influence of Middle English literature on medieval Catalan writing is, perhaps, merely nominal. In the dedication of *Tirant lo Blanc* (1460–64) to Ferrando de Portugal, Joanot Martorell masquerades as a translator of a nonexistent English novel:

> E com la dita hystòria e actes del dit Tirant sien en lengua anglesa, e a vostra il·lustra senyoria sia stat grat voler-me pregar la giràs en lengua portoguesa, opinant, per yo ésser stat algun temps en la illa de Anglaterra, degués millor saber aquella lengua que altri...me atreviré expondre no solament de lengua anglesa en portoguesa, mas encara de portoguesa en vulgar valenciana, per ço que la nació d'on yo só natural se'n puxa alegrar.
>
> [And since the above-mentioned chronicle and deeds of Tirant are found in English, and your Illustrious Lordship finds pleasure in my translating them into Portuguese (bearing in mind that, since I have spent some time in the Island of England, I should have a better command of English than anyone else)...I shall dare to translate not only from English into Portuguese, but from Portuguese into the vernacular of Valencia, so that the nation in which I was born will enjoy it.][1]

It was an age-old trick to present a piece of fiction as a truthful account—as old as Geoffrey of Monmouth's *Historia regum Britanniae*. In the case of

Martorell, however, the trick was backed by some real data: he had spent at least one year in England, and one may well assume that he had acquired a reasonable command of English; his *Guillem de Vàroic* and later the first part of *Tirant* followed the plot of the Anglo-Norman *Gui de Warewic* (in any of its versions); and Tirant, a Continental Breton hero, whose lineage reaches back to a certain captain and relative of Uther Pendragon who married an illegitimate daughter of the king of France, comes of age at the English court and is knighted by King Enric (chaps. 58–59)—a cross between Henry VI, whom Martorell met in real life and who possibly knighted him, and Edward III, who had instituted the Order of the Garter in 1348.[2] Indeed, Tirant is granted membership of the Garter as the top knight (chap. 85), whereas Martorell keeps the honor of being the earliest author to commit to paper the legend that accounts for the motto *Honi soit qui mal y pense*. All this notwithstanding, it has been suggested by Martí de Riquer that the influence of *Gui de Warewic* must have come via a late prose version in French, and not through the fourteenth-century English texts that Joseph A. Vaeth collated with Martorell's work.[3]

But there are avenues to pursue other than textual borrowing in order to detect the existence of a British influence in Catalan writing. Such influence mostly came through the Continent, and, I would argue, attention to mediation, rather than focus on direct contacts, will shed new light on Catalan works with British roots. I shall limit the following notes to those aspects of British writing which had an effect on the vernacular, particularly when they become eventually relevant to Martorell's *Tirant*.

The Latin Circuit and the English Friars

The impact of British scholarship in medieval Aragonese libraries can be easily documented. Pioneering research in notarial archives, even though limited to fourteenth-century Barcelona, gives us an insight into the early introduction in private libraries of famous British scholars in both the Arts and Theology (such as Roger Bacon, Robert Grosseteste, Robert Kildwardby, Richard of Middleton, and John Peckham) and of well-known encyclopedias (such as Bartholomaeus Anglicus's *De proprietatibus rerum*).[4] Three references to the younger Peter of Blois (the earliest from 1322) highlight the pervasiveness of letter-writing handbooks.[5] A glance at the towering figures of Ramon Llull (1232–1316) and Arnau de Vilanova (1240?–1311) confirms the Catalan adscription to the Latin international circuit at an early stage. Vilanova is well known for having left a mark on the Faculty school of medical science at Montpellier, including the work of Bernard de Gordon, which was to enjoy a wide success in the Iberian peninsula. Llull's scholarly work has had to struggle with his reputation as an *illuminatus* who was out of his time. However, he visited Paris on several occasions and often stayed at Montpellier, which was then part of Llull's homeland, the independent Kingdom of Majorca. Ruiz Simon has shown that Llull's *Ars* is a conscious reply to the defects of contemporary Aristotelianism, and has pointed to interesting parallels with Kildwardby's thought.[6] Likewise, recent scholarship is just unearthing the hidden background of Llull's more popular writings, as in the case of Bartholomaeus Anglicus's imprint on Lullian natural analogies.[7]

The mature works of both Llull and Vilanova were written during the reign of Jaume II (1291–1327). At this stage, translations from Latin were still rare.[8] Only one version from an English author into Catalan can be dated around those years: the 1320 version of H. of Saltrey's *Tractatus de Purgatorio Sancti Patricii* by Ramon Ros; its purpose was to edify the wife of a local nobleman, for she found pleasure "in reading the Holy Books which speak of God and his deeds."[9] One item in a modest inventory from 1322 belongs in the same popular level: "Storie cuiusdam anime que transmigraverat ab hoc seculo et rediit in hoc mundum" [Accounts of a certain soul who had migrated from this world and returned to it].[10] By 1337 John of Wales's *Breviloquium de virtutibus* was being imitated (in Latin) in religious circles, and his *Communiloquium* might have reached (in Latin and, perhaps, Aragonese) the court of Jaume II;[11] the Catalan version of this compendium was produced much later.[12] A partial translation of Geoffrey of Monmouth's *Historia*, which was supplemented by chapter 24 of Bede's *Historia Ecclesiastica Gentis Anglorum*, might have been copied in the first half of the fourteenth-century.[13] A marked interest in historical works and the romances of the *matière de Bretagne* remains the most distinctive feature of this early stage of lay literacy in the Crown of Aragon—a stage when practical matters (science, law, devotion) were still dominant.[14]

From the reigns of Pere III (1336–87), also known as Pedro IV, and his sons Joan I (1387–96) and Martí I (1396–1410), the data about cultural growth are more consistent, because there is an abundance of documents, one might argue, but also because of royal patronage, and because an interest for the classics started pervading the vernacular world. The British friars who followed John of Salisbury's path made a significant contribution to this general phenomenon: from John of Wales onward, they transmitted to the fourteenth century their medieval enthusiasm for Antiquity on a par with their genuinely Christian ends, particularly in the field of political thought; their impact reached as far as Italy.[15]

There is no comprehensive study of schooling at the Faculty schools in the Crown of Aragon.[16] Even so, the mere existence of the *studium generale* at Lleida, which was founded by Jaume II (1300), and of the mendicant *studia*, furthers our understanding of an educational network which was capable of producing graduate students aiming at a higher degree in law or theology. That elite was to be absorbed by the court and the mendicant orders. Thanks to the international structure of these orders students could be sent abroad to feed a self-reinforcing educational system. Thus Antoni Canals (ca. 1352–ca. 1419) was educated at the Dominican provincial *studium* and at the *studium generale* in Toulouse (and, possibly, at Paris); he then taught at the Dominican convent in Lleida (1387) and, thanks to the king's uncle, Cardinal Jaume d'Aragó, held a chair in Theology at the Cathedral of Valencia (1395–98). It is in those years when King Joan's interest in the services of Canals as translator is documented (before 1391), and when such services resulted in his position as chaplain and lecturer of King Martí's court (1398/99).[17] This courtly environment is the setting for Canals's reminiscing in the prologue to his *Libre de Sènecha De providentia*: he recalls his theological discussions with King Martí and some courtly men who were far too well read.[18] The same concern for the instruction of the court accounts for his eulogy of books and learning in the preface of his version of the Pseudo-Bernard *Carta de sant Bernat a sa germana*, which he addressed to King Martí's *camarlenc*. Canals copied there entire passages of Richard de Bury's *Philobiblon*, his attitude thus recalling that of the English friars.[19] We may also suspect a fair amount of pragmatism and attribute his choice to the need to ease his labor. Canals used to resort to sources that were not within easy reach of his audience. For instance, his *Scipio e Aníbal* renders a fragment of Petrarch's *Africa* while presenting the version as being largely based on Livy.[20] In 1314 Jaume II was already trying to get a copy of Livy's work, which was still a must-read at the time of King Joan.[21] Canals played with such interest for a work that was regarded as an ancient *speculum principum*, and turned Petrarch's fragment into an *ad status* sermon on Providence and the fall of princes for Alfons d'Aragó. Likewise, regarding the use of Richard de Bury's *Philobiblon*, we should tone down Canals's enthusiasm for classical learning, judging from the selection of borrowings and the nature of the following *Carta*.[22]

A cursory glance at the list of Aragonese friars who traveled abroad, according to a sample of documents from the Arxiu Reial, confirms that Paris and Toulouse, and later on Avignon, were the most usual destinations for those wanting a doctorate in theology.[23] A few students, however, went to England, and it is worth noticing that these entries tend to refer to gray friars. The link with the Franciscan *studium* at Oxford has been highlighted.[24] Cambridge was also an option. For instance, in 1383 Pere III asked the duke of Lancaster to recommend Lluís de Fonts, who had been sent to Cambridge by the Franciscan Chapter "ad legendum Sententias," so that the chancellor and the *magistri* did their best and the friar would soon become a master "in theologica facultate."[25] Royal protection was necessary in more than one respect. Thanks to Prince Joan's letters and the king's subsidies, Friar Nicolau Sacosta eventually managed to obtain his doctorate at Paris after spending three unfruitful years at Cambridge; he later became Queen Violant's confessor.[26]

Sir Richard Southern has summed up the financial problems that the average student had to face on his way toward a higher degree, thus explaining why so high a proportion of the few who succeeded had to follow a long, tortuous road:

> Normally he [the student] would be a Master of Arts by the time he was twenty-five, and he would then have to make his career in the practical world of secular or ecclesiastical administration before he could return to the university to study for a higher degree in theology or law. By the time he was a Doctor of Theology he would probably be about forty, and he would be ready for promotion to the higher offices of church and state.[27]

The career of the Franciscan Francesc Eiximenis (ca. 1330–1409) fits nicely into this pattern. He was well in his forties by the time he took his doctorate in theology at Toulouse (1374), thanks to royal patronage.[28] Former studies, according to his own words, had taken him to Paris and Oxford.[29] Being already a master, and here the pattern would seem to collapse, he settled down at Valencia and turned down a post as confessor to Prince Joan (1384), but he later became confessor to Queen Maria and died bishop of Elna. His time abroad made him the best Catalan depository of that repeatedly mentioned British tradition that Beryl Smalley noncommittally christened the "classicising" friars.[30]

Eiximenis's admiration for foreign scholarship is crystal-clear in his prideful recollection of one of the *libri naturales*, Aristotle's *De caelo et mundo*, "which is neither found in Catalonia, nor is familiar to us; you will find it, however, in the universities of Paris and England."[31] The benefits of his training as a member of an international order are best displayed by the inventory of his large library (1409), which was remarkably specialized in theology: its wide-ranging set of commentaries on the *Libri sententiarum*, theological *quaestiones*, and biblical handbooks included works by William Ockham and John Duns Scotus, of course, but also volumes by Adam Wodeham, John Dumbleton, Robert Holkot, and Thomas Buckingham.[32]

The intellectual fate of Eiximenis led him not to a life entirely devoted to writing Latin scholarly tracts, as he might at first have envisaged, but to hard labor in the field of vernacular compendia. Because of that, the array of *auctores* he mentions must be taken with a grain of salt, as suggested by many a coincidence with Thomas of Ireland's *Manipulus florum*.[33] More significant is the case of Holkot, from whom Eiximenis took some mythological lore, though disguising it as the saying of a "Lucius Lucanus, poeta" of his own making.[34] Reading through the variegated chapters of Eiximenis's encyclopedia for the laity, one finds more than the odd reference to English society. Thus part 5, on rulership, of his *Dotzè del Crestià o Regiment de príncipes e de comunitats* ends with a section dealing with the Cortes; its final chapter explains what should be dealt with in Cortes "according to English usage."[35] The focus is on the control of both church dignitaries and the king and his officials: "so that the kingdom would never be destroyed by the king's vicious life." It is then deemed necessary to scrutinize the royal officials' ruling, for "it is here that has to be seen whether the king and the rest [of the society] abide by the laws and statutes of the kingdom..., or whether anything contrary to justice has been forced upon anyone."[36] Albert Hauf has convincingly argued that Eiximenis's political thought was not at all original, let alone progressive, in its theoretical foundations, and has judiciously advised against turning him into an advocate of John of Salisbury's otherwise rather ambivalent doctrine of tyrannicide.[37] This issue is dealt with in chapters 607–09 of the *Dotzè*. They must be read with care, since they report a debate between the Patriarch of Alexandria and the Pisans—their views may not be Eiximenis's, but all the same he chose to place this *exemplum* as his final word on tyranny. The Patriarch puts forward a Christian merciful attitude in chapter 607, while the contrary arguments, in chapter 608, include the Sicilian rebellion against Charles d'Anjou as well as the hypothetical case, "as stated by Policratus," of a tyrant who broke up the deal with his vassals; in that instance, "even if he were not deposed by law," he would *de facto* cease to be their lord, thereby his people would not be breaking their sworn fealty "if they rise up against him and kill him."[38] The *solutio* in chapter 609 is clear enough: "the people's tyranny is far worse," concludes the Patriarch, for "government is proper to noblemen, and not to commoners"; and yet, in the case of the Sicilian Vespers, he eventually sanctions popular rebellion as a means of fighting tyranny: "it is not wrong doing; on the contrary, it ought to be done, and the ruler should meekly take on such correction. The Holy Church does not oppose it," although the Sicilians are still to blame for having disobeyed the pope's decision in favor of Charles.[39] Certainly Eiximenis shows little sympathy for the populace, but neither his attitude in chapter 675 nor the way he deals with tyrannicide is a monarchic manifesto either. Writing from Valencia, he might have felt free to express the political position of the city councils in their struggle to curtail the power of the king's officials.[40]

Much as in Canals's case, Eiximenis's "classicising" learning helped him a long way toward meeting more practical ends. John of Salisbury's *Policraticus* came to him via John of Wales's *Communiloquium*, a major source of the *Dotzè* and one that eased Eiximenis's arduous compilation.[41]

There are four extant manuscripts of the Catalan translation of the *Communiloquium*.[42] The edition of the early-fifteenth-century version of John of Wales's *Breviloquium* was based on three manuscripts.[43] Three more have been found since.[44] Such dissemination ranges across the social spectrum, from the queen to a humble wool carder.[45] The Welshman's works provided his audience with a wealth of ancient anecdotes, as if he were a Franciscan equivalent of Valerius Maximus. Eiximenis, who tended to hide his immediate sources, gave this away when advising the *princeps* to read, next to a carefully selected list of *auctores* (Vegetius, Valerius Maximus, Livy, and Boethius), Hugh of Saint Victor's *Didascalicon* and the "*Summa de collections*, as well as various short works by friar Johannes Gallensis."[46] The mixing of classical authors with their medieval followers promoted both sets of works as essential reading in the political and literary background of any educated man. In this respect both *Scipió e Aníbal*, the *Dotzè*, and the Catalan *Breviloqui* were right on target, and thus they figure among the sources of Martorell's *Tirant*, although the friars involved would have refused to be part of the fabrics of fiction in the company of numerous borrowings from, say, Ovid and Seneca's tragedies.[47]

Occasionally, the connection with the classical world was less convoluted. Bernat Metge (1340/46–1413) was brought up in the Royal Chancery in Eiximenis's time: he was to become one of those highly ranked members of the royal household who, according to the *Dotzè*, ought to be cross-examined in parliament. Metge's Latinate writing and his closeness, via Avignon, to the Latin works of so conspicuous a member of the papal court as Petrarch are well known. Here it is worth highlighting Metge's use in *Lo somni* (1399) of Seneca's *Hercules furens*, as well as his acquaintance with other Senecan tragedies, with the commentary by Nicholas Trevet.[48] Later on, this corpus was translated into Catalan and made a full impact on Martorell's *Tirant* and Ausiàs March's poetry. *Lo somni* witnesses to a fourteenth-century novelty: the Senecan fashion which Lovato dei Lovati and Albertino Mussato had initiated in Italy and which had been expanded by other routes by Friar Trevet's glosses.[49] Metge, who in his fictional works admitted to being an Epicurean, was a natural target for both Canals and Eiximenis. But even if it were only for his direct access to Latin, his writings would be a pointer to an alternative way of approaching the Latin classics—one that was far less dependent on the friars' "classicising" interest.

The French Mediation: Books, Journeys, and War

After surveying the British influence on Catalan writings through Latin texts, we must turn to French as a channel of transmission. It was through

French writing that the Arthurian legend impregnated medieval Europe—the works of the *matière de Bretagne* were read, both in French and Catalan, from the early fourteenth century.[50] The legend of Arthur's survival, to take a positively British instance, found its way into *La faula* by Guillem de Torroella (before 1374). Torroella placed Arthur on an Enchanted Island, somewhere in the East, and produced the most detailed report ever written of a meeting with the surviving king. At one point, Torroella challenges Arthur, who speaks in French, by pointing out that his tombstone had been found long ago, "according to history" [segons que recompta la gesta], that is, *La mort le roi Artu*. The king's reply, for which no precise source has been yet found, informs us that his wounds were healed by bathing in a nearby source of waters flowing down from the Tigris river, thereby implying that the Isle was not far from the Earthly Paradise.[51]

Leaving aside commonplace references in chapters 114 and 182, King Arthur appears twice in *Tirant lo Blanc*, the second time in a celebrated episode (chaps. 189–202) in which Martorell recreated Torroella's tale. Arthur is now found at Constantinople by Morgana and four allegorical ladies, which seems an appropriate enough location for an Eastern wonder, even more so if we notice that Lady Hope had been baptized "in the Jordan river" (chap. 189) and Torroella had set out on John the Baptist's day. In his first apparition, instead, Arthur passes unnoticed to the modern reader. He has now been taken from history—that is, again *La mort le roi Artu*, though now through its sentimental recreation in *mossèn* Gras's *Tragèdia de Lançalot*. The sentence borrowed from Gras by Martorell in chapter 28 reveals the Arthurian background of *Tirant*.[52] We have already been told about Guillem de Vàroic's deeds, and Tirant is about to meet him to be duly instructed; both characters, as is well known, fill in the names of the anonymous hermit and squire who meet in the prologue of Llull's *Llibre de l'orde de cavalleria*—by giving them names Martorell created a historical framework for his fiction. But Martorell still needed a name for the "great noble king" to whose "tournament" the Lullian squire is going.[53] This king, in chapter 28, will be the "righteous king of England," that is, Enric, who replaces "King Arthur" in Gras's original sentence.[54] Likewise, Tirant will be attending Enric/Arthur's tournament as if he were a new Sir Lancelot. No wonder then that the founding of the Order of the Garter by the king of England is related to "the Order of the Round Table that good King Arthur instituted in those times" (chap. 84).

More Eastern wonders originally imagined in Britain ended up in *Tirant lo Blanc*. Martorell borrowed from chapters 3 and 4 of Sir John Mandeville's *Voyage* not only the legend of the isle of Lango but bits of information about Greek geography.[55] It is likely that his immediate source was not Mandeville's Anglo-Norman compilation but a Catalan translation (doc. 1410), of which the only extant fragments have come to us through some seventeenth-century encyclopedic works.[56] France had been a mediating presence. In 1380 Prince Joan had asked Charles V for three books written in French: some *Canòniques de França*, Livy's *Ab urbe condita* (in Pierre Bersuire's version), and the *Mendievila*.[57] It is unlikely that Joan established any difference "di genere o specie" within the set.[58] Whether from Charles or from the duchess of Bar, Prince Joan finally obtained a copy of the *Voyage*, which was bound with *Lo purgatori de sant Patrici*.[59] Hence there is every reason to believe that the latter was also regarded as a document primarily reporting on the wonders of remote lands, and that, since the arrival as a devotional reading of Saltrey's *Tractatus* in 1320, a cultural shift had taken place. Indeed, the crown prince twice resorted to Ramon de Perellós, a nobleman educated at the court of Charles V, to get historical reports of the same kind. In 1378, when Perellós was in Cyprus, his lord required from him a copy of *De mirabilius Terrae Sanctae*.[60] In 1386 Joan was looking for the narrative by a certain knight who had been to Saint Patrick's Purgatory, according to Perellós's information.[61] It has nearly always been assumed that "that knight you refer to" was Owein; Riquer is more cautious.[62] Among the pack of monastic visions of the Other World that were translated into Catalan, there is a fragment of Louis d'Auxerre's journey to Saint Patrick's Purgatory (1358).[63]

Some years later, after the death of his lord, Perellós followed in Owein's and Louis d'Auxerre's footsteps. To convince his readers that he had really been to the Other World, he wrote a report of his journey to Ireland.[64] By that time going to Lough Derg had become a chivalric adventure. Perellós left Avignon in September 1397 and was back around March 1398. His journey was instrumental in finding the deceased king in purgatory in order to belie rumors that the king, having had no time to confess, was in hell. Indeed, a handful of Joan's counselors, including Metge and Perellós, were accused of corruption and of having encouraged, regardless of the king's poor health, the liking for hunting that caused his accidental death. Speaking from purgatory, on his way to salvation, King Joan implicitly admits to nepotism—a detail that is never given the importance it merits—and Perellós, we must assume, is cleansed by the purging nature of his ordeal.[65] That he really made the trip to Donegal is hardly to be doubted, although his description of Irish customs might have owed something to Gerald of Wales's *Topographia Hibernica*.[66] After transcribing Richard II's permit authorizing Perellós "in regnum nostrum Angliae venire, et per idem regnum versus terram nostram Hiberniae ad Purgatorium Sancti Patricii ibidem videndum at visitandum" [to come to our Kingdom of England and, crossing it, to proceed to our Hibernian land with a view to see and visit Saint Patrick's Purgatory], Riquer confidently states that the traveler did enter the cave in Lough Derg, where gases would have made him fall asleep.[67] Riquer trusts Froissart's reporting that Guillaume de l'Île and a certain English knight had told him that, on descending, "chaleur nous prit en les têtes" [we felt great heat in our heads], and so they fell sound asleep and "entrèrent en imaginations moult grandes et en songes merveilleux" [they got into great imaginings and wonderful dreams]. The English printer and publisher, William Caxton, a skilled translator of French works, seconds it: "And in lyke wise tolde to me a worshipful knyght of Bruggis named sir John de Banste that he had been therin in lyke wise and see none other thying but as afore is sayd [marvelous dreams]."[68] The only established fact is that Perellós borrowed his feigned experience of the Other World from Saltrey's *Tractatus* via an intermediate French version.[69]

Thousands of pilgrims congregate at Station Island every year. From the earliest printing (Toulouse 1484), Perellós's *Viatge* has been read as a devotional and eschatological popular work.[70] For Perellós, the supplier of King Joan's interest in exotic history, travel writing seems to have come first. In the prologue, he justified his journey by recalling both the *mirabilia* he had listened to in his youth at the French court and his traveling experience, to which he could testify "per vertadera fe" [as an eyewitness]—a phrase to which the chronicler Ramon Muntaner would have subscribed. The *Viatge*, in consequence, was addressed to those "who are eager to know about strange and wonderful things."[71] It is worth recalling that Gerald of Wales's *Topographia* was regarded as "a book that deals with the wonders of the Hibernian land," as its Occitan version states.[72] Through the *Topographia*, Saint Patrick's Purgatory found a place, among other wonders of Ireland, in the widely spread *Image du monde*.

So far I have been dealing with the Catalan reception of British works. An account of travels with no literary outcome falls out of the present scope, however interesting they may be for a better understanding of Martorell's stay in England.[73] Equally important is the involvement of England in the politics of the Continent, in as much as it was reflected in literary works, but this would require an article in its own right. The Hundred Years' War, to take the most prominent example, became the archetypal war between Christian powers (as in Bernat de So's *Vesió*, 1381–82) and so was present in the background of a climactic episode in the anonymous chivalric romance *Curial e Güelfa* (ca. 1430–45). Curial joins King Pere II the Great, "the best knight in the world," at an international tournament held at Melun—King Pere is, of course, the valiant knight who "d'ogne valor portò cinta la corda."[74] Curial, speaking under the influence of Mars, thinks of defying the English and the whole *matière de Bretagne*: "Soon we will see if the Bretons and the English are up to their pride, for they believe there are no other knights in the world but them."[75] King Pere, instead, "held a grudge" [havia un poc lo ventrell gros] against the French, since Charles d'Anjou, his rival in the struggle to dominate Sicily, had killed his father-in-law.[76] Hence the tournament stages a sort of Hundred Years' War fight all the way up to a fictional outcome: Pere and Curial's overall victory—though the former, it is remarked, hated the French as much as "he was close to the English side" [amava de cor los angleses].[77] A similar inclination is found in *Tirant lo Blanc* when Guillem de Vàroic reverses the course of history and prevents the fall of Rouen.[78] Martorell remained partisan to his country of adoption throughout the novel. In its final chapter, the heir to the newly reconquered Eastern Empire unexpectedly marries the daughter of the king of England. It is time we come full circle to reassess Martorell's command of English.

The crux of the matter is the precise source of Martorell's acquaintance with the deeds of Guy of Warwick. Hauf has rightly retrieved from Vaeth the idea that Tirant replicates the young Guy when Tirant goes to Byzantium and prevents Constantinople from falling to the Turk; however, the passages he quotes from one English version of the romance do not seem to me closer to Martorell's words than their French equivalents in *Le Rommant de Guy de Warwik et de Herolt d'Ardenne*.[79] For instance, when the emperor says in chapter 115 of *Tirant* that the bulk of the Greek Empire has been invaded, and states (my emphasis) "la gran pèrdua que havem fet de ciutats, *viles i castells*" [the great loss of cities, towns and castles that we have suffered], the French version reads: "Si lui ont prinses et abatues ses *villes et forteresses*" [they have taken and dominated his towns and castles], whereas the English text has: "Ther ys not lefte in that cuntre / Castell, towre nor cyte, / But hyt ys brente and stroyed all."[80] In *Tirant* the main culprit is "lo soldà," who is fully identified as the "soldà de Babilònia" in chapter 135; the *Rommant* has "le grand soudam de Babilonie et de Crenne," whereas in English he is "The ryche sowdan of Sysane."[81] For the time being it seems advisable to keep to Riquer's hypothesis that Martorell had a copy in French prose of the Guy of Warwick narrative.[82]

Such a supposition would not contradict in the least our knowledge of Martorell's sources: they are always in a Romance language. This is not to deny that he had developed a command of English. Even if he was no linguist, documents tell us that he stayed in England from March 1438 to February 1439, and he is not recorded back in Valencia until October 1440. Furthermore, the following sentence in the dedication of *Tirant* rings true: "for, if there are any shortcomings, certainly, my Lord, the blame is to be partly put on the English language, *the nature of which makes it impossible to translate adequately some words*" (my emphasis).[83] But Martorell used to enjoy playing with fact and fiction, and the language issue could be just another instance of that inclination. His real experience of England, however, comes to light on several occasions to enliven the novel. Thus Tirant (or rather Martorell, who must have been used to the dryness of Valencia) reports, in chapter 44, that warming beverages ("green ginger and malmsey") had been prepared for the dancers: "and they do so because the climate is so cold." Not much further down he remarks, as any present-day southerner would have done, "and they had provided wooden shelters and tents, in case it rained."

Tirant lo Blanc was not translated into Middle English, but its first Catalan source was: Caxton printed Llull's *Book of the Ordre of Chyvalry* after translating it, inevitably, from a French version.[84] It may well be the earliest case of a lasting influence of Catalan writing on English literature. Caxton also printed the *Mirrour of the World*, translating it from a French manuscript written at Bruges in 1464, which had been copied from another one owned by the duke of Berry.[85] This line of descent explains why chapter 12 included Cyprus, Sicily, Naples, Catalonia, Galicia, Navarre, and Portugal in a bizarre list of African "regyons and countrees."[86] Caxton added Aragon to the sequence and put things straight by making the following remark: "And how be it that the Auctour of this book saye that thise contrees ben in Afryke, yet, as I vnderstonde, alle thise ben within the lymytes and boundes of Europe."[87]

The English connection of *Tirant* is evident; some of its roots in British writing are not—John of Wales and his Catalan followers are needed to complete the picture, as much as some French version of *Gui de Warevic* and the Arthurian legend as turned into a *Tragèdia* by *mossèn* Gras in the shadow of Friar Trevet. All these works are demanded for the complex fabrics of *Tirant*. All these authors wrote, indeed, "within the lymytes and boundes of Europe."

Notes

1. Joanot Martorell (and Martí Joan de Galba?), *Tirant lo Blanch*, ed. Albert G. Hauf and Vicent Josep Escartí, 2 vols. (Valencia: Conselleria de Cultura de la Generalitat Valenciana, 1990), 1:1–2. All quotations from *Tirant* (with only the indication of chapter number for ease of reference) are from this edition. For "expondre" meaning "to translate," see Josep Pujol, *La memòria literària de Joanot Martorell: models i escriptura en el "Tirant lo Blanc"* (Barcelona: Curial and Publicacions de l'Abadia de Montserrat, 2002), pp. 24–26. All translations are my own.
2. See Martín de Riquer, *"Tirant lo Blanc," novela de historia y ficción* (Barcelona: Sirmio, 1992), pp. 91–96 and 103.
3. See Martí de Riquer, *Aproximació al "Tirant lo Blanc"* (Barcelona: Quaderns Crema, 1990), pp. 266–70, and Joseph A. Vaeth, *"Tirant lo Blanch": A Study*

of Its Authorship, Principal Sources and Historical Setting (New York: Columbia University Press, 1918). Albert G. Hauf, "La dama de Rodes: tècnica i 'energia boccaciana' en un novellino del Tirant lo Blanc," in Miscel·lània Joan Fuster, 8 vols., ed. Antoni Ferrando and Albert G. Hauf (Barcelona: Publicacions de l'Abadia de Montserrat, 1989–94), vol. 8, pp. 90–97 [79–118], has insisted on the English source. I shall come back to this issue at the end of the present essay.

4. Josep Hernando, Llibres i lectors a la Barcelona del s. XIV, 2 vols. (Barcelona: Fundació Noguera, 1995).

5. According to Hernando, Llibres i lectors, 2:752, one of them contained Peter of Blois's Libellus de arte dictandi rhetorice (1182/85). The Libellus was a brief preface to Peter of Blois's letter collection: see R.W. Southern, Scholastic Humanism and the Unification of Europe, 3 vols., The Heroic Age, with notes and additions by Lesley Smith and Benedicta Ward (Oxford: Blackwell, 2001), 2:183.

6. Josep M. Ruiz Simon, L'Art de Ramon Llull i la teoria escolàstica de la ciència (Barcelona: Quaderns Crema, 1999), pp. 105–07 and 118–27.

7. Mark D. Johnston, The Evangelical Rhetoric of Ramon Llull: Lay Learning and Piety in the Christian West around 1300 (New York: Oxford University Press, 1996), p. 77.

8. Martí de Barcelona, "La cultura catalana durant el regnat de Jaume II," Estudis Franciscans 91 (1990): 225–32 [215–95 and 92 (1991): 383–492].

9. Ramon Miquel y Planas, ed., Llegendes de l'altra vida (Barcelona: Biblioteca Catalana, 1914), p. 3.

10. Hernando, Llibres i lectors, 1:100.

11. See Joan de Gal·les, Breviloqui, ed., Norbert d'Ordal, Els Nostres Clàssics, A28 (Barcelona: Barcino, 1930), p. 1, and Conrado Guardiola Alcover, "Juan de Gales, Cataluña y Eiximenis," Antonianum 64 (1989): 340–42 [330–65].

12. See Curt J. Wittlin, "La Suma de Colaciones de Juan de Gales en Cataluña," Estudios Franciscanos 72 (1971): 193 [189–203], and Guardiola, "Juan de Gales," p. 347. Martí de Barcelona, "La cultura catalana," p. 231, dates the translation in the reign of Jaume II by mistake.

13. Pere Bohigas, Sobre manuscrits i biblioteques (Barcelona: Curial and Publicacions de l'Abadia de Montserrat, 1985), p. 180.

14. See Lola Badia, "Traduccions al català dels segles XIV i XV i innovació cultural i literària," Estudi General 11 (1991): 41 [31–50], and Martí de Barcelona, "La cultura catalana," p. 231.

15. David d'Avray, "Another Friar and Antiquity," in Religion and Humanism: Papers Read at the Eighteenth Summer Meeting and the Nineteenth Winter Meeting of the Ecclesiastical History Society, ed. Keith Robbins (Oxford: Blackwell and The Ecclesiastical History Society, 1981), pp. 49–58.

16. See, in general, Joan Josep Busqueta Riu and Juan Pemán Gavín, eds., Les universitats de la Corona d'Aragó, ahir i avui: estudis històrics (Barcelona: Pòrtic, 2002).

17. For Canals's biography, see Martí de Riquer, Història de la literatura catalana: part antiga, 3 vols. (Barcelona: Ariel, 1964), 2:433–36, and Antoni Canals,

trans., *Scipió e Aníbal. De providència (de Sèneca). De arra de ànima (d'Hug de Sant Víctor)*, ed. Martí de Riquer, Els Nostres Clàssics, A49 (Barcelona: Barcino, 1935), pp. 5–8.
18. Canals, *Scipió e Aníbal*, p. 86.
19. Riquer, *Història de la literatura catalana*, 2:442–45.
20. Francisco Rico, "Antoni Canals y Petrarca: para la fecha y las fuentes de *Scipió e Aníbal*," in *Estudios en memoria del profesor Manuel Sanchis Guarner*, 2 vols., ed. Emili Casanova (Valencia: Universidad de Valencia, 1984), 1:285–88.
21. Francisco Rico, "Nobiltà del Medioevo, nobiltà dell'Umanesimo," in *Gli Umanesimi medievali. Atti del II Congresso dell' Internationales Mittellateinerkomitee (Firenze, Certosa del Galluzzo, 11–15 settembre 1993)*, ed. Claudio Leonardi (Florence: SISMEL and Edizioni del Galluzzo, 1998), pp. 561–62 [559–66], remarks that King Joan was still looking for a copy of Livy, but is not certain that Livy's work was not available in the court of Jaume II. According to Martí de Barcelona, "La cultura catalana," p. 423, in 1322 Jaume II asked Friar Pedro Fernández de Híjar for "quendam librum Istoriarum Romanarum quem habetis."
22. Stefano M. Cingolani, *El somni d'una cultura: "Lo somni" de Bernat Metge* (Barcelona: Quaderns Crema, 2002), pp. 66–67.
23. Antoni Rubió i Lluch, *Documents per l'historia de la cultura catalana mig-eval*, 2 vols. (Barcelona: Institut d'Estudis Catalans, 1908–21), 2:lxxix–cxv.
24. Albert G. Hauf, *D'Eiximenis a sor Isabel de Villena: aportació a l'estudi de la nostra cultura medieval* (Barcelona: IFV and Publicacions de l'Abadia de Montserrat, 1990), p. 63.
25. Rubió i Lluch, *Documents*, 2:lxxxviii.
26. Rubió i Lluch, *Documents*, 2:lxxxvi–vii.
27. R.W. Southern, *Western Society and the Church in the Middle Ages* (London: Penguin, 1970), p. 294.
28. For Eiximenis's biography, see Martí de Barcelona, "Fra Francesc Eiximenis, O.F.M. (1340?–1409?): la seva vida, els seus escrits, la seva personalitat literària," *Estudis Franciscans* 40 (1928): 437–500; repr. in Emili Grahit et al., *Studia bibliographica* (Girona: Col·legi Universitari de Girona and Diputació de Girona, 1991), and Hauf, *D'Eiximenis a sor Isabel de Villena*, pp. 59–82.
29. Hauf, *D'Eiximenis a sor Isabel de Villena*, p. 156.
30. Beryl Smalley, *English Friars and Antiquity in the Early Fourteenth Century* (Oxford: Blackwell, 1960), p. 1.
31. Hauf, *D'Eiximenis a sor Isabel de Villena*, p. 63.
32. Jacques Monfrin, "La Bibliothèque du Francesc Eiximenis (1409)," *Bibliothèque d'Humanisme et Renaissance* 29 (1967): 447–87, as reprinted, with an appendix, in Grahit et al., *Studia bibliographica*, pp. 241–87.
33. Hauf, *D'Eiximenis a sor Isabel de Villena*, pp. 110–11.
34. Xavier Renedo, "Una imatge de la memòria entre les *Moralitates* de Robert Holcot i el *Dotzè* d'Eiximenis," *Annals de l'Institut d'Estudis Gironins* 31 (1990–91): 53–61.

35. Francesc Eiximenis, *Dotzè llibre del Crestià*, 2.5.675, ed. Curt Wittlin et al., 2 vols. (Girona: Col·legi Universitari de Girona and Diputació de Girona, 1987), 2.1:499.
36. Eiximenis, *Dotzè*, 2.5.675, ed. Wittlin, p. 500.
37. Hauf, *D'Eiximenis a sor Isabel de Villena*, pp. 116–23.
38. Eiximenis, *Dotzè*, 2.5.608, ed. Wittlin, pp. 329–30.
39. Eiximenis, *Dotzè*, 2.5.609, ed. Wittlin, pp. 333–34.
40. For a survey of this conflict, see Cingolani, *El somni d'una cultura*, pp. 91–97. In 1396 Eiximenis wrote to King Martí, soon after his accession to the throne: "Your High Lordship, the noble cities and towns should be close to your heart, for, in the long run, they will remove you from mud and will uphold your position." See Sadurní Martí, "Les cartes autògrafes de Francesc Eiximenis," *Estudi General* 22 (2002): 248. I am grateful to Jaume Torró for calling my attention to this letter.
41. Hauf, *D'Eiximenis a sor Isabel de Villena*, pp. 125–49. See also Guardiola, "Juan de Gales," pp. 354–61.
42. Ruth Leslie, "A Source for Juan Fernández de Heredia's *Ram de flores*," *Studia Neophilologica* 45 (1973): 159–60.
43. Joan de Gal·les, *Breviloqui*, pp. 15–17.
44. See Alexandre Olivar, "Sobre un manuscrit poc conegut de la versió catalana antiga del *Breviloquium de virtutibus* de Joan de Gal·les," in *Studia in honorem prof. M. de Riquer*, 3 vols. (Barcelona: Quaderns Crema, 1988), 3:87–95; Guardiola, "Juan de Gales," pp. 338–39; and Pere March, *Obra completa*, ed. Lluís Cabré, Els Nostres Clàssics, A132 (Barcelona: Barcino, 1993), p. 37.
45. Olivar, "Sobre un manuscrit," in *Studia M. de Riquer*, p. 91. See additional data on readership in Guardiola, "Juan de Gales," pp. 341–54, and March, *Obra completa*, p. 42. John of Wales's *Compendiloquium* and *Tractatus de VII vitiis* may have also been translated into Catalan, according to Guardiola, "Juan de Gales," pp. 340 and 349.
46. Francesc Eiximenis, *La societat catalana al segle XIV*, ed. Jill Webster, Antologia Catalana, 30 (Barcelona: Edicions 62, 1967), p. 37.
47. Pujol, *La memòria literària*, pp. 215–19. The *Breviloqui* was copied along with fragments of a Catalan version of Seneca's tragedies: see Joan de Gal·les, *Breviloqui*, pp. 16–17. This manuscript was not located by Tomàs Martínez in his edition of L.A. Sèneca, *"Tragèdies": traducció catalana medieval amb comentaris del segle XIV de Nicolau Trevet*, 2 vols., Els Nostres Clàssics, B14–15 (Barcelona: Barcino, 1995), 1:78, and is probably lost. See Olivar, "Sobre un manuscrit," in *Studia M. de Riquer*, p. 94 n4, and Guardiola, "Juan de Gales," p. 339 n20.
48. See, respectively, Lola Badia, "Bernat Metge i els *auctores*: del material de construcció al producte elaborat," *Boletín de la Real Academia de Buenas Letras de Barcelona* 43 (1991–92): 25–40, and Cingolani, *El somni d'una cultura*, pp. 79 and 81.
49. Giuseppe Billanovich, *I primi umanisti e le tradizioni dei classici latini: prolusione al corso di letteratura italiana detta il 2 febbraio 1951* (Freiburg, Switzerland: Edizioni

Universitarie, 1953). Trevet's glossing endeavor also found its way into Catalan through Pierre Bersuire's partial version of Livy and Raoul de Presles's *Cité de Dieu*, with additional exegesis by Thomas Waleys. See Curt J. Wittlin, "La traducció catalana anònima de les *Històries romanes* I–VIII de Titus Livi," *Estudis Romànics* 13 (1963–68): 277–315, and his "Traductions et commentaries médiévaux de la *Cité de Dieu* de saint Augustin," *Travaux de Linguistique et de Littérature* 16 (1978): 532–33 [531–55].

50. Martí de Barcelona, "La cultura catalana," p. 231, and Pujol, *La memòria literària*, p. 40.
51. For an updated account of Torroella's work, see Lola Badia, ed., *Tres contes meravellosos del segle XIV* (Barcelona: Quaderns Crema, 2003). The case for an Eastern location had been convincingly argued by Roger Sherman Loomis, "The Legend of Arthur's Survival," in his edited collection, *Arthurian Literature in the Middle Ages: A Collaborative History* (Oxford: Clarendon, 1959), p. 68, which seems to rule out the odd coincidence with Gervase of Tilbury's *Otia imperialia*.
52. Júlia Butinyà, "Una nova font del *Tirant lo Blanc*," *Revista de Filología Románica* 7 (1990): 191–96.
53. Ramon Llull, *Llibre de l'orde de cavalleria*, ed. Albert Soler Llopart, Els Nostres Clàssics, A127 (Barcelona: Barcino, 1988), p. 162.
54. Mossèn Gras, *Tragèdia de Lançalot*, ed. Martí de Riquer (Barcelona: Quaderns Crema, 1984), pp. 4–5.
55. Martí de Riquer, "El *Voyage* de sir John Mandeville en català," in *Miscel·lània d'homenatge a Enric Moreu Rey*, ed. Albert Manent and Joan Veny, 3 vols. (Barcelona: Publicacions de l'Abadia de Montserrat, 1988), 3:151–62, and Riquer, *Aproximació al "Tirant lo Blanc*," pp. 302–06.
56. Riquer, "El *Voyage* de sir John Mandeville," in *Miscel·lània Enric Moreu Rey*, p. 152.
57. Rubió i Lluch, *Documents*, 2:221.
58. Rico, "Nobiltà del Medioevo," in *Gli umanesimi medievali*, p. 561.
59. Riquer, "El *Voyage* de sir John Mandeville," in *Miscel·lània Enric Moreu Rey*, p. 156.
60. Riquer, *Història de la literatura catalana*, 2:310.
61. Rubió i Lluch, *Documents*, 1:342.
62. Riquer, *Història de la literatura catalana*, 2:311.
63. This fragment was identified by L.L. Hammerich, "Le pélerinage du Louis d'Auxerre au Purgatoire de S. Patrice: correction du text latin par une traduction catalane," *Romania* 55 (1929): 118–24. I owe this bibliographical reference to Jane Whetnall.
64. Riquer, *Història de la literatura catalana*, 2:309–32, remains the best overall account of Perellós's *Viatge*. See also Dorothy M. Carpenter, "The Pilgrim from Catalonia/Aragon: Ramon de Perellós, 1397," in *The Medieval Pilgrimage to Saint Patrick's Purgatory: Lough Derg and the European Tradition*, ed. Michael Haren and Yolande de Pontfarcy (Enniskillen: Clogher Historical Society, 1988), pp. 190–201.

65. For Perellós's encounter with King Joan, see Arseni Pacheco, ed., *Viatges a l'altre món: dos relats dels segles XIV i XVI* (Barcelona: Edicions 62, 1973), p. 45.
66. Joan M. Ribera, "Una altra lectura de Ramon de Perellós prèvia al seu viatge," *Revista de l'Alguer* 8 (1997): 233–51 and 9 (1998): 273–89, provides only small coincidences between Perellós's description and the *Topographia*.
67. Riquer, *Història de la literatura catalana*, 2:328–30.
68. Oliver H. Prior, ed., *Caxton's Mirrour of the World*, EETS, Extra Series 110 (London: The Early English Text Society, 1913), p. 99.
69. D.D.R. Owen, *The Vision of Hell: Infernal Journeys in Medieval French Literature* (Edinburgh: Scottish Academic Press, 1970), p. 221. See also Jordi Ainaud, "Un traductor al Purgatori: a propòsit del *Viatge al Purgatori de sant Patrici* de Ramon de Perellós," in *Traducció i literatura: homenatge a Ángel Crespo*, ed. G. González and F. Lafarga (Vic: EUMO, 1997), pp. 133–41.
70. Barry Taylor, "Los libros de viajes en la Edad Media hispánica: bibliografía y recepción," in *Actas do IV Congresso da Associação Hispânica de Literatura Medieval (Lisboa, 1–5 outubro 1991)*, ed. Aires A. Nascimiento and Cristina Almeida Ribeiro, 3 vols. (Lisbon: Cosmos, 1991), 1:64 [57–70].
71. Pacheco, *Viatges a l'altre món*, p. 27.
72. London, BL, MS Add. 17920, fol. 19v.
73. For their connection with Martorell, mention must be made of *mossèn* Felip Boïl and Vicenç Climent. See Martí de Riquer, ed., *Lletres de batalla*, 3 vols. (Barcelona: Barcino, 1968), 3:19–28; Riquer, *"Tirant lo Blanc," novela de historia y ficción*, pp. 46–55; and Robert B. Tate, "Joanot Martorell in England," *Estudis Romànics* 10 (1962): 277–79.
74. Dante Alighieri, *La "Commedia" secondo l'antica Vulgata*, ed. Giorgio Petrocchi, 4 vols. (Milan: Mondadori, 1966–67), *Purgatorio*, vol. 3, VII, line 114.
75. Ramon Aramon, ed., *Curial e Güelfa*, 3 vols. (Barcelona: Barcino, 1930–33), 2:86.
76. Aramon, *Curial e Güelfa*, 2:114.
77. Aramon, *Curial e Güelfa*, 2:144.
78. Pujol, *La memòria literària*, pp. 47–48.
79. See note 3 above, and Hauf, "La dama de Rodes," in *Miscel·lània Joan Fuster*, 8:92–97.
80. D.J. Conlon, ed., *Le Rommant de Guy de Warwik et de Herolt d'Ardenne* (Chapel Hill: The University of North Carolina Press, 1969), p. 154; Julius Zupitza, ed., *"The Romance of Guy of Warwick": The Second or 15th-century Version, Edited from the Paper Ms. Ff. 2.38. in the University Library, Cambridge*, 2 vols., EETS 25–26 (London: The Early English Text Society, 1875–76), vol. 1, ll. 2735–37.
81. Conlon, *Le Rommant de Guy de Warwik*, p. 154; Zupitza, *The Romance of Guy of Warwick*, vol. 1, l. 2729.
82. See again Riquer, *Aproximació al "Tirant lo Blanc,"* pp. 266–70. However, in chapter 135 of *Tirant* the Greek emperor bears the name Enric, which, as is implied in William J. Entwistle, "*Tirant lo Blanch* and the Social Order of

the End of the 15th Century," *Estudis Romànics* 2 (1949–50): 162, and Riquer, *"Tirant lo Blanc," novela de historia y ficción*, p. 120, could be a bad reading of Hernis, the emperor's name in both the Anglo-Norman version and the English texts: see Alfred Ewert, ed., *"Gui de Warevic," roman du XIIIe siècle*, 2 vols. (Paris: Champion, 1933), 1:89; Zupitza, *The Romance of Guy of Warwick*, 1:101; and Julius Zupitza, ed., *"The Romance of Guy of Warwick": Edited from the Auchinlek Ms. in the Advocate's Library, Edinburgh, and from Ms. 107 in Caius College, Cambridge*, 2 vols., EETS 42 and 49 (London: The Early English Text Society, 1883–87), 1:164. The *Rommant* reads "Hermym," according to Conlon, *Le Rommant de Guy de Warwik*, p. 172.
83. William J. Entwistle, "Observacions sobre la dedicatòria i la primera part del *Tirant lo Blanc*," *Revista de Catalunya* 7 (1927): 381–98, remains the main asset to assess Martorell's first-hand acquaintance with English society: see Riquer, *"Tirant lo Blanc," novela de historia y ficción*, p. 92 n4, and cf. his footnotes in Vol. 1 of Joanot Martorell and Martí Joan de Galba, *"Tirante el Blanco": versión castellana impresa en Valladolid en 1511*, 5 vols., ed. Martín de Riquer (Madrid: Espasa Calpe, 1974). According to Entwistle, "Observacions," p. 389, Martorell transliterated toponyms and title names most exactly. To substantiate such a statement, these should be checked against medieval language by a student of Middle English; see, for instance, "Grànug" (chap. 42), a term spelled "Grenewych," and only possibly pronounced as a three-syllabic word, in Chaucer's "The Reeve's Prologue," *The Canterbury Tales*, I.3907, in *The Riverside Chaucer*, ed. Larry D. Benson (Boston: Houghton Mifflin, 1987).
84. Llull, *Llibre de l'orde de cavalleria*, p. 65.
85. Prior, *Caxton's Mirrour of the World*, pp. vii–viii.
86. Prior, *Caxton's Mirrour of the World*, p. 93 n6.
87. Prior, *Caxton's Mirrour of the World*, pp. 93–94.

CHAPTER 3

THE SHRINE AS MEDIATOR: ENGLAND, CASTILE, AND THE PILGRIMAGE TO COMPOSTELA

Ana Echevarría Arsuaga

This essay focuses on the role of the shrine of Saint James in Compostela as a catalyst of the relations between England and Castile during the fourteenth and the beginning of the fifteenth centuries, when diplomatic and military contacts were adversely affected because of the Hundred Years' War.

The Origins of English Pilgrimage to Santiago

During the Middle Ages, pilgrimage was a way of evoking and establishing identity, as it had been since ancient times. The Christian Church fostered this activity once it became officially accepted as a way to strengthen cohesion among its followers. A number of holy places where relics of Jesus, Mary, saints and martyrs could be visited helped to draw a sacred map of Christendom throughout the lands of the former Roman Empire. The creation of routes in which pilgrimage sites were organized in a hierarchical order marked a cornerstone in the foundations of medieval Christianity. The sanctuaries and their routes had an important role in structuring space and the economic activities of the medieval population, and therefore became exceptionally important for the rulers of both the states and the Church.[1]

The three main sites of pilgrimage during the early Middle Ages— Jerusalem, Rome, and Constantinople—respond to a centralized religious pattern, linked to the expansion of early Christendom, monasticism, and the diffusion of the Roman ritual under an imperial power. However, after the ninth century, what may be termed "national sanctuaries" appeared, related to the emergence of powerful monarchies with a need for legitimization, often provided by religious sanction conferred by a holy mission linked in some way to a religious object. In the late Middle Ages, the unstable situation of the Roman Pontificate—it had first moved to Avignon and was later divided by schism—contributed to enhance the popular aspects of religious life, including pilgrimage. Destinations had multiplied by then and holy sites had to compete for pilgrims. Rulers tried to control the development of pilgrimage routes and, at the same time, to obtain profit from this movement. The aims of pilgrims became, thus, the object of laws and taxes, of diplomatic encounters and treaties, unrelated to religious concerns. A *pilgrim* was identified with a *traveler*, and the term was used for anybody who left his home. Legal protection was offered in these conditions for the *traveler* in a wide sense.

As Constance C. Storrs shows, English pilgrimage to Santiago de Compostela provides an interesting case study which allows us to explore the importance of pilgrimage routes and their links to the political and economic interests of the countries involved.[2] The fact that there was both a maritime and a land route adds to the complexity of the relations established there. The sea route was probably the first used by English and Irish pilgrims, based on the itinerary followed by the Vikings as early as the ninth century. Even Carolingian France might have been aware of the "discovery" of Apostle Santiago's shrine in this way. The sea was not a geographical barrier between England and Spain, or the *Finis Terrae* as defined by Franks or Italians, but rather part of the itinerary which linked Northern European ports with the Mediterranean, where the Iberian Peninsula was always a convenient intermediate stop. Given the traditional enthusiasm of the British people for pilgrimage to Rome and Jerusalem, it is easy to understand the success of Santiago de Compostela as a destination for their holy pilgrimages.[3]

Starting a trip from England, Ireland, Norway or Sweden to Santiago always involved taking a ship to cross the straits or channels. Therefore, travelers could consider easily that going by sea to Galicia was preferable than traveling first by sea, and then by land, to join the main route of the road to Santiago. In fact, despite its risks, the sea itinerary was safer, cheaper, and faster than the land route, as sailing from England to La Coruña, the main port of Santiago, did take only about four days since the thirteenth century. Those who chose that option and sailed across the Spanish Sea left from London, Plymouth, Bristol, and Southampton. A radial network was created between Santiago and the most important ports in Galicia: Vivero, La Coruña, Laxe, Muxía, and Noya. Storms and trade could divert this traffic to other ports such as Santander, Castro Urdiales, or Bilbao.

Once arrived at the Iberian shores, pilgrims could either continue walking close to the coast toward Galicia, or else travel inland to join the main route to Santiago, with all its holy sites and relics. The coastal way was difficult because of the mountains, but it had a special appeal, as the pilgrim could then visit the important church of San Salvador de Oviedo, without much hindrance. The connections to the inland route have not been traced. Such detours as the route that goes through the valley of Mena (Burgos) might have been one of those secondary roads from Castro Urdiales or Bilbao to one of the sites of the main road in the Palencia section.[4]

The sea itinerary was the oldest one followed by pilgrims traveling to Galicia. Undoubtedly, the traffic of Celtic and Anglo-Saxon monks going to the Continent had taken that form as early as the sixth century. It is not surprising then that the literary genres that speak about this route were accounts of miracles and hagiographies of local saints, devised for the saints' honor and to convince the simple folk to engage in such an arduous trip. The first Anglo-Saxon to take the Spanish Sea route was Saint Godric of Finchale, whose life and miracles were compiled around 1170. He was said to have made several pilgrimages to Rome and Jerusalem during his life, but he also visited some local sanctuaries such as Saint Andrews in Scotland, or Compostela in the Iberian Peninsula, before settling in Finchale, near Durham.

The miracles of Saint William of Norwich share this scope but add another quality to the pilgrimage: a healing sphere, which was forgotten, as Santiago became the Patron saint of Reconquest ideology. Several accounts show how pilgrims traveled to Santiago to recover from illness, paying one penny as exvote. But in all cases, it was the local saint who healed them when they returned.[5]

Another possibility developed during the Angevin period. A pilgrim could start in the same English ports, or from Irish towns such as Galway, Waterford, or Kinsale,[6] to arrive at Bordeaux or Gascony. Then he would take the traditional French Road to Saint-Jean Pied de Port, Roncesvalles, and then to Compostela.[7] This was a much longer way, but it served two purposes: visiting the most famous holy sites on French soil and tightening the links with the area of France that was under Plantagenet power. Noblemen could either cross the Channel for holy reasons or, rather, make good use of their stay on French soil—in order to fight a war or to supervise their lands—to join the pilgrimage. Since the land route through Europe via the French Road could sometimes take months to complete, it was not rare to find pilgrims who sought any ship that could leave them in closer ports on the French shores, to save them some days or weeks of marching.

Most of the documents about English pilgrims from the eleventh to the thirteenth centuries—preserved in abbeys of the French Road—reveal that they followed this route. Starting in 1064, these pilgrims had in common their noble origins and their possession of lands in England, which they graciously granted to the monasteries where they were lodged on their way to Santiago. The records of Sainte Marie de la Sauve Majeur, near Bordeaux, provide several examples, such as Robert II, earl of Derby (ca. 1139–59), William, earl of Lincoln (ca. 1141–53), or the great bishop of Winchester, Henry of Blois (1151). Other cases include that of Richard Mauleverer, a Yorkshire landowner who lodged in Marmoutier Abbey, near Tours, and granted the abbot some lands in Yorkshire (ca. 1100–04).[8] Less important landlords also made their way to Santiago and the influence of Jacobean imagery in remote English churches reveals the impact pilgrimage had in the diffusion of ideas.

As miracle accounts and hagiographies of Norman saints replaced those of the native Anglo-Saxons, the subject of the pilgrimage to Compostela started to appear in these Norman sources as well, with the motif of storms in the Channel while the pilgrims crossed to France. The final intention of the accounts was, however, to enhance the figure of English saints with respect to the generally acclaimed Santiago. The construction of pilgrimage mentality in England using nonlocal saints had very much to do with the process of formation of almost "national" identities in the Christian realms. The collection of miracles of Saint Thomas Becket presents accounts of pilgrims traveling to Santiago and going back to offer crosses to the English saint instead.

It is in this same period when the first bond between the English crown and Compostela may be established. Henry II Plantagenet had asked Ferdinand II of Leon for a safe-conduct to travel to Santiago (1177), but unfortunately he could not perform his pilgrimage, which might have been made years later by one of his sons.[9] Henry II had just judged the dispute between Alfonso VIII of Castile and Sancho VI of Navarre, who had occupied Castilian lands, so his implication in Iberian affairs might have prompted the inclusion of his name in the long list of promoters of Santiago's cult.

During the wars fought by King John I (1199–1216), pilgrims were dissuaded to travel due to both internal and external circumstances. Only Philip, bishop of Durham, is recorded to have traveled via Dover, Wissant, and Chinon in 1201, enjoying the protection of the Church. The next reference is only fifteen years later, when Lord Ralph of Normanville asked for permission to cross to Santiago. He was asked to leave his elder sons as hosts in England to take part in the campaign against the king of France and to take the quickest route so that he could be back in Easter. Unfortunately, we ignore whether Lord Ralph was able to fulfill his vote, but war did not end until September 1217, making roads and navigation very unsafe. After that date, when the French army withdrew, pilgrimage flourished again and written records with it.

Apart from donations, another main source of knowledge about English pilgrims is administrative records, such as royal licenses and safe-conducts. Royal officers could not leave the country without the king's permission, in the same way that noblemen were not supposed to leave armed service while there was any suspicion of attack. The general conditions established in these licenses included limiting the allowed absence to periods between four months and a year, provided that there was someone to substitute the pilgrim in his office. In the case of Roger of Zouchea, his license also specified that, if he died during his journey, his heirs would have one year to arrange for the payment of his debts. It was common for these royal officers to try to have all the due salaries paid by the royal treasure before their departure, but sometimes they only got guarantees or bills of exchange for the way. The rest of the population of the kingdom could move more freely and, therefore, have left few traces of their displacements.

The diplomatic relations established by Alfonso X of Castile and Henry III of England, concerning the dispute for Gascony, resulted in the most important peace treaty signed between the two countries (March 1254). It also contributed to enliven the traffic of English pilgrims to Santiago, protected by Alfonso's legislation, contained in the treaty and in more general works such as the *Partidas* and the *Fuero Real*.[10] He also permitted that whoever had started pilgrimage without writing a testament could do so while in Castile without any legal hindrance.

In the midst of negotiations concerning the Crusades, Clement IV summoned his legate in England, Ottobuoni, cardinal of Saint Adrian. Ottobuoni was commanded to make a pilgrimage to Compostela in order to assess the state of the Castilian Church. After some months passed without any attempts on the part of the legate to start his journey, the pope insisted. If he reached Castile, he had to exhort Alfonso X to give his aid to the Holy Land. Otherwise, the cardinal should delegate a Spanish priest for this mission.[11]

A year later (1269), the negotiations for the renewal of a truce between Theobald II of Navarre and Henry III of England, by request of Saint Louis show an interest on the part of Edward, prince of Wales, to travel through Navarre to perform his pilgrimage to Compostela. Theobald II offered to protect him and his retinue and to provide them with the most necessary things they might need during their journey.[12]

Edward II's reign was the last during which English pilgrims could travel with a certain ease, once the royal license had been provided. This is the case of the king's gamekeeper in Trent, Radulph of Monte Hermeri, who was authorized to leave his office for six months in 1315 to travel to

Compostela. The prestige of hospitals on the road to Santiago helped to attract donations from throughout Christendom. Thus, in 1321 Edward II gave a safe-conduct to the legates in charge of asking for alms for the hospital of Saint Mary of Roncesvalles, "given the benefices constantly received in that hospital by poor pilgrims who travel to visit the shrine of the Apostle Santiago."[13]

Jacobean Pilgrimage from England in the Fourteenth and Fifteenth Centuries

During the fourteenth and fifteenth centuries, the routes which had been followed by pilgrims traveling to Santiago in the former centuries were severely threatened by the Hundred Years' War (1337–1453), so the itineraries changed. Prohibitions to travel became generalized according to pro- or anti-English alliances negotiated by the Castilian kings. But because it was a religious journey, it was also affected by the Great Schism that divided the Roman Church between 1378 and 1417. Once unity had been destroyed, the struggle of shrines to keep their status among pilgrims was shattered. The role of Saint James as mediator was questioned due to other religious issues, and his characteristic performance as "Muslim-killer" was no longer necessary, as military ideology turned against other Christians instead of Muslims. Despite those events, this was a golden age for written itineraries and accounts of pilgrims, due in part to the increase in literacy among the nobility and burgesses who performed the pilgrimage. Three fundamental sources relate to the English pilgrims: the English translation of the *Pilgrim's Guide*, the English *Itinerary* in verse published by Purchas in the seventeenth century, but attributed to the fourteenth, which places the pilgrimage to Santiago in close relation to a wider route joining Compostela to Rome and Jerusalem, and, finally, the account of the fellow of Eton William Wey, who followed this same route in 1456.[14]

The situation in the twelfth century, when the French route crossing the Angevin realms enabled the traffic of English subjects to Compostela just by crossing the Channel had completely changed to a complex map of English domains in France during the fourteenth century. If the spoiled French land and the constant moves of armies did not dissuade the prospective pilgrim, the levies of troops limited royal licenses for non-warlike purposes. Moreover, limitations on commerce stopped many merchants from engaging in their regular activities to provide for the needs of the armies. As a natural consequence, those English pilgrims who dared and could perform a pilgrimage to Santiago preferred to avoid the dangerous French Road and to travel by sea, despite climate, pirate attacks, or contending fleets. Thus, the most frequent itinerary was the sea route to La Coruña, rather far from the more conflictive routes of the Channel and the Gulf of Biscay. Being in the area of influence of the English and Portuguese fleets, English vessels felt safer in the Atlantic coast.

Other pilgrims used their diplomatic missions as an excuse to visit the shrine, traveling through some of the kingdoms unaffected by war. Several Englishmen asked the king of Aragon for safe-conducts to go to Santiago in 1382 and 1399, and none of them asked for a return document, so it may be assumed that they found a place to sail back in one of the ships starting at the Atlantic ports.[15]

"Chivalric" pilgrimages had by then replaced part of the pious motives of the trip to Compostela. The journey around the European courts making war, learning new customs, jousting, and stretching alliances among the noblemen might include a visit to the most important shrines in Europe. Knights and squires appear frequently in individual safe-conducts, whereas collective pilgrimage was left for those who could not afford the long trip by land and who preferred the fast journey by sea.[16]

Merchants and shipowners joined this last group, as they obtained economic profits from the expeditions. The road to Compostela had always been privileged scenery for trade, both by sea and land. The *Pilgrim's Guide* warned the wayfarers not to take too much money or goods to sell on the way, given the penitential purpose of the journey, although the *Liber de miraculis* includes three references to merchants in the twenty-two miracles recorded. It seems that trade is an admitted evil, whereas the merchants' greed and deception were thoroughly condemned.[17]

With the development of guilds, those pilgrims who had traveled to Santiago started to get organized in groups to celebrate annual meetings. First, it was a mass to remember their journey, and later, they started to build chapels, order stained-glass windows and altars with the effigy of Saint James, founded hospitals for pilgrims, or helped to assist the members of the guild itself. Hence, their feast was celebrated on July 25 with a huge banquet and, often, theatre plays about the life of the saint. Apart from the French cities and towns such as Paris, Bordeaux, Moissac, Saint Quentin or Compiègne, closely linked to the French Road, Jacobean guilds spread to the main trade-centers in Europe, such as Gaunt, Douai, or Saint Trond in Flanders, and many others in Germany. The textile industry, one of the main exports in Northern European economy, which linked Flanders, England, and Castile, seems to have supported the cult of Saint James and fostered a pilgrimage favored by regular trade in the northern coast of the Iberian Peninsula. It is not surprising, then, that Jacobean pilgrimage in England was supported by non-Jacobean guilds formed by textile workers. For instance, in Lincoln, the Fullers' Guild (1297) and the Confraternity of Resurrection (1374) argued that if any of their members wanted to make the journey to Rome, Santiago in Galicia, or the Holy Land, the other members of the guild had to walk them to the town's gate and give them at least half a penny to contribute to the expenses.[18] The figure of Chaucer's Wife of Bath, a well-known weaver herself, may suggest a relationship between the English textile sector and Santiago, a connection which needs to be studied further.[19]

Towns on the road to Santiago were soon affected by war. The Cathedral chapter in Lugo was ready to reduce the rate of renting the altar and wine of Saint Mary's feasts to one hundred *maravedis* if the kings of France and England started to wage war against each other between February and May 1345, a period of great traffic of pilgrims.[20]

Several English kings and noblemen—starting with Edward III, the earl of March, and others—took their vote to visit Saint James's shrine during the war, and had to abandon their plans. In 1355, the pope accorded them a delay, just before an expedition to Calais, where all these men had been engaged. Relief was also found when a bishop accepted the cost of pilgrimage to found a chapel, an altar, or a window in honor of Saint James within the borders of England, a device which was widely used in these times of peril. Those were the cases of Agnes de Hulme, from Bacton-in-Lonsadale, persuaded by Bishop Thoresby of York to give her money for a window in his cathedral, dedicated to Saint James and Saint Catherine (1361), or the five pilgrims who offered an altar and guild to Saint James in Saint Peters's church in Burgh, Lincolnshire (1365).[21]

Systematic research into English official records was undertaken by Storrs in the 1960s, and provides first-hand information about individual pilgrims and large numbers of ships traveling to Santiago in the fourteenth and fifteenth centuries, which complements materials from Spanish sources. The Close, Patent and Treaty Rolls include letters of protection, safe-conducts, letters of attorney, and permissions to leave the country for intended pilgrims. However, they cannot be regarded as proof that every journey envisaged was actually made. Three Exchequer records also contain valuable information on the English side: the expense account of John Sheppey, prior of Rochester, who in 1346 combined pilgrimage with a diplomatic mission; the list of payments made by John Haytfield for John of Gaunt's expedition; and a Bristol Customs Account for 1396–97, which needs to be studied further.[22]

Despite the efforts made by Edward III to sign a marriage treaty with Castile between 1330 and 1340, Alfonso XI chose to accept a French alliance while maintaining peace with England. Both England and France developed their foreign policies with regard to Castile around the powerful merchant fleet, and the regulations concerning merchants and piracy of course were an important part of the negotiations. As a result of Alfonso's choice, his son Pedro I (1350–69) inherited a hidden conflict with England, which was later manifested in Edward III's belligerent policies by means of piracy. Castilian northern ports had to sign individual truces with Edward and the inhabitants of Bayonne, from where pirate attacks used to start. Only after 1362, when France openly backed Pedro's half-brother, Enrique of Trastamara, who claimed the crown of Castile, did Pedro I sign a treaty with Edward, prince of Wales, in which he decidedly accepted the English alliance. Although Storrs claimed the period after the treaty of Brétigny (1361) and the Anglo-Castilian alliance to be "one of respite... during which the pressure of shipping was temporarily reduced,"[23] it is also possible to think that the civil war that scourged Castile during the following six years did little to foster pilgrimage to Santiago's shrine.[24] And yet, the list of English pilgrims traveling to Santiago between 1361 and 1367 is remarkable, although usually they combine diplomatic affairs with pilgrimage.[25]

When Enrique managed to kill Pedro I in the battlefield of Montiel (1369), he was back to the pro-French policies devised by their father, and pilgrimage became almost impossible for the next twenty years. According to the 1454 Anglo-Castilian treaty, after Enrique II won his throne, he was obliged by the French king to sign a treaty according to which travelers were forbidden to cross from Castile to England and vice versa without safe-conducts and permission given by the king of France.[26] No more than twenty English knights could reach the coast of Castile at a time without the king of France being informed. Moreover, Castile was not free to negotiate or establish any kind of agreement with England, not even for their common interests concerning trade in the Atlantic and Northern Sea, until the truces of Leulingham (1389) made a certain approach possible.

During the earlier part of Richard II's reign, Franco-Castilian raids on the southern coast of England became common, and yet pilgrimage did not stop completely despite the difficult conditions of the sea route. The nobleman Galfrid of Poulglon was authorized to travel to the sanctuary of Our Lady of Rocheamadour, in France, and to Compostela, with all his retinue—including his wife and two daughters, the clerk master Robert Brocherioul, pages, servants, horses, and anything else they needed for their journey (July 13, 1383). It is impossible to know whether the retinue sailed from port, but at least the intention to maintain the traffic in the pilgrimage routes across Europe may be noticed. Since the journey brought the knight first into France and, later, to Castile, one might assume that the king of France could give his own safe-conduct for the second part of the trip. Safe-conducts of this kind were repeated throughout Richard II's reign. They stipulated the duration of royal protection, normally for one year, enough for the round trip.[27] Richard's uncle, John of Gaunt, duke of Lancaster, was the most powerful man in the realm, but never appointed as regent due to his unpopularity among magnates and the common people. However, his journey to Santiago de Compostela started a new trend in the (former) English pilgrimage to the holy site.

John of Gaunt's arrival in Castile must be understood in the context of Anglo-Castilian foreign policies.[28] Whereas Pedro I of Castile and Enrique II Trastamara found support in England and France, respectively, the Castilian navy had taken sides in the conflict, always against England. On the other hand, the Portuguese fleet, allied to the Englishmen, was comparatively small, so any intervention from the Castilian navy would alter the effectiveness of any land attack on the part of England against France. Therefore, the Franco-Castilian alliance was based on the funding and support of armed squadrons of Castilian galleys in the Channel and the Atlantic, attacking English ports between 1370 and 1380. The pressure was so big that, around 1384, Richard II authorized some coastal towns to pay a rescue for their own safety. At that point, John of Gaunt, married to Pedro I's daughter and heiress, Constanza, suggested he could claim the Castilian throne for his family. The Portuguese triumph at Aljubarrota helped him to push his suggestion forward, as João I was ready to engage in war against Castile as well. Both Richard II and the Parliament agreed to help the duke of Lancaster and his wife by lending them enormous sums of money and giving licenses to the men who volunteered to fight with them.

Although Labarge considers the duke of Lancaster's visit to Santiago's shrine as a "fortuitous activity" within his military campaign against Juan I of Castile, the symbolic importance of such movement suggests a careful planning on the part of John of Gaunt and his Castilian supporters. It should be remembered that the Apostle Santiago, Patron saint of Castile, was the figure chosen to ratify newly anointed kings. An articulated effigy of the saint was used to knight the king when he was proclaimed since Alfonso XI's reign, as no other knight in the country was considered worthy of such honor. It may be assumed that John of Gaunt's arrival at La Coruña on July 25, 1386, to start his conquest of Castile from there, was meaningful. The English fleet was said to have docked on the day of the local feast—suspiciously enough—and all the "royal" family went in solemn procession to the Apostle's shrine, as their first deed. Citizens accepted to receive them as lords if they agreed to stay in the city and garrison it. However, the court was later moved to Orense. Duchess Constanza and her two daughters—Philippa and Catalina—lived in the monastery of Celanova while the army attempted to conquer Castile. Froissart's version differs slightly from that of the Spanish *Crónica de Juan I*, for he argues that a month had elapsed between John of Gaunt's arrival at La Coruña and his entry in Santiago. Meanwhile, a group of French knights, who were themselves on pilgrimage to the holy site, learnt of Gaunt's intentions and rode swiftly to La Coruña to help resist the invasion.[29] We need not concern ourselves here with the development of the campaign and its results. It may be asserted, however, that the engagement and subsequent wedding of the heirs of both parts of the conflict—that is, Enrique, heir to Juan I of Castile, and Catalina of Lancaster, one of the duke's daughters— meant a rapprochement not only in political issues but in cultural and religious mentalities.[30] And this could only mean an increase in the number of pilgrims to Compostela.

However, another question overshadowed the horizon of pilgrimage at the end of the fourteenth century: the papal Schism. Once the division of the Christian pontificate was settled, the interruption of the Hundred Years' War did not help to solve the problem by means of arms. The effects were felt in all the courts of Europe, including England and Castile, who supported different sides. The Treaty of Bayonne permitted Catalina of Lancaster to keep her support of Pope Urban VI in private, in consideration of the position of England in the Schism, opposed to Castile and France. However, the princess had to change her views after becoming queen, in 1391.

But the problems posed by the Schism did not affect the royal family only. In 1389, Richard II of England ordered all his subjects to suspend any journey to Spain—*Hispania*, using the term employed by the pontifical chancery—due to the excommunication hanging over the kingdom. The excommunication had been dictated by the Roman pope, obeyed by England—the recently elected Boniface IX—but refused by Castile and France. Obviously, any bull sanctioning the graces obtained by pilgrimage issued by the Avignon pope Clement VII was unacceptable to the English Church, as were all the delays or cancellation of pilgrim votes accorded by this pope. Therefore, Richard declared all Spaniards schismatic, as well as his enemies. He commanded the warden of the passage in the port of London to stop anybody trying to sail to Castile, especially those merchants they knew.[31] The crisis had to do with Richard II's situation in his realm rather than with his foreign policies. His uncle, John of Gaunt, was still in his French domains when the king had to face the lords appellant and his uncle, the duke of Gloucester, who opposed him in 1387–88. Richard achieved a reassertion of his royal authority in May 1389 and was probably still unsure of John of Gaunt's reaction back in France when he issued the decree.[32]

Enrique III of Castile had a similar confrontation with the members of his Royal Council in 1393. After what can be defined as a real *coup*, he stood at the head of the kingdom and undertook the regularization of diplomatic relations with England. Because of Queen Catalina's family links, the traffic between England and Santiago de Compostela was reestablished successfully.

It appears, then, that at the end of the fourteenth century Compostela was one of the favorite destinations of English pilgrims again, as the numbers of ships and people arriving at Galician ports show.

A new legal settlement brought this apogee. The renewal of the Franco-Castilian alliance in 1391 permitted Enrique III to device independent policies concerning England, without having to ask for the acquiescence of the French monarchs. Soon after, the signature of a twenty-eight-year-long truce between France and England opened new perspectives (1396). A perpetual peace between Castile and England started to be discussed in 1393, when Enrique III's minority finished and he could start to negotiate his own policies at all levels.

The consequences of the facts we have mentioned above were a revival of Jacobean pilgrimage manifested in the number and quality of the licenses granted to shipowners sailing to Santiago. From 1394 and more or less frequently until 1456, there are a number of licenses to launch ships for pilgrims whose destination was Compostela from the most important ports of south England. Those collective return journeys were relatively easy and safe compared to other ways of traveling, especially for the inhabitants of this area of the island. The fact that the Crown used to give collective safe-conducts to shipowners was also very convenient. The information required included the names of the owner and captain, the name of the ship, and the number of pilgrims he was authorized to transport.

Following the truces of Leulingham, between 1390 and 1399, around fifty licenses were enrolled, twenty-nine of them corresponding to the Jubilee Year of 1395.[33] The first permission was granted to Otto Chambernoun, William Gilbert, and Richard Gilbert to embark on one hundred pilgrims on their ship called "la Charité de Paynton," commanded by Peter Cok, at Dartmouth, to take the pilgrims to Santiago de Compostela "ad vota sua ibidem facienda" [to fulfill his votes], and bring them back to England. All the pilgrims had to be in fealty and obedience to the king, be lay, and not use this permission to take from England any gold, silver, or money of any kind.[34] From February to July 1395, Richard II granted licenses to sail to no less than 1,630 pilgrims, plus two more ships sailing from Bristol, whose passengers were not counted. Each captain had to obtain six pennies from each pilgrim for the King's Treasure, for the license.[35] In 1397, Sir Philip of Courtenay received permission to travel forth and back from Compostela in his "bargea," called *James de Eymouth*.[36]

After Richard II's fall in 1399, diplomatic contacts between England and Castile became even more fluid because the new king, Henry IV, was the half-brother of Catalina of Lancaster, the Castilian queen. Given that the alliance with France did not contemplate another alliance with England, other alternatives were sought to guarantee peace between both kingdoms. Piracy had become a serious threat to navigation. It was thought that annual truces, in the style of those signed with Granada, would lead to peace in the sea routes and, therefore, to improve commerce among Castile, England, and Flanders—which allied itself to England—as it happened in fact. The clauses of this kind of truces were defined in a treaty which permitted the subjects of both kingdoms to move freely and travel without fear of reprisals (1403). The treaty authorized any personal trip without limitation, and going to any destination. Although merchants were mentioned specifically, the number of pilgrims traveling to La Coruña shows that the truces also benefited pious trips.[37]

As soon as Queen Catalina became regent (1406), she favored the continuation of Anglo-Castilian truces (1410–16), combined with an active correspondence about matters such as final peace, commerce, and legates.[38] Embassies kept traveling while executing some commercial missions; for instance, Squire Juan Rodríguez de Buenaventura, captain of the ship Trinidad, arrived in London with letters from the queen. He was granted a safe-conduct for one year for his ship, sailors, and servants, until the following Easter.[39]

When the French arrived in Castile for the renewal of their agreements with Castile (1408), a new wording of the treaty was conceived to replace that of 1369. Castile had the legal capacity to reach annual truces with England acknowledged formally, yet still no free negotiation could be undertaken for a definitive peace. On the January 4, 1410, two Castilian legates met in Fuenterrabía with Henry IV's envoys to give liberty of commerce. A court of four members was established to judge pledges addressed by sailors. Renewal of the truces was almost automatic until 1416 but, on the part of England, perpetual peace was still sought for. Henry IV asked his counselors to find a model for this agreement. They had to go back to the treaty signed by Alfonso X and Henry III, which appears again among Henry IV's records in 1414.[40]

The peak of Jacobean pilgrimage in this period may be explained by these favorable political conditions. Under Henry IV, the licenses granted to English ships transporting pilgrims add up to three in 1413: one to Edward, son of the earl of Devon, for forty pilgrims to sail in the vessel *Marie de Kyngeswere*; another to Edward Courtenay, for fifty, in the *Margarete de Plymmouth*; the third, for Walter Willy, captain of the *Elen de Levant*, to sail with forty pilgrims. On the following year, John Russell of Fowey, captain and owner of the ship *James de Fowy*, was authorized to carry another fifty pilgrims. In 1415 Richard Nicholl was granted a license to transport twenty-four pilgrims in the vessel *Marie de Pensans*, like Peter July, captain of the *Trinité de Falmouth*, owned by Henry Tremayn.[41]

Henry V's brief reign was more dedicated to war on French soil than to any other activity, and therefore it was his son, Henry VI, who implemented pilgrimage policies after 1422. The financial needs of the English crown were the reasons for a number of measures to ensure that the income produced by pilgrimage would reach the king as much as individual investors. Henry VI prohibited any ship to sail from English ports unless they had satisfied the required amount of six pennies per person, to the point that Cardinal Beaufort had to ask the Royal Council for a special license to leave, so that he could fulfill his pilgrimage votes (1426). Nor was this the only tax English pilgrims had to pay; after 1433, Henry VI appointed a collector for the commissions on foreign exchange: two pennies for each noble exchanged by travelers going to Rome, Jerusalem, or any other pilgrimage shrines.[42]

Despite the increase in travel costs caused by these measures, during the 1434 Jubilee—or rather "year of forgivance" (*año de perdonança*), as it was then called—royal licenses multiplied. Forty-nine were given on that particular year, for the passage of 2,310 pilgrims. The archbishop of Santiago, who collected the anchorage taxes of La Coruña, received that year no less than 405 crowns of the French coin, equivalent to around 14,000 *maravedis* instead of the usual average of 2,000 in other normal years.

On the other hand, King Juan II of Castile had approved a new law of reprisals the year before, in an attempt to control the traffic of spies and partisans of his rebel cousins, the *infantes* of Aragon. Any traveler could be imprisoned and deprived of his belongings without any warning or motive. Given the impact this law would have on pilgrimage, he issued a series of exemptions at the request of the clergy, in order to avoid a decrease in the number of pilgrims. He accepted all of them under his special protection. Therefore, he ordered the Great Admiral of the Seas and his officers, as well as all his subjects, to permit the passage of all the persons who traveled to Santiago de Compostela to obtain the graces of the Jubilee. Once the term expired, reprisals were applied consistently. For instance, the inhabitants of La Coruña captured the vessel *Catalina*, arriving from England with a group of pilgrims in 1440. Its passengers were released and recovered their possessions only after the archbishop and chapter of Compostela had appealed to the town council, citing the privileges accorded to pilgrims.

The following Jacobean Jubilee was celebrated in 1445. Juan II of Castile issued the same privileges for this purpose. As far as England is concerned, the prior of Winchester authorized Viceprior Robert Puryton to make a pilgrimage to Compostela to offer King Henry VI's alms equivalent to fifteen golden nobles. In response to such a generous donation, the chapter of the Cathedral celebrated a solemn mass in the main altar of the basilica, attended by Robert and a great number of pilgrims, among them the Englishmen. This ceremony was seldom possible to celebrate due to the excessive amount of pilgrims concentrated in the sanctuary on the year of the Jubilee. Moreover, the English royal family was accepted in the confraternity (*hermandad*) of Saint James. Although from that year on, royal licenses for pilgrimage were fewer, the increasing loading capacity of ships resulted in the same or even higher numbers of pilgrims. Whereas none of the former licenses included more than eighty pilgrims on each vessel, the permissions granted in the 1440s were often referred to one, or even two, hundred people. For instance, twenty-nine licenses issued in 1445 throw a figure of 1,700 pilgrims. The total amount decreased in 1451, with only eleven licenses for 594 people. In 1455 there was just one, for fifty people, whereas in 1456, there were fifteen, for around 770 pilgrims.[43]

The accession to the throne of Enrique IV of Castile saw another turning of the screw concerning Jacobean pilgrimage in the renewal of the Franco-Castilian alliance. First, the end of the Hundred Years' War left all the parts free to start new approaches to their foreign policies. The second reason was that Enrique IV was a well-considered monarch at the beginning of his reign, so his negotiating capacities were intact. In the 1454 treaty, Louis XI conceded that Castile could issue safe-conducts for at least twenty English vessels a year without French interference. The clause affected pilgrims to Saint James's shrine and merchants above all. Furthermore, the French king would have no say in the concession of licenses for Englishmen to cross Castile for commercial purposes, as he had before. Safe-conducts issued by Charles VII of France caused the complaints of Castilian ambassadors only a year later.[44] Soon, English merchant ships bringing goods to La Coruña did so by means of a safe-conduct issued by the Municipality. An agreement between La Coruña and Bristol, incorporating a royal license of the previous year, provided for mutual free entry into each other's ports for several ships, which is also recorded among the English Chancery enrolments for 1456.[45]

Likewise, the port of La Coruña was full of foreign vessels from most of the nations of Northern Europe, eighty-four ships according to the account written by William Wey, a fellow of Eton, whose estimated number of pilgrims might add up to 4,000 people. Given that La Coruña was just one of the ports receiving pilgrims and that the sea route could be used for several months during spring and summer—Wey sailed from England in May and returned in June—whereas the trip only lasted for one week, it is easy to conclude that thousands of pilgrims disembarked in Castile that year. The ports became as cosmopolitan and crowded as the main towns in the French Road. Wey included in his account all kinds of testimonies and sources available to a Jacobean pilgrim in the middle of the fifteenth century.

Ranging from diverse anecdotes to music, from legends and traditions about Saint James to the description of all the relics kept in the sanctuary, some contemporary miracles or a list of the bulls issued for that year's pilgrimage, Wey's account is undoubtedly the most interesting of all sources dealing with or written by English pilgrims to Castile.[46]

This brief account of the developments of English pilgrimage to Compostela has tried to emphasize the importance of the political scenario in the creation of cultural ideologies. Pilgrimage has only been possible throughout history in moments of peace, and yet it did not stop completely at times of war. Three-side negotiations during the Hundred Years' War provide an interesting perspective on the role of religious unity in Christian Europe. Shrines such as that of Saint James in Compostela sometimes played the role of mediator. Visits to those shrines provided an excuse for exchanges that would have never been possible in the battlefield or the royal court. This in turn helps explain the success of the sea itinerary above the land route in the late Middle Ages.

Notes

1. See J.L. Barreiro Rivas, *La función política de los caminos de peregrinación en la Europa medieval: estudio del Camino de Santiago* (Madrid: Tecnos, 1997), pp. 15–20.
2. On the general subject of English pilgrims in Santiago, see Constance C. Storrs, *Jacobean Pilgrims from England from the Early Twelfth to the Late Fifteenth Century* (Santiago de Compostela: Xunta de Galicia, 1994).
3. See D.W. Lomax's chapter on "Los peregrinos ingleses a Santiago," in *Santiago. La Europa del peregrinaje*, ed. Robert Plötz et al. (Barcelona: Lunwerg, 1993), p. 373 [165–79].
4. A. Soria y Puig, "El Camino y los caminos de Santiago en España," in Plötz et al., *Santiago*, pp. 214–15 [195–232].
5. Lomax, "Los peregrinos ingleses a Santiago," p. 376.
6. J.G. Hartwell, "Celtic Britain and the Pilgrimage Movement," *Y Cymmrodor* 23 (1972): 255–65.
7. The itineraries were first studied by D.W. Lomax, "The First English Pilgrimages to Santiago de Compostela," *Studies in Medieval History Presented to R.H.C Davis*, ed. Henry Mayr-Harting and R.I. Moore (London: Hambledon, 1985), pp. 165–79; see also D.W. Lomax, "Algunos peregrinos ingleses a Santiago en la Edad Media," *Príncipe de Viana* 31 (1970): 156–69; and Storrs, *Jacobean Pilgrims*, pp. 87–108.
8. For these and other cases, see Luis Vázquez de Parga, José María Lacarra, and Juan Uría Ríu, *Las peregrinaciones a Santiago de Compostela*, 3 vols. (Oviedo: Diputación Provincial, 1981), p. 51; Lomax, "Los peregrinos ingleses a Santiago," p. 375.

9. This record does not appear in *Foedera, conventiones, litterae et cuiuscunque generis acta publicae inter reges Angliae et alios quosvis imperatores, reges, pontifices, principes vel communitates (1101–1654)*, ed. T. Rymer (Hague: Neaulme, 1739–45), but is mentioned by A. Viñayo González, *Caminos y peregrinos: huellas de la peregrinación jacobea* (León: Isidoriana, 1981), p. 103 without quote.
10. Matthew Paris, *Matthaei Parisiensis, Monachi Sancti Albani Chronica Majora*, ed. H.R. Luard, 7 vols. (London: Longman, 1866–69), 3:41, 472–74; *Foedera* (1739–45), 1.2:178–81. Studied in the context of Anglo-Castilian diplomatic relations, especially with respect to the crusades, by José Manuel Rodríguez García, "Henry III, Alfonso X of Castile and the Crusading Plans of the Thirteenth Century (1245–1272)," in *England and Europe in the Reign of Henry III (1216–1272)*, ed. B.K.U. Weiler and Ifor W. Rowlands (Aldershot: Ashgate, 2002), p. 103 [99–120].
11. *Documentos de Clemente IV (1265–1268): referentes a España*, ed. S. Domínguez Sánchez (León: Universidad de León, 1996), doc. 154, p. 192. The records are dated November 23, 1267 and June 22, 1268.
12. M.R. García Arancón, *Colección diplomática de los reyes de Navarra de la dinastía de Champaña. Vol. II: Teobaldo II (1253–1270)* (San Sebastián: Sociedad de Estudios Vascos, 1985), 2:144–45, doc. 70. I thank Dr. J.M. Rodríguez for calling my attention to these three records.
13. *Foedera* (1739–45), 2.1:91; L.Vázquez de Parga et al., eds., *Las peregrinaciones*, 1:77–78; 3:26. *Calendar of the Patent Rolls Preserved in the Public Record Office. Edward II (1321–1324)* (London: HMSO, 1894–1904), 4:15. See also M.W. Labarge, *Viajeros medievales. Los ricos y los insatisfechos* (Hondarribia: Nerea, 2000), p. 133.
14. For an interesting state of the art, see M. Dunn and L. Davidson, eds., *The Pilgrimage to Compostela in the Middle Ages* (New York: Routledge, 1996), pp. xxiii–xlviii. The bibliography compiled by these two authors is very useful to anybody interested in the latest research about Jacobean pilgrimage: *The Pilgrimage to Santiago de Compostela: A Comprehensive, Annotated Bibliography* (New York: Garland, 1994).
15. The safe-conducts were registered at the Aragonese royal chancery, and read as follows: William d'Angla, knight, October 30, 1382; John of Bighton, March 12, 1389; Henri Tudesco and John Nell, squires, August 3, 1398; William of Arundel, November 20, 1399. Vázquez de Parga et al., *Las peregrinaciones*, 1:82–83; 3:29–32.
16. R.G. Plötz, "Milites et nobilitates in itinere stellarum (saeculum XI ad saeculum XVI)" [Knights and Nobles on the Road of the Stars (Eleventh to Sixteenth Centuries)], in *Viajes y viajeros en la España Medieval. Actas del V Curso de Cultura Medieval* (Aguilar de Campoo: Centro de Estudios del Románico; Madrid: Polifemo, 1997), pp. 117–19 [109–19]. Luis Suárez Fernández, *Navegación y comercio en el Golfo de Vizcaya* (Madrid: CSIC, 1959), p. 20, quoting *Calendar of the Patent Rolls Preserved in the Public Record Office. Edward III (1367–1370)* (London: HMSO, 1913), 14:228, where

Edward III issued a travel license for the vessel "Thomas," from Bristol, to take pilgrims to Santiago.
17. F. Ruiz Gómez, "El Camino de Santiago: circulación de hombres, mercancías e ideas," *IV Semana de Estudios Medievales: Nájera, 2 al 6 de agosto de 1993* (Logroño: Instituto de Estudios Riojanos, 1993), p. 174 [167–88].
18. Vázquez de Parga et al., *Las peregrinaciones*, 1:247–52.
19. Her portrait in the "General Prologue" (lines 445–76) tells us that she was a weaver and that she went to many pilgrimage sites, including Saint James. See *The Riverside Chaucer*, ed. Larry D. Benson, 3rd ed. (Boston: Houghton Mifflin, 1987).
20. Vázquez de Parga et al., *Las peregrinaciones*, 1:79.
21. Lomax, "Los peregrinos ingleses a Santiago," p. 382; Labarge, *Viajeros medievales*, p. 114.
22. Storrs, *Jacobean Pilgrims*, pp. 17–19.
23. Storrs, *Jacobean Pilgrims*, p. 112.
24. On these developments, see Clara Estow, *Pedro the Cruel of Castile, 1350–1369* (Leiden: Brill, 1995) and José Manuel Rodríguez García, "Los enfrentamientos bélicos con Inglaterra y sus gentes: la visión castellana (1250–1515)," *Revista de Historia Militar* 84 (1998): 11–44, especially pp. 21–24.
25. Fourteen pilgrims, most of them attorneys. Among them were the bishop of St. Andrews, the abbot of Evesham, and Thomas, earl of Mar. *Calendar of the Patent Rolls (1367–1370)*, 14:122, 134, 135, 137, 140, 212; Storrs, *Jacobean Pilgrims*, pp. 111, 168.
26. J. Torres Fontes, *Estudio sobre la Crónica de Enrique IV del Dr. Galíndez de Carvajal* (Murcia: CSIC, 1946), pp. 78–79. There was also a ship shortage, since vessels were also needed for war purposes, and many of them were captured or burnt. Storrs, *Jacobean Pilgrims*, p. 112.
27. Vázquez de Parga et al., *Las peregrinaciones*, 1:81; 3:33.
28. See the essays by Jennifer Geouge, Joyce Coleman, and Amélia Hutchinson in this volume for discussions of John of Gaunt's Iberian policies with a focus on Portugal. See also the essay by R.F. Yeager for a discussion of John of Gaunt's policies toward Castile from a cultural and literary perspective.
29. Pedro López de Ayala, *Crónica del rey D. Juan I*, in *Crónicas de los reyes de Castilla*, ed. C. Rossell, 2 vols. (Madrid: Real Academia Española, 1953), 2:109 et seq.; J. de Wavrin, *Chroniques d'Angleterre*, British Library, Royal Ms. 14 E IV, f. 246; F. Lopes, *Crónica de D. João I*, 2 vols. (Porto: Livraria Civilizaçao, 1983), 2:214–16, 219–27, and Jean Froissart, *Oeuvres: Chroniques*, ed. Kervyn de Lettenhove, 25 vols. (Brussels: Victor Devaux, 1867–77), 11:339–49. All the records concerning arrangements for the campaign, in *Foedera* (1839–45), 3:150, 190–200; 4:11–16, 24–25, 31, 39–49, 61. See also Labarge, *Viajeros medievales*, p. 135.
30. R.F. Yeager's essay in this volume expands on this issue. Joyce Coleman's essay in this volume argues that a similar rapprochment occurred through another one of John of Gaunt's daughters, Philippa, in the case of Anglo-Portuguese relations.

31. *Foedera* (1839–45), 3.4:39. Dated June 15, 1389.
32. In matters dealing with Richard II's reign, I am following J.A.F. Thomson, *The Transformation of Medieval England, 1370–1529* (New York: Longman, 1983), pp. 148–65.
33. See list of licenses in Storrs, *Jacobean Pilgrims*, pp. 173–75.
34. *Foedera* (1839–45), 3.4:95. Cf. Vázquez de Parga et al., *Las peregrinaciones*, 1:84; 3:35.
35. *Calendar of the Patent Rolls Preserved in the Public Record Office. Richard II (1391–1396)* (London: HMSO, 1895–1909), 5:537–38, 565–66, 568, 572, 601–02; see also Labarge, *Viajeros medievales*, pp. 134–35; Storrs, *Jacobean Pilgrims*, pp. 112–13.
36. *Foedera* (1839–45), 3.4:128.
37. The agreement was established by the English Royal Council and the secretary of the king of Castile, but it was Henry IV of England himself who authorized it on request of "his brother the King [Enrique III] of Castile." *Foedera* (1839–45), 4.1:48.
38. *Foedera* (1839–45), 4.1:156, 165–68, 180, 198; 4.2:25, 57, 67–69, 78–79, 83.
39. *Calendar of Signet Letters of Henry IV and Henry V, 1399–1422*, ed. J.L. Kirby (London: HMSO, 1978). Dated March 27 and June 6, 1409.
40. *Foedera* (1839–45), 4.2:96.
41. Vázquez de Parga et al., *Las peregrinaciones*, 1:85.
42. *Calendar of the Patent Rolls Preserved in the Public Record Office. Henry VI (1429–1436)* (London: HMSO, 1901–10), 2:282, 471. See also Labarge, *Viajeros medievales*, p. 139; Storrs, *Jacobean Pilgrims*, pp. 122–23.
43. Vázquez de Parga et al., *Las peregrinaciones*, 1:85, 92–94; Storrs, *Jacobean Pilgrims*, pp. 124–25.
44. Torres Fontes, *Estudio sobre la Crónica*, pp. 78–79; Suárez Fernández, *Navegación y comercio*, pp. 207–09.
45. Storrs, *Jacobean Pilgrims*, p. 107. The agreement is published in pp. 193–96.
46. *The Itineraries of William Wey*, in Vázquez de Parga et al., *Las peregrinaciones*, 1:96, 238; 3:127–32, after the original English edition; Labarge, *Viajeros medievales*, p. 135; Storrs, *Jacobean Pilgrims*, pp. 146–49.

CHAPTER 4

LEONOR OF ENGLAND AND ELEANOR OF CASTILE: ANGLO-IBERIAN MARRIAGE AND CULTURAL EXCHANGE IN THE TWELFTH AND THIRTEENTH CENTURIES

Rose Walker

This essay examines the evidence for Anglo-Iberian cultural exchange within two royal marriages in the high Middle Ages through a consideration of manuscripts and memory.

This essay will examine two examples of cross-cultural exchange between England and Castile during the late twelfth and thirteenth centuries. The first is the marriage of Leonor, daughter of Henry II of England and of Eleanor of Aquitaine, to Alfonso VIII of Castile in 1170, which lasted until they both died, only a few weeks apart, in 1214. The second is the more famous marriage, in 1254, of Eleanor of Castile, daughter of Fernando III of León and Castile and his second queen, Jeanne of Ponthieu, to Edward, son of Henry III, who was to succeed him as Edward I of England in 1272. This marriage lasted until Eleanor's death in 1290.

Despite this apparent symmetry a comparison between the two Anglo-Iberian marriages is not a straightforward matter. History shows us two very different queens. Eleanor of Castile, lives for us quite vividly through considerable documentary and chronicle evidence, but Leonor of England remains a shadowy figure, as chroniclers talk only of her traditional queenly virtues of modesty and prudence. Eleanor was cosmopolitan in her tastes, both culinary and material. John Carmi Parsons and Thomas Tolley have shown us how she collected decorative arts from a wide range of countries, from France and Italy, as well as the Holy Land, Damascus, and Tripoli.[1] We know that Aragonese gardeners worked on Eleanor's gardens at her manor of Langley in 1289,[2] and in the same year a Castilian ship docked at Southampton provided her with pomegranates, lemons, oranges, and olive oil from her homeland.[3] We have no records of Leonor's belongings, and in any case she probably only visited England on one or two occasions. If she had any longing for childhood tastes and colors, these would probably have been rooted in Normandy, perhaps around Domfront where she was born, or in Anjou.[4] It is thus difficult even to identify her as English; instead, she belonged to the wider Plantagenet world. There is only one tantalizingly intimate reference that tells us that in 1180 Henry II sent Leonor a small vessel or chalice and some fabrics.[5]

Yet there are some striking similarities between the lives of the two queens, perhaps most obviously the importance of each queen's lineage for her own identity and for her subjects. From the Iberian perspective the designations used by Castilian scribes show that they did think of her as "English." They called her "*Anglica Elionor*" and later *filia regis Angliae*, emphasizing her exalted status as daughter of the king of England regardless of where she was born or spent her childhood.[6] Likewise, when a Westminster Chronicler recorded Eleanor's death, it was as daughter of the illustrious King Ferdinand of Castile; for the Dunstable annalist Edward I's wife was "a Spaniard by birth"; and for Matthew Paris, her Spanish nationality was sufficient to provoke derisive laughter among the people.[7]

There is no direct evidence for Leonor as a patron, although, in the Spanish manner, she was associated with nearly all Alfonso VIII's charter donations, and thus with his extensive promotion of the Cistercian Order. Most famously Alfonso VIII and Leonor founded Las Huelgas, the Cistercian nunnery on the outskirts of Burgos in 1187. I have questioned elsewhere the independent role so often assigned to Leonor in this foundation, although she does seem to have been an active partner.[8] Eleanor of Castile, on the other hand, was the most prolific royal foundress in England since the previous century and not dependent on Edward I for a lead. She concentrated her attention on the Dominicans and established priories for them in London and Chichester. She also re-founded Rhuddlan and gave major donations to the priories at Salisbury and Northampton.[9]

Thomas Tolley has tackled this difficult subject through an evocative, and he admits quite speculative, study of Eleanor of Castile and the "Spanish" style in England primarily in relation to textiles and decorative devices.[10] I am going to use such suppositions about Eleanor as a point of reference against which to measure potential cultural exchange within the marriage of Leonor of England. First I shall consider manuscripts, because the transmission of manuscripts has a special place in discussions of cultural exchange between royal women. It provides the surest and most convincing evidence for a network of female patronage that has seen queens commission, present, and pass on manuscripts to their daughters and other female relatives.[11] The dynastic links between the English and French courts in the mid-thirteenth century provide, for example, a plausible nexus for the exchange of the famous Bibles Moralisées.[12] The second part of the essay will focus on the memorialization of each queen through the form and decoration of her tomb.

Books and Ownership

Eleanor of Castile figures prominently in discussions about royal women and artistic exchange, as she is particularly noted for her patronage of manuscripts. She had her own scriptorium, and her accounts name two scribes, Roger and Philip, and an illuminator, Godfrey, who purchased vellum, ink, gold, and pigments including *Gumma alba de Ispannia*, probably mucilage for gold-leaf.[13] Eleanor's interests encompassed chivalric culture and history, which was popular at the Castilian, English, and French courts.[14] She commissioned several books in the vernacular, and her main focus of interest seems to have been the Ponthevin romance, and in this she followed her mother's taste.

Beyond this we know that Eleanor owned an unillustrated copy of Archbishop Pecham's treatise on pseudo-Dionysius's *De Celesti Hierarchia*,[15] and that she was almost certainly sent codices by her half-brother, Alfonso X, probably including a copy of his 1264 version of the Arabic *Ladder of Mohammed*.[16] In addition her household accounts say that Eleanor owned copies of *vitae* of Saint Thomas Becket and of Saint Edward the Confessor that needed repair by 1288, and it is here that we can start to identify surviving codices.[17] One copy of *La Estoire de Seint Aedward le Rei*, most likely written and illustrated by Matthew Paris in the 1240s, had been presented to her mother-in-law Queen Eleanor of Provence. The only extant copy (Cambridge University Library MS Ee.3.59) may have been made for Eleanor of Castile on the occasion of her marriage in 1254 in Burgos or for her arrival in England.[18] Such a gift would certainly fit with her swift induction into the Plantagenet dynastic cult and it would have matched the taste of other female members of the royal circle around 1250.[19]

The Douce Apocalypse (Oxford, Bodleian Library, Douce MS 180) is the only surviving illuminated manuscript that is clearly associated with Eleanor and Edward, as it includes donor portraits of them. But another earlier, mid-thirteenth century, Apocalypse, the Trinity Apocalypse (Cambridge, Trinity College, MS R 16 2), is more relevant to our purpose, as it, unlike Douce, contains Castilian "symptoms" and it has been dated by

Nigel Morgan to the years around Eleanor's arrival in England, ca. 1252–57.[20] George Henderson has indicated sufficient links between the Trinity Apocalypse and the Douce Apocalypse to be certain that Trinity was available to the artist of Douce, which suggests a possible connection between this manuscript and Eleanor of Castile.[21] The prominent queenly figures depicted in this manuscript point to a female royal patron, but some scholars have linked it with Eleanor of Provence because it shows slightly more interest in the Franciscans than the Dominicans.[22] However, an illuminated commentary on the Apocalypse would have made a very appropriate gift for, or commission by, a Spanish princess, as the Beatus Apocalypse manuscripts were such noted high-status and luxury products of Iberian manuscript illumination. Indeed they were almost emblematic of the earlier Anglo-Iberian marriage of Alfonso VIII and Leonor, as their reign had seen such a significant and remarkable resurgence of that tradition at monastic institutions that flourished under their patronage.

Yet the Trinity Apocalypse does not have the Beatus text, but uses instead the commentary of Berengaudus in Anglo-Norman French.[23] Nor do its miniatures on the whole reflect the Spanish tradition, although there are some idiosyncratic aspects to the manuscript that suggest quite detailed knowledge of that tradition. Trinity is unusual among English Apocalypses because of its large size, which is much more commensurate with the surviving Castilian codices of the late twelfth century.[24] As Henderson highlighted, it also follows Iberian examples in the way that it varies its illustrations in size and in location on the page.[25] Most striking in this respect is the design and iconography of the miniature of the Heavenly Jerusalem (fol. 25v.), which has been regarded by most scholars as the single example of the work of one artist.[26] It depicts the City as a four-sided cloister viewed from above and is very similar in form to the late-twelfth-century and early-thirteenth-century miniatures from the late flowering of the Beatus tradition in Castile. Yet it differs from the Iberian examples in that it merges the subjects of the typical Beatus double-page spread.[27] The four-cloister elevations remain, like an opened out plan, and they still feature crenellations and arcades, albeit in the Trinity manuscript with Gothic arches, and detailed brickwork. The center of the garth in the Beatus examples is usually occupied by a figure of John, the author of the book of the Apocalypse, with one of the Seven Angels and the Lamb of God. On the facing recto in the Iberian manuscripts, there is a representation of the River of Life, flowing from Christ enthroned in a mandorla and watering the Tree of Life, with the Angel and John standing on raised ground, to one side, viewing the scene. In the single miniature in Trinity, however, the mandorla, the River, and the Tree of Life have been moved with the Angel into the center of the garth, and the symbol of the Lamb of God now sits on Christ's right hand within the mandorla. The figures of John and the angel stand in the bottom left-hand corner of the margin and overlay that part of the cloister.

Other miniatures in Trinity also reflect the Iberian tradition, at least in its twelfth-century manifestation, not in style or iconography, but through a preference for geometrical order in their design.[28] There is nothing, however, in the execution of any of the miniatures to suggest the involvement of an Iberian-trained scribe, although we know that there was at least one Spanish painter, a Master Peter, at Henry III's court and that he worked on a hanging and on panels at Westminster Abbey between 1251 and 1258. Although Master Peter could have been responsible for introducing Iberian elements into artistic practices of the royal circle, there is no record of him working on manuscripts.[29] Instead the explanation for these Iberian "symptoms" could lie with Eleanor of Castile herself, if she brought an Iberian Apocalypse manuscript with her on her marriage, and it was made available to one of the artists working on the Trinity Apocalypse.[30] However, no such manuscript has survived, unlike the new impetus to Apocalypse illumination represented by Trinity, which survives concretely in the form of several imposing English Apocalypse manuscripts.

It is harder to find manuscripts definitively associated with Leonor of England in Castile. Instead we have a set of fragmented allusions to "English" style, including elements of the Bible of Burgos and of the San Pedro de Cardeña Beatus. We have seen that Eleanor was given a copy of the *Vita* of Saint Edward, a fundamental text for Henry III's English dynastic identity, and Leonor may have literally carried an embodiment of an earlier form of that identity with her to Castile. This was probably in the form of a manuscript of the *Historia regum Britanniae* attributed to Geoffrey of Monmouth, which recounts legends of early kings of the English including those of Arthur.[31] The early-twentieth-century scholar William Entwistle believed that a copy was used in the court of Leonor's son, King Enrique I, to add a reference to King Arthur to the *Anales Toledanos Primeros*, and that Leonor's great-grandson, Alfonso X, also used the *Historia*. Despite the other ways in which the Castilian court could have acquired a copy of the *Historia*, it is quite probable that Leonor transmitted this text to Castile. It would have made a very suitable marriage gift in the same vein as the *Vita* of Saint Edward given to Eleanor of Castile. The new kingdom of Castile, separated from León only in 1157, had no equivalent mythologized history when Leonor arrived in 1170, but by the early thirteenth century Alfonso VIII's court provided the milieu for the production of the great Castilian epic *Poema de Mio Cid*. Alfonso and Leonor's reign also saw the remarkable revival in the production of Beatus manuscripts mentioned above, this time linked emphatically to Castile and likely products of royal patronage.

Manuscripts make up the core of the arguments in favor of the absorption of aspects of English art into Castile at the turn of the twelfth century. As the Cistercian monastery of Las Huelgas has the strongest association with Leonor, it may be helpful to concentrate on a small group of Castilian manuscripts linked with that house and on the more famous codices often attributed to its near neighbor San Pedro de Cardeña, which may well have produced manuscripts for Las Huelgas. In any case these two groups constitute the bulk of the surviving illuminated manuscripts from Alfonso VIII's Castile.

Unfortunately none of the Las Huelgas manuscripts can be positively localized to that house, and we do not know if it even had a scriptorium. There are six manuscripts that could belong to the first decades of the abbey's existence now in the abbey's library, but I shall concentrate on the Antiphoner (Burgos, Archivo de Las Huelgas MS 10).[32] San Pedro de Cardeña, on the other hand, was an established Benedictine house that almost definitely had its own scriptorium. It probably produced, around 1180, its famous, and now fragmented, Beatus manuscript (Madrid, Museo Arqueológico Nacional, MS 2; New York, Metropolitan Museum of Art; Madrid, Coll. Francisco de Zabálburu y Basabe; Girona, Museu d'Art de Girona, Num. Inv.47), as well as the Bible of Burgos (Biblioteca Provincial de Burgos, MS 846), of which one leaf from the, now lost, second volume is bound into the Bible of Las Huelgas.[33] Yarza Luaces has rightly pointed out that one artist worked both on the Burgos Bible and on the Las Huelgas Lectionary (Burgos, Archivo de Las Huelgas, MS 9), so there were close links between the two institutions.

Scholars of Iberian manuscripts, and most notably Yarza Luaces, have identified close stylistic parallels between these Beatus and Bible manuscripts that have led him to attribute them to Cardeña, and some of these lead in turn to English manuscripts. The Cardeña Beatus has two very different figurative styles that appear throughout the manuscript. One uses heavily outlined tear-drop damp-fold shapes, which are familiar from English manuscripts associated with Master Hugo and Bury St Edmunds in the first half of the twelfth century.[34] Damp-fold drapery remained a distinctive characteristic of English illumination until around 1150, and can be found, for example, in the Lambeth Bible, and in the work of the Master of the Leaping Figures in the Winchester Bible.[35] The itinerant artist of the Lambeth Bible also worked in Hainault, and some elements of his style persisted in that area, but English damp-fold did not take hold on the Continent.[36] However, some twenty-five years later, this heavily outlined "English" damp-fold is found in Castile throughout the Cardeña Beatus and, as an isolated instance, on the figure of God in the upper register of the only full-page miniature in the Bible of Burgos (fol. 12v.).[37] In the Cardeña

Beatus the tear-drop folds are transformed into a vibrant decorative pattern that suggests drapery through the use of multicolored repeated outlines. It is the distinctive appearance of damp-fold in Castile that most surely indicates English models. We do not know how this "English" stylistic feature was introduced into Castile, but given the likely dates for the manuscripts that contain it, that is ca. 1175, it seems plausible to suggest that one or more models came with Leonor on the occasion of her marriage to Alfonso VIII. Certainly the "English" features that were introduced into Castile around the time of the marriage were those that had been employed in England for many years. They are distinct from the style probably executed by a group of itinerant artists, which is found in later manuscripts associated with the royal circle, for example, in parts of the Winchester Bible dated to post-1170 and in the wall paintings in the chapter house at Sigena in Aragón ca. 1200.[38]

At this point it is appropriate to invoke our comparison. In both cases we have found evidence for a new awareness of the foreign style or composition within five years of the marriage. In both the Trinity Apocalypse and the Burgos Bible the imported element is most obvious in a defined and isolated part of the manuscript, the iconography of the depiction of Heavenly Jerusalem in the former and the style of God clothing Adam and Eve in the latter. On the other hand the damp-fold in the Cardeña Beatus has been totally absorbed and reinvented as a very Iberian flat decorative design, and some scholars see likewise a pervasive awareness of Iberian design in the Trinity Apocalypse. Did Leonor's father, Henry II, perhaps continue to send her manuscripts, in the same way that Eleanor of Castile's brother sent codices to her a century later? The Paris Psalter has to be a serious candidate for such a gift, as it was probably produced at Canterbury and later sent to Spain ca. 1180. We know that it definitely came to Spain, because its miniatures were completed in Catalonia in the fourteenth century, but we cannot be sure when it traveled to the Peninsula, in what circumstances, or whether it went directly to Catalonia.[39]

If we turn now to Las Huelgas, we must take into account Yarza Luaces's view, which has inclined toward an English origin for its Antiphoner. However, Yarza has also admitted the possibility that it could be from Northern France or indeed an Iberian product with strong foreign influence.[40] Sonsoles Herrero, who is one of the few people to have had access to these manuscripts, stated that it was a foreign product of the so-called Channel Style, although it lacks the gamboling white lions that characterize the most meaningful use of that term. Weseley Jordan has studied the musical notation of the Antiphoner as well as its paleography and decoration, and he concluded that the manuscript was written in Spain by French chaplains at Las Huelgas. Although we do not know of any

French chaplains at Las Huelgas at the end of the twelfth century, there is little doubt that the quadratic notation of the Antiphoner derives from the Ile de France, and that it is quite unlike the Aquitanian notation previously used in Castile in the twelfth century. The Cistercian Order, to which Las Huelgas belonged, had adopted the new musical notation with enthusiasm. It also attached great importance to having a "correct" Antiphoner, more than any other liturgical book,[41] so we would expect one owned by such a prominent royal foundation as Las Huelgas to have been copied from a good Cistercian exemplar, possibly even from Cîteaux itself, and the exceptionally large size of this manuscript (415 × 275 mm.) marks it as an important possession. This expectation fits with the conformist nature of the contents of this Antiphoner, and its Cistercian calendar, and the order of the antiphons, responses, and canticles argue for a date at the end of the twelfth century.[42] Jordan's assessment of the paleography is quite cursory, but he does seem to be correct in noticing the particular form of the letter "z" used in the Antiphoner, which is found elsewhere in the Spanish kingdoms, but not in France or England. In itself this is a small detail, but Jordan is also right to highlight the elongated ascenders of some letters and some of the abbreviations employed. This evidence suggests that the text and the musical notation were copied in Castile from a Cistercian exemplar with a good pedigree, perhaps from Cîteaux itself. The illumination, however, is a more complex matter.

The fine illuminated letter "A" of *Aspiciens* on the Antiphoner's first folio immediately calls to mind the profusion of splendid illuminated letter "A"s in the history of Iberian illumination that combine foliate interlace and fauna.[43] Most are found in Beatus Apocalypse manuscripts, but a Castilian missal (Salamanca, MS 2637) of the second half of the twelfth century shows that the predilection for these opening initial "A"s had already migrated to liturgical codices. However, the exact nature of the decoration in the Las Huelgas Antiphoner, which is a spectacular display of "octopus" flowers and interlocking circles, argues at first sight against a Castilian origin.

Many words have been written about octopus flowers by Jalabert and others, which locate them in an early form in the Bury Bible (Cambridge, Corpus Christi College, MS 2), in the Winchester Psalter, and later in the Winchester Bible and in the Paris Psalter (Paris, Bibliothèque Nationale, MS Lat. 8846). By the later twelfth century octopus flowers were generically too prevalent to do more than place manuscripts that exhibit them in the ambit of an international style that spread across Plantagenet and French lands.[44] However, the octopus flowers in the Antiphoner have some distinctive features: five or seven shell-like petals with serrated edges that spring directly from the stem; one or two of the petals on most of the flowers formed by a row of small nascent leaves; and cross-hatched fruits that nestle within the petals. Many other octopus flowers have two tiers or other more complex constructions, and there are comparatively few flatter patterns. The closest parallels for these elements can be found in the same English manuscript tradition, for example in the work of the Master of the Lambeth Bible in the, now lost, Liessies Gospel Book, that we have already found reflected in Castilian manuscripts. Indeed simple, flat octopus flowers can be found in friezes along the lower borders of the Cardeña Beatus and the Burgos Bible. Other aspects of the Las Huelgas letter "A" also appear in the Cardeña Beatus, for example, a framed "S" initial (fol. 19v.) is formed by the schematic body of a dragon, just as dragons' bodies form the "A" in the Las Huelgas manuscript.

The matter is complicated, however, because the fashion for comparatively simple octopus flowers continued in later English manuscripts, including initials in the Winchester Bible and in the Paris Psalter (fol. 6r.), where significantly they can be seen in conjunction with the dominant feature of the Antiphoner initial, geometric concentric and interlocking spirals. The Master of the Genesis Initial in the Winchester Bible executed a fine framed letter "S" to begin the Prologue to Jonah (fol. 204r.),[45] which combines a dragon's sinuous body with geometric interlocking circles and simple octopus flowers. However, this artist produced a more molded effect especially on the dragon's tail than the work found at Las Huelgas, which is flat and decorative in the Iberian tradition and relies on beading to add interest.

An isolated example of concentric geometric circles in a fragment from the Pontigny Bible of ca. 1195 (Paris, Bibl. Nat. de Fr., nouv.acq. Lat. 2525, fol. 1) should make us pause at this point. This needs to be considered together with other fragments, probably from the same manuscript, that have some of the features that we have identified in the Las Huelgas Antiphoner initial, including flat, open "octopus" flowers and beading (London, V & A, Ms 8985 A). So is it possible that the illumination of the Las Huelgas Antiphoner, like its text and music, followed a Cistercian model. Although Las Huelgas was a daughter house of Cîteaux and not of Pontigny, very few Cîteaux manuscripts date from the end of the twelfth century, which suggests that it may have turned to other scriptoria for its needs and indeed for books to send to new daughter houses.[46] The difficulty with this approach is that this is one circle and not a pattern of interlocking circles and more importantly that the additional element in the illumination, the little white lions of the "Channel Style," do not appear in the Las Huelgas Antiphoner.

So in summary, taking into consideration the different kinds of evidence in the Las Huelgas Antiphoner—the musical notation, the paleography, and the decoration—I wish to propose a date of 1180–1200 and Castilian production probably at San Pedro de Cardeña. Whereas the scribe adhered closely to the text and notation of a Cistercian model produced in or near the Île de France, the illuminator worked in a decorative style already established at Cardeña in the previous decade in response to English manuscripts of the mid-twelfth century. He further developed the style to include the geometric interlocking circles that feature in later English manuscripts. And it is possible to envisage him doing this in response to sight of the work of an artist like the Master of the Genesis Initial, whose hand is, of course, one of those that Oakeshott famously identified in the wall paintings in the chapter house at Sigena in Aragón ca. 1200. This does not enable us to be certain about Leonor's role, but it does indicate that manuscripts in the style employed in England in the last two decades of the twelfth century—or the itinerant artists who produced them—traveled to Castile.

Although we cannot rule out an English origin for the Las Huelgas Martyrology (Burgos, Archivo de Las Huelgas, MS 1), it is much more likely that its "Channel Style" illumination was produced in Paris or northeastern France in the early thirteenth century. It thus falls outside the scope of this essay and probably needs to be considered as part of a study of links between Castile and that region whether through the Cistercians or through the marriage of Leonor and Alfonso VIII's daughter Blanche of Castile to the future Louis VIII of France.

Burial: Two Queens United in Memory?

Much has been written about the death of Eleanor of Castile in 1290 and on the rituals that led to her burial in Westminster Abbey (figure 4.1). It was an emphatically royal dynastic burial from the heraldry on the tomb chest and on the cushion under the effigy's head to the scepter in its hand and the paste jewels in her crown and robe.[47] Even within the tomb the body was dressed in royal robes, crown, and scepter.[48] Her gilt-bronze tomb effigy, the largest so far produced in England, was pioneering and executed with remarkable refinement.[49] The tomb was commissioned by her husband at the time of her death together with another image of her for Lincoln. At the same time he ordered a new effigy of his father Henry III, who had been buried at Westminster twenty years earlier. The heraldry on Eleanor's tomb gives due prominence to her Castilian origin as well as acknowledging her maternal legacy and her marriage into the Plantagenet house. Beyond the heraldry there is nothing Castilian about Eleanor's memorial. Its conceptual and stylistic roots lay with the series of royal effigies produced for St-Denis in the mid-1260s.[50] Eleanor's memory was in the care of the monks of Westminster Abbey and the Plantagenets; it was expressed in dynastic form on her tomb and through the proximity of the

Figure 4.1 Westminster Abbey, tomb of Eleanor of Castile. Conway Library Courtauld Institute of Art.

tomb of her father-in-law, Henry III, and to the shrine of Saint Edward the Confessor.

Leonor's tomb is decidedly a retrospective tomb, although its date is disputed and suggestions have varied from mid-thirteenth century to early fourteenth. The tomb cannot be considered in isolation as it was conceived with the tomb of Alfonso VIII as a pair of gabled tomb chests. The two

Figure 4.2 Las Huelgas, tombs of Alfonso VIII and Leonor of England (west). Conway Library Courtauld Institute of Art.

sarcophagi are almost identical in form and even joined together. Heraldry is extremely prominent: the castle, symbol of Castile, is found within a trefoil under a round arch on the sides and gables of both tombs and on both ends of Alfonso VIII's tomb, whilst the head and foot of Leonor's tomb bear shields with three Plantagenet leopards (figures 4.2 and 4.3). Historiated scenes fill the gable ends of both tombs: two angels bear Leonor's regal soul to heaven; angels on Alfonso's tomb hold the triumphal cross, perhaps recalling the victory at Las Navas de Tolosa. At the foot of Leonor's tomb there is a crucifixion scene; the foot of Alfonso VIII's tomb has the king handing over the foundation document of Las Huelgas.

This choice of low relief sculpture and narrative scenes is relatively unusual at this time outside Las Huelgas. Elsewhere effigy tombs were much in fashion by the mid-thirteenth century, as evidenced not only by those for Henry III and Eleanor of Castile, but even in Burgos Cathedral itself by the enameled image of Bishop Maurice of Burgos. Yet the royal and noble tombs of Las Huelgas never followed that lead, but continued to favor tomb chests or tomb niches. The design of the tomb of Leonor and Alfonso derives to some extent from that of the tomb of Berenguela, a sister of Alfonso X (and of Eleanor of Castile), who entered Las Huelgas as a nun in the 1240s.[51] Until her death in 1279, she was *senora* and *domina* of the monastery, and a re-dedication of Alfonso's tomb also in 1279 is attributed to her direction in a notice that survives only in an eighteenth-century copy.[52]

Figure 4.3 Las Huelgas, tombs of Alfonso VIII and Leonor of England (east). Conway Library Courtauld Institute of Art.

Berenguela's own tomb, which now sits close to that of the founders, is also a gabled tomb chest with historiated scenes of the infancy of Christ and the Coronation of the Virgin, although in this case the scenes are set under enclosed trefoils and extend along the sides of the sarcophagus and the gable in an almost antique manner. There is only minimal use of heraldry, which was to be so prominent on the tombs of Leonor and Alfonso VIII. By the early fourteenth century there was a firm preference at Las Huelgas for heraldic tombs with developed repetitive heraldic designs that resemble sculpted fabric, perhaps permanent funeral palls. The most notable examples of this genre are the tombs of Doña Blanca of Portugal (d. 1321) and of Alfonso de la Cerda (d. 1333), which date from the early fourteenth century. Rocío Sánchez has demonstrated convincingly that the tombs of Leonor and Alfonso VIII belong stylistically with this group and historically with the knighting of Alfonso XI in 1331 at Las Huelgas.[53]

This was the first time that this ceremony had taken place at Las Huelgas since the future Edward I of England was knighted there in 1254. Las Huelgas had begun to lose its preeminence after the death of Fernando III and his decision to be buried in the cathedral in Seville in 1252. Berenguela's brother, Alfonso X, was not only to follow his example, but also in 1279 to translate the body of his mother, Beatriz, away from Las Huelgas.[54] Indeed Alfonso X had never again been as generous to Las Huelgas as he had been at the time of the marriage of Eleanor of Castile to the future Edward I of England. There was thus every reason in the context of renewed interest from Alfonso XI for the nuns of Las Huelgas to set about reestablishing its role as a royal burial place and simultaneously boosting the status of the monastery by promoting its association with its royal founders. They could draw on the links with England that had been beneficial in the late twelfth century and renewed by the mid-thirteenth-century marriage and thus reinforce their right to provide spiritual support and intercession for the royal family of Castile.[55]

A link with a tomb in Burgos Cathedral and its use of sculpture further supports this dating. Most of the sculpture surviving from thirteenth-century Burgos comes from the cathedral. Deknatel's comparison between the sculpture on the south transept door, the *Puerta del Sarmental* at Burgos, of ca. 1240, and work on the west front of Amiens Cathedral remains rightly unchallenged. So we can be as sure as a stylistic comparison can make us that two masons from Amiens came to set up a workshop in Burgos not long after work started on the Cathedral.[56] The later north portal, the *Puerta de la Coronería*, introduces a new heavier drapery style that belongs with, but does not straightforwardly derive from, ateliers that mainly worked in Paris, Chartres, and Reims, and there is a sweetness, for example, in the faces of the angels, that bears comparison with the angels in the Sainte Chapelle.[57] Yet the resonances with Amiens do not entirely disappear, and this has some relevance for the Las Huelgas tombs. The style of the *Puerta de la Coronería* continues in different manifestations in the towers of the Cathedral and in the new cloister, both of which belong mainly to the later decades of the thirteenth century.

Amid these manifold developments it is possible to suggest one stylistic link between Leonor's tomb and the sculpture of Burgos Cathedral. The small figures of Mary and John in the crucifixion scene on Leonor's tomb are paralleled by another figure of Mary, part of an Annunciation, now found on the wall of a tomb located outside the *Puerta del Sarmental* (figure 4.4). The tomb is in a bad state of repair and it has been moved, allegedly from the *capilla de San Antolín*. The inscription on the tomb says that it belongs to don Pedro Díaz de Peñafiel and that he died in 1333. However, the sculpture does not seem to be part of the tomb but instead reused older fragments, and each figure is carved on a bracket that is now embedded, somewhat awkwardly, into the wall. If we look at other sculptures in the cloister, it is possible to identify some common features albeit at a much higher level of execution. Brackets of the same shape are used to support figures on the cloister portal. Elsewhere a princely figure in the cloister holds on to the belt of his robes, a feature familiar, for example, from Rheims, and found again on the Mary on the Peñafiel tomb.

Figure 4.4 Burgos Cathedral, tomb of Díaz Peñafiel, figure of Mary from an Annunciation. Photo: Julian Gardner. Conway Library, Courtauld Institute of Art.

This suggests that the fragments may belong to the same period as the cloister sculpture, that is, the last decades of the thirteenth century, and consequently that there may have been an interest in the use of such archaic figures in a funerary context at that time.

Comparisons between the figures from the Peñafiel tomb and the cloister sculpture are difficult because of differences in scale and quality, but when the Peñafiel figures are compared with the sculpture on Leonor's tomb the resemblance is more striking. In particular the drapery on the figure of John and the head-dress on the figure of Mary at Las Huelgas seem almost identical to that used on the Peñafiel tomb figures. Both belong stylistically to International Gothic of the mid-thirteenth century and hark back, for example, to a female figure on the front of the tomb of Adela of Champagne, now at Joigny. This could have indicated that the Las Huelgas tomb belonged with the late-thirteenth-century sculpture of the Burgos Cathedral cloister. Instead I think it demonstrates a similar interest in archaism shared by both the Peñafiel tomb and the tombs of Leonor and Alfonso VIII in the first half of the fourteenth century. Moreover this archaism focuses on the mid-thirteenth century of Eleanor of Castile rather than on the late twelfth and early thirteenth centuries of Leonor of England.

Another possibly archaic reference is the form of the Castilian heraldry on Leonor and Alfonso VIII's tombs. Some aspects of the castle image including its central tower, two side towers, and distinctive triangular crenellations are in line with the form of the motif found elsewhere in Las Huelgas, for example, embroidered in gold on a red silk textile and in the stuccowork on the ceiling of the Cloister of San Fernando.[58] The image of the castle on the tombs, however, is not just larger but also more elaborate in its detailing than the other examples. Several of the windows have quatrefoil or trefoil tracery and the large central doorway has rich polylobe decoration with crocket terminations. The polylobing is immediately reminiscent of that found on the three portals on the west front of Amiens cathedral, which has in turn links to Burgos Cathedral, while the micro-architectural detailing could find a counterpart on the *trumeau* of the central portal of the west front at Amiens, although that example retains some plainer Romanesque arches.

Whilst the imagery of Castile dominates the surfaces of both tombs, Leonor's tomb makes explicit reference to her dynastic origins. The Plantagenet heraldic shield with its three leopards is prominently displayed on both ends of the sarcophagus, but it has one unusual detail in that the leopards are shown wearing crowns, when normally the Plantagenet leopards had only tufts of hair. This error could stem from an attempt to distinguish the leopards from the lion of León or from copying a treasured but worn original, perhaps a fabric, where the tufted heads of the leopards could have been mistaken for crowns. There is indeed one reference to Leonor wearing what sounds like a heraldic motif in a poem by the Catalan troubadour, Raimon Vidal of Besalú. He describes Queen Leonor as "wrapped in a cloak of scarlet sisclaton silk with a silver border and a golden lion embroidered on it." We can only speculate whether this distinctive cloth, perhaps bearing the Plantagenet leopard motif, was not mere poetic licence but a cloth actually worn by Leonor and perhaps one of the fabrics sent by her father.[59] However, the developed form of the Plantagenet leopards belongs not to the late twelfth but to the thirteenth and fourteenth centuries and featured for example on the tombs and other memorials to Eleanor of Castile from the 1290s. So it is more likely that the sculptors were copying an example preserved from the visit of Edward on his marriage to Eleanor of Castile in 1254 or perhaps a later gift from Eleanor to her sister, Berenguela.

One aspect of Alfonso VIII's tomb sculpture may also refer to Henry III and the marriage of Edward to Eleanor of Castile. In the representation of Alfonso VIII handing over the foundation charter to the nuns, the two lions, one on each side of the throne, mark it as the throne of Solomon. This was a designation to which kings often aspired, but Henry III of England took a particular interest in this biblical reference, as he not only commissioned bronze leopards to stand on either side of this throne but also depicted them on his Great Seal.[60] Moreover, it is quite possible that Las Huelgas had a copy of that Great Seal, because Alfonso X had attached great importance to the idea that the negotiated arrangements for the marriage between Eleanor of Castile and Edward of England should be sealed by it.[61]

The historiated scenes in the end gables of Leonor's tomb reflect two approaches to depicting her royal piety. The crucifixion scene had a precedent within Alfonso VIII's family as it recalled the tomb of his mother Blanca at Nájera, whereas the Marian quality of the royal soul ascending to heaven resonated in a modest way with the same quality in the effigy on Eleanor's Westminster tomb.

The marriage of Eleanor of Castile and Edward I and the associated knighting of Edward seem to sit behind the inspiration for the joint tombs of Alfonso VIII and Leonor. The decoration of the tombs is indeed a series of quotations from that event and its historical context. Thus the dynastically important Anglo-Iberian marriage of 1254 gave new impetus to the distinguished memory of the founders of Las Huelgas and to their successful union of 1170. Both would have added luster to the rising fortunes of Las Huelgas and of Alfonso XI in the 1330s.

In summary each memorial reflects the power and wealth of the kingdoms involved in the marriages. Leonor of England, still defined by her distinguished Plantagenet ancestry, lay symbolically beside her husband, Alfonso VIII of Castile, in their foundation of Las Huelgas, her marriage reinvented through the marriage of Eleanor of Castile and Edward of England. Eleanor of Castile was to lie in Henry III's Westminster Abbey adorned with her heraldic identity, but in reality owing very little to her Iberian inheritance.

Notes

1. John Carmi Parsons, *The Court and Household of Eleanor of Castile in 1290. An Edition of British Library, Additional Manuscript 35294 with Introduction and Notes* (Toronto: Pontifical Institute of Medieval Studies, 1977), p. 53. Thomas Tolley, "Eleanor of Castile and the 'Spanish' Style in England," in *England in the Thirteenth Century. Proceedings of the 1989 Harlaxton Symposium*, ed. W.M. Ormrod (Stamford: Paul Watkins, 1991), p. 170 [167–200].
2. Parsons, *Court and Household*, p. 53.
3. Parsons, *Court and Household*, p. 12; John Carmi Parsons, *Eleanor of Castile. Queen and Society in Thirteenth-Century England* (Basingstoke: Macmillan, 1994), p. 54.
4. Edmond-René Labande, "Les filles d'Aliénor de'Aquitaine: étude comparative," in *Cahiers de Civilisation Médiévale* 29 (1986): 105–11.
5. Theresa M. Vann, "The Theory and Practice of Medieval Castilian Queenship," in *Queens, Regents and Potentates*, ed. Theresa M. Vann (Dallas: Academia Press, 1993), p. 131 [125–47]; *The Great Roll of the Pipe for the Twenty-Sixth Year of the Reign of King Henry the Second: AD 1179–80* (London: Wyman and Sons, 1930), p. 157.
6. Julio González González, *El reino de Castilla en la época de Alfonso VIII*, 3 vols. (Madrid: Consejo Superior de Investigaciones Científicas, Escuela de Estudios Medievales, 1960), 1:191.
7. Matthew Paris, *Matthaei Parisiensis, Monachi Sancti Albani Chronica Majora*, ed. Henry Richard Luard (London: Longman, 1872–83), v. 513. See also Parsons, *Eleanor*, pp. 63–65.
8. Rose Walker, "Leonor of England, Plantagenet Queen of King Alfonso VIII of Castile, and Her Foundation of the Cistercian Abbey of Las Huelgas in Imitation of Fontevraud?" in *Journal of Medieval History*, 31 (2005): 346–68.
9. Parsons, *Eleanor of Castile*, p. 57.
10. Tolley, "Eleanor of Castile and the 'Spanish' Style," pp. 178–92.
11. Susan Groag Bell, "Medieval Women Book Owners: Arbiters of Lay Piety and Ambassadors of Culture," in *Women and Power in the Middle Ages*, ed. M. Erler and M. Kowaleski (Athens, GA: University of Georgia Press, 1988); Margaret Howell, *Eleanor of Provence, Queenship in Thirteenth-Century England* (Oxford: Blackwell, 1998), pp. 82–92.
12. John Lowden, *The Making of the Bibles Moralisées, 1. The Manuscripts* (Philadelphia, PA: The Pennsylvania State University Press, 2000), pp. 185–86 and 216.
13. Parsons, *Court and Household*, pp. 13 and 86. Tolley, "Eleanor of Castile and the 'Spanish' Style," p. 171.
14. Parsons, *Eleanor*, pp. 55–56. Parsons, *Court and Household*, pp. 13, 90.
15. Parsons, *Eleanor*, pp. 57–58. Tolley, "Eleanor of Castile and the 'Spanish' Style," pp. 171–72.
16. Parsons, *Court and Household*, pp. 28–29.

17. Paul Binski, "Reflections on *La estoire de Seint Aedward le rei*: Hagiography and Kingship in Thirteenth-Century England," *Journal of Medieval History* 16 (1990): 339–40 [333–50].
18. *Age of Chivalry, Art in Plantagenet England, 1200–1400*, ed. Jonathan Alexander and Paul Binski (London: Royal Academy of Arts, Weidenfeld and Nicolson, 1987), cat. no. 39, pp. 216–17. Parsons, *Court and Household*, p. 13 n39.
19. George Henderson, "Studies in English Manuscript Illumination, I-II," *Journal of the Warburg and Courtauld Institutes* 30 (1967): 79 [71–104].
20. David McKitterick, Nigel Morgan, Ian Short, and Teresa Webber, *The Trinity Apocalypse (Trinity College Cambridge, MS R.16.2)* (London and Toronto: The British Library and University of Toronto Press, 2005), pp. 4–5 and 29–30.
21. Henderson, "Studies," p. 128.
22. Howell, *Eleanor of Provence*, pp. 90–91. Peter H. Brieger, *The Trinity College Apocalypse: An Introduction and Description* (London: Eugrammia Press, 1967), p. 14.
23. Frances Carey, *The Apocalypse and the Shape of Things to Come* (London: The British Museum, 1999), no.10, pp. 75–78.
24. Henderson, "Studies," p. 128; McKitterick, Morgan, Short, and Webber, *The Trinity Apocalypse*, pp. 4 and 34–35.
25. Henderson, "Studies," pp. 129.
26. McKitterick et al., *The Trinity Apocalypse*, plate 20.
27. See, for example, the early-thirteenth-century Arroyo Beatus in John Williams, *The Illustrated Beatus*, 5 vols., *The Twelfth and Thirteenth Centuries*, Vol. 5 (London: Harvey Miller, 2003), plates 520 and 521.
28. Brieger, *The Trinity College Apocalypse*, pp. 9–13.
29. J.G. Noppen, "Westminster Paintings and Master Peter," *The Burlington Magazine* 91 (1949): 305–09.
30. McKitterick et al., *The Trinity Apocalypse*, p. 30. Nigel Morgan favors this option in this recent book, or the possibility of Simon de Montfort, over Eleanor of Provence.
31. William J. Entwistle, *The Arthurian Legend in the Literatures of the Spanish Peninsula* (London and Toronto: J.M. Dent, 1925), pp. 32–35.
32. *Manuscritos e impresos del monasterio de Las Huelgas Reales de Burgos, Catálogo de la Real Biblioteca, Catálogo de los Reales Patronatos 14.2* (Madrid: Patrimonio Nacional, 1999), pp. 19–26.
33. *Art of Medieval Spain A.D. 500–1200* (New York: The Metropolitan Museum of Art, 1993), cat. no. 152, pp. 299–300, which includes a reproduction.
34. *Art of Medieval Spain*, cat. no. 153, 300–01. William D. Wixom and Margaret Lawson, *Painting the Apocalypse: Illustrated Leaves from a Medieval Spanish Manuscript* (New York: The Metropolitan Museum of Art, 2002), pp. 9–12.
35. Joaquín Yarza Luaces, "Las Miniaturas de la Biblia de Burgos," *Archivo español de arte* 42 (1969): 185–203. *English Romanesque Art 1066–1200*, ed. George Zarnecki, Janet Holt, and Tristram Holland (London: Arts Council of Great Britain with Weidenfeld and Nicolson, 1984), cat. no. 54, p. 116.

36. Walter Cahn, *Romanesque Manuscripts. The Twelfth Century*, 2 vols. (London: Harvey Miller, 1996), 1: no.106, 255–256, 2:128–130; Joaquín Yarza Luaces, "La miniatura en Galicia, León, y Castilla en tiempos de Maestro Mateo," in *Actas do Simposio Internacional sobre "O Portico da la Gloria e a Arte do seu Tiempo" (Santiago de Compostela, 3–8 do outobro de 1988)* (Santiago de Compostela: Dirección Xeral de Cultura, 1991), p. 321 [319–40]; *Art of Medieval Spain*, cat. no. 152, pp. 299–300.
37. *Art of Medieval Spain*, cat. no. 152, pp. 299–300.
38. Walter Oakeshott, *Sigena: Romanesque Paintings in Spain and the Winchester Bible Artists* (London: Harvey Miller and Medcalf, 1972).
39. *The Utrecht Psalter in Medieval Art. Picturing the Psalms of David*, ed. Koert van der Horst, William Noel, and Wilhelmina C.M. Wüstefeld (Utrecht: HES Publishers, 1996), no. 30, pp. 240–41.
40. Yarza Luaces, "La miniatura," pp. 327–29.
41. David Chadd, "Liturgy and Liturgical Music: The Limits of Uniformity," in *Cistercian Art and Architecture in the British Isles*, ed. Christopher Norton and David Park (Cambridge: Cambridge University Press, 1986), pp. 299–314, esp. p. 301
42. Weseley D. Jordan, "Four Twelfth-Century Musico-Liturgical Manuscripts from the Cistercian Monastery of Las Huelgas, Burgos," *Manuscripta* 37 (1993): 21–70.
43. Sonsoles Herrero González, *Códices Miniados en el Real Monasterio de Las Huelgas* (Madrid and Barcelona: Patrimonio Nacional and Lunwerg Editores, 1988), pp. 69–80 and figure 52.
44. M-M. Gauthier, "Le goût plantagenêt et les arts dans la France du Sud-Ouest," in *Stil und Überlieferung in der Kunst des Abendlandes I. Akten des 21. Internationalen Kongress für Kunstgeschichte, Bonn, 14–19 Sept. 1964* (Berlin: Mann, 1967), pp. 139–55.
45. Walter Oakeshott, *The Two Winchester Bibles* (Oxford: Clarendon Press, 1981), plate 125.
46. Yolanta Zaluska, *L'enluminure et le scriptorium de Cîteaux au XIIe siècle* (Cîteaux: Centre National de la Recherche Scientifique du Centre National des Lettres, 1989), pp. 165–67.
47. Parsons, *Eleanor*, p. 207. Paul Binski, *Westminster Abbey and the Plantagenets: Kingship and the Representation of Power, 1200–1400* (New Haven: Yale University Press, 1995), pp. 107–10.
48. Parsons, *Eleanor*, p. 60.
49. Phillip Lindley, "The Sculptural Memorials of Queen Eleanor and their Context," in *Eleanor of Castile 1290–1990: Essays to Commemorate the 700th Anniversary of her death: 28 November 1290*, ed. David Parsons (Stamford: Paul Watkins, 1991), pp. 69–92.
50. Paul Williamson, "Sculpture," in *Age of Chivalry: Art in Plantagenet England 1200–1400*, pp. 102–03 [98–106], and cat. no. 377, pp. 364–65.
51. Andrea Gayoso, "The Lady of Las Huelgas. A Royal Abbey and Its Patronage," *Cîteaux: commentarii cistercienses* 51 (2000): 1–2 and 91–115.

52. José Manuel Lizoaín Garrido, *Documentación del monasterio de las Huelgas de Burgos (1263–83)*, Fuentes medievales castellano-leonesas, 32 (Burgos: J.M. Garrido Garrido, 1990), doc. 596, pp. 112–13; Elie Lambert, *L'art gothique en Espagne aux XIIe et XIIIe siècles* (Paris: Henri Laurens, 1931), p. 200; Henrik Karge, "Die königliche Zisterzienserinnenabtei Las Huelgas de Burgos und die Anfäge der gotischen Architektur in Spanien," in *Gotische Architektur in Spanien. Akten des Kolloquiums der Carl Justi-Vereinigung und des Kunstgeschichtlichen Seminars der Universität Göttingen, 4–6. Februar 1994*, ed. Christian Freigang (Frankfurt am Main: Vervuert; Madrid: Iberoamericana, 1999), p. 27 [13–40, 373–76].
53. Rocío Sánchez Ameijeiras, "La memoria de un rey victorioso: los sepulcros de Alfonso VIII y la fiesta del triunfo de la Santa Cruz," in *Grabkunst und Sepulkralkultur in Spanien und Portugal*, ed. Barbara Borngässer, Henrik Karge, and Bruno Klein (Frankfurt am Main: Vervuert, 2006), pp. 289–315.
54. Lizoaín Garrido, *Documentación*, doc. 596, pp. 112–13.
55. Anne McGee Morganstern, *Gothic Tombs of Kinship in France, The Low Countries, and England* (Philadelphia, PA: The Pennsylvania State University Press, 2000), p. 150.
56. Frederick B. Deknatel, "The Thirteenth Century Gothic Sculpture of the Cathedrals of Burgos and Leon," *Art Bulletin* 17 (1935): 260–62 [243–389].
57. Paul Williamson, *Gothic Sculpture 1140–1300* (New Haven: Yale University Press, 1995), pp. 228–30.
58. L. Torres Balbás, "Las yeserías descubiertas recientemente en Las Huelgas de Burgos. Contribución al estudio de la decoración arquitectónica hispano-musulmana," *Al-Andalus* 3 (1943): 21–66.
59. González, *El reino de Castilla*, 1:193. Linda M. Paterson, *The World of the Troubadours in Medieval Occitan Society c.1100–c.1300* (Cambridge: Cambridge University Press, 1993), pp. 116–17 and 166. (The translation from Vidal is mine and is based on Vidal's text in Paterson.)
60. *Age of Chivalry: Art in Plantagenet England 1200–1400*, p. 316, cat. 276.
61. Parsons, *Eleanor*, pp. 14–16.

CHAPTER 5

A CASTILIAN IN KING EDWARD'S COURT:
THE CAREER OF GILES DESPAGNE, 1313–27

Cynthia L. Chamberlin

By examining the career of Giles Despagne, a yeoman in the service of Edward II of England, this essay investigates the king's great regard for his maternal Castilian heritage and his use of this heritage to strengthen his position, especially in international affairs.

Edward II of England long has been known as a king embroiled throughout his reign in bitter struggles with his nobles, most often provoked by Edward's penchant for "favorites."[1] Baronial opposition to royal favorites, although expressed in the language of intimate personal relationships, essentially was based on socioeconomic competition for royal patronage. Occasionally, when a baronial coalition decided that mere political methods were ineffective, such attempts to gain control went to the lengths of armed rebellion against the king, represented as "rescuing" him from the "evil advisers" who had been causing him to distribute patronage incorrectly and otherwise behave unbecomingly. An aspect of Edward II's reign that has been little studied, however, is the great regard he had for his Castilian heritage and how he used the dynastic links forged by this heritage in attempts to strengthen his position, especially in international affairs. Moreover, playing an important role in Edward's disputes with his barons were a number of Castilians in his service, some of them his kin and others, unrelated, with links to the Castilian merchant community trading with England.[2] As Edward's Castilian retainers occupied positions of great confidence and proximity to the king, an examination of their careers in his service provides new perspectives on key events and developments in his turbulent reign and its aftermath.

Despite remarkably profuse survival and publication of medieval English records containing data concerning the activities of Edward II's Castilian retainers on his behalf, less accessible in most cases is information about these men's personal lives and backgrounds or their continuing links with Iberia. Usually it is only in the public arenas of politics and trade that they become visible, in either English or Iberian sources. Interesting studies nonetheless can be made of individuals such as Edward II's first cousin Master James of Spain, a clerical pluralist on a wide scale despite his illegitimate birth and lack of ordination. Yet Master James was also an Oxford scholar; and if he was chronically absent from his collection of benefices, it was because he held key positions in his cousin the king's fiscal administration, in precisely the years in which Edward II's financial reforms were determining the ultimate fate of his reign.[3] Another kinsman, Rodrigo de España, was an official of Edward's household from the future king's boyhood. He maintained close ties with Castilian merchants in England, who doubtless assisted him as he undertook diplomatic errands to Castile for the king in the early years of the reign. Rodrigo died while on one of these missions in 1312, and Edward II took the time, amidst his first really serious clash with his nobles, to write to his cousin Fernando IV of Castile about the welfare of Rodrigo's widow and children. He also took an interest in the settlement of Rodrigo's estate—of which prominent Burgos merchant and occasional diplomat Andrés Pérez de Castrogeriz was an executor—as Rodrigo had been administering a number of estates and other business transactions for the king at the time of his death.[4] But perhaps the most rewarding figure to study, in terms of insight into the crucial developments of Edward II's reign and relations between England and the Christian kingdoms of Iberia during this period, is a Castilian who was not the king's kinsman, Giles Despagne.

The personal relationship between Edward II and his yeoman Giles Despagne can be traced only in its outlines, through their public actions as reported in official records. One element of it must have been Edward's predilection for things Castilian or for anyone associated with his mother, Eleanor of Castile. Edward had not known his mother well, for he largely was not brought up under her care and she died when he was only six. Nevertheless he invested her memory, and by extension her family and native land, with considerable significance. Possibly this was in part psychological compensation for the difficult, unrewarding relationships he had with most of his English kin; he may have idealized his Castilian relatives, safely distanced from him by space or time, as more supportive and affectionate toward him than his severely critical paternal ones were in everyday life. He also may have been inspired by the deeds of his Castilian and Leonese ancestors, particularly those of his maternal grandfather, Fernando III, recounted by Rodrigo Jiménez de Rada in *De rebus Hispaniae*. A copy of this book was noted in a 1320 inventory of the Exchequer; it may have been brought to England by Eleanor upon her marriage to Edward I in 1254, or else sent for later, for she shared her natal family's cultivation of literature. Archbishop de Rada was Fernando III's older contemporary and had written about that king's accomplishments on the battlefield and in the council chamber mostly from an eyewitness perspective. At the end of the book, he even recorded Eleanor's birth. Reading this book, Edward II would have felt himself linked by that mention of his mother to his illustrious grandfather and all the generations of Iberian royalty preceding them.[5]

Another part of Edward II's attachment to his Castilian heritage was inculcated in him by the expectations of a society that laid great emphasis on both agnatic and cognatic kinship. For example, when Cardinal Petrus Hispanus—born Pedro Rodríguez and formerly bishop of Burgos—visited England as a papal legate early in 1307, Edward I sent his son and heir to welcome him, commenting in a letter to the pope that the cardinal would have special affection for the prince because the cardinal was a Castilian and Prince Edward of Castilian descent. Presumably this ethnically inspired affection was to work both ways. According to a perhaps not very reliable contemporary report, one of the cardinal's purposes in visiting was to bring an offer from "the nobility of Spain" that, if Fernando IV should die without issue, the crown of Castile and Leon should go to Prince Edward by virtue of his being Eleanor's son. While such an offer may not have been impossible, given the complexities of Castilian dynastic rivalries in this period, it is more likely that the unknown correspondent who made this report had heard some garbled version of discussions between England and Castile regarding Gascony and the prince's right as heir to his mother, to whom all Castilian claims to Gascony had been relinquished long before.[6]

By some reports, Prince Edward even would have preferred a Castilian bride for himself,[7] but he was obliged instead to marry French princess Isabelle, daughter of Philippe IV, as part of a papally mediated end to yet another war between England and France over Gascony. Otherwise known to contemporaries as the duchy of Guyenne, Gascony was part of the inheritance of England's kings since the time of their ancestor Eleanor of Aquitaine. In their capacity as dukes of Guyenne, however, they were supposed to acknowledge the French kings as their overlords with rights to intervene in the duchy under certain circumstances, a situation that did not reconcile well with their simultaneous identities as sovereign kings in England.[8] The tensions inherent in this ambivalent relationship, although supposedly resolved by Edward II's marriage to Isabelle, in time would result in one of the final crises of his reign. In that crisis, Edward would turn to Castile—the land from which he reputedly would have preferred a bride in the first place—and to other Iberian kingdoms for aid.

In addition to his dynastic attachment to Castile, Edward II showed marked favor to Iberian merchants, particularly Castilians, both before and after coming to the throne.[9] It is most likely in this context that Giles Despagne became known to him and entered his service.[10] Giles Despagne's origins are more obscure than those of Edward II's cousins, James of Spain and Rodrigo de España. Unlike both James and Rodrigo, Giles never is referred to in English records as a royal relation; so, even though in many cases he performed duties similar to Rodrigo's, including carrying out diplomatic missions, he probably was not a blood relation of either Rodrigo or the English kings. There were other contemporaries in English records surnamed "of Spain" (*de Ispannia*, Despagne) who were not related to the royal family, who may have been Giles's kin.[11] It is not known whether he was born in England or in Iberia, and if the latter, in which of the Christian kingdoms there. The most likely surmise is that he was Castilian, either in actual birth or in background.[12] Based on his early associations with Castilian merchants and his later diplomatic missions for Edward II and Edward III, he clearly spoke Castilian as well as the French used in English elite circles. Less certain is whether or not he also spoke Portuguese. Giles was sent on at least two diplomatic missions to Portugal; but as Castilian was employed as a sort of Iberian *lingua franca* in the fourteenth century, it would not have been strictly necessary for him to have spoken Portuguese to have been able to discharge those duties.

Giles assuredly was not the "shadowy character" or "professional bounty hunter" that he has been termed in a recent account of Edward II's reign.[13] Yet this neglect is scarcely unique. Whereas Giles occasionally receives a summary line or two in accounts of Edward III's pursuit of his father's accused assassins, modern historians of the period hardly mention Giles's previous career in Edward II's service. He had a long, adventurous career in Edward II's service before Edward III employed him in the 1330s to apprehend a number of the men accused of the alleged murder of Edward II in 1327 and the judicial murder of the earl of Kent in 1330. Moreover, the notable loyalty that Giles displayed toward his first royal English master, in addition to his other qualifications as a warrior and diplomat, must have inspired Edward III's choice of him to go to Castile to retrieve the fugitive Sir Thomas Gourney. Edward III seems to have inherited the loyalty Giles bore his father, as he employed Giles on diplomatic missions to Iberia even after the round-up of fugitives was completed.

Giles first appears in English crown records on November 6, 1313, as one of a company of foreigners—most of them identifiable as merchants doing business in England—who agreed to stand surety for merchants and seafarers from Castro Urdiales, Santander, and Laredo desirous of coming to England to trade. Several English merchants based in Southampton had been conducting a campaign of reprisals against merchants of the Cantabrian ports for past actions against their own ships and goods in those parts, with the result that Castilian merchants were refusing to come to England any longer, for fear of arrest, lawsuits, or worse. The Castilian merchants therefore had petitioned Edward II for a royal safe-conduct against his own subjects' harassment, which the king granted for the space of a year, given the support of the ten named guarantors, including Giles Despagne. A condition attached to the safe-conduct was that the ten guarantors have the Castilian merchants protected by it make some sort of proper amends to those of Southampton for their countrymen's past offenses. One of the guarantors, Juan Sánchez, almost certainly was the same man who had held Rodrigo de España's power of attorney in 1311, while Rodrigo was on one of his missions to Castile. This indicates that Giles belonged to the same merchant circles with which Rodrigo had such close connections.[14]

It is not apparent from this record if Giles was already in King Edward's service at the time he acted as guarantor for the Castilian merchants, but it is likely that he entered the king's service around this time. He certainly was a royal yeoman less than a year later, when he lost valuable horses fighting beside the king at the disastrous (for the English) battle of Bannockburn in 1314, although he was not reimbursed for them until over two years later.[15]

Giles Despagne's position in Edward II's household was that of sergeant-at-arms (*serviens ad arma*) or yeoman (*vallettus*), terms used interchangeably to indicate a non-knightly member of the king's household cavalry. There were about thirty sergeants-at-arms in this body during Edward II's reign, a good proportion of them foreigners. Each was required to have three horses—an ordinary riding horse, a warhorse, and a packhorse—and the warhorses, at least, were issued, like other military equipment, from the king's Wardrobe. A sergeant-at-arms earned 12d. a day serving inside England and 2s. a day when on the king's service overseas; these figures are faithfully reflected in the expense accounts Giles kept of some of his later missions. If any of the sergeant's three horses were lacking, however, he would have his wages stopped until he replaced it, as he was considered incapable of performing his duties without them.

As might be expected, based on these criteria, one of the yeoman's main duties was to serve as the king's personal bodyguard on all occasions. When the king was in residence, the sergeants-at-arms guarded his rooms; when he traveled, they formed his immediate escort; and on the battlefield they were the troops directly surrounding and defending his person. They undoubtedly were the most loyal body of soldiers at his command. Yet they were not merely a band of privileged thugs; king's yeomen generally came from elite families and possessed social skills, education, and standing appropriate to persons who spent most of their time in close proximity to the king. Some of the yeomen of Edward's household when he was prince of Wales, for example, were his own cousins, as well as unrelated young men of lesser birth. Individual yeomen frequently were used for tasks such as carrying confidential diplomatic correspondence, administering royal estates or the lands of royal wards, and conducting purveyances. They have been described as "perhaps the most faithful and useful section of the [king's] household."[16] When Edward II needed practical results, it was often to his sergeants-at-arms that he turned, especially if getting those results might require potentially adventurous physical activity—as nearly all a royal yeoman's duties might, even the administrative ones.

These unusually close ties between king and yeomen meant, as a consequence, that the royal sergeants-at-arms were the personnel on whom the king could rely for enforcement of unpopular actions and policies. Purveyances were a case in point. All medieval governments in Europe used some form of the purveyance system, as did the households of great nobles. The system itself, therefore, rarely was questioned, but complaints about abuses of it by individual officials or even particular households were legion. Some doubtless were due to the inherent inefficiency of the system, but many were justified, as the system practically invited corruption and arbitrary displays of power by the purveying officials. Edward II's household had a notably bad reputation where abuses of purveyance were concerned. At least in the earlier years of his reign, the abuses may have been in part unavoidable, as his government was chronically short of funds, yet his household had to be fed somehow. On the other hand, his purveyors—who were under great pressure to get results, without which they themselves would not eat—seem to have been high-handed and insensitive to the plight of the supplies' original owners, even during the dreadful famine years of 1315–17. Edward himself notoriously would overlook even the most outrageous conduct by his household officials, so long as it produced results. This eventually extended beyond purveyances to nearly all aspects of his fiscal administration and amounted in some cases to toleration of overtly criminal, violent behavior by his officials.[17]

There is no record that Giles was personally responsible for such abuses, but he very well might have been. Undeniably, he was part of a close-knit organization that was, namely Edward II's household. There must have been a strong "us versus them" component in the household's mentality, contributing to the ties of loyalty binding the king and his personal retainers. This would have been especially marked in the relationship of Edward with his sergeants-at-arms, most so with those sergeants of foreign origin, like Giles. In this mentality resulting from Edward's frequently embattled kingship, in combination with Edward's noted partiality for Castilians, probably lie the origins of the extraordinary loyalty Giles displayed toward his master throughout his career.

As a member of Edward II's personal bodyguard and household cavalry, Giles would have been among those who bodily dragged the king off the field of Bannockburn when it became apparent the English cause was lost and who then protected him from the Scots' pursuit as he was obliged to flee. During this forced withdrawal from the battlefield, the king had one horse killed under him and had to be given another by one of his companions, and one of his household knights was taken prisoner. His privy seal and his personal shield both were lost in the course of this rout, although the victorious Robert Bruce subsequently returned them by messenger. The English royal party first sought safety inside Stirling Castle, but its castellan dared not give them shelter, so they were obliged to ride on across country, pursued by Sir James Douglas and sixty horsemen, to Dunbar Castle. There they boarded a boat and finally escaped to Berwick.[18]

Giles certainly received material rewards for his service. In 1317 Edward II gave him a substantial house at a place called La Forde or Old Ford, outside London. Giles was permitted to bequeath this property to his children, if he had any, although it would revert to the crown at his death if he did not.[19] It is unknown if Giles had a family at the time of this grant, but he had acquired a wife, at least, by the time Edward II bestowed a series of properties on him in 1321. The king's gift of Reading, Burghfield, Whitley, Early, Barton Winyard, Sonning, and lands previously owned by the late William de Montreuil in an unspecified location was bestowed jointly upon Giles and his wife Laurencia for their lifetimes.[20] Unfortunately, nothing further is known about this lady, even whether she was English or Castilian.[21] She probably lived at least until the 1330s, however, for when Giles departed on his protracted diplomatic missions for the crown in 1324–25, 1331–32, 1333–34, and 1336, he does not seem to have taken out powers of attorney for someone to administer his property and financial affairs in his absence. This suggests he already had someone to administer them, and the most likely person would have been his wife.[22] There is no record of whether Giles and Laurencia had children. In 1322 Giles was granted further land at Old Ford; this property probably adjoined that which he had been given in 1317. Unlike the first parcel, this grant was Giles's to dispose of as he pleased, without legal strings attached.[23]

It is significant that two out of the three grants were made to Giles in the period 1321–22, for that was when Edward II, after years of political struggles with the larger part of his nobility, finally achieved the definitive upper hand. He did so, however, only by giving up on political maneuvering, which on the whole had not served him well, and resorting to armed force. He conducted a series of divide-and-conquer campaigns that picked off opposition leaders a few at a time in widely separated regions of the kingdom. Once defeated, his opponents and their chief supporters ended up in prison, dead on the battlefield, or, increasingly, executed following treason trials of rather dubious legality. In all cases, their estates were confiscated to the king's personal administrative office, the Chamber, rather than to the Exchequer. This resulted in Edward II's becoming for the first time not only fiscally stable but actually quite wealthy.[24] While in these campaigns Edward did enjoy the military support of a few nobles with whom he had been on good terms for years, the forces organized and led by his household knights, esquires, and sergeants-at-arms were key in achieving many of his victories, thanks to their efficiency, esprit de corps, and reliability.[25]

A significant military role was played as well in the final battle of the conflict, at Boroughbridge in Yorkshire on March 16, 1322, by levies from the northern shires. The northerners had become convinced, possibly with good reason, that the long-time leader of the noble opposition, the king's cousin Thomas, earl of Lancaster, had gone so far in his efforts to restrain Edward's oppressive tendencies as to enter into treasonous correspondence with the Scots. To inhabitants of Yorkshire, Cumberland, Westmorland, and Northumbria, terrorized for years by Scottish guerrilla warfare, there could be no greater crime. Some of Lancaster's supporters were slain on the field, Lancaster himself captured. After a show trial at which neither he nor anyone else was allowed to speak in his defense, Lancaster was promptly beheaded and his vast estates confiscated. Despite his less than virtuous personal life and extremely modest talent for governance when he was in power,[26] Lancaster had been a steadfast leader of the opposition to all Edward II's unpopular policies and abuses. In combination with the blatantly unjust manner of his death, this earned him a posthumous reputation as a martyr. The never officially sanctioned cult of "Saint Thomas" of Lancaster would provide Edward II's enemies with a rallying point in the future, just as the living earl had done before March 16, 1322.[27]

As his forces were closing in on the rebellious nobles before Boroughbridge, Edward II dispatched Giles and the household knight Sir John Sturmy to Tutbury Priory to confiscate all the valuable moveable goods Lancaster and his allies had left there for safekeeping shortly before the battle. The local sheriff was ordered to assist them in bringing this treasure to the king.[28] This likely means that Giles was not personally present at either the battle or Lancaster's execution, as collecting, inventorying, and transporting the rebels' valuables would have occupied some time. Nevertheless, he was performing very useful services for his heretofore cash-poor royal master, one which the fiscally obsessed king would not have entrusted to anyone but retainers he considered highly loyal and not inclined to embezzlement. Giles probably had participated in some of the earlier campaigns in 1321, however, as evidenced by the generous land grant he and Laurencia received that year.

Edward II's ruthless moves against his fractious nobles coincided with the rise to power of his latest, and ultimately most despised, favorites, the father-and-son team of the elder and younger Hugh Despenser. Unlike the king's previous favorites, who virtually all had been foreigners, the Despensers were members of the English nobility. They typified the best and worst characteristics of Edward II's household. They were vigorous, administratively very capable, and devotedly loyal. Unfortunately, they also were avaricious in the extreme, markedly jealous of their influence over the king, and ruthless in both their pursuit of wealth and their elimination of political rivals. Hugh the younger seems to have been, in addition, remarkably arrogant. Scholars argue over how great an influence they wielded over Edward II, versus how much the divisive and deeply resented policies of the last years of his reign were his own doing, but it is safe to say they encouraged him in both his centralizing administrative reforms and his ruthless assertions of power. In return, he essentially gave *carte blanche* to their acquisitiveness and elimination of their rivals, so long as he also benefited by them. Whatever the actual balance of power in their relationship, the Despensers soon were regarded throughout England as the perfect archetypes of "the king's evil advisers" and roundly hated. Those of their enemies among the English elites who could do so, fled into exile, congregating mostly in France. Their number consisted particularly of the remaining Lancastrian sympathizers.

Having in the first part of his reign suffered from the profound disadvantage of inadequate funds, from 1322 on Edward II was resolved never to find himself in that vulnerable fiscal position again. In addition to confiscating all the rebels' lands and moveables he could appropriate and then not regranting them—except to the Despensers and a few other select supporters—he devoted his administration to acquiring as much wealth as possible. Besides rigorous collection of existing taxes, fees, fines, and dues, new ones were imposed and tactics amounting to extortion were employed, even on some of the king's own, less favored, relatives. Simultaneously, expenditures were cut in many areas. On the one hand, Edward II in just a few years became astonishingly wealthy for a medieval ruler and likewise free from open domestic dissent. On the other, he had achieved this through what was essentially tyranny. In seeking to eradicate all the usual political, military, and fiscal challenges to authority common to medieval rulers, he only succeeded in driving dissent underground, where it would grow to dangerous proportions unseen.

Likely royal yeomen like Giles were not perceived by the Despensers as either threats to their political ascendancy or possessors of wealth sufficient to be worth taking from them. The yeomen's stout fidelity to their king must have struck the favorites as quite useful, in fact. Regrettably, there is no indication of what Giles's private opinion of the Despensers was—whether he approved of their ruthlessly effective support of the king, so like his own but on a much grander scale, or dreaded the eventual consequences of the resentment their excesses were building up—but their working relationship appears to have been excellent. Not only did Giles's place in the king's regard suffer no diminution during their supremacy at court, it actually seems to have risen. He began to be used on diplomatic missions abroad, of which there was no record before this point; and that never would have happened, had the Despensers disapproved of him. Yet his advancement in Edward II's service shows no signs of having been owed to Despenser patronage, for his name never appears in any documentary contexts that would suggest he had become their client. Therefore Giles's increased prominence was the result of meritorious service to the king, especially during the crisis of 1321–22, and also of international political developments at this time that created a heretofore unanticipated increase in the number and urgency of Edward II's diplomatic contacts with the Christian kingdoms of Iberia. Suddenly confidential emissaries familiar with the languages and ways of that peninsula—Castilian, in particular—found themselves a valuable strategic commodity. At Edward's court, that meant essentially Giles and his fellow sergeant-at-arms Bernal Pelegrín.[29]

Philippe V died in 1322, and the last of Edward II's brothers-in-law came to the French throne as Charles IV.[30] He demanded that Edward come to France to perform homage for Gascony. Busy putting an end to his nobles' rebellions and absorbing their estates into a newly powerful personal administration, Edward asked for a postponement. One was granted; but when Edward—as was his practice when confronted with demands to do homage for the duchy—attempted to avoid the new deadline, Charles IV proved less patient than had his predecessors over his brother-in-law's delaying tactics. He was only too ready to declare Edward in default, especially as tensions between various prominent Gascons and their nominal French overlord already were at a height that demanded resolving. A pretext for occupying Gascony on the grounds of its duke's dereliction of duty soon presented itself, in the mishandling by Edward II's officials of a jurisdictional dispute in the Agen, at a priory called St.-Sardos. In August 1324, Charles's forces moved in, inaugurating the War of St.-Sardos.[31]

Both Edward II and his Gascon administration seemed unprepared for this war, and it did not go well for the English. In addition to the obvious responses of raising forces to defend the duchy and sending a high-ranking embassy to Paris to negotiate, Edward's strategic reaction was to seek allies in Iberia. Initially he wrote to Jaume II of Aragon and to various members of the Castilian royal family who were claiming simultaneously to exercise regental powers for the thirteen-year-old Alfonso XI, requesting military aid against France.[32] Such inspiration to look to Iberia for allies may have come from inconclusive negotiations for a double marriage with Aragon conducted in 1321–22.[33] The strategic locations of Castile and Aragon vis-à-vis Gascony also had much to do with it. Given Edward II's sentiments about his Castilian heritage, though, it must have seemed natural to him to expect help from his kinsfolk there. His overtures to various members of the Castilian royal family stressed their mutual kinship in excess of what was required by diplomatic convention.[34] His invocation of the Anglo-Castilian treaty of 1254 that had married his mother to his father, thereby resulting in his own existence, was likewise reiterated to a striking degree, as if Edward expected it to have real power even after seventy years.

The Castilian notables initially so addressed were, for formality's sake, Alfonso XI himself; the regent Don Juan, son of the late Prince Juan and María de Haro; Don Juan's mother, the lady of Biscay; and the latter's cousin, Fernando Díaz de Haro. Edward II at this juncture either was not fully informed of the complexities of the Castilian regency situation—for he failed to address rival regents Prince Felipe and Don Juan Manuel—or, more likely, he had made a conscious decision to seek help only from Don Juan of Biscay and his adherents, who controlled those portions of Alfonso XI's realms nearest Gascony. Prince Felipe's power bases were in the west, in Galicia, and south, in Andalusia; Juan Manuel's were in central Castile and the southeast, in Murcia. Typically, Alfonso XI, Don Juan of Biscay,[35] and Doña María de Haro all were addressed as "the king's dearest kinsman" or "kinswoman."[36] An initial commission appointed for the negotiations consisted of Edward II's half-brother Edmund, earl of Kent; the archbishop of Dublin; the seneschal of Gascony, Sir Ralph Basset; and a prominent law professor, Master William Weston, canon of Lincoln. Kent, the archbishop, and Basset, however, already constituted the embassy sent to negotiate with Charles IV concerning the war—and were not distinguishing themselves in that capacity—so Weston became one of Edward II's major envoys to the Iberian kingdoms.[37]

Edward's diplomatic goals in both Aragon and Castile were twofold. From each kingdom he desired immediate military aid against the French, both men and supplies, and a more permanent alliance to be cemented by a royal marriage. To Aragon, he again proposed that his eldest son and heir,

Edward, marry Jaume II's youngest daughter, Yolande.[38] To Castile, he proposed that Alfonso XI marry his eldest daughter, Eleanor. These strategies were characterized in correspondence between Hugh Despenser the younger and English officials in Gascony during the autumn of 1324 as offering the best chances of discomfiting the French.[39]

Castile's response at first was positive, with Burgos merchants Andrés Pérez de Castrogeriz and Pedro Juanes quickly sent to England as *ad hoc* envoys.[40] Meanwhile, Don Juan of Biscay waxed grandiloquent to emissaries sent by the earl of Kent on Edward II's behalf. They accordingly "spoke to the said Don Juan the fairest words they could," yet expressed skepticism in their private report to Kent on the likelihood of Don Juan's ever following through on his promises. Acknowledging their caution, Kent instructed them on their subsequent mission to try to get Don Juan's promises in writing, or else what military aid from him they could.[41] In the meantime, more pragmatically, Edward II's government sought the Castilian government's permission to buy and export horses, arms, and provisions from Castile to support the war in Gascony.[42] To encourage the grant of this permission, Edward II conceded his safe-conduct and tax exemptions for all merchants from Alfonso XI's domains coming to trade in English territory.[43]

By January 1325, Edward II had learned that the Aragonese king did not favor a marriage between his daughter and the English king's heir.[44] Jaume II declared that his personal and political ties to France were too strong ever to consider joining an anti-French alliance. He would be delighted, however, to mediate a peace between England and France, if their respective kings consented. His heir, Prince Anfós, seemed more sympathetic, yet nevertheless declined to make his forces available unless Edward II paid handsomely to support them.[45] Edward then began to pursue the idea of a marriage between his eldest son and Alfonso XI's sister, Princess Leonor, instead. Weston was assigned to this embassy also, in company with royal justiciar Sir John Stonor; Arnau Guillem de Béarn, lord of Lescun in the Pyrenees; and Master Pers Galicien, treasurer of the Agen. They also were to continue negotiations for the marriage of Eleanor to Alfonso XI.[46] Meanwhile, Giles's friend and fellow sergeant-at-arms Bernal Pelegrín had placed another Castilian regent, Don Juan Manuel, in touch with the English king. Edward II thanked Juan Manuel for his letters, which Bernal had brought to him, and apologized for sending Andrés Pérez with his reply instead of "our dear hired man-at-arms (*stratilatem*), your client, Bernal Pelegrín," as the latter was needed "for other difficult business of ours elsewhere," which Andrés would explain.[47]

The mission to Castile in February 1325 was one of Giles Despagne's first diplomatic undertakings for Edward II. Expense accounts for the embassy indicate that Galicien and Lescun never made the journey but instead were replaced by Giles. Together with Stonor and Weston, he departed England on February 15 and returned on August 27, while Galicien and Lescun instead undertook an embassy to Aragon.[48] The decision to send Giles to Castile seems to have been connected to the fact that he already had been chosen for a mission to Portugal that had potential bearing on the war in Gascony. The Genoese Antonio Pessagno, formerly Edward II's favorite merchant-banker and one-time seneschal of Gascony, had parted ways with the king around 1320, possibly squeezed out of favor by the rise of Despenser *père et fils*, and he had gone to France. By early 1325, rumors reached the English court that Pessagno intended to persuade his brother Manuele, admiral of Portugal since 1317, to bring the Portuguese fleet into the war on the side of France. Appalled at the prospect, Edward II wrote to the new king of Portugal, Afonso IV, beseeching him not to permit his admiral to do any such thing. Giles Despagne was chosen to bear the letter to Portugal.[49] Whether as a result of this request, or simply because the rumor never had had any substance, the Portuguese fleet stayed out of the war.[50]

Since Giles already was headed to that part of the world, it evidently made sense for him to join the embassy to Castile, along with Andrés Pérez. The latter, however, was detailed to communicate with Juan Manuel and María de Haro, whereas Stonor, Weston, and Giles met with Alfonso XI's own negotiators: the bishops of Burgos and Avila, the *scholasticus* of Toledo cathedral, Alfonso's justiciar Martín Fernández, and the knight Fernán Sánchez de Valladolid.[51] Only the latter two seem to have been regularly involved in the substantive negotiations, as counterparts to Stonor and Weston. The seals of these four appeared on a transcript summarizing their negotiations, prepared in Valladolid on May 22, 1325, along with that of Lescun, who evidently had rejoined the English envoys by that point.[52] Giles's seal did not appear on the transcript, nor was his name mentioned in it. Therefore, he must have taken no leading part in the negotiations, but he probably served in an adjunct role, perhaps as a translator for the Englishmen Stonor and Weston.

It was common practice for members of the king's household, especially those with a military background like Giles's, to be used as diplomatic couriers. But Giles's real value in this capacity was his Iberian background, as having a courier who knew the geography, customs, and above all the language of the country to which he was sent was far more desirable than making do with a messenger who, even if of more elevated rank, did not possess such knowledge. The English government had few persons in its employ thus qualified when it came to diplomatic exchanges with the Iberian kingdoms, and none of high rank. Therefore, from the mid-1320s, Giles and his colleague Bernal Pelegrín frequently were employed on missions to Castile,

Aragon, and Portugal. Another solution was to use leading merchants whose business took them back and forth on a regular basis between England and Iberia, and who thereby were bilingual, such as Andrés Pérez de Castrogeriz. Once two kingdoms agreed to begin an important negotiation, however, higher-ranking envoys were considered necessary to give the proceedings proper cachet,[53] such as Master Pers Galicien, the lord of Lescun, or Sir John Stonor. Yet these higher-ranking negotiators often may not have had the requisite fluency for discussion of fine points, which made having someone like Giles along to translate at need would have been extremely useful in delicate negotiations such as Edward II's pursuit of a double marriage alliance with Castile during the War of St.-Sardos. Giles's military experience also would not come amiss as an escort in the frequently dangerous journeys to and from their assignment.

Castile was in a situation very similar to England's with regard to finding envoys with adequate language skills and so happily made use of the bilingual messengers England had managed to find, such as Andrés Pérez and Bernal Pelegrín, who were originally Castilian subjects. There seemed to be little official concern over possible conflicts of interest in using the same people as messengers or even as negotiators. As noted above, Bernal Pelegrín could be simultaneously the "client" of Castilian regent Juan Manuel and the hired retainer of England's king. Giles Despagne, however, never was considered to be in anyone's service but that of the king of England.

By May 1325, Anglo-Castilian negotiations had yet to reach any firm agreement. The English were supplicants, somewhat desperate ones, as their king needed help in his war and had not much to offer in return, except money—which, by some reports, he was self-destructively reluctant to spend.[54] Castile was cautious. Its domestic political situation was unstable, with the kingdom effectively divided among three mutually antagonistic regents—Don Juan Manuel, Prince Felipe, and Don Juan of Biscay—with public order broken down as opportunists of every stripe took advantage of the resultant chaos to pursue their own profit. A fourth party was on the horizon as well, that of young King Alfonso XI himself, only months away from attaining his legal majority.[55] It was, in fact, with this fourth party that Edward II's envoys negotiated, despite scrupulously maintaining diplomatic correspondence with all the regents.[56] The young king's negotiators' responses to the English proposals were vastly different in tone than Don Juan's chivalric fanfaronade of the previous autumn. They were not uninterested, but they also were aware of the potential dangers involved and of the limitations of their own position.

The English envoys made a formal request that the 1254 treaty of alliance between their country and Castile be considered still in force and augmented by a marriage between Alfonso XI and Eleanor of England. They also reiterated the offer of a marriage between Princess Leonor and Edward II's heir, if Alfonso XI was interested,[57] proposing that each king provide the bride coming to his shores with dower lands equivalent in worth to those the other bride would receive. Finally the English presented their king's urgent request for 3,000 Castilian cavalry for the defense of Gascony.

To their dismay, but probably not to their surprise, the Castilians rejected out of hand the idea that the 1254 treaty could be considered still effective; any alliance could be based on a new marriage or marriages only. Furthermore, the Castilians were not impressed by the proposal that the respective brides be given equivalent dowers. They thought Princess Leonor ought to have a dower worth more than Eleanor's, and that Eleanor should bring a dowry larger than the one Leonor would take away. As the Castilians accurately pointed out, their country in making these marriage alliances with England would incur France's enmity, which it did not presently have. England already was France's enemy, so making the marriages would leave the English no worse off in that respect than they currently were. Although not stated directly, the implication was clear: if Edward II wanted Castile's help, he had better be prepared to pay handsomely for it, to offset the risks Castile would run in going to war with France.[58]

The Castilians surely knew Edward had become an unusually wealthy ruler. With wealth basically all he had to offer, the Castilian negotiators were determined to get as much of it as they could in return for their help, especially as Alfonso XI's own finances were in a grievous state. His regents and their respective supporters effectively had been plundering his realms for the past dozen years, and the young king needed funds in order to have a hope of ever asserting power over them once he reached his majority. As added incentive, the Castilians mentioned that the English king's daughter was not the only bride currently on offer to their ruler.[59] The English envoys, defensively, argued that their king would not give larger dowries or dowers for his children than he got in return and could not afford to pay more than his original offer.[60] While the national pride underlying the first statement likely was understandable to the Castilians and only to be expected as a bargaining tactic, the latter excuse must have rung hollow, given the notoriety of Edward II's wealth.

Nevertheless, the Castilians were prepared to give the English another chance and moved on to the matter of military aid. They could not, they explained, furnish the 3,000 cavalry Edward III was requesting. Their king had too many enemies of his own closer to home for him to so denude his realms of defenses. They could offer 2,000, though, if the English king would pay their expenses during the campaign. Yet the amount being offered by the English was insufficient even for that.[61] Once again, Alfonso XI's negotiators, with their master's future as king in mind, were demanding a steep price. They realized that their political position vis-à-vis Castile's regents and other magnates was not one of strength, making it doubly risky to go to war with a foreign power. What would improve that position most quickly was the main thing Edward II had to offer, namely large sums of cash. The problem lay in persuading the increasingly tightfisted Edward and the Despensers to pay over amounts sufficient to make the risks worth Castile's while.

Evidently unprepared to answer this approach, the English envoys claimed inability to exceed their instructions. The Castilians countered by falling back on a position they freely admitted having taken with the previous English embassy in 1324, declaring that Alfonso XI, as a minor, could not enter into such negotiations or produce such military aid without his guardians' consent. This time, however, they added the encouragement that, after Alfonso had held a parliament planned for All Saints' Day to discuss these and other matters—by which time he would have attained his majority—King Edward could write again and receive a fully informed reply. With little more to say, both sides agreed to have a summary drawn up of their negotiations to date, for each side to peruse pending further negotiations.[62]

In the meantime, developments in England and France rapidly were changing the situation against which the Anglo-Castilian and Anglo-Aragonese negotiations were taking place. The war never had gone well for England, and with Iberian military aid so far not materializing, the best temporary solution seemed to be to make a truce with France. Charles IV proved amenable, and it was suggested that Edward II's wife, Isabelle of France, would be the ideal person to negotiate a more permanent solution between her husband and her brother. Both kings agreed, and she traveled to France in the spring of 1325 to begin negotiations.[63] The ultimate result of Isabelle's mission to France, however, was to be Edward II's downfall.

Isabelle personally found the Despensers as loathsome as the rest of England did. Thanks to her previous loyalty and good counsel, the queen had been one of Edward II's closest advisers before the Despensers' rise to power, but now they were doing all they could to destroy her influence, motivated by Hugh the Younger's extreme jealousy of his influence with the king.[64] The Despensers' ultimately fatal mistake was believing that, as a woman and a foreigner in England, Isabelle could or would do nothing to fight back. Once in France, she reached a set of acceptable compromises with her brother, but the one sticking-point remained Charles IV's insistence that homage had to be fully and properly performed to him for Gascony. Edward II, however, declined to leave England to do so, claiming sudden ill health.[65] So a different solution was suggested that seemed acceptable to all parties: the English king would create his twelve-year-old heir duke of

Guyenne in his place, and the boy would go to France to perform the homage. That way, English royal authority remained officially unimpaired, Charles IV received acknowledgment of his overlordship in Gascony, and Edward II could continue to control the duchy in his capacity as father of its minor duke. Young Edward went to France, Gascony was formally confiscated from his father and re-bestowed on him, and he did homage in September 1325.

Up to this point, neither Edward II nor the Despensers seemed unduly worried by their knowledge that Charles IV had been outraged to learn of Isabelle's treatment in England or that he considered Edward's efforts to make anti-French alliances with Castile and Aragon virtually treasonous.[66] Indeed, even after his son's installation as duke of Guyenne, Edward II continued to pursue the Castilian marriage projects and send out feelers to Prince Anfós of Aragon, consisting of Pers Galicien and, in a subordinate capacity, Giles Despagne and two merchants from Burgos. Mindful that now the king of Castile was legally of age and would be holding his planned first parliament before the English envoys could arrive, Edward II provided his emissaries with a letter suggesting that Alfonso finally might wish to make a decision about the proposals of marriage and alliance. He also solicited the support of the three former regents, the bishops of Burgos and Avila, and the Castilian chancellor. He even wrote to various cardinals in Avignon, urging them to support the issuance of dispensations for the double marriage with Castile.[67]

Yet, even though their business in France ostensibly had been concluded, Queen Isabelle and the heir to England failed to return home in a timely manner. Edward II sent them commands to return. Isabelle flatly refused, so long as the Despensers remained in power. The news grew worse and worse for Edward II: Isabelle had joined forces with the Lancastrian exiles in France, led by Sir Roger Mortimer. The king's own half-brother, Kent, in France as one of the English negotiators, joined the dissidents as well. Word of all this was leaking back to England, despite Edward's and the Despensers' concerted efforts to intercept letters and agents, and the anti-Despenser cause espoused by queen and exiles was gaining a very sympathetic response in the kingdom. Civil unrest and minor rebellions began breaking out. Word also came eventually that Isabelle's relationship with Mortimer had become much more than merely a political alliance.[68]

The young duke of Guyenne was completely under the control of his mother and her new allies, especially Mortimer, who were trying to use his marriage to gain a useful foreign alliance, even as his father had done during the war and continued to do throughout this fresh crisis. Some news of these competing marriage strategies reached Castile while Galicien's and

Giles's embassy was there in the autumn of 1325. On New Year's Day 1326, Edward II wrote to reassure the Castilian court lady Mayor García that any rumors she might have heard about his heir's plans to marry a Frenchwoman were unfounded. He intended no marriage for his son but the one currently being negotiated with Castile.[69]

That may have been true, but now the Castilians were negotiating very cautiously, thanks to the conflicting reports they were getting out of England and France. Alfonso XI did not want to send his beloved only sister into what soon might become a civil war—and by now the marriage between Princess Leonor and the duke of Guyenne was the only one on the table. By the early autumn of 1325, alarmed at the prospect of a confederation between his former regents Juan Manuel and Juan of Biscay, to be cemented by the latter's marriage with the former's only legitimate child, seven-year-old Constanza, Alfonso XI had acted on his councilors' cynical advice and offered to marry Constanza himself. His pride and ambition stimulated by the thought of being the king's father-in-law, Juan Manuel did not hesitate to abandon his compact with Juan of Biscay. Galicien and Giles likely arrived in Castile just in time to attend the royal wedding held on November 28, 1325, during the parliament in Valladolid—the same parliament at which Edward II had hoped Alfonso would be advised to marry his daughter Eleanor.[70] Under the circumstances, they did not stay long. Edward II's attempt to extricate himself from the Gascony crisis with the help of his Castilian relatives had foundered on the exigencies of the domestic Castilian political situation and on Edward's own shortsighted unwillingness to spend the wealth amassed from suppressing his rebellious nobles.

Edward II and his advisors knew that an invasion by the English exiles was imminent, but they were uncertain as to where it might try to land and also distracted by the resumption of fighting against the French in Gascony from June onward. In the end, they were not able to intercept it. On September 24, 1326, Isabelle's and Mortimer's small force of Hainaulter mercenaries slipped past Edward's defenses and landed in Suffolk. They immediately began sending out messages to rally support to their cause. In the traditional manner, this was proclaimed to be the liberation of King Edward from his evil advisers the Despensers, and the response was overwhelmingly in the queen's favor.[71]

Overwhelmed and dismayed by the extent to which they were losing control of the kingdom, with defections to the queen's advancing forces on every side, Edward II and the Despensers made the fateful decision to abandon an increasingly mutinous London and head west to the Despensers' power base in Wales. There they hoped to raise loyal forces, which still did exist in scattered areas, to combat the rebels' invasion. With them they brought an immense treasure in cash and jewels, at a minimum valued at £29,000—and this was only a part of the king's fiscal resources—as well as the most important royal records. To guard it all, they brought a small but intensely loyal force consisting of the king's and the Despensers' sergeants-at-arms and a few knights. Giles Despagne was among them, his service as a diplomat now subsumed into service to his master as a soldier.[72] In the king's absence, London imploded into anarchy. Queen Isabelle and Mortimer, with their by now sizeable forces, therefore avoided the capital and veered west in pursuit of the king and his "evil advisers." Behind them, in London, mobs ran amok, plundering the houses of foreign merchants and assassinating any royal officials who previously had incurred their hatred through too thorough enforcement of Edward II's oppressive fiscal policies.[73]

Leaving the senior Despenser to try to hold Gloucester for them, Edward II and Hugh the younger sought refuge in southern Wales. Although a number of the king's ranking household officers, including his steward, deserted along the way, the royal sergeants-at-arms and Hugh Despenser's men never did. At the end of October, they holed up in Despenser's virtually impregnable castle at Caerphilly.[74] For reasons that are not clear, Edward II and Despenser by October 31 made a decision to leave the treasure, the royal records, and most of their men here and push on with just a handful of attendants. The castle nominally was entrusted to Despenser's teenaged son, but the real commander of its defenses was an experienced Despenser retainer, John Felton. In addition to Felton and Despenser's son, Caerphilly's defenders numbered at least 122 men, Giles Despagne among them, along with three other identifiable Iberians.[75]

Where exactly the fugitive king and his companions went in Wales after that is not always possible to trace. Their plans, whatever those were, went awry, due in large part to miserable weather. On November 16, their pursuers, including Thomas of Lancaster's brother Henry, at last caught up with them.[76] The captured king was treated relatively well, housed not uncomfortably at Kenilworth Castle. The same could not be said for his companions, who were taken to the queen and Mortimer. After parading him humiliatingly through the streets of Hereford, Isabelle and Mortimer had Despenser hanged, drawn, and beheaded. The others were either executed or else committed to prisons from which they never emerged alive.[77] The Hainaulter mercenaries then were committed to besiege Caerphilly Castle, where the last of Edward II's supporters, including Giles Despagne, had been left guarding his treasure.

Despite the queen's and her confederates' claims that they had come only to rid King Edward of his "evil advisers," they did not now restore the king to his throne surrounded by "virtuous" councilors, namely themselves. Instead, Edward was left at Kenilworth, and the new rulers of the realm called an assembly at Westminster for the purpose of deposing him. As of January 25, 1327, Edward II no longer was recognized as king of England. The young duke of Guyenne, now fourteen, was crowned Edward III on February 1.[78] Real power, however, remained in the hands of Queen Isabelle and her lover, Roger Mortimer.

Even then, in a remarkable display of loyalty to the deposed king, Caerphilly Castle declined to surrender, despite the siege and accompanying negotiations going on since November 1326. The new regime ardently wanted the treasure and records inside the castle. Yet even when the defenders were apprised that Edward II's cause was lost, they refused to yield until the new government issued pardons to every one of them and solemnly swore not to execute Despenser's son. Their demands were not met until March 20, 1327, and only then did Caerphilly submit.[79]

After that date, when his name appeared on the pardons list, Giles Despagne disappears from English crown records for the next three years. There is no indication that he was given any important employment by Isabelle and Mortimer, although his colleague Bernal Pelegrín was sent on occasional diplomatic missions.[80] Whether Giles even continued as a yeoman of the new king is unknown. It is not impossible that the queen and Mortimer did not care to have in that confidential position someone whose conspicuous loyalty to Edward II rendered him suspect in their eyes; conversely, Giles himself may not have cared to serve them.

A peculiar, tense situation existed in England after Edward III's coronation. Edward II might have abdicated his throne—or, practically speaking, been deposed from it—but his marriage certainly had not been annulled by the church. Nevertheless, although the Despensers had been definitively and gruesomely removed, the queen made no move to join her spouse in his enforced retirement at Kenilworth.[81] Not only had Isabelle no wish to relinquish her lover for a husband she had dethroned and imprisoned, but she also had no intention of giving up the power she now enjoyed as *de facto* joint ruler of England with Mortimer. Both Isabelle and her unofficial consort had profited enormously from their seizure of the government, as had their key supporters. Worse, their regime rapidly was demonstrating itself to be as greedy, jealous, and despotic as the Despensers' ever had been. Many who had supported them when their proclaimed goal was to overthrow bad government and install good now grew disenchanted.

Under these circumstances, the former king's continued existence was a liability. Given a choice of oppressive governments, Edward II's now seemed to some people the lesser of two evils. There were whispers of plots to rescue him and restore him to the throne. The church was preparing to deliver an official opinion that Isabelle should go live with her husband, as every good Christian wife ought to do. By spring, the former king was transferred to the custody of Mortimer's supporter Lord Thomas Berkeley, at Berkeley Castle near Bristol.[82]

The threatened rescue plots started materializing. On July 9 a group of armed men led by Stephen Dunhead and his brother, Friar Thomas, forced their way into Berkeley Castle and rescued the former king.[83] Edward does seem to have been recaptured subsequently, although his temporary rescuers got away.[84] It was after this profoundly unnerving event that Mortimer sent another of his own retainers, the former Lancastrian Sir Thomas Gourney, to Berkeley Castle to assist in the problem of assuring the former king's security. Nonetheless, a new rescue plot, originating in Wales, sprang up around this time. According to a later declaration by one of the participants, it was discovered and reported to Mortimer on September 14.[85] Probably to few people's surprise, it was announced on September 28, at a parliament being held at Lincoln, that the former king had departed this life a week earlier, on September 21, at Berkeley Castle. Natural causes were alleged; which ones, was not specified, at least to the general public.[86] A full state funeral was held on December 21.[87] That, Mortimer and Isabelle surely hoped, would be an end of the matter.

As things transpired, however, it was not. In November of 1330, Edward III overthrew his mother's regime in a palace coup, executing Mortimer for treason and regicide, while dispatching Isabelle to enforced retirement in the countryside. Gourney and others implicated in Edward II's death promptly fled the country; and when their presence was discovered in Burgos only a few months later, it was his father's loyal sergeant-at-arms Giles Despagne whom the young king sent to Castile to handle the delicate business of extraditing Edward II's accused murderers back to England. This mission to Castile in 1331 is the point at which Giles ordinarily makes his brief appearance in the history books—yet only an examination of his previous career in Edward II's service reveals why Edward III chose him for the task.

Unlike many of Edward II's English subjects, Giles had remained scrupulously loyal—at times, even above and beyond what might have been expected, as in the siege of Caerphilly Castle. Unfortunately, none of the administrative records from which Giles's career has been reconstructed shed much light on the reasons for Giles's extraordinary loyalty. Why was Giles so loyal to a king so unpopular for his oppressive governance, political solecisms, and military failures that he ended up deposed by a coalition led by his own wife, brothers, and cousins? Part of the reason must have been the material rewards and status that Giles received during Edward II's reign. Another factor probably was the intense *esprit de corps* among the king's sergeants-at-arms, amounting to an "us versus them" outlook with regard to Edward's resentful subjects, especially the nobles, whose attempts to restrain the king's perceived excesses usually took the form of trying to control and limit his personal household and finances. Giles undoubtedly also responded to Edward II's predilection for Castilians, which was not shared by the majority of xenophobic Englishmen. Yet there must have been a strong element of personal loyalty as well in their relationship. For all his faults as a ruler, Edward II had certain charms as a human being. He was good-looking, vigorous, and physically courageous. He was convivial, sometimes to an extreme considered unbecoming in a king; fond of music and plays; and possessed of a quirky sense of humor that seems to have eluded some of his graver, traditionally minded contemporaries.[88] Above all, though, he was devotedly loyal to his friends. Indeed, had his loyalties been less unrelenting—had he been more cynically expedient and less stubborn about giving up advisers and retainers on whom he had set his heart—he probably would have had a more successful reign. But something in his character would not allow him to retract his loyalties, once given.

It may have been this quality of devoted loyalty in Edward II that called forth an answering devotion in those on whom he bestowed his personal friendship and patronage. Neither his notorious first favorite, Pers Gavaston, nor the Despensers ever abandoned him, even if they showed few scruples about exploiting Edward's favor to their own material advantage, without apparent regard for the consequences it would bring him. Edward's favorite religious order, the Dominicans, remained devoted to him even after his deposition; several English preaching friars were involved in the plots to rescue him from Berkeley Castle. Archbishop Melton of York and Bishop Gravesend of London likewise remained well disposed to Edward after the deposition, which made them targets for Mortimer's and Isabelle's malicious intrigues. Giles Despagne's attachment to Edward II, like the Dominicans' and the prelates', continued apparently even after Edward's reported death in 1327. Its persistence was reflected most concretely in Giles's remarkable pursuit of Gourney and others implicated in Edward's end, despite a daunting array of bureaucratic, diplomatic, and other obstacles. The records generated by this pursuit, like those of Giles's other missions for his king, provide valuable insight for historians into the practical mechanics of diplomacy between England and Castile, of the personalities and motivations involved, and of the other factors influencing Anglo-Iberian relations in this period just before the Hundred Years' War.

Notes

1. Natalie Fryde, *The Tyranny and Fall of Edward II, 1321–1326* (Cambridge: Cambridge University Press, 1979), p. 13; Joel T. Rosenthal, "The King's 'Wicked Advisers' and Medieval Baronial Rebellions," *Political Science Quarterly* 82 (1967): 595–618.

GILES DESPAGNE 111

2. Members of this community hailed almost entirely from the economically interaffiliated regions of Burgos and the Cantabrian ports. See Teófilo F. Ruiz, "Castilian Merchants in England, 1248–1350," in *The City and the Realm: Burgos and Castile, 1080–1492*, Variorum Collected Studies, 375 (Aldershot, UK, and Brookfield, VT, 1992), study no. 9; "Burgos y el comercio castellano en la Baja Edad Media: economía y mentalidad," in Ruiz, *The City and the Realm*, Study no. 3:38–51; "The Economic Structure of the Area of Burgos, 1200–1350," in *The City and the Realm*, study no. 2:3–4; "The Transformation of the Castilian Municipalities: the Case of Burgos, 1248–1350," in *The City and the Realm*, study no. 7:5. (The essays or studies in Ruiz, *The City and the Realm*, are facsimile reproductions of previously published essays. The book has no continuous pagination. Each essay has its own original page numbers; those are the ones given.) See also Wendy R. Childs, *Anglo-Castilian Trade in the Later Middle Ages* (Manchester and Totowa, NJ: Manchester University Press, 1978).
3. Master James's exact parentage is not known, although in documentation he is frequently referred to as the nephew of Edward II's mother, Eleanor of Castile, and she is called his paternal aunt. His age seems such that he may have been the son of Queen Eleanor's half-brother, Prince Enrique, who lived in England on and off in 1256–59; see Jean-Paul Trabut-Cussac, "Don Enrique de Castille en Angleterre," *Mélanges de la Casa de Velázquez* 2 (1966): 51–58. For highlights of James's ecclesiastical and bureaucratic careers, see *The Registers of Walter Bromescombe (A.D. 1257–1280) and Peter Quivil (A.D. 1280–1291), Bishops of Exeter, with Some Records of the Episcopate of Bishop Thomas de Bytton (A.D. 1292–1307), also the Taxation of Pope Nicholas IV, A.D. 1291 (Diocese of Exeter)*, ed. F.C. Hingeston-Randolph (London: George Bell & Sons, 1889), pp. 335, 344, 390–91; *Registrum Epistolarum Fratris Johannis Peckham, Archiepiscopi Cantuariensis*, ed. Charles Trice Martin, 3 vols., Rerum Britannicarum Medii Aevi Scriptores, 77, pts. 1–3 (London: Public Record Office, 1882–85; repr. Wiesbaden, Germany: Kraus Reprints, 1965), docs. 423–24, 428–31; *Registrum Roberti Winchelsey, Archiepiscopi Cantuariensis*, ed. Rose Graham, 2 vols. (Oxford: Oxford University Press, 1917–31), 1:453–54; Hilda Johnstone, ed. *Letters of Edward Prince of Wales, 1304–1305* (Cambridge: Cambridge University Press/Roxburghe Club, 1931), pp. 119, 159–60; *Les Registres de Benoît XI. Recueil des bulles de ce pape, publiées ou analysées d'après les manuscrits originaux des Archives du Vatican*, ed. Charles Grandjean (Paris: Ernest Thorin, 1883–1905), doc. 470; Great Britain, *Calendar of Entries in the Papal Registers Relating to Great Britain and Ireland. Papal Letters*, 16 vols. (London, 1893–1986), 1:612, 2:11, 144; T.F. Tout, *Chapters in the Administrative History of Mediaeval England. The Wardrobe, the Chamber and the Small Seals*, 6 vols., Publications of the University of Manchester, Historical Series, 34–35, 48–49, 57, 64 (Manchester: Manchester University Press, 1928–37), 2:211, 338–40, 343, 347; James Conway Davies, *The Baronial Opposition to Edward II, Its Character and Policy. A Study in Administrative History* (Cambridge: Cambridge University Press, 1918), pp. 195, 232–33;

C.L. Shadwell and H.E. Salter, *Oriel College Records*, Oxford Historical Society, 85 (Oxford: Clarendon Press, 1926), pp. 114–15, 117–21; Great Britain, *Calendar of the Patent Rolls Preserved in the Public Record Office*, 71 vols. (London, 1891–1973), 1313–17, p. 618 (hereafter abbreviated *CPR*); *CPR*, 1321–1324, p. 269. Also see A.B. Emden, *Biographical Register of the University of Oxford to 1500*, 3 vols. (Oxford: Clarendon, 1957–59) 3:1736–38.

4. For highlights of Rodrigo's career in England, see Johnstone, *Letters*, pp. 11–12, 61, 70–71; Beriah Botfield, ed., *Manners and Household Expenses of England in the Thirteenth and Fifteenth Centuries, Illustrated by Original Records* (London: W. Nicol, 1841), p. 96; John Carmi Parsons, *The Court and Household of Eleanor of Castile in 1290. An Edition of British Library, Additional Manuscript 35294, with Introduction and Notes*, Pontifical Institute of Mediaeval Studies, Studies and Texts, 37 (Toronto: Pontifical Institute of Medieval Studies, 1977), p. 76 and n85, pp. 126, 157; Great Britain. Court of Chancery, *Calendar of Chancery Warrants, A. D. 1244–1326*, preserved in the Public Record Office (London: His Majesty's Stationery Office, 1927), p. 151; *Calendar of the Close Rolls*, preserved in the Public Record Office, 64 vols. (London: H.M. Stationery Office, 1833–1963), 1296–1302, p. 68 (hereafter abbreviated *CCR*); *CCR*, 1302–07, p. 482; *CPR*, 1307–13, p. 139; *CPR*, 1324–27, p. 83; *Foedera, conventiones, literae, et cujuscunque generis acta publica, inter reges Angliae et alios quosvis imperatores, reges, pontifices, principes, vel communitates, ab ineunte saeculo duo–decimo, viz ab anno 1101, ad nostra usque tempora habita aut tractata. . .*, Thomas Rymer, ed., 3rd ed., 10 vols. (The Hague: Neaulme, 1739–45), p. 316.

5. John Carmi Parsons, *Eleanor of Castile. Queen and Society in Thirteenth-Century England* (Basingstoke, UK: Macmillan, 1994), pp. 38–42, 91; Roy Martin Haines, *King Edward II. Edward of Caernarfon, His Life, His Reign, and Its Aftermath, 1284–1330* (Montreal: McGill-Queen's University Press, 2003), p. 4; Johnstone, *Letters*, pp. xxxviii–xl; M.T. Clanchy, *From Memory to Written Record. England, 1066–1307*, 2nd ed. (Oxford: Blackwell, 1993), p. 162; Rodrigo Jiménez de Rada, *Historia de rebus Hispaniae, sive Historia Gothica*, ed. Juan Fernández Valverde, Corpus Christianorum, Continuatio Medievalis, 72A (Turnholt, Belgium: Brepols, 1987), 9.18.301.

6. Hilda Johnstone, *Edward of Carnarvon, 1284–1307*, Publications of the University of Manchester, 295 (Manchester: Manchester University Press, 1946), pp. 120–21; Peter Linehan, "The English Mission of Cardinal Petrus Hispanus, the Chronicle of Walter of Guisborough, and News from Castile at Carlisle (1307)," *English Historical Review* 117 (2002): 605–21; Parsons, *Eleanor*, pp. 7, 11–12, 15.

7. A candidate at one time was Fernando IV's sister Isabel.

8. Fryde, *Tyranny*, pp. 18, 135–37; Haines, *King Edward II*, pp. 303–06; Elizabeth A.R. Brown, "The Political Repercussions of Family Ties in the Early Fourteenth Century: The Marriage of Edward II of England and Isabelle of France," *Speculum* 63 (1988): 573–95.

9. Johnstone, *Letters*, pp. 23, 47, 72–73, 95; Childs, *Anglo-Castilian Trade*, pp. 6, 11–12, 19–22, 183, 194, 216, 229–30; Ruiz, "Castilian Merchants," pp. 177–78; *CPR*, 1307–13, pp. 451, 486; *CPR*, 1313–17, pp. 116, 299, 300; *CPR*, 1324–27, pp. 16, 32, 306.
10. His name in Castilian Spanish would have been Gil. Since he seems to have spent most of his adult life in England, however, this essay refers to him by the anglicized version of his name, Giles. In no record is he accorded any surname except "of Spain," *de Ispannia*, or Despagne.
11. Great Britain, Public Record Office, *Calendar of Fine Rolls Preserved in the Public Record Office*, 13 vols. (London: H.M.'s Stationery Office, 1911–62; repr. Nedeln, Lichtenstein: Kraus Reprints, 1971), 2:269 (hereafter abbreviated *CFR*); *CPR*, 1313–17, pp. 64, 577, 626; *CPR*, 1321–24, pp. 55, 338. The most prominent individual bearing a variant of this surname probably was the wine merchant and financier Arnau Despanha, who was, however, from Gascony; see *CPR*, 1317–21, pp. 38, 377, 379.
12. Spain, España, or *Ispannia* was most frequently understood by those outside the Iberian Peninsula to mean Castile and Leon as a single kingdom; Alfonso XI, like other rulers of Castile-Leon, generally was designated *rex Ispanniae* in diplomatic correspondence from England and France. Within the peninsula, however, "Spain" sometimes could mean Castile-Leon but more often was an inclusive geographical term for all of the peninsula that was not part of Portugal; in intra-Iberian diplomacy, Alfonso XI was king of Castile, Leon, and so on. Yet occasionally even Portuguese individuals came to be known, outside of Iberia, by the sobriquet *Hispanus*, for example, the thirteenth-century Petrus Hispanus (né Pedro Julian) who became Pope John XXI.
13. Paul Doherty, *Isabella and the Strange Death of Edward II* (London: Constable & Robinson, 2003), pp. 166–67.
14. *CPR*, 1313–17, p. 34. For Juan Sánchez otherwise, see *CPR*, 1313–17, p. 92; *CPR*, 1307–13, p. 303.
15. *CPR*, 1313–17, p. 606; *Rôles gascons, transcrits et publiés par Francisque Michel*, 4 vols., Collection de documents inédits sur l'histoire de France, 4th ser. Histoire politique (Paris, 1885–1962), 4:575, item 6.
16. Conway Davies, *The Baronial Opposition to Edward II*, p. 223; Tout, *Chapters in the Administrative History*, 2:135–36; Johnstone, *Letters*, pp. xv–xvi.
17. Michael Prestwich, *The Three Edwards. War and State in England, 1272–1377*, repr. ed. (London: Routledge, 1993), pp. 94–95, 101–03; Fryde, *Tyranny*, pp. 106–18.
18. G.W.S. Barrow, *Robert Bruce and the Community of the Realm of Scotland*, 3rd ed. (Edinburgh: Edinburgh University Press, 1988), pp. 228–31.
19. *CPR*, 1317–21, p. 28.
20. *CPR*, 1321–24, p. 34.
21. "Laurencia" was not a common female name in either country in the early fourteenth century. It would have been "Lorenza" in Castilian Spanish or "Lawrencia" in English; but in the absence of more information about her

background, in this essay her name has been left in the Latinized form used in the original letters patent and maintained by the *CPR*'s editors.
22. For examples of contemporary confirmations of powers of attorney, see, for instance, *CPR*, 1330–34, pp. 70, 400.
23. *CPR*, 1321–24, p. 220.
24. Fryde, *Tyranny*, pp. 69–105; Tout, *Chapters*, 2:338–40; Prestwich, pp. 93, 104–07.
25. Conway Davies, *The Baronial Opposition to Edward II*, p. 223.
26. See Fryde, *Tyranny*, pp. 19–20; Tout, "Captivity," p. 147; Haines, *King Edward II*, pp. 95, 107–08, 188.
27. John Edwards, "The Cult of 'St.' Thomas of Lancaster and its Iconography," *Yorkshire Archaeological Journal* 64 (1992): 103–22; John M. Theilmann, "Political Canonization and Political Symbolism in Medieval England," *Journal of British Studies* 29 (1990): 241–66; Fryde, *Tyranny*, pp. 58–60; Haines, *King Edward II*, pp. 14–141, 188.
28. *Calendar of Fine Rolls Preserved in the Public Record Office*, 13 vols. (London: H.M.'s Stationery Office, 1911–62; repr. Nedeln, Lichtenstein: Kraus Reprints, 1971), 3:106 (hereafter *CFR*).
29. For Bernal Pelegrín, see *CCR*, 1313–18, pp. 118, 454, 483; *CCR*, 1318–23, pp. 121, 210, 229, 696, 701. His name is rendered in various ways in English records: Bernardus Pelegrini, Bernard Pelegrym or Pelerin, and so on. Although the Christian name, in the form Bernat, was more common in Occitan-speaking lands such as Gascony, Catalonia, and Languedoc than it was in either England or Castile, there was one area of Castile where it was used with some frequency: the commercially linked zones of inland Burgos and the Cantabrian ports. There, men named Bernal or Bernalte were not uncommon; Ruiz, "Burgos," pp. 49, 53–54, and "The Transformation," p. 10. Another possibility is that Bernal was from Murcia, where much of the population was Catalan-speaking. This is suggested by his identification in one letter as the "client" of Castilian regent Juan Manuel, whose power bases were in Murcia and central Castile; see n47, below. If Bernal did speak Catalan as well as Castilian, it would explain why he often was sent to the Catalan-speaking court of Jaume II.
30. Fryde, *Tyranny*, p. 134.
31. Chaplais, *War*, pp. ix–xiii. Some scholars believe that the jurisdictional dispute was deliberately manufactured by the French government, either as a means of pressing the issue and forcing Edward to do homage or else as a ploy to regain the Agen for France; see Fryde, *Tyranny*, p. 141.
32. *Foedera*, 3rd ed., 2.2.113.
33. See Pierre Chaplais, *English Medieval Diplomatic Practice, Part I, Documents and Interpretation*, 2 vols. (London: Her Majesty's Stationery Office, 1982), 1:63–66.
34. *Foedera*, 3rd ed., 2.2.124, 126.
35. Known in the *Crónica del muy alto et muy católico rey don Alfonso el Onceno deste nombre, que venció la batalla del Río Salado, et ganó a las Algeciras*,

ed. Cayetano Rosell, Biblioteca de Autores Españoles, 66 (Madrid: Rivadeneyra, 1953) (hereafter *CAXI*), and many subsequent histories as Juan *el Tuerto*, Juan the One–Eyed.
36. Don Fernando was merely "the king's kinsman," reflecting his lesser political status, as Don Juan and his mother controlled Biscay, while Fernando belonged to a cadet branch of the Haro family.
37. *Foedera*, 3rd ed., 2.2.113–14; Chaplais, *War*, pp. xii–xiii. For Weston's career, see Fredric Cheyette, "The Professional Papers of an English Ambassador on the Eve of the Hundred Years' War," in *Economies et Sociétés au Moyen Age. Mélanges offerts à Edouard Perroy*, Publications de la Sorbonne, Etudes, 5 (Paris: Publications de la Sorbonne, 1973), pp. 400–13.
38. For Yolande, see J. Ernesto Martínez Ferrando, *Jaime II de Aragón. Su vida familiar*. Consejo Superior de Investigaciones Científicas, Escuela de Estudios Medievales, Publicaciones de la Sección de Barcelona, 10 (Barcelona: Consejo Superior de Investigaciones Científicas, 1948), 1:183–89. A marriage between these two had been suggested earlier but without result; *Acta Aragonensia. Quellen zur deutschen, italienischen, französischen, spanischen, zur Kirchen- und Kulturgeschichte aus der diplomatischen Korrespondez Jaymes II (1291–1327)*, ed. Heinrich Finke, 3 vols. (Berlin and Leipzig: Walther Rothschild, 1908–22), 1:499–500 (incorrectly dated 1324 instead of 1322); Chaplais, *English Medieval Diplomatic Practice*, 1:63–66.
39. Chaplais, *War*, docs. 57, 60, 81, 85.
40. Chaplais, *War*, 98n; *Foedera*, 3rd ed., 2.2.124.
41. Chaplais, *War*, docs. 96, 109. For the 1254 treaty between Castile and England see Parsons, *Eleanor*, pp. 11–12, 15.
42. Chaplais, *War*, doc. 102 and p. 114 n1. For generations, export of such goods from Castile had been prohibited without special licence from the king, as Castile considered them essential matériel for defense (or aggression) against the Muslims of Granada and North Africa; see Ruiz, "Castilian Merchants," pp. 181–82; Childs, *Anglo-Castilian Trade*, pp. 120–22.
43. *Foedera*, 3rd ed., 2.2.123.
44. *Foedera*, 3rd ed., 2.2.124, 127–28; *Acta Aragonensia*, 1:487–88, 501–02; Chaplais, *War*, doc. 196 and appendix V, docs. 1–3; Haines, *King Edward II*, p. 323.
45. Chaplais, *War*, doc. 196, and appendix V, docs. 1–3; Martínez Ferrando, 1:185–87; *Acta Aragonensia*, 1:487–88.
46. *Foedera*, 3rd ed., 2.2.124–26; also n33, above.
47. *Foedera*, 3rd ed., 2.2.126; *CCR*, 1323–27, p. 359.
48. Chaplais, *War*, p. 141 n1.
49. Chaplais, *War*, doc. 127 and p. 134 n1; Natalie Fryde, "Antonio Pessagno of Genoa, King's Merchant of Edward II of England," in *Studi in Memoria di Federigo Melis*, ed. Luigi da Rosa, Vol. 2 (Naples: Giannini, 1978), esp. p. 175.
50. In fact, on May 7, 1325, Edward II wrote again to Afonso IV and his mother, Isabel of Aragon, asking that his sergeant-at-arms Pers Bernat de Pensol be allowed to purchase for export wheat and other provisions. Like

Castile, Portugal traditionally forbade the export of such goods on the grounds of domestic military necessity.

51. For the latter, see Julio Puyol, "El presunto cronista Fernán Sánchez de Valladolid," *Boletín de la Real Academia de la Historia* 77 (1920): 516–33.
52. Chaplais, *War*, doc. 178.
53. Chaplais, *English Diplomatic Practice*, pp. 78–81, 133–41, 152–55.
54. Fryde, *Tyranny*, pp. 144–45; Haines, *King Edward II*, p. 322.
55. He would turn fourteen on August 13, 1325, and almost immediately move to assume personal rule.
56. Or, in the case of Don Juan of Biscay, usually with the regent's powerful mother, until her death later in 1325.
57. For Leonor of Castile, see Chaplais, *War*, doc. 132; H.T. Sturcken, "The Unconsummated Marriage of Jaime of Aragon and Leonor of Castile (October 1319)," *Journal of Medieval History* 5 (1979): 185–201; Martínez Ferrando, *Jaime II de Aragón*, 1:187.
58. Chaplais, *War*, doc. 178.
59. Chaplais, *War*, doc. 178; Martínez Ferrando, 1:187; *CAXI*, chap. 60.
60. Chaplais, *War*, doc. 178.
61. Chaplais, *War*, doc. 178.
62. Chaplais, *War*, doc. 178. Weston kept a copy of the summary, alongside a copy of the instructions from mid-February, among his professional reference papers; see Cheyette, "The Professional Papers of an English Ambassador," p. 410.
63. Haines, *King Edward II*, pp. 169, 324–25.
64. Haines, *King Edward II*, pp. 163, 325; Fryde, *Tyranny*, p. 147; Tout, "Captivity," p. 157; Herbert Maxwell, ed. and trans., *The Chronicle of Lanercost, 1272–1346* (Glasgow: James Maclehose and Sons, 1913), p. 249.
65. Haines, *King Edward II*, pp. 168–69.
66. Haines, *King Edward II*, pp. 322–24 and n135.
67. *Foedera*, 3rd ed., 2.2.144–46; *CPR, 1324–27*, pp. 180–81; Ruiz, "Castilian Merchants," p. 179; Childs, *Anglo-Castilian Trade*, pp. 227–28.
68. Haines, *King Edward II*, pp. 169–73; Fryde, *Tyranny*, pp. 145–48, 177–82; Ian Mortimer, *The Greatest Traitor: The Life of Sir Roger Mortimer, 1st Earl of March, Ruler of England, 1327–1330* (London: Jonathan Cape, 2003), pp. 141 and n20, 142, 145.
69. *Foedera*, 3rd ed., 2.2.149. Edward II's letters to non-royal members of the Castilian court are another mark of his interest in relations with his mother's homeland; see *Foedera*, 3rd ed., 2.2.125, 145.
70. *CAXI*, chaps. 41–42; Andrés Giménez Soler, *Don Juan Manuel. Biografía y estudio crítico* (Saragossa: La Académica, 1932), docs. 400–01, 406, 409, 413. For the dramatic sequelae to this marriage, see *CAXI*, chap. 48; Giménez Soler, doc. 420.
71. Fryde, *Tyranny*, pp. 180–87; Haines, *King Edward II*, pp. 172–78.
72. Bernal Pelegrín apparently was not part of this guard; his whereabouts at the time are not recorded, but his name does not appear on the list of those later pardoned for defending Caerphilly; see nn79–80, below.

73. Fryde, *Tyranny*, pp. 188–89, 193–94; Haines, *King Edward II*, pp. 179, 182–83.
74. Fryde, *Tyranny*, pp. 189–91; Haines, *King Edward II*, pp. 181–82, 184. For Caerphilly Castle's history and defenses, see Jeffrey L. Thomas, "Caerphilly Castle," http://www.castlewales.com/caerphil.html.
75. Fryde, *Tyranny*, p. 191; Haines, *King Edward II*, pp. 184, 186; *CPR*, 1327–30, pp. 37–39.
76. *Adae Murimuth Continuatio chronicarum. Robertus de Avesbury De gestis mirabilibus regis Edwardi Tertii*, ed. Edward Maunde Thompson, Rerum Britannicarum Medii Aevi Scriptores, 93 (London: Longman, 1889; repr. Wiesbaden, Germany: Kraus Reprints, 1965), p. 49.
77. Fryde, *Tyranny*, pp. 191–93; Haines, *King Edward II*, pp. 184–86; Friedrich W.D. Brie, ed., *The Brut, or the Chronicles of England*, 2 vols., Early English Text Society, 131, 136 (London: Kegan Paul, Trench, Trübner, 1906–08), 1:239–41; Thomas Hog, ed., *Adami Murimuthensis Chronica sui temporis, nunc primum per decem annos aucta, M.CCC.III.–M.CCC.XLVI. cum eorundem continuatione ad M.CCC.LXXX. a quodam anonymo* (London: Sumptibus Societatis, 1846), pp. 49–51; *Annales Paulini*, in Stubbs, 1:318–19.
78. Fryde, *Tyranny*, pp. 195–200; Haines, *King Edward II*, pp. 187–94; Claire Valente, "The Deposition and Abdication of Edward II," *English Historical Review* 113 (1998): 852–81.
79. Fryde, *Tyranny*, pp. 209–10; *CPR*, 1327–30, pp. 10, 15, 18, 20, 37–39.
80. *CPR*, 1327–30, p. 19.
81. *Adae Murimuth*, p. 52.
82. Tout, "Captivity," pp. 151–53, 155–56; Brie, *The Brut*, 1:249; Haines, *King Edward II*, p. 224.
83. Frédéric J. Tanquerey, "The Conspiracy of Thomas Dunheved, 1327," *English Historical Review* 31 (1916): 119–24; also Tout, "Captivity," pp. 157–61, 163; Haines, *King Edward II*, p. 224 n21.
84. Haines, *King Edward II*, pp. 224–26.
85. Tout, "Captivity," p. 184.
86. Mortimer, *The Greatest Traitor*, pp. 185–86; Fryde, *Tyranny*, pp. 201–02; Tout, "Captivity," p. 170.
87. Tout, "Captivity," pp. 168–70.
88. Prestwich, *The Three Edwards*, pp. 79–81; Haines, *King Edward II*, p. 47; Doherty, *Isabella*, pp. 24, 28, 31.

CHAPTER 6

ANGLO-PORTUGUESE TRADE DURING THE REIGN OF JOÃO I OF PORTUGAL, 1385–1433

Jennifer C. Geouge

This essay examines the conditions of Anglo-Portuguese trade during the reign of João I, highlighting the problems encountered by merchants and the vicissitudes of trade relations.

It is generally accepted that Portugal was a leader of what is termed "The Golden Age of Exploration." One wonders how Portugal, which controlled little territory on the European Continent and had a small population, was able to become a powerful force. During the course of the Reconquista, the kingdom of Castile had absorbed the lion's share of the territory on the Iberian Peninsula, which left Portugal with only a thin strip of territory along the Atlantic coast. Yet by 1500, the Portuguese trade empire reached the Far East and would reach Japan in the 1540s.

The Portuguese were more than happy to let foreign ships, including English ships and their captains, take the risks of trade, which could include the usual economic risks of supply and demand as well as the more physically dangerous risks of shipwreck and piracy. This calculated policy permitted the Portuguese fleet to be engaged in the enterprise of exploration and expansion rather than focus on European trade. The policy also permitted Portugal to develop its identity in an Atlantic that was quickly being redefined.

Anglo-Portuguese trade provides an example of the way the Portuguese pursued European trade, despite setbacks. A study of Anglo-Portuguese trade relations shows that the relations between the two countries have not always been ideal. Although treaties between the two nations were sealed, the actual practice of trade was quite unstable. There were periods of relative calm and safety for merchants and traders, and times when the threat of war loomed ominously over the relations. In spite of the difficulties encountered in trade, the alliance somehow managed to remain alive well into the modern period.

It might be useful to discuss briefly the state of research in the field, or perhaps the state of non-research in the field. Western history texts frequently overlook the role of Portugal in the late medieval period. Portugal seems to emerge only in the discussion of the age of expansion and exploration. Sadly, it is not only those specializing in Continental European history who overlook Portugal. Such prominent scholars of medieval Iberia as Joseph O'Callaghan and Angus MacKay spend only a few pages discussing Portugal. Ramón Menendez Pidal's monumental series offers only a cursory treatment of medieval Portugal. Among Portuguese historians, there is only a handful who study Portuguese trade in the Middle Ages.

This is not to say that all scholars have ignored the trade relationships that existed during the Middle Ages between Portugal and the rest of Europe, especially England. Perhaps the earliest of the twentieth-century scholars of Anglo-Iberian relations was Violet Shillington. Her book, titled *Commercial Relations of England with Portugal* was published in 1907.[1] The text is still the most comprehensive work on Anglo-Portuguese relations, and is frequently given mention by those few scholars of Portuguese history who deign to mention the development of the Anglo-Portuguese trade. She comments that "the Portuguese have received comparatively very little notice in connection with English foreign trade in the Middle Ages."[2] Even though there has been a concerted effort by Portuguese scholars to make more of the primary texts accessible to scholars, her statement is still true today.

Of the handful of writers who have written on the topic of Portuguese trade in recent years, the most prominent is Luis Adão da Fonseca, at the University of Porto, who has written numerous books and articles dealing with various aspects of Portuguese trade, including Anglo-Portuguese relations. In 1986, he wrote a brief study on the Treaty of Windsor and its implications. In it, he states that the treaty was the basis for economic changes in Portugal during the fifteenth century and that the treaty had permitted Portugal to fortify itself with the English alliance. However, he notes in his bibliography that we still lack an adequate study of the Anglo-Portuguese alliance. He refers to Shillington's work as one of the few available.[3] A few other scholars, including Wendy Childs, Francisco Ribeiro da Silva, and Luis Miguel Duarte, have published articles in the past several years regarding Anglo-Portuguese relations.[4]

Some question the breadth of Anglo-Portuguese trade because of lack of mentions in English customs records of a great number of Portuguese ships.

However, this point of view does not take into consideration the fact that there was a significant presence of English merchants in Portugal, both in Porto and in Lisbon, as well as the presence of Portuguese merchants in England. Nor does it take into consideration Portuguese goods carried on English ships as evidence of Portuguese involvement in trade. Moreover, it does not take into account the numerous references to Portuguese denizens in English records, such as the *Close Rolls* and *Patent Rolls*, or the mentions of English denizens in Portuguese records, such as *Descobrimentos* and *Quadro Elementar*. The preponderance of the matters of trade issues in these documents is sufficient to show that trade between England and Portugal was a "going business."

In most cases, whenever English trade relations are mentioned in most texts, the assumption goes along the lines of "everyone knows there were good relations." This raises two concerns: how does everyone know and, more importantly, were the relations really that good? This essay will ease the first and help to answer the second question. While the respective monarchs seemed to be interested in maintaining friendly relations, the actual practice of trade was unstable, at best. This essay will focus on the often turbulent trade relations with England during João's reign, using as sources published diplomatic records and calendar rolls.

Portuguese trade ties with England date back to the time of the Crusades and the era of Richard I "Lionheart," when English crusaders helped to expel the last of the Muslim invaders from Portugal, thereby completing the Portuguese Reconquest. A good trade relationship ensued, with primary exports from Portugal including such medieval staples as cork and wax.[5] However, the early period of Anglo-Portuguese ties is not where my interest lies.

The beginnings of truly intriguing and turbulent trade relations start with the reign of João I. The English had supported his claim to the throne of Portugal politically, militarily, and religiously. Both the English and the Portuguese supported the Roman pope, whereas the Spanish and the French supported the pope in Avignon.[6] João was appreciative of the English support. When he became king, he surrounded himself with talented advisors, such as Nun Alvarez,[7] who encouraged ties that would help to legitimize João's rule and guarantee Portuguese sovereignty. One means of securing these ties was active pursuance of growth of trade, both foreign and domestic. A major focus of both João's trade policy and his diplomatic policy was England, whose king and magnates, especially the Lancastrians, he believed would help him achieve his goals.

The strong Anglo Portuguese ties that were established during the reign of João, especially in conjunction with the later efforts of Henry IV, gave Portugal security. England could provide Portugal with a reliable source of grain and wool, two essential staples which Portugal was unable to produce in sufficient quantity. Later in the century, the English trade was so favored that Portuguese merchants actually petitioned for an edict, which was issued in Portugal, prohibiting the importation of any cloth which did not come from England.[8] English merchants were also involved in the very lucrative business of selling arms. The Anglo-Portuguese trade was not one-sided, though. Portugal was able to provide the English with highly valued trade goods, including oil, wax, figs, resins, honey, dates, salt, hides, and such. They also provided the highly desired commodity of wine.

These goods were traded at numerous ports in England, especially London and Bristol, which were the most important in Portuguese trade. Other English ports engaged in Portuguese trade included Southampton, Barnstaple, Dartmouth, Plymouth, Tenby, Milford, Chichester.[9] Portugal had far fewer ports than England. Most of the English trade came through either Porto or Lisbon. Porto was a center of trade for the wine industry. Lisbon was more important for other trade industries, including the cloth trade. In order for merchants to carry goods to and from other parts of Portugal, special licenses had to be purchased at a premium price. Because of this, Lisbon, which had been a small city, was as large as London by 1450. The centralization of trade out of Lisbon made control of levies, duties, and the like, much more efficient. It also made it easier to keep an eye on what merchants and customs officers were doing—in a way that the decentralized English trade was not able to accomplish.[10]

The long-standing goodwill between England and Portugal was formalized in 1386 with the signing of the Treaty of Windsor.[11] It also served to bind them together against common enemies, perhaps with the idea that the enemy of my enemy is my friend. England promised to send assistance to Portugal if it were invaded or attacked, and Portugal was to do the same if England were attacked. The treaty also guaranteed unmolested trade between the two countries.[12] This treaty promised permanent alliance, and included a clause that successive monarchs—on each side—were to confirm the treaty within a year of accession to the throne.[13] The 1386 alliance was strengthened further in 1387 with the dynastic marriage of João to Philippa, the elder daughter of John of Gaunt, duke of Lancaster, by his wife Blanche of Lancaster.

João continued his policy of friendly contact with the English. Within a short period of the signing of the treaty, João appealed to Richard II for assistance against a threatened Castilian invasion, basing his request for assistance on the terms of the treaty. Although many Englishmen were reluctant to expend even more money on the Iberian problem,[14] some English magnates and merchants provided loans, in the name of João, to help defend Portugal against hostile neighbors. When João's agents were slow in making repayment, English merchants took matters into their own hands in clear violation of the treaty, which laid out means of redress. Portuguese ships and goods were seized at sea, and Portuguese denizens were arrested, including João's half-brother, the infante Dinis.[15] Numerous complaints were sent to João by Portuguese merchants trying to do business in England. Their goods were being seized by English merchants, in lieu of payment by João of his debts. Although this was a standard practice among merchants, João sent letters to Richard complaining of such treatment, calling it scandalous. After all, the two nations were allied and had sworn perpetual friendship. Should there not be some benefits and protection that arise from such an alliance?[16]

In addition to the seizure of goods to recover debts, salvage rights were another prickly point in Anglo-Portuguese trade. The Portuguese were upset by the frequent ignoring of the prevailing custom of salvage by the English. The custom was that goods would be left unmolested as long as there was even a sole survivor of the wreck. Unfortunately, what often happened was that goods were seized anyway, often violently. This was especially true if the survivor was in no condition to give any resistance. In 1387, merchants from Porto on a ship called *Seint Nicholas* wrecked at Kindsdown by Dover during a storm, and their goods were seized, including the rigging. The mayor and bailiff of Sandwich were ordered to ensure that all their goods "as were salved" as well as the rigging and gear of the ship should be restored to the merchants from "whose hands soever found." If the goods were not found, they were to be restored the value of the goods—less the king's custom.[17]

Portuguese goods, including wine, were also being seized upon the open sea by English sailors. This prompted João to demand restitution.[18] He complained that in some cases, goods were seized for several years. The restitution he asked for came to quite a hefty total. He estimated that approximately 100 tuns of wine recently had been seized. The value of the wine, at a modest estimate, was placed at 100 escudos and 5 marks per tun. Thus, a fair restitution amount would total over 10,000 escudos.[19]

Richard wanted to maintain a steady flow of Portuguese goods into England. However, Richard, who was strapped for cash,[20] was not interested in paying financial restitution to the Portuguese. Instead, he responded by creating a new system of proctors. English merchants who were owed debts by the Portuguese could bring their claims in front of the proctors to determine if the claims were valid and if action could be taken. The system included the implicit understanding that goods of Portuguese merchants were not to be seized if they were not party to the original debts.[21] João clearly believed that the treaty was not just empty words, and he was interested in maintaining good relations with England, so he gave the proctor system a chance to work. The system seemed to stabilize the relationship for a time. However, in part owing to its slowness, by 1394 harassment of Portuguese merchants in England had resumed.

João also maintained good relations by keeping content the numerous Englishmen and Englishwomen who had arrived in Portugal after his marriage to Philippa. Because of the long-standing goodwill between the countries, there was already a sizable contingent of Englishmen in Portugal, and many of the recent arrivals took up more or less permanent residence in Portugal, wanting to take advantage of trade possibilities. Although the English were attacking Portuguese ships off the coast of England, João believed that those merchants who were in Portugal were not responsible for the actions of their countrymen. Thus, in one of his early actions that set the tone for the treatment of Englishmen in Portugal, he issued edicts in 1389 which granted English merchants increased privileges "like unto those offered to the Genoese."[22]

Not surprisingly, Portuguese merchants were not happy with the new privileges, especially since they were not being given the same rights in England. Merchants in Porto began to clamor for the rights to attach the property of English merchants in Portugal as a means to compensate for the losses suffered by their countrymen by English hands. João was, understandably, quite concerned with this new turn of events. He was deeply concerned that such action against English merchants would harm the new alliance with England. He even issued laws and regulations limiting the rights of Portuguese merchants to attach property of English merchants unless they were directly involved in the seizure of Portuguese ships and property.[23]

Merchants in Portugal began attaching property of English merchants, although by more peaceful means than the English were using on the Portuguese, seizing the goods in port rather than attacking ships on th seas. João, at this point, issued an edict forbidding the insulting or molesting of foreigners in Portugal for the purpose of trade. The duty on goods imported to Portugal was also decreased, leaving the Portuguese merchants to bear most of the brunt of the unequal trade system. Portuguese merchants were not happy with the restrictions being placed upon them. The "good men" of the council of Porto issued a complaint about the terms and demanded a return to the old rights.[24]

One might think that the different perceptions of the English and the Portuguese toward the importance of the alliance would be the beginning of the end of a short-lived friendship. However, in 1397–98 there was an uprising in Portugal, encouraged by Castile, whose king was planning an incursion into Portugal. João turned to the English for assistance and received English aid in the form of English men at arms and archers to repel the threat. Richard was willing to help militarily, viewing the treaty primarily as a military alliance. Richard understood war as a chance to enrich his coffers and successful military action as a means to glorify himself.[25] Richard granted the ambassador of Portugal the right to purchase 500 lances and transport them to Portugal.[26] He later granted permission for 20 knights and 400 additional lances to be sent to Portugal.[27]

However, Richard was not willing to help the situation of Portuguese merchants in England. Instead he chose to take advantage of the situation to fill the royal purse. Richard raised import duties on wine. He was able to justify raising the duties by claiming that he was spending the revenue to help João, although not much money was actually spent on aiding the Portuguese. The new duties on wine hurt the Portuguese trade, since wine was by this point the premier export to England. Adding insult to injury, Portuguese merchants continued to find themselves detained in ports. Some local merchants, being fairly certain that nothing would be done about the detentions, used them as a means to force the Portuguese merchants to sell goods at reduced prices, rather than permit them to spoil.

Richard gave only limited support to the alliance, perhaps because Richard was still struggling to free himself from Lancastrian influence and John of Gaunt had played an important role in establishing the alliance. The future of the alliance was greatly enhanced when Richard was deposed in 1399 by his cousin, Henry Bolingbroke, duke of Lancaster, son of John of Gaunt.[28] The relationship between England and Portugal improved significantly thereafter. Henry IV, whose sister was married to João, quickly acted to reaffirm the Treaty of Windsor. Henry was almost as keen as João was to keep the alliance strong, perhaps due to familial ties, but more likely due to trade ties and a common support for the Roman pope. He even insisted that England be included in any treaties signed by the Portuguese. When Portugal signed a truce with Castile in 1400, Henry sent word to João that he wanted to be included in the treaty as an ally of Portugal. Henry also inducted João into the Order of the Garter, making him the first foreigner to receive that honor. This tradition of inducting members of the house of Avis would be continued by future Lancastrian kings of England.

Although the relationship between Henry and João was much more amicable and familiar than the relationship with Richard had been, the relationship was not unmarred by turmoil. In an incident in August, only months after Henry assumed the throne, the Portuguese merchant, Lewis Gonsalyn,[29] had to petition the crown for the right to lade English goods that had already been contracted. Apparently the customs collectors had been giving him a bit of trouble, raising the customs tax and denying that it had been paid. Gonsalyn was able to produce proof that it had been paid, and was allowed to lade his ships after a few more delays.

Although Henry issued edicts in 1403 and 1404 prohibiting the harassment of Portuguese denizens, including those in England for the purpose of trade, and specifically mentions that their goods were not to be seized in recompense for debts owed by João's agents,[30] many Portuguese still encountered problems. Portuguese merchants appealing to English authorities often were ignored. The English local officials were often either unable or unwilling to do anything, sometimes both; a few were even involved in the harassment. When the matters were brought before the king's justices and the crown, the decrees were often ignored. In 1403, John Botewelle, a merchant of Lusshebone (Lisbon),[31] was carrying a load of wine to England. His ship ran into bad weather. Rather than waiting for the fickle weather to clear, he landed at Waterford, but did not unload his ship. When the weather improved, he sailed for Dartmouth, his original destination. The winemaster from Waterford claimed a customs fee, although the fee had already been paid at Dartmouth. Botewelle, who had been double-billed, sought restitution. The law stated that customs could only be charged at ports where goods were unloaded, and Botewelle knew that the only way to gain recompense was to take the matter to court. The winemaster at Waterford was reprimanded for trying to collect customs on wine that had neither been unloaded nor offered for sale at his port.

Another incident during the reign of Henry IV shows that sometimes the harassment did not involve the loading and unloading of goods of Portuguese ships nor the demand for payment of unfair customs by Portuguese merchants. John de Lere had returned home to Portugal on business and had left his possessions in England. His personal goods were seized from the house in which he had been staying.[32] The list of goods seized includes a mantle, hose, a coat, a table, boots, and shirts. It is stated in the complaint that the goods were seized because of the debt owed by Portuguese officials.

It was not only common merchants who were molested. Even João's ambassadors and emissaries were subject to harassment. Lawrence da Sousa, "a servant of the king of Portugal," brought a shipload of fruits to England for the purpose of selling them as a means of giving financial support to the Portuguese ambassador. He was required to pay customs, which was not too objectionable. However, merchants at port tried to force him to spend the money from the sale of the fruits on other merchandise. Da Sousa took his grievance before the king's justices, and he was granted unspecified relief because the "king's will is to shew the said Lawrence special favor."[33]

On several occasions, Henry had to issue special letters granting the ambassadors freedom to leave England, unmolested, and with all of their goods. A letter granting Martim Dossem, the ambassador, free passage stated that there were twenty five people and fifteen horses in the group.[34]

This group was to be allowed to leave, and the coffers, bags, and other things belonging to the ambassador were not to be opened.

The nearly constant antagonism between England and France during the Hundred Years' War also caused problems for Portuguese merchant ships. It was quite common for English ships, in the name of defending their country, to seize foreign ships, even if they were from countries that were friendly. John Pynell, of Portugal, fell victim to just such an occurrence. His ship, "laden with diverse goods," was captured at sea. Although he protested that the action was against the truce between England and Portugal, the captors insisted that he was, in fact, not Portuguese, but rather was Breton.[35]

Numerous Portuguese ships were attacked and run aground on the premise that they were hostile ships. Complaints were brought by captains and merchants. In one interesting case, the ship of Fonsus Martyn and Rigo Gonsalvez was captured off the Isle of Wight by "the king's enemies of France." The ship was rescued in short order. However, the rescuers held onto the goods and had to be ordered to release the goods to the Portuguese sailors and the owner of the ship.[36]

In spite of the turbulent trade, the alliance held. The alliance even takes another military turn in 1404–05. In the past, England had helped Portugal defend itself against threats. João, in an effort to show his good faith, allowed Portuguese knights, led by his illegitimate son Alfonso, to assist Henry in his "wars in the northern parts."[37] After 1405, Henry, the most serious of the internal crises solved, was able to focus more of his attention on the problems of the Portuguese merchants. An edict was issued, primarily directed to the sheriff of Bristol, but also to the sheriffs of Southampton, Kent, and Devon, that "under pain of his wrath and the pains thereupon incumbent" ships and cargoes of Portuguese ships were not to be detained or harassed in any way. Portuguese persons were also not to be harassed.[38]

Hoping to strengthen the alliance, João supported the marriage of his natural daughter, Beatrice, to Thomas, earl of Arundel, in 1405. This helped further to strengthen the ties between England and Portugal. However, the debt problem still loomed over this new diplomatic alliance. There was concern on the parts of both Henry and João that the shipment of the dowry would be interfered with and seized by English merchants, who wanted to collect on the old debt owed by João, because the dowry was a ready source of coin and easily converted plate. Consequently, special letters of passage were drawn up for the merchants who were to deliver the dowry to England, so that they would not be harassed.[39]

The relations after 1405 were usually quite friendly, although there was still the potential for lawless acts. In addition, there were still occasional government officials who overstepped their authority. Sometimes officials failed in their duties to preserve the king's peace. John Dorsele, a Portuguese merchant, was forced by stress of weather to make port at Dartmouth. His goods were detained with the knowledge of the local officials, and Dorsele brought action before the king's justice. A judgment was issued to ensure that the goods would be kept safe.[40]

When João complained, once again, about the treatment of Portuguese merchants, Henry reminded him that part of the problem was the old debt. The system of proctors had been set up during the reign of Richard II to consider claims, but many debts had yet to be repaid. However, Henry did somewhat oblige his brother-in-law by offering slightly more equitable treatment of Portuguese denizens, although the English never granted the same level of special privileges to Portuguese denizens that the English king's subjects received in Portugal. In 1406, Henry issued an edict that all Portuguese merchants should be permitted to come and go freely in all the domains of the king of England.[41]

Occasionally, Portuguese denizens were specifically exempted from paying the usual customs fees. In the case of John Vasques, described as a "knight of Portugal," nine tuns of wine laded on a Portuguese ship were ordered to be delivered to him "now and there" without taking the usual custom.[42] Henry also reminded the port masters that any Portuguese merchants coming to England and trading in good faith were not to be held liable for the debts of the king of Portugal or his emissaries.[43] These mandates regarding Portugal were Henry's attempt to secure fair and just treatment of Portuguese merchants. Although these regulations did not offer any special privileges to the Portuguese traders and merchants, the basic rights that were afforded, combined with the growing Portuguese dependence on foreign grain, were enough to justify a booming Anglo-Portuguese trade.[44]

The new laws were, however, largely ignored. The Portuguese merchants remained unsatisfied with their continued mistreatment at the hands of the English. They, therefore, turned to their own king to seek assistance in the matter. João again treated with Henry to enforce the laws regarding the treatment of Portuguese merchants. He reminded Henry of the favorable treatment that English merchants in Portugal had received.

The benefits and privileges João offered to English merchants provided them with more freedom from duties and customs than native Portuguese merchants. Generally, when English traders had complained of slow release of goods, slow payment of moneys owed, and of unscrupulous traders, João had acted to help. In the early stages of trade, the Portuguese merchants were willing to bear the burden, but many Portuguese merchants were beginning to complain that the English were receiving too many benefits.

Perhaps the most significant benefit offered to the English merchants was the establishment of a system of brokers. English merchants had complained about delays caused by disputes over quality. João established a system of neutral brokers who were to be present when wool was sold. The brokers were to inspect the seals on the cases and be present when the cases were opened. Disputes and complaints were turned over to a specially appointed custom-house judge who would decide the issue forthwith.[45] This judge was to be knowledgeable about commerce. English merchants were to give him a list of all those who bought from them and how much they owed. If the Portuguese merchants were slow in making payments, their goods were to be held for up to nine days, after which point the goods would be sold in order to permit the English merchants to collect their money.

The English also benefited from low import tariffs. Even a town as far inland as Bragança passed laws permitting foreign traders to conduct business.[46] Although João tried very hard to protect English interests in Portugal, he was somewhat bound by the fact that the urban merchant class had been essential to his rise to power. He did not want to encroach too much on their commercial interests and risk alienating a part of his power base.

In some cases, João was not able to prevent English ships and goods from being seized. In 1409, the ship of Thomas Fauconer, a Londoner, was seized by two of João's officials. The goods were taken, Fauconer was kept prisoner, and was subjected to "tormentos." He was held in prison for several months. In 1412, Henry wrote a "very affectionate" letter to his sister, Philippa, the queen of Portugal, asking for her intervention in the case of another ship that was unjustly seized asking for prompt justice.[47] This case was quickly settled, and restitution was made.

After the death in 1413 of Henry, with whom João had a friendly relationship, relations cooled somewhat, since the family tie was now one of uncle to nephew rather than between brothers-in-law. There is little record of correspondence or legal actions concerning Anglo-Portuguese trade during the reign of Henry V (1413–22).[48] This may be due to the fact that Henry seems to have concerned himself mainly with the war against France. The arms trade, however, seems to have caught Henry's attention, as several permits for the transportation of arms were issued.[49] As long as the English had decent access to Portuguese trade, either by Portuguese traders coming to England or by English traders in Portugal, neither João nor Henry had cause to be concerned about trade relations.

During the reign of Henry VI (1422–61, 1470–71),[50] many of the old difficulties of trade resurfaced. By this point, the old debts owed by João had long been paid. Most of the complaints during the early years of Henry's reign seem to be related to the problem of shipwrecks. In some cases, ships were run aground because of weather, and the goods were carried away.[51] In other cases, such as the ship the *Seintmarie de Portaferro* of Lisbon, English ships took the ship at sea, in a clear act of piracy.[52] The ship was then run aground, "suffering her after being so taken to be wrecked, and taking the goods when cast ashore."

A similar incident occurred a few years later. This time, it involved the running aground of five ships, "laden with wine, figs, raisins, and other merchandise," which were then seized. These goods had been destined from Portugal to Flanders. The goods taken from the ships were carried to Falmouth, "in breach of the amity between the king and the Flemish."[53] In some instances, justice was served by demanding the return of the goods, or money equal to the value of the goods. In other instances, justice was served by the issuance of arrest warrants against the perpetrators of the piracy.

However, João was still very interested in maintaining ties with England. He continued to look for ways to strengthen his alliance with England. Near the end of his reign, another of his daughters, Isabella, married Phillip the Good of Burgundy, in an attempt to strengthen the Anglo-Portuguese alliance. England had strong ties with Burgundy, and João was hoping to use the tie both for his benefit and also to show his desire to ally Portugal with the English. However when the Anglo-Burgundian alliance fell apart, it would become evident to João's successors that the marriage alliance would not yield the results that João intended.[54]

The intentions were good on the part of the Portuguese and the English. However, relations were often bad. Yet, in spite of all the twist and turns of the trade, the alliance remained intact. When João died, his son Duarte continued the alliance with England, which remained mostly amicable. The Portuguese were more than happy to let the English ships and their captains take the risks of trade, only occasionally carrying goods to England themselves. Serious problems did not arise until 1470, when Portuguese ships became caught in the middle of the readeption of Henry VI,[55] at which point Portugal declared war on England and renounced all treaties with England. The declaration was short-lived, because by that point, Edward IV (1461–70, 1471–83) had regained the throne and was very conciliatory toward Alfonso. He also reissued the Treaty of Windsor, which would endure through most of the modern period, as long as there was a Portuguese monarch and an English monarch. There were two significant breaks: once when the Portuguese throne fell under Spanish control for dynastic reasons (hence no Portuguese monarch) and once during the protectorate of Cromwell (hence no English monarch). The six hundredth anniversary of the Treaty of Windsor was celebrated in 1986.

The Portuguese continued to actively pursue foreign trade in the fifteenth and sixteenth centuries. However, the focus of trade shifted from

Europe to Asia and Africa, and later to the western hemisphere. Because the Portuguese were more than happy to let foreign ships, including the English, take the risks of trade, the Portuguese were able to focus their energy elsewhere and extend their trade ties throughout much of Asia and Africa. This refocus of energy became the Age of Exploration.

Notes

1. Cowritten with A.B. Wallis Chapman, who wrote the section dealing with modern trade.
2. V.M. Shillington, *The Commercial Relations of England and Portugal* (1907; repr., New York: Burt Franklin, 1970), p. vii.
3. Luis Adão da Fonseca, *O essencial sobre o Tratado de Windsor* (Lisbon: Imprensa Nacional/Casa da Moeda, 1986), p. 59. T.H. Lloyd, *Alien Merchants in England in the High Middle Ages* (Sussex: The Harvester Press, 1982), notes in his footnotes that Shillington's book is the only study of medieval Anglo-Portuguese trade.
4. Wendy R. Childs, "Anglo-Portuguese Trade in the Fifteenth Century," *Transactions of the Royal Historical Society*, 6th ser., 2 (1992): 195–219. Luis Miguel Duarte, "Aspectos menos conhecidos das relações entre Portugal e a Inglaterra na segunda metade do século XV," *Congresso Internacional: Bartolomeu Dias e sua Epoca. Actas*, Vol. 3 (Porto: University of Porto, 1989), pp. 551–61. Francisco Ribeiro Da Silva, "Portugal e o curso no Atlantico Norte na segunda metade do século XV. Alguns aspectos," *Congresso Internacional: Bartolomeu Dias e sua Época. Actas*, Vol. 3 (Porto: University of Porto. 1989), pp. 541–49.
5. Shillington, *Commercial Relations*, p. 29.
6. For a detailed account on English involvement in Iberia, consult P.E. Russell's *The English Intervention in Spain and Portugal in the Time of Edward III and Richard II* (Oxford: Clarendon Press, 1955).
7. For more on the political beliefs of Nun Alvarez, consult A. do Carmo Reis, *Introdução ao Pensamento Político de Nun'Álvares* (Vila do Conde: Edições Linear, 1982). A good general text on fifteenth-century Portugal is A.H. de Oliveira Marques's *Portugal na Crise dos Séculos XIV e XV* (Lisbon: Editorial Presença, 1987). Unfortunately, there is no adequate general text for this period available in English. There are also no recent works on the reign of João I.
8. Visconde de Santarém, *Quadro Elementar das relações politicas e diplomaticas de Portugal com as diversas potencias do mundo* (Paris: J.P. Aillaud, 1842), 19:226.
9. Although the trade seems to have been focused at the southern ports, there is a handful of references to northern English traders wanting access to Portuguese goods. Goods would be re-laden in southern ports and then taken north to York or Kingston, as in the case mentioned in the *Calendar of the Close Rolls, Richard II* (Nedeln: Kraus Reprint, 1971), 3:368.

10. Perhaps the centralization was one of the reasons for the significantly lower number of Portuguese attacks on English interests, since it is more difficult to misbehave when under supervision.
11. The text of the treaty is included in its entirety in *As Gavetas da Tore do Tombo* (Lisbon: Centro de Estudos Ultramarinos, 1970), 8:312–20.
12. Luis Adão da Fonseca, *O Tratado de Tordesilhas e a Diplomacia Luso-Castelhana no Século XV* (Lisbon: Edições Inapa, 1991), p. 15.
13. Santarém, *Quadro Elementar*, 19:91.
14. For a detailed account of English involvement in Iberia, see Russell's *English Intervention in Spain and Portugal*.
15. *Close Rolls*, Richard II, 3:518.
16. Santarém, *Quadro Elementar*, 19:120.
17. *Close Rolls*, Richard II, 3:205. This must have been a difficult winter. There are a few records of ships wrecked and goods seized within a little over a month. Sometimes the wrecks are blamed on the carelessness of the seamen in a storm.
18. Santarém, *Quadro Elementar*, 19:123.
19. Santarém, *Quadro Elementar*, 19:124.
20. Richard II was a monarch known for an over-inflated sense of his own regality, and he expended a considerable amount of both time and money to enhance his image. For a brief history of late medieval England, consult Maurice H. Keen, *England in the Later Middle Ages* (London: Routledge, 1973). For a more detailed account of the reign of Richard II, consult Nigel Saul, *Richard II* (New Haven: Yale University Press, 1997).
21. Santarém, *Quadro Elementar*, 19:122.
22. Santarém, *Quadro Elementar*, 6:68 and 19:122.
23. Santarém, *Quadro Elementar*, 14:122.
24. João Martins da Silva Marques, ed., *Descobrimentos portugueses, documentos para a sua história* (Lisbon: Edição do Instituto de Alta Cultura, 1971), 1:213.
25. For an interesting discussion on Richard's personality disorder, refer to A. Compton Reeves, "Richard II: A Case of Narcissistic Personality Disorder?" *Medieval Life* 12 (1999): 19–22.
26. Santarém, *Quadro Elementar*, 19:128.
27. Santarém, *Quadro Elementar*, 19:129.
28. The standard text for the reign of Henry IV is J.L. Kirby's, *Henry IV* (London: Constable, 1970).
29. *Close Rolls*, Henry IV (Nedeln: Kraus Reprint, 1971), 1:87.
30. Santarém, *Quadro Elementar*, 19:150–51.
31. *Close Rolls*, Henry IV, 2:89.
32. *Close Rolls*, Henry IV, 2:236.
33. *Close Rolls*, Henry IV, 2:264.
34. Santarém, *Quadro Elementar*, 19:143. One almost wonders whether the group would have been harassed if a different number of people showed up.
35. *Calendar of the Patent Rolls*, Henry IV (Nedeln: Kraus Reprint, 1971), 2:357.
36. *Calendar of the Patent Rolls*, Henry IV, 2:277. Also listed on the same page is another similar incident regarding the *Katerine*, perhaps an indication that this action was not uncommon.

37. *Close Rolls*, Henry IV, 3:23. Santarém, *Quadro Elementar*, 19:165. Although Alfonso was João's bastard son, the records do not make note of it. The fractious nobles, some of whom had helped Henry oust Richard II, turned against him. Among the nobles were the Percys of Northumberland and Richard Scrope, archbishop of York.
38. *Close Rolls*, Henry IV, 2:317. Santarém, *Quadro Elementar*, 6:69.
39. *Royal and Historical Letters during the Reign of Henry IV, King of England and of France, and Lord of Ireland*, ed. F.C. Hingeston, 2 vols. (New York: Kraus Reprint, 1964–66), 2:84. Santarém lists the dowry as 6,250 marks of English currency and property valued at 6,280 marks of English currency. *Quadro Elementar*, 19:cxxxi and 155. After the death of Arundel, she was granted the right to enjoy her dower "as though she had been born in England" (*Rotuli Parliamentorum*, London: 1832), 4:130.
40. *Close Rolls*, Henry IV, 3:340.
41. *Transcript of Foreign Records*, ser. 2, no.153. Quoted in Shillington, *Commercial Relations*, p. 92.
42. *Close Rolls*, Henry IV, 4:167. In another instance, customs officials from sandwich were ordered to permit four loads (fothers) to be taken to Portugal without payment of custom. *Close Rolls*, Henry IV, 2:441.
43. *Patent Rolls*, Henry IV, 4:234.
44. Ironically, the dependence on foreign grain increased as a result of the boom in trade. As trade increased, Portuguese farmers turned over more of their acreage to vineyards instead of growing grain, making the Portuguese even more dependent on an import trade in grain.
45. Santarém, *Quadro Elementar*, 6:67.
46. The law did not apply specifically to English traders, but is an indication of trade interest in outlying areas. Hirondino da Paixão Fernandes, *Bibliografia do Distrito de Bragança. Documentos (textos) Publicados* (Bragança: Instituto Superior Politécnico de Bragança, 1996), p. 77.
47. Santarém, *Quadro Elementar*, 19:131, 171.
48. A good reference for the reign of Henry V is C.T. Allmand's *Henry V* (Berkeley: University of California Press, 1992).
49. Santarém, *Quadro Elementar*, 19:174–75.
50. A good reference for the reign of Henry VI is Ralph Griffiths's *The Reign of King Henry VI: The Exercise of Royal Authority, 1422–1461* (Berkeley: University of California Press, 1981).
51. *Patent Rolls*, Henry VI, 1:546.
52. *Patent Rolls*, Henry VI, 1:548.
53. *Patent Rolls*, Henry VI, 2:527.
54. The Anglo-Burgundian alliance unraveled shortly after João's death. For more information on the trade aspects of the Anglo-Burgundian Alliance, see John Munro, *Wool, Cloth and Gold: The Struggle for Bullion in Anglo-Burgundian Trade, ca. 1340–1478* (Toronto: University of Toronto Press, 1973).
55. Edward IV seized the throne in 1461. Henry, with the help of Warwick, briefly regained control in 1470–71, which is referred to as the readeption.

CHAPTER 7

PHILIPPA OF LANCASTER, QUEEN OF PORTUGAL—AND PATRON OF THE GOWER TRANSLATIONS?

Joyce Coleman

This essay traces Philippa of Lancaster's career as queen of Portugal (r. 1387–1415), emphasizing her policy of promoting Anglo-Portuguese interchange and relating that policy to the Iberian translations of John Gower's "Confessio Amantis"

This essay is part literary history and part soap opera. It features a strong female lead who survives a rich but chaotic childhood and a series of failed betrothals to marry a man whom she comes to love, to produce a famous generation of children, and incidentally to be the means of textual migration and translation in no fewer than four countries and five languages. She brought French literature to Chaucer and Chaucerian literature, possibly, to Portugal; she did her best to persuade the clergy of her adopted country to embrace the Latin Use of Sarum; and it was arguably she who sponsored the translation of John Gower's *Confessio Amantis* into Portuguese and Castilian.[1]

To date, Philippa of Lancaster has had no more than a walk-on role in history. The oldest legitimate daughter of John of Gaunt, she is most famous for marrying João I of Portugal, as a preliminary to a joint English–Portuguese invasion meant to place her father on the throne of Castile. After the failure of that expedition, and after marrying Philippa's half-sister Catherine to the heir-apparent to Castile, John could return to England and contemplate the prospect (which came true) of his grandsons ruling in the

Iberian Peninsula. The historians' emphasis has always been on Gaunt, and indeed there is no question that he was the operative force behind these alliances. The arranging of marriages—his own and those of his siblings or children—was a political tool to which he returned again and again throughout his career. Philippa's marriage to João came after at least five previous attempts to marry her off to powerful French, English, and Flemish lords.[2] Each betrothal was designed to extend John's, and usually England's, influence in key areas—and each was ultimately terminated, either by the proposed spouse or by powerful nobles in his region who wished to avoid precisely such extensions of English, or Lancastrian, influence. Yet while literally a puppet in her father's hands, Philippa had a personality and an intelligence that emerges through the corners of the chronicles, and that found expression particularly once she had her own establishment far from her father. This essay has two related goals. One is to present, to an English-reading audience largely unfamiliar with it, the story of Philippa's life and accomplishments in Portugal. The other is to relate that life to the debate over Philippa's responsibility for the Gower translations.

The most detailed account we have of Philippa's habits and character comes from Fernão Lopes, keeper of the Portuguese Royal Archives, writing on commission from Philippa's son Duarte in 1434. It is worth quoting this in full:

> She always prayed the canonical hours according to the Use of Sarum and although this observance was by no means easy to arrange, she was so keen on this that she taught it to her chaplains and other worthy persons. Every Friday it was her custom to read the Book of Psalms and she would speak to no one until she had quite finished it. When she was prevented from doing so through illness or through giving birth, somebody would read to her all that she was wont to read on that particular day; and she would listen devoutly and without interruption. There is no need to speak at length about fasting or the practice of reading the Holy Scriptures at convenient times; for all this was a regular part of her life and ordered so wisely that idleness could gain no foothold in her imagination.
>
> She cared for the poor and needy, giving alms most liberally to churches and monasteries. She loved the noblest of husbands most faithfully. She made great efforts never to annoy him, and set great store by the education and sound upbringing of her children. Nothing she did was done out of rancour or hatred. On the contrary, all her actions were dictated by love of God and of her neighbour.
>
> Her conversation was plain, and often helpful without showing any pride in her royal rank; and her way of speaking was sweet, gracious and most pleasing to all who heard her. In order not to appear too cut off from others, she delighted sometimes in relaxing with her maidens in those lawful games in which no trickery could be involved and which were seemly for any honest

person. So if the perfect manner in which she lived could be recorded in detail, any woman could study it with profit, no matter how high her rank.

[Ella rezaua sempre as oras canonicas pello costume de Saresbri; e por o el seia nom bem ligeiro dordenar, assy hera em esto atemta, que seus capellaães e ourtras honestas pessoas reçebiam nelle pera ella emsinamça. Todallas sestas feiras tinha costume rezar o psalteiro, nom fallamdo a nenhuuma pessoa ataa que o acabaua de todo; e quando era embargada per doemça ou constramgida per empedimento de parto, açera de ssy lhe rezauom todo o que ella auje em husamça, ouuyndo deuotamente sem nenhuuma outra toruaçam. Dos jejuuns nom compre fazer sermom, nem do leer das Santas Scprituras em conuenhauees tempos; ca assy era todo repartido com tam madura discriçom que nunca a oçiosidade em sua maginaçam achaua morada.

[Era cuidadossa açera dos pobres e mynguados, fazendo largas esmollas aas egrejas e moesteiros. Amou bem fielmente o sseu muy nobre marido, teemdo gram semtido de o nunca anojar, e da boa emsinamça e criaçam de seus filhos. Nom fazia cousa alguuma com ramcor nem odio, mas todas suas obras eram feitas com amor de Deus e do proximo.

[Em ella auia huuma chaã conuersaçam, proueitosa a muytos sem oufana de seu real estado, com doçes e graçiosas pallauras a todos praziuees douuir. Allegraua-sse alguumas (vezes), por nom pareçer de todo apartada despaçar com suas domzellas em jogos sem sospeita demgano licitos e conuinhaaues a toda onesta pessoa; assy que, semdo seus perfeitos costumes em que muyto floreçeo per meudo postos em scprito, assaz seriam dabatosa emsinança pera quaaesquer molheres, posto que de moor estado fossem.]³

One wonders if Philippa was an early reader and follower of Christine de Pizan's advice to prudent queens, in the *Trésor de la Cité des Dames* (1405). Prudence, at least in personal affairs, is not the quality that characterized Philippa's early home life. Born in Leicester on March 31, 1360, she suffered a series of childhood traumas: her mother, Blanche of Lancaster, died when she was eight; she acquired a foreign stepmother, Constanza of Castile, when she was eleven; and from about age twelve she (and Constanza) had to watch her father conduct a long-running affair with her governess, Katherine Swynford (see figure 7.1). Philippa and her two full siblings, Elizabeth and Henry (the future Henry IV), were joined in the extended household by John's illegitimate daughter Blanche (product of an early affair with one of his mother's chamber-ladies); by John's daughter with Constanza, Catherine or Catalina; and by the four Beaufort children produced by Gaunt and Swynford, along with Swynford's two children by her husband. Despite the multiplicity of liaisons and offspring, however, the duke seems to have taken care with his daughters' education. Both Philippa and Elizabeth were taught to read and write,⁴ and religious guidance seems to have been at least on offer: Lopes asserts that "in her youth this blessed queen [Philippa] was

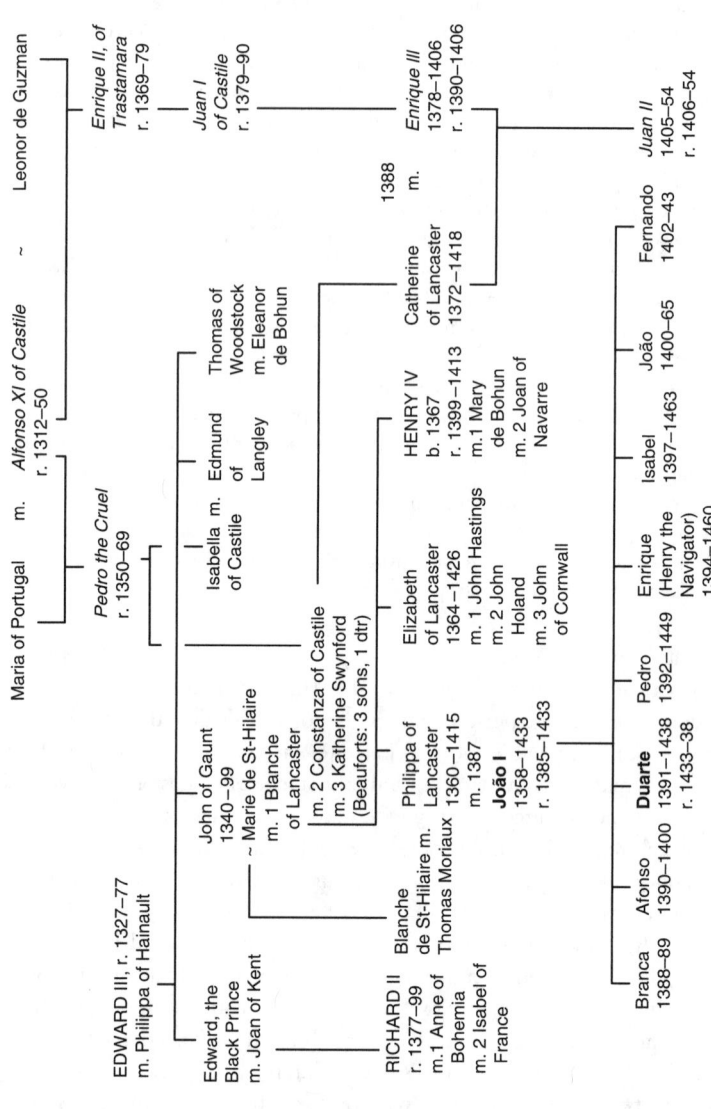

Figure 7.1 Lancastrian and Anglo-Iberian alliances.

Note: Kings of England given in ALL CAPS; kings of Portugal in **boldface**; kings of Castile in *italics*.

devout and had a good knowledge of the divine liturgy."⁵ John of Gaunt's relations with Swynford may even have increased his closeness with his daughter, since instead of leaving Philippa and Elizabeth with a settled older woman, as he did with Henry and Catherine, John may have had them with him more often in order to have Swynford with him as well.⁶

Philippa seems to have been her father's favorite daughter, judging from the presents he gave her⁷ and from the quality of the men to whom he kept trying to marry her off. One of these, the Flemish count William of Ostrevant, is said to have regretted the collapse of their betrothal because he had fallen in love with her.⁸ She must have earned a reputation for admirable or lovable qualities, since in late 1384 or early 1385 the dukes of Berry, Burgundy, and Bourbon considered her as a possible bride for their nephew, the young Charles VI of France. An offshoot of that otherwise unsuccessful idea was a complimentary ballade (number 765) written in her honor by Eustache Deschamps. The poem employs the conceit of competitive Orders of the Flower and the Leaf to praise Philippa as the chief Flower. As I have argued in a previous article, this poem might have furnished the occasion for Philippa's first act of literary patronage. Shortly after she would have received it, three English works were begun that each use the Flower and Leaf motif: the F prologue to Geoffrey Chaucer's *Legend of Good Women*, John Gower's *Confessio Amantis*, and (to a lesser extent) John Clanvowe's *Boke of Cupide*.⁹ It is easy to assume that Philippa had passed copies of Deschamps's ballade to Chaucer, long an associate in her father's court, and to her cousin Richard II or his wife Anne. Either the motif made its way into three poetic works simultaneously through such coterie circulation or, more likely, Richard found he liked the idea so much that he commissioned three poets to create complimentary Flower and Leaf poems for his own wife.¹⁰

A Lancastrian Princess in Portugal

By the time Philippa was reading and sharing her charming poem from Deschamps, her father was already negotiating with the man who would become her husband, João of Portugal. The story of Philippa's marriage gets told, when it does, primarily as an adjunct to the story of Gaunt's attempt to make himself king of Castile. John of Gaunt had married Constanza of Castile, the heir-in-exile to the Castilian throne, in September 1371. Constanza's father, Pedro the Cruel, had been overthrown in 1369 by his bastard half-brother Enrique of Trastamara. By marrying the Spanish princess, Gaunt made himself the legitimate king of Castile, a status quickly recognized in England.¹¹ By 1385, as his eighteen-year-old nephew Richard II was assuming increasing control of his realm, and exhibiting increasing impatience with his uncle's guardianship, John decided the time was ripe to go claim his crown. Also influencing that decision was the accession of a new king of Portugal intent on defeating Castile's ambition to conquer and absorb his country.

João I had emerged as a strong leader amid the chaos following King Fernando's death on October 22, 1383 (see figure 7.1). As a bastard son of Pedro I, Fernando's father, João had been made the master of the military Order of Aviz.[12] Fernando's only legitimate heir, meanwhile, was his daughter Beatriz, who had been married to Juan I of Castile. With his father-in-law dead, Juan prepared to invade and assimilate Portugal. The only approach to a central authority in that endangered country was Fernando's widow, Leonor, who was immersed in an affair with the Galician noble Juan Fernándes Andeiro. João made his first mark on Portuguese history on December 6, 1383, by striding into Leonor's chamber and killing her lover. The city council of Lisbon responded by appointing him regent of Portugal. As a Castilian invasion threatened, João sent an embassy to England, which was allowed to recruit English men-at-arms and archers (at Portuguese expense). With these en route to Portugal by March 1385, João summoned a meeting of the Cortes (the Portuguese parliament), and persuaded them to elect him king (on April 6, 1385). One of his first moves as king was to instruct his ambassadors in London to invite Gaunt to come seize his Castilian crown.

Meanwhile, Juan of Castile was marching toward Lisbon. João, his constable Nuno Alvares Pereira, the Portuguese forces, and the English archers met the Castilian invaders on the road from Aljubarrota, where their much smaller but better-captained army won a stunning victory (August 14, 1385). Aware that the Castilians would regroup and return, with French reinforcements, João renewed his invitations to John of Gaunt. This time Gaunt, backed by parliamentary funding, agreed. A further suggestion from João was that they should seal their alliance by his marriage to one of the duke's daughters. Gaunt seems to have accepted this idea as well, for his expeditionary force included both of his marriageable daughters, Philippa and Catherine. On July 9, 1386, Gaunt's party set sail from Plymouth, arriving at La Coruña, in Galicia, on July 25. The English company advanced on Santiago de Compostela, which quickly ceded itself to them; by September Gaunt and Constanza had established their new Spanish court at the Benedictine monastery of Celanova, south of Orense.[13]

The story of Philippa's life after her arrival in Iberia comes primarily from Fernão Lopes's *Crónica del Rei Dom João de boa memoria* ("Chronicle of the Lord King João of Good Memory") and from its sequel, the *Crónica da tomada de Ceuta por El-Rei D. João I* ("Chronicle of the Capture of Ceuta by the Lord King João I"), written by Lopes's successor as royal archivist,

Gomes Eanes de Zurara.[14] Like all earlier historians, both men tend to embroider speeches and heighten drama; and writing as they did for the sons and grandson of Philippa, their portraits of her come close to hagiography. However, their positions meant that they were also close to reliable sources, both documentary and oral. I will follow the accounts of these chroniclers, assuming that events happened more or less as described, even if enhanced in the telling.

João had already consulted his council about his proposed marriage even before the Lancastrian court was set up at Celanova. Most of the councilors argued strongly that he should wed Catherine, since with her he would acquire a claim to rule Castile himself. Wary of such dynastic entanglements, however, João chose Philippa instead. The prospective father- and son-in-law met for the first time on November 1, 1386, at Ponte do Mouro, and over the next three days agreed plans for their mutual invasion of Castile in early 1387, to be preceded by João's marriage to Philippa at Oporto. Both projects suffered delays, owing to a variety of problems at João's end. For one thing, he was waiting to receive a papal dispensation from the vow of celibacy he had taken as master of the Order of Aviz. Although this vow had not prevented him from having two children with a mistress, Ines (or Agnes) Pires, it would clash with the sacrament of marriage. Word of the pope's preliminary approval arrived at Ponte do Mouro, apparently resolving the problem, but other difficulties arose and the final release was held up.[15] According to Jean Froissart, João hesitated as well because of rumors, spread by the French allies of Castile, that France's planned invasion of England had succeeded (in fact, the preparations dragged on too long and were ultimately abandoned). If England were under French control, João's councilors reminded him, marriage to Philippa "would be worthless to him."[16] There was also the constant fear that Gaunt would make a separate arrangement with Castile, leaving Portugal (and Philippa) to its fate.

Under pressure from Gaunt, João dispatched Laurenço Vicente, archbishop of Braga, and Bishop João Rodrigues de Sá to Celanova. On November 11, according to Lopes, the bishops and the Lancaster party reaffirmed the marriage arrangement.[17] Froissart claims that a proxy marriage took place, with the archbishop presiding and the bishop standing in for João. At the conclusion of the ceremony, he goes on, the new bride lay down with the proxy groom "on a bed, in courteous fashion, just as a husband and wife ought to be."[18] After five failed betrothals and a long journey to Galicia to be bartered and debated over, Philippa of Lancaster thus found herself a wedded woman at last—lying stiffly in bed next to a Portuguese bishop. Her feelings about the sequence of events that brought her to that bed are not, of course recorded. She was probably pleased at the idea of having a husband and her own establishment at last, but the prospect of never seeing her father or her native land again must have called up some of the emotions that Chaucer was soon to ascribe to Constance in the "Man of Law's Tale":

> Allas, what wonder is it thogh she wepte,
> That shal be sent to strange nacioun
> Fro freendes that so tendrely hire kepte,
> And to be bounden under subjeccioun
> Of oon, she knoweth nat his condicioun?[19]

Fortunately for Philippa, João turned out to be a more successful dynastic partner than Constance's Sowdan of Surrye, though he was not ready to marry her in person quite yet. While the bishops were in Celanova, the king was off mustering his army. Gaunt took the initiative in December of sending Philippa to Oporto. João arrived there in late December, and the proxy spouses met for the first time, in the bishop's palace.[20] No one mentions what language they spoke; perhaps João knew French, or they both knew enough church-Latin to communicate, or Philippa managed as well as she could with what Romance roots she could muster. A few days later, João left again.[21] Time passed, and Gaunt wrote to remind João that marriages were forbidden during Lent, which meant they had to complete the rite of the *sponsalia* (formal betrothal) by February 3. Apparently deciding to ignore the vow-of-celibacy problem,[22] João agreed to go ahead—which he did at the last possible moment, riding all night from Guimarães to Oporto on February 2. He and Philippa performed the *sponsalia* in the cathedral on the third, and the marriage itself finally took place on a date reminiscent of Chaucer's Valentine poetry, the fourteenth.[23]

"Neither of them took precedence," says Lopes, describing the pair's ride to the cathedral for the ceremony; "rather they rode in complete equality [*ambos jguall*]."[24] John of Gaunt wasn't there; neither was Duchess Constanza. Both, says Lopes, were too busy assembling their forces for the coming invasion of Castile. Over the period of celebration following his marriage, João set up a household for Philippa, delegating officials, chamber-ladies, and sources of income. Then he headed back to his army, accompanied by his new wife. After two days of visits and meals Philippa left for Coimbra, while her father and husband set about invading Castile.[25]

The invasion of Castile, according to Peter Russell, was "a tremendous fiasco, . . . the most incompetently conducted of all Lancaster's campaigns."[26] Gaunt and the remnant of his army returned to Portugal in June 1387, where the duke visited his now-pregnant daughter at Coimbra. João, having completed a pilgrimage to Guimarães, was en route to join them when he fell seriously ill with a fever, at a place called Curval. "The Queen loved him very much," says Lopes,

> and when she heard this news of her beloved husband, she set out in haste for that place accompanied by her father the Duke. When they arrived there and saw the King so weak and helpless that he could barely speak, they were so terribly upset, especially the Queen, that she had a miscarriage. This was hardly surprising because there she was, in a foreign land, recently married and in a position of such great honour, and if her husband were to die so soon she would consider herself the most unfortunate woman in the world. Turning all this over and over in her heart made her weep continually, begging Death to carry her off.
>
> [A Raynha, como taaes nouas ouuyo do seu muyto amado marido que ella tamto preçaua, trigosamente partio pera aquelle logar, e o Duque seu padre com ella. E quando chegarom e o virom tam fraco e sem esforço que adur lhe pode fallar, ficaram tam nojosos e tristes, espeçialmente a Rainha, quanto se dizer nom pode, de guissa que logo moueo huuma criamça, e nom sem razom, ca se uia em terra estranha casada de pouco, posta em tam gramde homra, e falleçer-lhe logo assy çedo, bem se tinha por malaventuirada amtre as molheres do mundo. E cuidamdo esto em sua alma e spritu, nom çessaua de chorar, pedimdo aa morte que a leuasse.][27]

João made his will while his nobles despaired: "they could see no future for the kingdom except the clear and obvious one that through his death Portugal would be totally destroyed." Philippa stayed by his bed to comfort him, weeping and praying to Mary "to have pity on her own forsaken state and, as Mistress of Mercy, to restore her beloved husband to health."[28] And Mary, or something, did: João began to improve and was soon out of danger.[29] The crisis over, Gaunt and his wife prepared to withdraw to Bayonne, where they would hold negotiations with the representatives of Castile. They lingered in Oporto, however, "so that the Duke could enjoy the company of his daughter the Queen, for he did not know when he might see her again."[30] He never did, after he and his company set sail in late September.[31]

In his detailed account of the invasion of Castile, Russell blames its failure in part on João's repeated deference to the ideas and schemes of his new father-in-law.[32] Though it led to the defeat of Gaunt's ambitions, this deference is an interesting early measure of João's feelings about his new relations. Lopes's description of João and Philippa riding to their wedding "in complete equality" is another indication, as are his generous marriage gifts.[33] Once they began having children, the spouses alternated names from their respective families. Given his own illegitimate birth, João had good reason to value his new wife—possessor, in Russell's words, of "some of the bluest blood in Europe."³⁴ Philippa's practical value no doubt increased considerably in 1399, when her brother, unexpectedly, became king of England.

As the account of João's illness and her miscarriage implies, Philippa quickly committed herself emotionally to her new husband; God, as Lopes puts it, had "granted her a husband to her taste."³⁵ Despite his delays in committing himself to her, João also came to value Philippa for more than her family connections. Perhaps her genuine grief when he was near death, and the apparent efficacy of her prayers, helped turn his affections toward her. In the years immediately following their wedding, the king brought the queen to witness his assaults on Melgaço and Tui, and in 1390 he came to Santarém to be at the birth of their second child, and first son, staying on for four months.³⁶ João's pre-Philippa mistress, Pires, was shipped off to become superior of a convent,³⁷ while the king—despite having "a great house full of beautiful women," notes Lopes, "amongst whom he could have freely fulfilled such [sexual] desire if he had so wished"—continued to honor and love his wife "with an honest and pure love."³⁸

Like Philippa, João was both devout and intellectual. Writing to inform Henry IV and his council that he had negotiated a truce with Castile, for example, he began with a cascade of biblical quotations in praise of peace.³⁹ According to Lopes, João himself translated the hours of the Virgin into Portuguese and had his clerks translate the Gospels, the Acts of the Apostles, the Epistles of St. Paul, and various saints' lives, to increase the piety of his people.⁴⁰ He had a library of eighty-three volumes,⁴¹ and specially admired Saint Augustine.⁴² At the same time, again like Philippa, João was ready to enjoy more secular forms of entertainment. An acquaintance with fashionable European literature is indicated by his judgment that "Guillaume de Machaut did not create such a beautiful concord of melody, no matter how fine it may be, as the dogs produce when they are running well."⁴³ The comment occurs in João's *Livro da montaria*, which united information about hunting, horsemanship, and courtly life with advice to princes. This text and other records make it clear that João's bookishness combined with a strong athletic nature: he sings the praises of boar-hunting in the mountains; he explains that one needs *ligeirices* (agility, rapidity, lightness) to jump onto a horse or over obstacles, and how handball (*péla*) keeps the limbs supple. Mental agility is also important for a knight or general, and chess is recommended as a means of learning to think strategically. Also useful, and enjoyable in itself, was dancing; João "speaks with delight of the rooms decorated for the balls of his time," and commissioned instrumental pieces from the musicians attached to his court.⁴⁴ Disparate in background, the two spouses thus turned out to be compatible in intelligence and temperament.

One important piece of Anglo-Portuguese policy, implemented soon after João and Philippa had commenced conjugal life, was to reform the dissolute court atmosphere promoted under the bad old days of Fernando and Leonor (and Leonor's lover). According to Lopes, João and Philippa arbitrarily matched up some of the unmarried ladies and gentlemen of their household—with less than blissful results. The designated men were simply told to turn up the next day to be married, and when they did—no doubt in a state of high curiosity—"the King himself led the bridegrooms to the chamber of the Queen and there told each one that woman whom he should receive in marriage, to whose command there was no contradiction." Only one woman managed to marry the man she liked; the other couples were so persistent in their discontent that João swore off all future matchmaking.[45] His dislike of promiscuity had grown so intense, however, that when a favorite courtier persisted in an affair with a lady, the king had him burned at the stake.[46] What H.V. Livermore called the "new austerity" affected other behavior as well; in 1391 sumptuary laws "forbade all save doctors and prelates to wear gold or gilt brass and velvet on the person or mount, except on three high days."[47]

The years following Philippa's marriage saw a steady stream of pregnancies. Twenty-seven was a fairly advanced age to start bearing children, and two more early deaths followed the miscarriage in Curval (see figure 7.1). Branca (named after Philippa's mother, Blanche), born in 1388, lived only eight months; she was buried in a sepulcher at the foot of her great-grandfather Afonso IV's tomb. The next child, Afonso, born in 1390, was named after the same king. João welcomed the birth of his heir with much celebration; the grief must have been great, too, when the boy died at the age of ten.[48] The year 1391, however, saw the birth of the son who ultimately became João's heir, Duarte (named after Edward III), and over the next eleven years, until she was forty-two, Philippa produced five more children—Pedro, Enrique, Isabel, João, and Fernando—named, presumably, after João's father; Philippa's grandfather (Henry duke of Lancaster) and/or brother;[49] Philippa's aunt Isabelle de Coucy; João himself; and João's half-brother and royal predecessor.

The Anglo-Portuguese Court

The Valentine's Day marriage became an essential element in what developed into João and Philippa's joint myth as founders of the Golden Age of Portugal.[50] Another element of that myth is the rigorous but loving manner in which they raised and educated their children.[51] We don't have a book-list for their schooling, but as Russell notes, "[t]he education they received...was plainly of good quality."[52] In adult years, perhaps reflecting his own education, Duarte recommended that sons "be taught right from the beginning to read, write, and speak Latin, continuing with good books in Latin and in the vernacular as good guidance for a virtuous life." They should further read moral philosophy as well as books on war and "the approved chronicles."[53] Duarte himself wrote two books, one a moral–political treatise (*Leal conselhiero*, "The Loyal Counselor") and the other a guide to horsemanship (*Livro da ensinança de bem cavalgar toda sela*, "The Book of Learning to Ride Well with Any Saddle"); while Pedro created a florilegium based on Seneca and other classical writers (*Virtuosa bemfeitoria*, "The Virtuous Benefactor") and translated Cicero's *De officiis*. Both princes have left written "white papers" demonstrating their ability to analyze political situations. Enrique ("Henry the Navigator") went farther, conceiving what was possibly Europe's first systematic research project— the exploration and mapping of the coast of West Africa, which paved the way for Portugal's later maritime dominance.[54] Isabel, like her mother a "cultural ambassador"[55] married off to Duke Philip the Good of Burgundy, became a notable sponsor of translations into and out of several languages.[56] Together these offspring earned Camoens's sobriquet of a "marvelous generation";[57] more recently, Charity Cannon Willard has labeled them "an ambitious, talented, and energetic family."[58]

Philippa's devotion to her children became the focus of the famous story of her death, related in heart-rending (and suspiciously full) detail by Zurara. In order to initiate their three oldest sons into knighthood, João planned an invasion of, or crusade to, Ceuta, in Morocco. Philippa accompanied her husband and sons to Restello, intending to join the expedition and witness her sons knighted on the field of battle with swords she had ordered made for them. Her anxiety about their survival she subsumed into fasting and prayer, and into the distribution of largesse to monks and other worthy persons in exchange for their prayers. While her men were preparing the fleet, Philippa spent most of her time in church—where, as it happened, her fellow-supplicants included refugees from an outbreak of the plague in Lisbon. Her family and doctors warned that, weakened by her austerities, she was susceptible to infection, but she refused to leave. She was an old woman, she declared (she was fifty-five), and did not fear death. The plague struck soon after. If it seems ironic that the only family casualty of the Ceuta invasion was the noncombatant queen, one almost gets the sense from Zurara that this was the deal Philippa was after: that she had bargained her life with God in exchange for those of her husband and sons.[59]

Preparations stopped as all attention turned to what was surely one of the Middle Ages' most exemplary deaths. João was devastated to think "of the loss that would follow the death of so good a wife, to whom he had been married for twenty-seven years with no intervention of discord, . . .but rather much love and concord." He could neither eat nor sleep, and those around him feared he would contract the disease himself; only his great physical strength saved him, says Zurara.[60] From her deathbed Philippa presented each son with a fragment of the Holy Cross and with the sword she had prepared for their knighting. In her last hours she joined her hands and addressed the Virgin Mary, whom she seemed to see above her. The priests administered Extreme Unction and intoned the mass of the dead—with Philippa correcting their Latin. Then raising her eyes to Heaven, she died.[61] It was July 18, 1415.

The invasion of Morocco proved successful, and João knighted each son on the field with the sword provided by his mother. Each adopted an Anglo-Norman motto "as if to proclaim to the world that, where chivalry was concerned, they intended particularly to invite comparison with their English relatives."[62] Philippa was buried in the monastery of Odivelas, where her body reportedly gave off a fragrant smell. On October 15, 1416, it was disinterred, transported to Batalha—the monastery built in honor of João's victory at Aljubarrota—and buried in the Founder's Chapel.[63] For Anthony Goodman, Philippa's "role in Portugal is symbolised in her effigy on her tomb in the monastery at Batalha; she clasps her husband João I with one hand and a liturgical book with the other."[64]

Contact with England

Although Philippa apparently settled well into her Portuguese career, her personal staff was largely English, and her English friends and relations remained a strong presence in her life.[65] Writing some ten years after her marriage to ask Richard II to find an English benefice for her chancellor, Adam Davenport, Philippa may have reflected some feeling of homesickness. "Everyone who finds himself outside his own country," she noted, "naturally wishes to return."[66] Philippa never did return home, but old family relationships were maintained and new ones developed nonetheless. In the early 1390s Philippa sent Richard II a lion, which he added to his menagerie in the Tower.[67] In 1392–93 Philippa requested and Richard granted a pardon, "at the supplication of our beloved cousin the queen of Portugal," of an official at the tollbooth in Bishop's (now King's) Lynn, who had killed a boatman, perhaps in a quarrel over tolls.[68] João sent his herald to visit his brother-in-law Henry before the latter's duel with Mowbray in September 1398.[69] Philippa kept her brother informed of her childrens' birth;[70] in 1401 the new King Henry sent the ten-year-old Duarte eight gold collars worth £250.[71] Henry also continued to order and, presumably, send Garter gowns to his sister;[72] and although it was unusual to enroll non-English members, he inducted João into the Order in 1400,[73] while his grandson Henry VI inducted Pedro in 1428, Duarte in 1436, Enrique in 1443, and Duarte's heir Afonso V in 1447.[74] Both Pedro's and Enrique's tombs display the Order's arms.[75] Philippa also concocted or supported a plan to marry João's illegitimate daughter, Beatriz, to Thomas Fitzalan, earl of Arundel.[76] The financial arrangements generated considerable correspondence among Philippa, João, João's agents, Arundel, and Henry, both before and after the marriage on November 26, 1405.[77] In these letters João repeatedly addresses Henry as "Irmaão" ("brother").[78]

Surviving letters also reveal Philippa's surprising friendship with the controversial bishop of Norwich, Henry Despenser. Despenser had won fame for suppressing the Peasants' Revolt in Cambridgeshire, and notoriety for leading an ill-fated "crusade" in 1383 against the Flemish supporters of the anti-pope Clement VII. He was also one of the few magnates to stand by Richard II in his last days.[79] It was bold of Philippa, therefore, to write Archbishop Arundel in 1399, asking him to resolve the ill-will between her brother Henry and Despenser, "a man from whom we have received great kindness and many favors."[80] She notes that she is writing to Henry as well. Some time after, still in 1399, Despenser wrote to thank her for her intervention. He has been ill, he says, but her letters have revived him. The bearer of these letters was Philippa's chamber-lady, Elizabeth Elmham, a native of his diocese, whom he promises to help in some unstated affairs. (Despenser would have had his own reasons for helping Elizabeth: the only Norfolk magnate to join the bishop in support of Richard was Sir William Elmham, who was probably Elizabeth's father.)[81] An undated letter from some calmer time has Philippa thanking Despenser for his second gift to her of cloth of Rennes and fine linen ("drape de Reines et de laune") along with "little purses" ("petitz burses") brought by Arundel Herald and her treasurer, Thomas Payn.[82]

Most of these letters close by informing the recipient that the bearer of the letter will fill them in on further news and details, suggesting a flow not only of practical information but also of court news and gossip.[83] Apart from these personal and familial letters, of course, there was also a constant exchange of communications and embassies between Portugal and England concerning political and mercantile affairs. "Ambassadors frequently stayed for weeks," points out Wendy Childs, "and might be used repeatedly, thus becoming 'specialists' in each other's country, able to pick up news, lifestyle, literature, and ideas, if they were so inclined."[84] Some of the ambassadors were already familiar faces for Philippa or her English household. The courtier-poet John Clanvowe, to whom her father had given a rosary in 1373,[85] shuttled between England and Iberia in 1386, setting up relations with the new rulers.[86] Roger Elmham, a clerk in the Office of the Privy

Seal and a brother or other close male relation of Philippa's chamber-lady Elizabeth Elmham, acted as ambassador to Portugal throughout the 1390s. He had previously served as clerk of the king's works, until succeeded in 1389 by Geoffrey Chaucer.[87] Finally, commerce between Portugal and England kept up a steady interchange of goods and personnel, facilitated by the trade guarantees incorporated in Anglo-Portuguese treaties.[88]

A Policy of Anglophilia

The *Dictionary of National Biography* records approvingly of Philippa of Lancaster that she "enjoyed the reputation of a perfect wife and mother,"[89] and other encomia are not lacking. She was "a model of womanly goodness" to James Hamilton Wylie and "an ensample of godly living" to Sydney Armitage-Smith.[90] Less noticed is Philippa's two-pronged policy, supported by her husband and her brother, of promoting Portugal's national identity and its contacts with England. These policies converged, since the way Philippa could promote national identity for Portugal—and thus assist João's efforts to distinguish it from Castile culturally as well as politically—was by importing elements of her own culture of origin. Isolated at the western tip of Europe, Portugal was eager to cultivate its political and mercantile relations with England, while it was clearly in England's interest to maintain a strong ally on the borders of Castile—a traditional ally of England's traditional enemy, France. An examination of the intricate relations Philippa fostered between her two "home countries" will make an important background against which to evaluate her role in the Gower translations.

Family Stories

Anglophilia seems to have been bred into Philippa's children. The high regard in which they held her, plus the many stories of her family and native country she apparently told them, shaped their characters, and with their characters, their country. Peter Russell, in his biography of Enrique, notes: "It is safe to presume that the young Prince Henry, like his brothers, was much influenced in his formative years by his English mother and the tales she told them of the military victories and the famous deeds of chivalry performed by their Plantagenet ancestors."[91] Duarte grew up with a lively admiration for English military acumen and discipline, which he encouraged Enrique to emulate when planning the invasion of Tangier in 1437. "Bear in mind," he wrote his brother,

> the example of the English who, principally for this reason, continuously win their battles. They make use of [training] in such a way that, wherever they

find themselves and even if they are few and without a captain, they rapidly take up such effective positions that their enemies are made very afraid.[92]

Enrique and Pedro became the first Portuguese dukes, honored by their father with a title imported from England.[93] Pedro displayed his enthusiasm for England by visiting it in 1425, during a tour of Europe; in 1428, to be installed as a knight of the Garter; and in 1429, to attend the coronation of Henry VI. His sister Isabel, as duchess of Burgundy, played a significant role in Anglo-Burgundian relations for several decades after her marriage in 1430.[94]

Cultural Patronage

The familial strategy extended to the royal household and dependencies as well. We have already encountered Philippa's advocacy of the Use of Sarum. "[A]lthough this observance was by no means easy to arrange," as Lopes remarked, she persuaded her chaplains "and other worthy persons" to embrace it.[95] Her sons continued the usage in their private devotions after her death.[96] One other piece of literature may be associated with Philippa's Anglo-inflected piety. The *Orto do esposo* ("Garden of the Spouse"), dated to the late fourteenth or early fifteenth century,[97] is a collection of religious and didactic exempla. One of these tells the story of four robbers who take refuge in a cave, where they find a tomb filled with treasure. One goes into town for food, his mates kill him when he returns, and then the murderers eat the poisoned food brought by their victim and die as well.[98] The resemblance to the "Pardoner's Tale" is clear. Copies of individual Canterbury tales, and/or of the entire collection, could easily have reached Portugal via the same channels that brought the *Confessio Amantis*. The author of the *Orto*, a Cistercian monk named Hermengildo de Tancos, belonged to the Royal Convent and Palace of Santa Maria de Alcobaça, an important center of learning, the burial-place of the preceding dynasty, and also a major owner of land. Religious or business dealings could have brought Hermengildo into contact with the royal household, where someone—perhaps the queen— could have told him the story of the "Pardoner's Tale" (the text would have done him little good, since presumably he did not read English). The *Orto* version may thus present Hermengildo's recollection of that tale, adapted, as exempla readily were, to a new literary context and audience.[99] Supporting the idea that Philippa was involved in such transmission is the fact that two of her sons, Duarte and Pedro, owned copies of the *Orto*.[100]

Another feature of Anglo-Portuguese piety that may be related to Philippa are the devotional sculptures made of Nottingham alabaster that began accumulating in Portuguese churches in the late fourteenth and early fifteenth centuries. Francis Cheetham's recent *Alabaster Images of Medieval England* catalogues fifty-six such plaques surviving in Portuguese churches or collections.[101] Despite their prevalence, very little is known about the provenance of these alabasters. One Coronation of the Virgin, dated to between 1380 and 1420 and found in the parish church of Cernache, near Coimbra, may have belonged to William Arnold, a member of Philippa's household who was given the seignory of Cernache by her son Pedro.[102] It seems logical to assume that other such alabasters found their way to Portugal as imports by Philippa or other English people in her household.

An even more visible product of English influence was Batalha (Battle) Monastery, the greatest monastic building of the period, which was apparently built to English designs. Affinities to English architecture were already visible in the work supervised by Batalha's first architect, the Portuguese Afonso Domingues. When he died in 1402, Philippa replaced him with an architect named Huguet, whose precise origins are obscure but who constructed the Founder's Chapel and other structures with clear English affiliations.[103] The master plans, along with masons to implement it, may have been supplied by Henry Yevele, the great English architect who also designed, among other structures, Westminster Hall and Blanche of Lancaster's tomb.[104] If Philippa didn't contact Yevele directly, she could have had access to him through her acquaintances Roger Elmham or Geoffrey Chaucer, successive clerks of the king's works around the time when Batalha was begun, in 1388.

Philippa's tolerance of or taste for more frivolous pursuits also manifested itself in the importation of those little purses supplied by her friend, Bishop Despenser. She had evidently asked for them, since she thanks him for remembering to send them, and she asks for more, because they are "en deintee" among the ladies of the court.[105] Not only did the queen thus propagate one form of the famous *opus anglicanum* but she also very effectively induced, among an influential population perhaps less interested in liturgies and monasteries, a lively admiration for and identification with English culture.

The Gower Translations

And finally we come to Gower. Scholars have known that a Portuguese translation of Gower's *Confessio Amantis* existed from the headnote of the Castilian translation, which survives as Madrid, Escorial ms. G.II.19:

> This book is called *Confisyon del Amante*, which was written by John Gower, native of the kingdom of England; and it was turned into the Portuguese language by Robert Payne, native of said kingdom, and canon of the city of

Lisbon; and later it was put into the Castilian language by John of Cuenca, householder of the city of Huete.

[{E}ste libro es llamado *confisyon del amante*, el qual conpuso juan goer, natural del rreyno de ynglaterra; e fue tornado en lenguaje portogues por rroberto paym, natural del dicho rreyno e canonjgo de la çibdad de lixboa; e despues fue sacada en lenguaje castellano por juan de cuenca, vesjno de la çibdad de huete.][106]

Linguistic analysis makes it clear that the Castilian was, as the headnote implies, translated from Portuguese, rather than directly from English.[107] In 1995 Antonio Cortijo Ocaña announced that Angel Gómez Moreno had discovered a manuscript in the Biblioteca Real de Palacio of Madrid, which Cortijo Ocaña was able to identify as a copy of the Portuguese translation of the *Confessio*.[108] Palacio II-3088 lacks any headnote explaining the origin of the translation but does include a colophon stating that the manuscript was created in 1430 for Fernando de Castro the Younger ("o Moço"), son of the governor of Ceuta.[109] Both manuscripts are copies from earlier exemplars. The text follows Gower's closely, while replacing his poetry with prose, omitting most of the Latin elements, and condensing throughout.[110]

Peter Russell has found two Portuguese references to a Robert Payn: one from 1402 identifying Ruberte Paym as a well-paid official of Queen Philippa's household; and a Lisbon house-lease from 1430. Payn's name is absent from a later list of Philippa's household, drawn up probably a few years after 1402 but definitely before 1414. Russell hypothesizes that Payn left Philippa's employ some time after 1402 to become a canon at Lisbon Cathedral, at which point he began his translation. The Escorial headnote describes Payn as a native (*natural*) of England, but his Portuguese was so good that he may have grown up among the English merchant colony resident in Lisbon.[111] John Matthews Manly connected the translator with the "Robert Payn, of Whitby, clerk" who left England in early 1390 to seek a benefice from the pope. The connection seems weak; the records do not say whether the Whitby clerk succeeded, or where this benefice was. Manly also found a Robert Payn who "in 1416, shortly after the death of Philippa in Portugal, was appointed rector of Aldeburgh by Sir Gerard Usflete, husband of Elizabeth Duchess of Norfolk, who had been in the household of John of Gaunt."[112] This could have been the translator, repatriating after the death of his patroness—in which case the Lisbon house-lease of 1430 would represent either him returning to Portugal, or the residence of a nephew named after him (see figure 7.2).

Although Payn is a common surname, a number of men of that name also turn up closely associated with Philippa, her brother, and/or royal service, suggesting a family network. A Sir Thomas or Thomas Elie or Thomelim Payn served as treasurer to Philippa and traveled to England on diplomatic missions for her husband; scholars have accepted it as "a reasonable hypothesis," to quote Russell, that Robert Payn was Thomas' son.[113] According to Russell and W.J. Entwistle, Thomas's wife was a Portuguese woman named Antónia Dias d'Arca.[114] Dias d'Arca may have been a second wife, married by a widowed Thomas Payn after he took up service with Philippa. It is also possible, however, that Thomas had married her before 1386 and that she was Robert's mother, supporting the suggestion that Thomas and therefore Robert Payn had experience with Portugal or at least the Portuguese language before Gaunt sailed from Plymouth.

Back in England, a John Payn from Helhoughton, Norfolk, was butler to Philippa's brother, Henry, in which capacity he had dealings with both Geoffrey Chaucer and John Gower.[115] Unremarked by scholars until now, a Robert Payn also served as groom of the royal chamber under both Richard II and Henry IV.[116] Another royal groom, mentioned with Robert in a record of 1400, was Thomas Elys.[117] Since Robert Payn the royal groom was a layman, and placed in England until at least 1400, he is unlikely to be the man who held a high position on Philippa's staff in 1402 and later became a canon of Lisbon. However, he was probably one of the family—as was, perhaps, Thomas Elys, who might hold the key to the mystery of the treasurer's middle name. Figure 7.2 presents a possible genealogy of the Payns (including other known sons of Thomas Payn).[118]

The connections with Philippa are strong: the translator of the *Confessio* was or had been in her household, his father was her treasurer, and other family members were in service with her brother. Philippa's son Duarte owned a copy of the Portuguese *Confessio*—or *Livro do Amante*, as he calls it; he quotes from it in his *Leal conselheiro* of 1438.[119] Fernando de Castro o Moço, the patron of the newly discovered manuscript, was associated with two of Duarte's brothers: he was in Fernando's service and he was related to an important official in Enrique's household.[120] From all these data it should

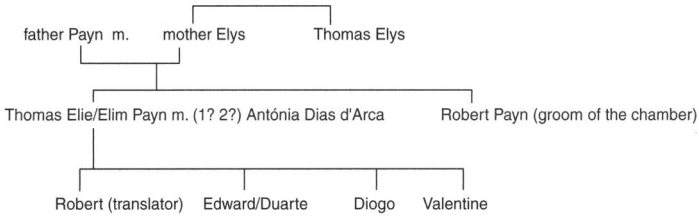

Figure 7.2 Hypothetical reconstruction of Robert Payn's genealogy.

be easy to assume that Philippa, having obtained a copy of the *Confessio* from one of her many English contacts, had then engaged Robert Payn to translate it as a present for her husband, and more generally their court, and that she further had the work translated from Portuguese into Castilian as a gift for her half-sister, Catherine, and her brother-in-law, Enrique III of Castile.

Many authoritative scholars, however, have searched for alternate explanations. In 1930 Manly suggested that Payn obtained and translated the work himself, as a bid for royal favor.[121] Peter Russell, in 1961, asserted that Payn must have translated the book after Philippa's death, in 1415, because his exemplar belonged to the first recension of the *Confessio*, which speaks favorably of the king whom her brother deposed in 1399.[122] In 1975 Robert Warren Hamm credited Philippa's father or brother, who could have intended the translation as "a velvet-gloved reminder of Lancastrian political power in that part of the world."[123] In 1991 Bernardo Santano Moreno argued that the Portuguese translation could not have been created before 1433, when Philippa's newly crowned son instituted regulations that could explain certain monetary values mentioned in the text. This dating led to the theory that King Duarte and his cousin Juan II of Castile may have collaborated on the bilingual translation project.[124] The discovery of Palacio II-3088—a later exemplar of the Portuguese translation whose colophon dates it to 1430—doesn't seem to have reduced the popularity of the Duarte–Juan theory in some circles. Most recently, R.F. Yeager has surveyed a wide range of potential initiators or sponsors of the translations, including Philippa, her father, her stepmother, her brother, her half-sister Catherine, her son Duarte, Payn himself, other unspecified members of Philippa's or Gaunt's entourages, English merchants resident in Lisbon, Richard II, and Gower's executor, Sir Arnold Savage.[125]

Can it be a coincidence that most of the alternative initiators proposed by these scholars are male? Not all of the scholars who speculate about the Iberian *Confessio*'s exclude Philippa, but none pays sufficient attention to the web of associations that link her to the Payn family and to the prospective owners and readers of the translations. Nor has any scholar—even Russell, who cowrote a short biography of Philippa in 1940[126]—discovered more in her than the hyper-pious and dutiful daughter, wife, and mother. The account of her life in Portugal assembled here allows us to broaden that perspective considerably. Philippa of Lancaster imported English liturgy, exempla, alabasters, architecture, and purses, spreading anglophilia across many levels of Portuguese society. She imbued all her children with pride in their Lancastrian lineage, building and maintaining their connections with their English relations. This was a policy motivated not only by personal loyalty and Plantagenet nostalgia, but very pragmatically by her desire to bolster Anglo-Portuguese relations and to foster a sense of Portuguese identity. Most of her importations combined popular appeal with a religious or didactic angle, a pattern into which Gower's *Confessio* fits seamlessly. The *Confessio* is precisely the sort of book Philippa and João would have enjoyed, and that they would have thought suitable for their children and for the Portuguese court upon which they were trying to impose their rather puritanical lifestyle.

The difficulties raised by various scholars are not hard to counter. It need not surprise us that the translations are based on the first recension of the *Confessio*. It isn't even necessary to argue that that was the version Philippa had received and therefore proceeded with, or that the translation was begun before the later recensions were created—though either or both statements may be true. The first recension was by far the most popular; it survives in twenty-five exemplars, while there are only seven of the second recension and fifteen of the third.[127] The *Confessio* manuscripts owned by Henry IV himself, and by his sons, were all either first or second recension.[128] It was the version with the best mix of "lust" and "lore";[129] Gower's later recensions became increasingly angry and didactic, with a consequent decline in entertainment value. Philippa had known Richard all her life, and though she surely supported her brother there is no reason to suppose she despised Richard, after or before 1399; remember the letters she wrote in defense of Bishop Despenser and her patronage of William Elmham's daughter, both men who had championed Richard to the end. And of course the first recension also includes a flattering reference to Philippa's brother, then earl of Derby.[130] Finally, Russell points to Richard's special status in Portuguese eyes: "For John I and his sons Richard II was the English king who had signed the 1386 alliance with Portugal, and had come to the aid of John I at a critical moment of the struggle to maintain Portuguese independence."[131]

While some scholars favor Duarte (r. 1433–38) as patron of the translations, no one has offered convincing evidence that would mandate a later dating. Manuel Alvar, author of a detailed linguistic examination of the Castilian translation, in the prologue to an edition of that translation, accepts without question the Portuguese version's association with Philippa of Lancaster.[132] Although often mixed into the discussion, the dates and relatively humble nature of the two surviving manuscripts are irrelevant, since both are copies of earlier exemplars. Moreover, if Robert Payn was mature enough to hold an important position in Philippa's household in 1402, how likely is it that over thirty years later he would be willing or able to translate Gower's lengthy book? Or that, long after his mother's death, Duarte would remember the *Confessio* and understand it well enough to decide to sponsor a lengthy and expensive translation process? Philippa had motive, method, and opportunity; the evidence associates the Portuguese translation and its propagation with people linked to her household. Occam's Razor makes her the most likely candidate.

The same argument extends easily to the Castilian translation. No one has been able to discover more about the translator, Juan de Cuenca, than what the Escorial manuscript tells us in its headnote. His hometown of Huete, however, is known to be associated with the Lancasters. As part of the peace-arrangements between John of Gaunt and Juan I in 1388, the Castilian king presented the town to Constanza of Castile.[133] Once Constanza returned to England, her daughter Catherine administered the property for her.[134] A Lancastrian looking for a Castilian–Portuguese bilingual, therefore, was perhaps more likely to look for one in Huete than elsewhere. The date of the translation is also uncertain. Bernardo Santano Moreno quotes an authority from 1788 who dated the work, citing the Escorial manuscript, to ca. 1404. Santano Moreno himself disputes this, pointing out that the Escorial headnote calls Huete a city (*çibdad*), a status it did not attain until July 26, 1428.[135] Since the Escorial manuscript is a copy of an earlier exemplar, however, we cannot be sure that the scribe who copied or created the headnote did not simply update this piece of information—if, indeed, we are to suppose that the distinction between city and town was maintained so rigorously in nonlegal contexts.

Yeager, like several other scholars, explores the idea of the two halfsisters operating in parallel, each commissioning a translation of the *Confessio*.[136] If Catherine had commissioned a Castilian rendition, however, surely the translator would have worked directly from the English. As Yeager amply proves, the Lancastrian household had long included Castilian members;[137] there would have been no difficulty in finding someone, either in Castile or England, who could turn Gower's English into Spanish. But the Spanish *Confessio* was, as its headnote tells us and as the linguistic evidence confirms, produced from the Portuguese version. At a minimum this means that whoever sponsored the Castilian translation was endorsing the Philippian text, even if Philippa herself was not directly involved. But given Philippa's pattern of commissioning and disseminating influential cultural artifacts, it seems likely enough that the Castilian *Confessio* was another such production— whether she had the book translated in Portugal, or sent it to Catherine for translation in Castile. Sisterly love could be one motivation for such a gift; the establishment and maintenance of good relations between rulers could be another, given that much of João's policy throughout his reign focused on creating a stable peace with Castile.

★ ★ ★

Anyone who has had the fortune and the time to read Froissart, Lopes, or Zurara would know how intimately the life of Philippa of Lancaster, and of many other women, was interwoven with history. For these medieval chroniclers, dynastic marriages were as important as battles, and the relations among spouses and children as crucial, at times, as those among rulers. Women's actions, modulated through their familial roles or exerted directly, had significant effect. All of this, oddly, vanishes when one reads the modern historians. Again and again I had the experience, in this research, of turning from a richly complex medieval account of events to a modern one, and finding that only the "hard" stuff, the battles and power struggles, had filtered through. Much of the account of Philippa's life given here has lain fallow in the medieval sources, simultaneously too "soft" or romantic and too powerful for the armor-plated machismo that has characterized much scholarship since the mid-twentieth century.

Literary scholars, too, have often contrived to edit Philippa out of the record. A good deal of effort has been expended to offset the most obvious and likely explanation for the existence of Portuguese and Castilian versions of Gower's *Confessio Amantis*—that is, the one crediting Philippa with the initiative of having the work translated. The reasons for ascribing one or both translations to other agents, or for placing them after Philippa's death, are not very substantial and seem sometimes to reflect the desire—also manifest in discussions of the propagation of the Flower and Leaf motif[138]—to avoid having to acknowledge a female as instigator of an important literary event.

Notes

1. According to G.C. Macaulay, Gower's first modern editor, the *Confessio* was thus "the earliest English book which made its way beyond the limits of its own language": "Introduction," in John Gower, *The English Works of John Gower*, ed. Macaulay, EETS e.s. 81, Vol. 1 (London: Kegan Paul, Trench, Trübner, 1900), p. vii [vii–clxxiv]. Peter Russell, noting the precedence of the *Ancrene Riwle*, reassuringly decides that "at any rate Gower's poem was probably the earliest work of pure literature in English to be translated into another language": "Robert Payn and Juan de Cuenca, Translators of John Gower's *Confessio Amantis*," *Medium Aevum* 30 (1961): 26 [26–32]. A discussion of this point, by a tableful of medievalists becalmed in the Kalamazoo airport in 2004, produced two further candidates, one at least of which also qualifies as "pure literature": the lost or unidentified English text that Marie de France cites as a source for her *Fables* (contributed by Erik Kooper), and *Olive and Landres*, a Scottish romance that survives only in Norwegian translation (contributed by Felicity Riddy).
2. For a discussion of Philippa's life and activities before arriving in Iberia, see my essay, "The Flower, the Leaf, and Philippa of Lancaster," in *Rethinking the "Legend of Good Women": Context and Reception*, ed. Carolyn Collette (Cambridge, UK: Boydell & Brewer, 2006), pp. 33–58.

3. Fernão Lopes, *Crónica del Rei Dom João de boa memoria*, ed. and trans. Derek W. Lomax and R.J. Oakley, in Lomax and Oakley, eds., *The English in Portugal, 1367–87* (Warminster, UK: Aris & Phillips, 1988), pp. 236–37 [155–356]. Lopes's encomium is echoed by a later chronicler: Gomes Eanes de Zurara, *Crónica da tomada da Ceuta por el rei D. João I*, ed. Francisco Maria Esteves Pereira (Lisbon: Academia das Sciências de Lisboa, 1915), pp. 141–43.
4. Sydney Armitage-Smith, *John of Gaunt: King of Castile and Leon, Duke of Aquitaine and Lancaster, Earl of Derby, Lincoln, and Leicester, Seneschal of England* (1904; repr. New York: Barnes & Noble, 1964), p. 415.
5. "...em sua moçidade era deuota e nos diuinaaes offiçios sperta": Lopes, *Crónica*, II, chap. 98; ed. and trans. Lomax and Oakley, pp. 236–37.
6. Ana Echevarría, "Catalina of Lancaster, the Castilian Monarchy and Coexistence," in *Medieval Spain: Culture, Conflict, and Coexistence: Studies in Honour of Angus MacKay*, ed. Roger Collins and Anthony Goodman (Houndmills, UK: Palgrave, 2002), p. 80 [79–122].
7. *John of Gaunt's Register*, ed. Sydney Armitage–Smith, 2 vols., Camden 3rd ser., vols. 20–21 (London: Camden Society, 1911), 2:191, 193, 296; *John of Gaunt's Register, 1379–1383*, 2 vols., ed. Eleanor C. Lodge and Robert Somerville, Camden 3rd ser., vols. 56–57 (London: Camden Society, 1937), 1:110, 111, 179, 230, 231; 2:297; Mary Anne Everett Wood, ed., *Letters of Royal and Illustrious Ladies of Great Britain, from the Commencement of the Twelfth Century to the Close of the Reign of Queen Mary*, 3 vols. (London: Colburn, 1846), 1:78.
8. A Flemish chronicle claims the count "amoit le fille au duc de Lenclastre" ("loved the duke of Lancaster's daughter"): *Istore et croniques de Flandres, d'après les textes de divers manuscrits*, ed. Kervyn de Lettenhove, 2 vols. (Brussels: Hayez, 1879–80), 2:384.
9. See Coleman, "The Flower, the Leaf, and Philippa of Lancaster"; see also Coleman, "'A bok for king Richardes sake': Royal Patronage, the *Confessio*, and the *Legend of Good Women*," in *John Gower: Essays at the Millennium*, ed. R.F. Yeager (Kalamazoo: Medieval Institute Publications, in press).
10. Geoffrey Chaucer, *The Riverside Chaucer*, 3rd ed., gen. ed. Larry D. Benson (Oxford: Oxford University Press, 1987), LGW F:72, see also G:69–70; John Gower, *The English Works of John Gower*, 2 vols., ed. G.C. Macaulay, EETS e.s. 81–82 (London: Kegan Paul, Trench, Trübner, 1900–1), CA 8:2467–68; Sir John Clanvowe, *The Works of Sir John Clanvowe*, ed. V.J. Scattergood (Cambridge, UK: Brewer, 1975), ll. 26–27.
11. P.E. Russell, *The English Intervention in Spain and Portugal in the Time of Edward III and Richard II* (Oxford: Clarendon Press, 1955), pp. 174–75.
12. Elias Ashmole, *The Institution, Laws & Ceremonies of the Most Noble Order of the Garter* (London, 1672; repr. Baltimore: Genealogical Publishing Co., 1971), pp. 69–70.
13. Russell, *The English Intervention*, pp. 352–439.
14. There is no complete English translation of Lopes or Zurara. I have used Derek Lomax and R.J. Oakley's partial, bilingual edition of Lopes, whose

Portuguese text is based on Entwistle's 1968 edition; Fernão Lopes, *Crónica del Rei Dom Joham I de boa memoria e dos reis de Portugal o decimo*, Part 2, ed. William J. Entwistle (Lisbon: Imprensa Nacional-Casa da Moeda, 1968). Other translations are from secondary sources, with the Portuguese provided from Entwistle. For Zurara I have used Edgar Prestage's *Chronicles of Fernão Lopes and Gomes Eanes de Zurara* (Watford, UK: Voss & Michael, 1928), along with Virginia de Castro e Almeida's unsatisfactory *Conquests and Discoveries of Henry the Navigator*, trans. Bernard Miall (London: Allen & Unwin, 1936) as well as secondary sources; the Portuguese comes from Pereira's edition of 1915. I provide chapters for all citations of Lopes and Zurara, so that readers can locate the texts in different editions. T.W.E. Roche's short biography *Philippa: Dona Filipa of Portugal* (London: Phillimore, 1971) was written by a journalist on commission from the Portuguese tourism board; like the shorter notices in E. Thornton Cook and Catherine Moran's *Royal Daughters* (London: Heath Cranton, 1935), pp. 46–64, and Rose Macaulay's *They Went to Portugal* (London: Jonathan Cape, 1946), pp. 34–44, the information provided is unreliable.
15. Russell, *The English Intervention*, pp. 438–50; see also Lopes, *Crónica*, II, chaps. 123–26; ed. and trans. Lomax and Oakley, pp. 308–29 and 353 n1 to chap. 94.
16. "...ne luy vaulroit riens": Jean Froissart, *Oeuvres: Chroniques*, Vol. 11: *1383–1386*, ed. Kervyn de Lettenhove (Brussels: Victor Devaux, 1870), pp. 430–33, quote from p. 431.
17. Lopes, *Crónica*, II, chap. 94; ed. and trans. Lomax and Oakley, pp. 226–27, 353 n2 to chap. 94.
18. "...sur ung lit courtoisement, ainsi comme espous et espouse doivent estre": Jean Froissart, *Oeuvres: Chroniques*, Vol. 12: *1386–1389*, ed. Kervyn de Lettenhove (Brussels: Devaux, 1871), pp. 90–91, quote from p. 91.
19. Chaucer, *Canterbury Tales*, 2:267–71.
20. Russell, *The English Intervention*, p. 450.
21. Lopes, *Crónica*, II, chap. 94; ed. and trans. Lomax and Oakley, pp. 228–29.
22. Just as well, since the papal approval didn't come through until 1391. See W.J. Entwistle and P.E. Russell, "A Rainha D. Felipa e a sua côrte," in *Congresso do mundo português, Memórias e comunicações apresentadas ao Congresso de História Medieval (II Congresso)*, Vol. 2 (Lisbon: Comissão Executiva dos Centenários, 1940), 326 [317–46]).
23. Russell, *The English Intervention*, pp. 450–51.
24. "...nom himdo aredados huum do outro, mas ambos jguall": Lopes, *Crónica*, II, chap. 96; ed. and trans. Lomax and Oakley, pp. 232–33.
25. Lopes, *Crónica*, II, chaps. 96–99; ed. and trans. Lomax and Oakley, pp. 232–41.
26. Russell, *The English Intervention*, pp. 486–87; Lopes, *Crónica*, II, chap. 115; ed. and trans. Lomax and Oakley, pp. 286–87.
27. Lopes, *Crónica*, II, chap. 116; ed. and trans. Lomax and Oakley, pp. 286–89.
28. "...nom fallauom em nenhuum cobro que ao regno poer podessem, saluo nos camjnhos claros e abertos, como Portugal per sua morte de todo

ponto era perdido"; "que se qujsesse amerçear do seu desemparo, e assy como Mestra de Mysericordia prouese de saude ao seu desejado marido" (Lopes, *Crónica*, II, chap. 116; ed. and trans. Lomax and Oakley, pp. 288–89).

29. Lopes, *Crónica*, II, chap. 116; ed. and trans. Lomax and Oakley, pp. 288–89; Russell, *The English Intervention*, pp. 490–93.
30. "...por sollaçar com a Rainha, sa filha, que nom sabia quamdo a auya de uer": Lopes, *Crónica*, II, chap. 118; ed. and trans. Lomax and Oakley, pp. 292–93.
31. Lopes, *Crónica*, II, chaps. 118–19; ed. and trans. Lomax and Oakley, 292–97.
32. Russell, *The English Intervention*, pp. 456–94.
33. Lopes, *Crónica*, II, chap. 97; ed. and trans. Lomax and Oakley, pp. 234–35.
34. Peter Russell, *Prince Henry "the Navigator": A Life* (New Haven: Yale University Press, 2000), p. 25.
35. "Deus outorgou marido comcordauell a sseu deseio": Lopes, *Crónica*, II, chap. 98; ed. and trans. Lomax and Oakley, pp. 236–37.
36. Lopes, *Crónica*, II, chaps. 136, 140, 141; ed. Entwistle, 2:277–80, 288, 290.
37. Lopes, *Crónica*, II, chap. 148; ed. Entwistle, 2:306.
38. "...posto que gram casa de fremosas molheres trouuesse quamto liuremente em semelhante feito podera comprir seu deseio. Homrou muyto e amou sua molher dhonesto e saão amor": Lopes, *Crónica*, II, Prologue; ed. Entwistle, 2:3; my thanks to Amélia Hutchinson for the translation.
39. London, BL Cotton Nero B.i, fols. 27–28v.; printed in F.C. Hingeston, ed. and trans., *Royal and Historical Letters during the Reign of Henry the Fourth, King of England and France and Lord of Ireland*, 2 vols., Rolls Series 18 (London, 1860 and 1965), Vol. 1, No. 83 [pp. 228–29].
40. Lopes, *Crónica*, II, Prologue; ed. Entwistle, 2:2.
41. A.H. de Oliveira Marques, *Daily Life in Portugal in the Late Middle Ages*, trans. S.S. Wyatt (Madison: University of Wisconsin Press, 1971), p. 236.
42. Charity Cannon Willard, "The Patronage of Isabel of Portugal," in *The Cultural Patronage of Medieval Women*, ed. June Hall McCash (Athens: University of Georgia Press, 1996), p. 310 [306–20].
43. "Guilherme de Machado nom fez tam fermosa concordança de melodia, nem que tam bem pareça, como a fazem os caães quando bem correm": Joao I, *Livro da montaria*, in *Obras dos príncipes de Avis*, ed. M. Lopes de Almeida (Porto: Lello & Irmão, 1981), p. 17 [1–232]; translated in de Oliveira Marques, *Daily Life*, p. 260.
44. De Oliveira Marques, *Daily Life*, pp. 244, 251–52, 261, quote from p. 257.
45. "...el-Rey consygo os noyuos a camara da Raynha, e ally dise a cada huum aquella que reçebesse; a cujo mamdado nam ouue contradiçam": Lopes, *Crónica*, II, chap. 139; ed. Entwistle, 2:283–84, quote from p. 283; translated in de Oliveira Marques, *Daily Life*, p. 173.
46. Lopes, *Crónica*, II, chap. 139; ed. Entwistle, 2:284–87.
47. H.V. Livermore, *A History of Portugal* (Cambridge, UK: Cambridge University Press, 1947), p. 181.
48. Lopes, *Crónica*, II, chap. 148; ed. Entwistle, 2:306.

49. Russell, *Prince Henry*, p. 14.
50. See, for example, Jorge de Sena, "O vitorianismo de Dona Filipa de Lancaster," in *Estudos de história e de cultura*, Ser. 1a, Vol. 1 (Lisbon: Edição Revista "Ocidente," 1963), pp. 93–100.
51. Rita Costa Gomes, *The Making of a Court Society: Kings and Nobles in Late Medieval Portugal*, trans. Alison Aiken (Cambridge, UK: Cambridge University Press, 2003), pp. 69–70.
52. Russell, *Prince Henry*, p. 19.
53. Trans. in de Oliveira Marques, *Daily Life*, p. 236.
54. Russell, *Prince Henry*, pp. 19–20.
55. Susan Groag Bell, "Medieval Women Book Owners: Arbiters of Lay Piety and Ambassadors of Culture," *Signs: Journal of Women in Culture and Society* 7 (1982): 742–68.
56. Charity Cannon Willard, "A Portuguese Translation of Christine de Pisan's *Livre des trois vertus*," *PMLA* 78 (1963): 459–64; Willard, "Isabel of Portugal and the French Translation of the *Triunfo de las donas*," *Revue belge de philologie et d'histoire* 43 (1965): 961–69; Willard, "The Patronage of Isabel of Portugal."
57. ". . .inclita geração"; cited in Anthony Goodman, *John of Gaunt: The Exercise of Princely Power in Fourteenth-Century Europe* (New York: St. Martin's Press, 1992), p. 136.
58. Willard, "The Patronage of Isabel of Portugal," p. 308.
59. Zurara, *Ceuta*, chaps. 37–38; ed. Pereira, pp. 116–22.
60. "Da quall cousa el Rey estaua muy anojado, como aquelle que conhecia a perda que sse lhe seguia per morte de tam boa molher, com a quall auia uijmte e sete annos que estaua casado, ssem nehũ amtrepoimento de desacordo, . . .amte mujto amor e comcordia": Zurara, *Ceuta*, chap. 39; ed. Pereira, p. 124; my translation.
61. Zurara, *Ceuta*, chaps. 44–45; ed. Pereira, pp. 134–40; trans. Prestage, pp. 76–79.
62. Russell, *Prince Henry*, p. 23.
63. James Hamilton Wylie, *History of England under Henry the Fourth*, 4 vols. (1894–98; repr. New York: AMS Press, 1969), 2:333.
64. Goodman, *John of Gaunt*, p. 364.
65. Russell, *The English Intervention*, pp. 542–43.
66. ". . .come chescun esteant hors de son propre paijs de naturele inclinacioun desire de resorter a ycelle": M. Dominica Legge, ed., *Anglo-Norman Letters and Petitions from All Souls MS. 182*, Anglo-Norman Text Society 3 (Oxford: Blackwell, 1941), no. 28 [pp. 73–74, quote from p. 73].
67. Goodman, *John of Gaunt*, p. 20.
68. The pardon, "ad supplicationem dilecte consanguinee nostre Regina portugalie," is dated January 5, 1393; National Archives, Public Record Office, Patent Rolls, C66/336, rot. 13; *CPR 1391–1396*, p. 206. Two more pardons "at the supplication of the queen" follow the Lynn one in the *Calendar of Patent Rolls*, but consultation of the roll itself reveals that the queen in question was Anne of Bohemia, not Philippa. There is no indication how Philippa came to know of this murder and to intercede on the murderer's

behalf; the bishop of Bishop's Lynn at the time, however, was her friend Henry Despenser (see below).
69. Michael Bennett, *Richard II and the Revolution of 1399* (Thrup: Sutton, 1999), p. 132.
70. Entwistle and Russell, "A Rainha D. Felipa," 335, 346 n3.
71. Wendy R. Childs, "Anglo-Portuguese Relations in the Fourteenth Century," in *The Age of Richard II*, ed. James L. Gillespie (Stroud: Sutton, 1997), p. 43 [27–49].
72. Philippa had been a member of the Order since 1379. See Hugh E.L. Collins, *The Order of the Garter, 1348–1461: Chivalry and Politics in Late Medieval England* (Oxford: Clarendon Press, 2000), p. 302. Records cited by George Frederick Beltz show Garter robes being ordered for both Philippa and João in 1401 and 1409, and for João alone in 1408; *Memorials of the Most Noble Order of the Garter, from Its Foundation to the Present Time* (London: Pickering, 1841), pp. xiv–xv, xvii.
73. Collins, *The Order of the Garter*, p. 179.
74. Childs, "Anglo-Portuguese Relations," 44.
75. Russell, *Prince Henry*, p. 409 n24.
76. Lopes, *Crónica*, II, chap. 204; ed. Entwistle, 2:458–61.
77. Philippa: London, BL Cotton Vesp. F.iii, fol. 47 (Hingeston, ed. and trans., *Royal and Historical Letters*, Vol. 2, No. 193 [pp. 99–102]); Alfonso Miedosa: London, BL Cotton Nero B.i, fols. 31–32v. (Hingeston, no. 192 [pp. 96–99]); João: Cotton Nero B.i, fols. 33–33v. (Hingeston, no. 190 [pp. 87–91], fols. 34–34v. (Hingeston, no. 189 [pp. 83–86]), fols. 35–35v. (Hingeston, no. 191 [pp. 92–95]); Thomas Fitzalan: BL Cotton Nero B.i, fols. 30–30v.
78. Hingeston, ed. and trans., *Royal and Historical Letters*, Vol. 2, No. 190, p. 88 (pp. 87–91); Vol. 2, No. 191, pp. 92–93 (pp. 92–95).
79. *Dictionary of National Biography*, 5:861–62.
80. "...un homme de qi nous avons receuz grande bien vuillance et pluseurs bienfaitz": Legge, ed., *Anglo-Norman Letters*, No. 287 (pp. 347–48, quote from p. 347).
81. Simon Walker, *The Lancastrian Affinity, 1361–1399* (Oxford: Clarendon Press, 1990), p. 206; Russell, *The English Intervention*, p. 542.
82. Legge, ed., *Anglo-Norman Letters*, No. 307 (pp. 372–73; quote from p. 372). Russell dates this letter to between 1400 and 1402 ("Robert Payn and Juan de Cuenca," p. 29).
83. See, for example, Legge, ed., *Anglo-Norman Letters*, No. 307, pp. 372–73.
84. Childs, "Anglo-Portuguese Relations," pp. 44–45.
85. *John of Gaunt's Register*, 2:192.
86. Thomas Rymer, *Foedera, conventiones, litterae, et cujuscunque generis acta publica inter reges Angliae, et alios quosvis imperatores, reges, pontifices, principes, vel communitates*, 3rd ed., rev. George Holmes (1740; repr. Farnborough, Hants.: Gregg Press, 1967), Vol. 3, Pt. 3, p. 200 (old style 8: 513–14); V.J. Scattergood, "Introduction," in Scattergood, ed., *The Works of Sir John Clanvowe* (Cambridge, UK: Brewer, 1975), p. 26 [9–31].

PHILIPPA OF LANCASTER 163

87. Edouard Perroy, ed., *The Diplomatic Correspondence of Richard II*, Camden 3rd Ser. 48 (London: Camden Society, 1933), pp. 91–93, 135, 140–41, 228–29; Martin M. Crow and Clair C. Olson, eds., *Chaucer Life-Records* (Austin: University of Texas Press, 1966), pp. 336 n1, 402, 404–08, 411–13; *Calendar of Patent Rolls 1385–1389*, p. 379; John H. Harvey, *Henry Yevele, c. 1320 to 1400: The Life of an English Architect*, 2nd ed. (London: Batsford, 1946), pp. 42–43.
88. Childs, "Anglo-Portuguese Relations," 40–41, 46.
89. *Dictionary of National Biography*, 15:1053.
90. Wylie, *History of England*, 2:332; Armitage-Smith, *John of Gaunt*, p. 178.
91. Russell, *Prince Henry*, p. 22.
92. Quoted and translated in Russell, *Prince Henry*, pp. 171–72.
93. *Dicionário de história de Portugal*, ed. Joel Serrã, Vol. 2 (Lisbon: Iniciativas Editoriais, 1975), p. 344.
94. C. Terlinden, "Les relations de famille entre les maisons souveraines de Belqique et de Portugal," in *Congresso do mundo português: Memórias e comunicações apresentadas ao Congresso de História Medieval (II Congresso)* (Lisbon: Comissão Executiva dos Centenários, 1940), pp. 214–18 [197–220]; Childs, "Anglo–Portuguese Relations," 44.
95. "...e por o el seia nom bem ligeiro dordenar, assy hera em esto atemta, que seus capellaães e outras honestas pessoas reçebiam nelle pera ella emsinamça": Lopes, *Crónica*, chap. 98; ed. and trans. Lomax and Oakley, pp. 236–37.
96. De Oliveira Marques, *Daily Life*, p. 221.
97. *Orto do esposo*, 2 vols., ed. Bertil Maler (Rio de Janeiro: Instituto Nactional do Livro, 1956).
98. *Orto do esposo*, ed. Maler, 1:240–41.
99. Frederick J. Williams, "Chaucer's 'The Pardoner's Tale' and 'The Tale of the Four Thieves' from Portugal's *Orto do Esposo* Compared," *Bulletin des études portugaises et bresiliennes* 44–45 (1983–85): 100–2 [93–109]. The notes in the *Riverside Chaucer* date the Pardoner's Introduction, Prologue, and Tale to the mid-1390s (Chaucer, *The Riverside Chaucer*, p. 905).
100. Julia Dias-Ferreira, "Another Portuguese Analogue of Chaucer's *Pardoner's Tale*," *Chaucer Review* 11 (1977): 258, 260 n4 [258–60]; João José Alves Dias, ed., *Livro dos conselhos de el-rei D. Duarte (Livro da cartuxa), edição diplomática*, rev. A.H. de Oliveira Marques and Teresa F. Rodrigues (Lisbon: Editorial Estampa, 1982), p. 208; see also Williams, "Chaucer's 'The Pardoner's Tale.'"
101. Francis Cheetham, *Alabaster Images of Medieval England* (Woodbridge: Boydell Press, 2004), pp. 204–05. A decade earlier, however, Alice Berkeley and Susan Lowndes, in *English Art in Portugal*, counted "nearly one hundred Nottingham alabasters in Portugal" (Lisbon: Edições Inapa, 1994), p. 33.
102. Pedro Dias, "Alabastros medievais ingleses em Portugal: Subsídios para a sua inventariação e estudo região das Beiras," *Biblos* 55 (1979): 270–71, 275 [259–87]; Berkeley and Lowndes, *English Art in Portugal*, pp. 30–34.

103. John Harvey, with Arthur Oswald, *English Medieval Architects: A Biographical Dictionary down to 1550* (Gloucester: Sutton, 1984), p. 152.
104. Harvey, *Henry Yevele*, pp. 13–14, 35, 45. See also Berkeley and Lowndes, *English Art in Portugal*, pp. 22–26.
105. Legge, *Anglo-Norman Letters*, No. 307, p. 372. R.F. Yeager assumes a more general fashion for the purses, interpreting the "trussyngcofres" Henry IV sent to his half-sister Catherine of Lancaster in 1411 as "small purses": "Gower's Lancastrian Affinity: The Iberian Connection," *Viator* 35 (2004): 492–93 n40 [483–515], citing the *Calendar of Close Rolls 1409–1413*, pp. 244–45. More likely, the "two pairs of great 'trussyngcofres' " cited in the Close Rolls (p. 245) were packing cases ("trussing coffers," *Oxford English Dictionary*, 2nd ed., 18:623) used to hold the fancy cloths Henry was sending his sister.
106. Madrid, Escorial G.II.19, fol. ir.a.1–b.1; cited and translated in Robert Warren Hamm, "An Analysis of the *Confisyon del Amante*, the Castilian Translation of Gower's *Confessio Amantis*," Ph.D. dissertation (University of Tennessee, 1975), p. 6.
107. Karl Pietschl, cited in John Matthews Manly, "On the Question of the Portuguese Translation of Gower's *Confessio Amantis*," *Modern Philology* 27 (1930): 467 [467–72].
108. Antonio Cortijo Ocaña, "La traducción portuguesa de la *Confessio Amantis* de John Gower," *Euphrosyne* n.s. 23 (1995): 458–59 [457–66].
109. Cortijo Ocaña, "La traducción portuguesa," 457–59; Antonio Cortijo Ocaña, "*O livro do Amante*: The Lost Portuguese Translation of John Gower's *Confessio Amantis* (Madrid, Biblioteca de Palacio, MS II–3088)," *Portuguese Studies* 13 (1997): 4 [1–6].
110. Hamm, "An Analysis," pp. iii–iv.
111. Russell, "Robert Payn and Juan de Cuenca," pp. 28–31.
112. Manly, "On the Question of the Portuguese Translation," pp. 470–71.
113. Manly, "On the Question of the Portuguese Translation," p. 467; Russell, "Robert Payn and Juan de Cuenca," pp. 29–30, quote from p. 30.
114. Entwistle and Russell, "A Rainha D. Felipa," p. 336.
115. Manly, "On the Question of the Portuguese Translation," 467–68; Walker, *The Lancastrian Affinity*, p. 203.
116. *Calendar of Patent Rolls 1381–1385*, p. 398; *CPR 1391–1396*, p. 469; *CPR 1399–1401*, pp. 323, 344. Manly discovered and listed these Patent Roll citations, but simply folded the groom of the royal chamber into his unexplicated category of five laymen named Robert Payn who "do not deserve individual record" ("On the Question of the Portuguese Translation," 469, 469 n3).
117. The *Calendar of Patent Rolls* entry, dated July 13, 1400, reads: "Notification that the king wishes the following, who receive fees and annuities from him, to stay on the service and about the body of his kinswoman the queen, to be excused from coming to him on his present journey to Scotland, viz. . . .Robert Payn, William Floure, Thomas Elys and Robert Jolyf, grooms of the chamber" (*CPR 1399–1401*, p. 323).

118. For Edward/Duarte and Diogo, see Russell, "Robert Payn and Juan de Cuenca," 29; for Valentine, see Mário Martins, "Dum poema inglês de John Gower e da sua tradução do português para o castelhano," *Didaskalia* 9 (1979): 413 [413–31].
119. Russell, "Robert Payn and Juan de Cuenca," 28. A list of Duarte's books, compiled between 1433 and 1438, includes one labeled "o amante": *Livro dos conselhos*, ed. Alves Dias, p. 207.
120. Cortijo Ocaña, "*O livro do Amante*," p. 4.
121. Manly, "On the Question of the Portuguese Translation," p. 471.
122. Russell, "Robert Payn and Juan de Cuenca," pp. 31–32.
123. Hamm, "An Analysis," p. 19.
124. Bernardo Santano Moreno, "The Fifteenth-Century Portuguese and Castilian Translations of John Gower, *Confessio Amantis*," *Manuscripta* 35 (1991): 31 [23–34].
125. Yeager, "Gower's Lancastrian Affinity."
126. Entwistle and Russell, "A Rainha D. Felipa."
127. Macaulay, "Introduction," pp. cxxxviii–clxvii.
128. Joel Fredell, "Reading the Dream Miniature in the *Confessio Amantis*," *Medievalia et Humanistica* n.s. 22 (1995): 63 [61–93].
129. Gower, *Confessio Amantis*, Prol.: 17, 19.
130. Gower, *Confessio Amantis*, 8: following l. 3172.
131. Russell, "Robert Payn and Juan de Cuenca," p. 31.
132. Manuel Alvar, "Prólogo," in *John Gower: Confesión del Amante. Traducción de Juan de Cuenca (s. xv)*, ed. Elena Alvar, Anejos del Boletín de la Real Academia Española 45 (Madrid, 1990), pp. 17–18 [1–134].
133. Russell, *The English Intervention*, p. 519.
134. Echevarría, "Catalina of Lancaster," p. 84.
135. Santano Moreno, "The Fifteenth-Century Portuguese and Castilian Translations," p. 27.
136. Yeager, "Gower's Lancastrian Affinity," pp. 484, 491–92, 512.
137. Yeager, "Gower's Lancastrian Affinity," pp. 501–05.
138. See Coleman, "The Flower, the Leaf, and Philippa of Lancaster."

CHAPTER 8

"OS DOZE DE INGLATERRA": A ROMANCE OF ANGLO-PORTUGUESE RELATIONS IN THE LATER MIDDLE AGES?

Amélia P. Hutchinson

This essay analyses the episode known as The Twelve of England as an icon of Anglo-Portuguese relations in the later Middle Ages

The episode known as "Os Doze de Inglaterra," The Twelve of England in English, can be considered an icon of Anglo-Portuguese relations at the end of the fourteenth century. Militarily, politically, and commercially, such relations are celebrated by the Treaty of Windsor signed in 1386. This was a comprehensive alliance with specific clauses sealing the friendship between the two maritime nations, strengthened by the marriage of João I of Portugal to Philippa of Lancaster, John of Gaunt's elder daughter by his first wife, Blanche of Lancaster.[1] Complementary trade interests, similar objectives, and shared enemies contributed to the success and longevity of the alliance, which has survived to the twenty-first century.

In the third quarter of the fourteenth century, England was seeking strategies to neutralize the role of Castile as a French ally, both nations representing an impending threat to British southern shores and territories on the Continent. John of Gaunt, the powerful duke of Lancaster, took a bold political initiative by marrying Constanza, daughter of the murdered Pedro the Cruel, and claiming the crown of Castile on behalf of his wife and himself. The Portuguese, on the other hand, wished to preserve the national integrity of their crown and territory by creating a protective shield represented by the specter of an Anglo-Portuguese military force, which Castile should not dare challenge lightly.

Despite its relevance for the politics of the age, the Treaty of Windsor was not a sudden new departure in Anglo-Portuguese relations. These had been initiated two centuries earlier when a contingent of English knights on their way to the Holy Land assisted King Afonso Henriques in the conquest of Lisbon in 1147. Soon after, the monarch enticed them to stay and continue their crusading mission by awarding them royal privileges and new land to settle. The next centuries saw the development of commercial and diplomatic exchanges frequently peppered by acrimony, as discussed in chapter 6 in this volume. By 1295, Edward I of England and Dinis of Portugal signed agreements already excluding Castile, and thus foreshadowing terms of the Treaty of Windsor. A century later, as a reflection of closer contacts, the English had become a reference in Portuguese culture. Queen Leonor Teles in Fernão Lopes's *Crónica de D. João I*, for instance, refers to the English habit of not wearing armor at court in time of peace;[2] King Duarte in his *Livro da ensinança de bem cavalgar toda sela* specifies how long the English wear their stirrups;[3] the organization of the Portuguese army and commanding ranks are influenced by English trends;[4] new English names such as Duarte, derived from Edward, are given to the royal princes, and even church rites are influenced by the scholarly piety of the English-born Queen Philippa.[5]

In very brief terms, the episode of The Twelve of England is the story of how twelve ladies of the House of Lancaster, having been insulted by as many English knights, ask the duke of Lancaster to help them defend their honor; and how the duke had to ask the king of Portugal, his son-in-law, to send him twelve of his best men. After the victory of the Portuguese in London, nine of them return to Portugal, but the other three travel throughout Europe in search of further adventure.

Like an icon, The Twelve of England crystallizes an ideal, perhaps imaginary moment of glory and international recognition for Portugal, highlighting its knights' chivalric valor as a national trait. Furthermore, these qualities are recognized by the English, their vital ally against the persistent Castilian threat of invasion. Nationally and internationally, the Treaty of Windsor was an additional affirmation of the newly established house of Aviz founded by King João I with his accession to the throne in 1385. The early days of the dynasty were difficult, being forced to meet many challenges, from the danger of Castilian invasion, to the struggle to ascertain itself. This called for a realignment of loyalties because João I was an illegitimate heir when there were other legitimate contenders still alive.[6]

The episode of The Twelve of England presents three main questions: (i) the establishment of the earliest extant version, (ii) the identification of the historical moment, which may have given rise to this national legend, and (iii) the reasons for the stereotypical Arthurian elements that flavor the narrative.

The most widely known version of The Twelve of England is to be found in Camões's *Lusíadas*, Canto VI, stanzas 42–69.[7] In this instance, the episode fills in a relaxing moment of story-telling, as Fernão Veloso entertains his fellow mariners during a long night shift in the course of their voyage of discovery of a sea route to India. But Camões is not its original source. There are at least two earlier pieces of evidence pointing to an *ur*-text estimated to date from the mid-fifteenth century. The first is the *Cavalarias de Alguns Fidalgos Portugueses*, preserved in MS 87 of the Biblioteca Municipal do Porto and possibly a copy of that earlier text.[8] The second is a brief reference to the incident in its essential elements recorded by Jorge Ferreira de Vasconcelos in his romance *Memorial das Proezas da Segunda Távola Redonda* of 1567.[9] The first edition of *Os Lusíadas* came to light five years later, 1572.

Joaquim Costa, author of the extensive introduction to Magalhães Basto's edition of the *Cavalarias de Alguns Fidalgos Portugueses*, believes that two other accounts of the narrative were based on a text, or texts, anteceding Camões's epic.[10] These belong respectively to Pedro Mariz's 1599 edition of his *Diálogos de Vária História*, and to Manuel Correia's *Lusiadas de Luiz de Camões Comnětados* published in 1613.[11] There are many other retellings and references to The Twelve of England such as in Francisco Soares Toscano's *Parallelos de Príncipes e Varões Illustres* (1623), Manuel Soeiro's *Los Anales de Flandes* (1624), Manuel de Faria e Sousa's *Lusiadas de Luis de Camoens Comentados* (1639), Dom Fernando de Meneses, count of Ericeira's *Vida e Acçoens d'El Rey Dom João I* (1677), Duperron de Castera's *La Lusiade de Camoens* (1768), and others.[12] Nevertheless, only the author of the *Cavalarias*, Camões, Ferreira de Vasconcelos, Pedro Mariz, and Manuel Correia seem to relate back to that *ur*-text, possibly the first transcription of an oral tradition still free from later influence or interpolation. Whereas later versions and authors present differences in circumstances, details, and even in the list of names of the twelve heroes, sometimes increased to thirteen, the five authors above consistently tell the same story. Manuel Correia, in fact, follows sections of the *Cavalarias* quite closely.

These five narratives also share a declared intention to present the episode as historical fact. The author of the *Cavalarias* states that there is a chronicle in England on this event: "E destas coisas há aí Crónica em Inglaterra que largamente trata dêstes Cavaleiros" [And there is a chronicle in England about these things, which extensively refers to these knights].[13] Camões referring to his epic narrative in general professes to tell only of true deeds and not *histórias enganosas* [false tales]. Through the voice of

Fernão Veloso, introducing the story of The Twelve of England to his fellow mariners, he further declares:

> Contarei (disse) sem que me reprendam
> De contar cousa fabulosa ou nova.
> E, por que os que me ouvirem daqui aprendam
> A fazer feitos grandes de alta prova,
> Dos nacidos direi na nossa terra,
> E estes sejam os Doze de Inglaterra.[14]
>
> [I will tell it (said he), without deserving rebuke for telling a fabulous fable or a tale of my invention; but so that those listening to me can learn from this and perform outstanding deeds, I will speak of those born in our homeland, and by them I mean the Twelve of England.]

Curiously, there is another connection between the *Cavalarias* and Camões's stanza above. Whereas the former is appended to a sixteenth-century copy of the *Crónica de D. João I* written by Fernão Lopes, Portugal's medieval chronicler par excellence, the latter, through Fernão Veloso, performs a function, which was commonly attributed to chronicles—to provide a true model of one's ancestors to be followed by younger generations. Furthermore, it was a model to be enjoyed at moments of leisure as a form of entertainment. Fernão Lopes's chronicles were read aloud for the enjoyment of the Portuguese court and as a confirmation of João I's kingship as the founder of the new house of Aviz.[15] Jorge Ferreira de Vasconcelos in his brief reference to The Twelve of England attributes the incident the same veracity as that awarded to Fernão Lopes's description of King João I and his closer knights at the siege of Coria, who identified themselves with heroes of the Round Table:

> E em tempo del-Rei dom João, de boa memória, sabemos que seus vassalos, no cerco de Guimarães [sic], se nomeavam por cavaleiros da Távola Redonda e ele por Rei Artur. E de sua corte mandou treze cavaleiros portugueses a Londres que se desafiaram em campo cerrado com outros tantos Ingleses, nobres e esforçados, por respeito das damas do duque de Alencastro.[16]
>
> [And in the times of king João I of Good Memory, we know that his knights in the siege of Guimarães [it actually should read Coria] identified themselves with knights of the Round Table, and he identified himself with King Arthur. And from his court he [João I] sent thirteen Portuguese knights to London, who fought an equal number of noble and brave English knights in a joust, on account of the ladies in the household of the duke of Lancaster.]

The connection made by Ferreira de Vasconcelos between Fernão Lopes and the story of The Twelve of England is also important because it implies that the *Cavalarias* may have been his source. As the narrative is appended to the end of the *Crónica de D. João I*, Part II, preserved in a copy estimated to date from about 1550, Vasconcelos may have assumed that it had the same authorship.

Pedro Mariz's statement of having found his source in a "Chronica antiqua huius temporis" [an old chronicle of that age] further supports the belief that The Twelve of England is historical fact.[17] Manuel Correia, on the other hand, presents the narrative as the actual source of Camões, though without offering further justification.[18] As noted above, Manuel Correia seems to have had direct access to the text of the *Cavalarias*, or to another version which reproduced it quite closely.

From the evidence of the five texts above, it can be argued that the *Cavalarias* is the earliest extant version of the adventures of The Twelve of England.[19] Unless other evidence comes to light, it will be difficult to prove whether the episode of The Twelve of England is fact or fiction. Modern historians such as Carlos Riley believe it to be a legend constructed to present Álvaro Gonçalves Coutinho, the central hero of the narrative, as the founder of his own house, and to signify reconciliation with the king, João I.[20] The penultimate paragraph of the manuscript states the following:

> E após isso [defeating the king of France's champion] querendo-se êle vir a Portugal, escreveram a El-Rei Dom João de Boa-Memória que fizesse muita honra e mercê, àquele Cavaleiro, porque pusera em liberdade o Condado de Flandres, e o livrara daquela sujeição de França; e El-Rei, por satisfação de tamanha coisa, lhe fêz muita mercê e o fez conde e foi o fundamento da Casa sua.[21]

> [And after that, as he wished to return to Portugal, they [the duke and duchess of Flanders] wrote to King João of Good Memory asking him to give much honor and favor to that knight because he had freed the County of Flanders, and had delivered it from its subjugation to France; and the king, in recognition of such great deed, awarded him much favor and made him a count, and that was the foundation of his own house.]

In that regard, the *Cavalarias* seems to derive also from the tradition of the *Livros de Linhagens*. These were the predecessors of Portuguese historiography, which included fantastic legends and fables to explain the foundation of some aristocratic houses of Western Iberia. Álvaro Gonçalves Coutinho's eldest brother became the first count of Marialva, and the Coutinho-Marialva family enjoyed increasing prestige in the fifteenth century. The same Álvaro Gonçalves was also distinguished by the privilege of belonging to the group of twenty knights with permanent residence in the Portuguese court.

Despite its brevity, the *Cavalarias* does not display a unity of plot. There are two clear sections: (i) the episode of The Twelve of England proper, and (ii) the subsequent adventures of two of the most notable of the twelve heroes: Álvaro de Almada, later count of Avranches, and Álvaro Gonçalves, nicknamed *Magriço*.

This clear division poses two possibilities: (i) either the section of The Twelve of England proper was written as a preamble to the adventures of Álvaro Gonçalves, and, therefore, both parts belong together; or (ii) the adventures of this knight were attached to another narrative already circulating in the oral tradition. According to Carlos Riley, the oral tradition of the narrative is betrayed by the variations in the list of heroes from version to version, the use of nicknames, such as *Magriço*, and the time when the combat in London is likely to have taken place according to internal evidence.[22] Álvaro Gonçalves's absence from the duke of Lancaster's campaign in the Iberian Peninsula is another important factor in considering different origins for the two sections of the narrative and their oral transmission. That being the case, the knight's chivalric spirit and bravery could not have influenced the duke in his selection.[23] Furthermore, the twelve knights of the *Cavalarias* are unlikely to have fought in London in the context of the episode, as pointed out by Riley because, with few exceptions, they belong to different generations. It is as if different traditions had been brought together through the thread of a narrative derived from family memories and other factual elements transmitted orally and finally shaped by literary, possibly even propagandistic concerns.

The text opens with the verbal form "Conta-se" [It is said] without making reference to the origin of the tale. It seems to betray a remote memory of the presence of the duke of Lancaster and his contingent in Portugal following the Portuguese victory over Castile at the battle of Aljubarrota, which led to a period of peace. These events are referred to in the first paragraph of the *Cavalarias* but, surprisingly, there is no mention of the Treaty of Windsor, despite its relevance and the references in the text to other contemporary detail.

The treaty of Windsor was equally important to the English. The intervention of John of Gaunt in the Iberian Peninsula had been part of his plan of the "chemin de Portyngale."[24] This strategy involved military aid to Portugal in her struggle against Castile with the objective of weakening French hostilities against England in the context of the Hundred Years' War.[25]

During the period preceding and subsequent to signing the Treaty, there was much diplomatic activity between the two signatories. The presence of Portuguese ambassadors in the royal entourage and in the ducal court of Lancaster, which had a double role as court of Castile in exile, offered many opportunities to construct memories and exchange cultural links between the two nations. The marriage of João I to the duke of Lancaster's daughter was another open door to the influence of English ways into the Portuguese court. João I was one of the first foreign kings to become a knight of the Garter.[26] He was followed by several of his children and by all his successors until King Manuel, who was invited but never installed. The Order of the Garter had been founded by Edward III, Lancaster's father and Philippa's grandfather, a fact that may have contributed to the image of the English as paragons of chivalry in the eyes of the Portuguese.

Philippa had received the same honor on her eighteenth birthday together with her sister Elizabeth and their stepmother Constanza.[27] Interestingly, Gomes Eanes de Zurara turned Philippa into another icon of the ideal of chivalry when in a poignant scene in the *Crónica da Tomada de Ceuta*, she calls her sons to her deathbed giving them swords with the recommendation to be always guided by the highest ideals of the order.[28] This took place on the eve of the expedition to Ceuta, North Africa, where the princes were to be knighted after taking the city, their chosen ordeal to prove themselves worthy of knighthood. Though closer to the generation of João I and Philippa's children, Álvaro Gonçalves Coutinho belongs instead to an interim generation grown after the battle of Aljubarrota, which traveled round Europe participating in many conflicts connected to the later stages of the Hundred Years' War. It is in that context that the *Cavalarias* shows Álvaro Gonçalves Coutinho fighting in Paris on behalf of the interests of the counts of Flanders, the duke and Duchess of Burgundy. The Duchess Isabel was a daughter of João I and Philippa of Portugal. In reality, this fight did not take place in the course of a decisive duel for the autonomy of the duchy, as stated in the *Cavalarias*, but during the ongoing struggle against the Armagnacs, namely at the taking of one of the main gates into Paris at Saint Cloud.[29] As this event took place in 1411 and Isabel only married Philip the Good of Burgundy in 1430, it becomes obvious that there is considerable time condensation and literary license in the arrangement of the elements of the narrative. This and other details seem to confirm once again that the *Cavalarias* is a combination of different memories and traditions recorded as a single narrative after receiving considerable literary treatment.

As the text of the *Cavalarias* is not widely known, a brief outline of the narrative could prove useful at this stage.

The opening lines convey a sense of peace and normality. John of Gaunt duke of Lancaster has already returned to England after his expedition to the Iberian Peninsula, where his daughter Philippa married João I of Portugal. The duke is pleased with the marriage and impressed by the bravery of the

Portuguese. This sense of harmony is suddenly broken when twelve English knights insult twelve ladies from his wife's retinue accusing them of being too ugly and, therefore, unworthy of being in the service of the duchess. Furthermore, they are ready to challenge anyone who dares contradict their word. Vexed by the insult, the twelve ladies plead with John of Gaunt, their lord and exponent of European chivalry, to help them find twelve champions ready to redress their shame. At first, John of Gaunt is unable to assist because his own knights are intimidated by the prowess of their prospective opponents. Then, remembering the bravery of the Portuguese, the duke tells each lady to write to one of the twelve best knights he had met during his campaign in the Iberian Peninsula. He also sends letters: one addressed jointly to all the knights, and another to João I of Portugal asking for his consent, which is readily granted. Eleven Portuguese knights travel directly to London by sea, catching a boat in the city of Porto, the main center of Anglo-Portuguese trade. The twelfth, Álvaro Gonçalves, nicknamed *Magriço*, travels by land guided by the spirit of adventure. His late arrival makes his lady fear for her honor, but the other eleven companions assure her that should *Magriço* be prevented from joining them, they would gladly fight against their twelve English opponents, thus clearing her name and accruing more honor. *Magriço* finally arrives a couple of days before the tournament from which the Portuguese come out victorious. Overjoyed, the ladies thank the defenders of their honor, but *Magriço* resists having his hands washed by his lady, as was the customary token of gratitude, because he believed them to be too hairy and offensive to the eyes of a woman.

After the tournament, the Portuguese are threatened by their defeated opponents. They complain to the duke of Lancaster and nine decide to return to Portugal; the other three, including Álvaro de Almada and Álvaro Gonçalves, the *Magriço*, decide to travel by land once again in search of adventure.[30] The narrative is now followed by a fairly distinct section containing the account of Álvaro de Almada's duel against a German in Basle, and ends with a relatively extensive description of the combat between Álvaro Gonçalves and a champion of the king of France to liberate the county of Flanders from French vassalage, as referred above.[31]

There is no historical evidence of any of these events as such, although there are points of contact with actual historical circumstances. The opening of the narrative is a reasonably accurate though brief account of John of Gaunt's presence in the Peninsula: "e, depois do Duque e El-Rei fazerem no Reino algumas coisas, ele se foi com os seus para Inglaterra" [And after the duke and the king accomplished a few deeds in the kingdom, he [the duke] went back to England with his followers].[32] The disappointment of the Portuguese with their ally's military action, however, is omitted despite the situation of discredit of João I before his subjects when his father-in-law unexpectedly signed terms with Castile.³³

Considerable emphasis is given to the marriage of Philippa of Lancaster to João I and to her father's satisfaction with her circumstances as queen of Portugal: "estando o Duque em muito contentamento, pela bondade que nos Portugueses vira, a quem deixava sua filha por senhora" [the duke was very happy with the kindness he had seen in the Portuguese, to whom he had entrusted his daughter as their queen].³⁴ In modern terms, this is a politically correct narrative where the Portuguese are praised without implying criticism against their English counterparts.

The accusation of ugliness directed at the twelve ladies seems too trifling to be taken seriously.³⁵ It sounds more like a pretext for a fight in a romance of chivalry than an incident requiring international intervention, unless it was meant as a disguised attack on the duke's interests and circumstances. Knowing that John of Gaunt was married to Constanza of Castile from 1371 to 1394 can help identify the origins, albeit remote, of the incident leading to the chivalrous feat of The Twelve of England. Three details acquire particular relevance—(i) the injured ladies belong to the duchess of Lancaster and not to the queen of England, as referred by later versions of the narrative, (ii) the duchess of Lancaster is a Castilian, surrounded by Castilian ladies-in-waiting, and (iii) John of Gaunt, his Castilian court at the Savoy and his political ambitions were not very popular in England. P.E. Russell observes that "there were many other Castilians, apart from Juan Gutierrez, in the domestic circle of the Pretender and Doña Constanza," enough "to give an appropriately exotic air to the Lancastrian household. Some were ladies-in-waiting who had attended the Castilian princesses during their exile in Gascony." One of them was appointed governess of the royal offspring. "Others probably belonged to the families of the various Castilian knights who had joined the Castilian Pretender."³⁶ Some of these spirited ladies, "noz demoiselles d'Espaigne," however, could be troublesome, and John of Gaunt was forced to send five of them to a more quiet residence in Nuneaton, from where they soon dismissed themselves in search of a more congenial and lively abode. P.E. Russell identifies a Sancha Garcia who eventually married Sir Walter Blount. Other Peninsular ladies married other members of the duke of Lancaster's personal retinue.³⁷ The numerous Castilian exiles residing in the court of the duke and duchess of Lancaster seem to have been the object of much suspicion. On December 22, 1379, the wife of Juan Fernandez of Spain, from Lancaster's retinue, was released from prison after being cleared of the suspicion of spying. On 1381 she was declared innocent of her husband's death.³⁸ And on the eve of the Peninsular campaign in 1387, there was a Castilian conspiracy to poison the duke.

The nationality of the duchess of Lancaster and her ladies-in-waiting, therefore, matters for the story of The Twelve of England. Important is also Manuel Correia's explanation that the English knights who refused to defend the ladies of the duchess did so on the grounds that they were "naturaes" [natives], meaning with the same nationality as their opponents.[39] This excuse only makes sense if Lancaster's English knights refused to fight against other Englishmen on behalf of foreigners, a real possibility between 1371 and 1394, the duration of the duke of Lancaster's marriage to his second wife Constanza.

The text of the *Cavalarias* says that "...vierão os fidallgos ingre/ses a dizer hum dia as damas da duquesa que/erão muito feas, e muito pouco para serem damas/de tam excellente senhora como a duquesa" [the English nobles came one day and told the ladies of the duchess that they were very ugly and not fit to be the ladies of such an excellent lady as the duchess].[40] The nobles who initiated the conflict are identified as English, but the ladies in question are identified solely by the personality to whose retinue they belong—the duchess. This explains why their first port of appeal was the duke of Lancaster and not the king. Interestingly, the brief summary in the *Memorial das Proezas da Segunda Távola Redonda* by Ferreira de Vasconcelos speaks of "damas do duque de Alencastro" [ladies of the duke of Lancaster].[41] This reference does not differ much from "damas da duquesa" [ladies of the duchess], as in the *Cavalarias*. In Pedro Mariz, Camões, and Manuel Correia, however, the ladies are identified with the court: "damas do Paço" [ladies of the court] in Pedro Mariz, "damas gentis da corte inglesa" [noble ladies of the English court] in Camões, and "damas da Raynha de Inglaterra" [ladies of the queen of England] in Manuel Correia.[42] The later the author of the reference, the greater the degree of variation in the identification of the ladies but, in any case, they are never called English. This detail seems to indicate that Jorge Ferreira de Vasconcelo's *Memorial* is the closest to the text of the *Cavalarias*, possibly his source, as referred earlier. The authors of the other versions either used a different source or distanced themselves from the original through paraphrasing and making the assumptions most obvious to them. Later versions, such as in Dom Fernando de Meneses's *Vida e Acçoens d'El Rey Dom João I* (1677), call them "Damas Inglezas" [English ladies], although Manoel Soeiro in his *Anales de Flandes* (1624) is more noncommittal by referring to them as "damas de palacio" [court ladies].[43]

As the text of the *Cavalarias* situates the incident with the ladies of the duchess some time after the Lancasters' return from the Peninsula, during a moment of quiet enjoyment of their achievement, it is now possible to narrow the timeframe for the origin of the story of The Twelve of England. This could have taken place between 1387, date of the truce between England, Castile, and Portugal, and 1394, the year of the death of Duchess Constanza. These dates, however, based on the internal evidence of the first part of the *Cavalarias*, detach it further from the second, as Álvaro Gonçalves's exploits in France can be placed at around 1411–14. During the years they held a Castilian court in exile (1371–87), the duke and duchess of Lancaster were surrounded by dissident Galicians and Castilians who professed to remain faithful to the heiress of Pedro the Cruel after his assassination in 1369. These were the *emperogilados*, the faction faithful to the murdered king Pedro. After 1387, however, when Constanza's daughter Catalina recovered her royal heritage on marrying the heir of Castile, many of these Peninsular noblemen returned home and only a few remained in the service of the Lancasters. Amongst them was Juan Guttierez, dean of Segovia and bishop of Dax from 1374 to 1392. He frequently engaged in ambassadorial duties, causing complaints to reach the ears of Richard II in 1382. After 1387, the duke of Lancaster would be short of young Peninsular blood to defend his wife's ladies. Calling for the assistance of his former Portuguese comrades in arms seems a logical and pragmatic decision.

Furthermore, it was not unusual to find Portuguese knights jousting throughout Europe or engaging in foreign battles during the Hundred Years' War, especially after hostilities with Castile subsided (1387, 1397) and a lasting peace was signed in 1411. In 1415, Soeiro da Costa, Rui Mendes Cerveira, and João Pereira Coutinho, names included in later versions of The Twelve of England, fought alongside Henry V at Agincourt. Between 1414 and 1415, Álvaro Gonçalves Coutinho, the *Magriço* of The Twelve of England, and other Portuguese knights are identified by Enguerrand de Monstrelet and Jean Lefevre as participants in various *faits d'armes* in Paris.[44] Even after the conquest of Ceuta in 1415, which marks the beginning of Portuguese expansion in Africa and was to absorb generations of ambitious young nobles born after hostilities ceased with Castile, it is still possible to find Portuguese knights in different battlegrounds in Europe. In 1435, João de Melo de Arras challenged the Burgundian Pierre de Beaufremont merely for the sake of glory.[45]

The next problem presented by The Twelve of England is the unlikely ease with which the duke of Lancaster wrote down the names of twelve Portuguese fellow warriors from his past experience in the Iberian Peninsula. To believe Froissart in his *Chronicles*, John of Gaunt would not have been able to do so. In the past, when Rui Fogaça, the Portuguese ambassador, announced the list of those fallen at the battle of Aljubarrota, the duke had found their names much too strange and awkward to pronounce.[46] Nevertheless, this was before the duke's Peninsular campaign. As Froissart does not make the same observation about French,

Castilian, or Gascon names, this passage could be interpreted as a symptom of the chronicler's own difficulties with the Portuguese language, judging from the distortions suffered by Portuguese patronymics in his chronicles. As John of Gaunt spent a few weeks in daily contact with his Portuguese allies, during their joint incursions into Castile in 1387, there is a remote possibility that he may have retained the names of his Portuguese companions. The other assumption is that the clear memory of the duke's Portuguese comrades and their names symbolizes familiarity and respect. This could be taken as another symptom of an earlier period of oral transmission of The Twelve of England. Unfortunately, John of Gaunt's letter to João I is not fully reproduced in the *Cavalarias* and thus his list of heroes and respective spelling remains unknown. Within the context of the narrative, however, it was accurate enough for the twelve Portuguese knights to respond with their presence at the combat in London.

Finally, there is the question of identifying what historical event may have been at the root of the combat between the twelve pairs of knights in London. The 1390 Saint Inglevert tournament is the first to come to mind. It was announced throughout Europe to attract competitors, which may have been interpreted by the author of the *Cavalarias* as the challenge. The competition required each of the sixty contesters to parade together with his lady through the streets of London before the tournament.[47] Is this the source of the pairing of the knights to as many ladies in The Twelve of England? Why twelve? Owing to its symbolic and formulaic nature, the number could be explained by association with other famous groups of twelve such as the twelve apostles, the twelve peers of France, perhaps even the twelve knights sent as messengers by the Roman emperor Lucius Liber to challenge King Arthur into becoming his subject. Interestingly, this is recorded in the Portuguese adaptation of Geoffrey of Monmouth's *Historia Regum Britaniae* in the *Livro das Linhagens* by Dom Pedro Count of Barcelos.[48] Carlos Riley, however, suggests another source. He argues that the number twelve and the mission to London to defend as many ladies, in what resembles a judicial court, evokes the order of L'Écu Vert à la Dame Blanche founded in 1399 by Jean Le Meingre, also known as Maréchal Boucicault. The objective of this order was to offer women of high birth a brotherhood of knights ready to defend their honor and to deliver them from any oppressor through direct combat.[49] Incidentally, as Carlos Riley points out, the number of members of this order was exactly thirteen, the same as The Twelve of England in some versions, plus *Magriço*, whose individual identity is thus singled out. The coincidence offers further evidence that the episode of The Twelve of England is a collage of different events and traditions with different chronologies pieced together round the figure of Álvaro Gonçalves, its main hero. Nevertheless, it is also a piece of political propaganda polished with touches of Arthurian romance, which enjoyed a period of revival in England and Portugal.[50] By giving the stage to King João I and his valiant knights, the setting and structure of The Twelve of England in the *Cavalarias* are presenting the newly founded Aviz dynasty, as a guarantor of peace, harmony, and justice out of the chaos which had preceded it. According to the Post-Vulgate *Merlin*, a copy of which existed in the Aviz library at least between 1433 and 1438 if not before, the young King Arthur had also brought a period of peace and prosperity after defeating the rebellious barons in his kingdom.[51] Although the narrative focuses primarily upon the insult addressed to the duchess of Lancaster's ladies in England, the fact that John of Gaunt can only find them champions amongst João I's subjects, inevitably brings the attention back to the Portuguese court and its dynastic head. The very opening of the narrative has as its chronological point of reference King João I's victory over the king of Castile at Aljubarrota (1385): "Conta-se que, depois que El-rei Dom João de Boa-Memória venceu na batalha a El-Rei de Castela" [It is said that after King João of Good Memory defeated the king of Castile at the battle [Aljubarrota]].[52] João I is also the next point of reference because the story about to unfold is situated after his marriage to the duke of Lancaster's daughter: "andando cá o Duque de Lencastre, com a filha do qual El-Rei de Portugal era casado, que lha trouxe ao Pôrto, onde se fizeram seus solenes desponsórios" [when the duke of Lancaster was here [in Portugal], whose daughter the king of Portugal had married, because he brought her to Porto, where they celebrated their sponsalia].[53] There is a third chronological reference to João I: "e, depois do Duque e El-Rei fazerem no reino algumas coisas, ele se foi com os seus para Inglaterra" [and after the duke and the king did a few things in the kingdom, he [the duke] returned with his followers to England].[54] From this point onward, the presence of the Portuguese monarch is still felt throughout the narrative, though indirectly, by means of the deference with which the duke of Lancaster asks for his permission, and the high standards of bravery observed by his knights. This technique resembles Arthurian romances where the presence of the mythical king is felt in the background even when his name is only mentioned in the opening scene, or not at all. *Sir Gawain and the Green Knight* is a typical example. After the opening stanzas in Carleon describing the Green Knight's challenge to participate in the beheading game, the plot leaves Arthur's court and follows the adventure of Sir Gawain. Nevertheless, King Arthur's virtual presence remains center-stage because Gawain must follow the code of behavior of the Round Table and meet its high standards of bravery and courtesy. Although there is no evidence that *Sir Gawain and the Green Knight* was ever in circulation in Portugal, at least in written form, Camões creates another parallel in his own version of The Twelve of England. João I's initial impulse is also to embark upon the adventure ahead, but unlike Arthur he does not need reminding that the duty of a monarch is to remain at the helm of his kingdom:

> Já chega a Portugal o mensageiro;
> Toda a corte alvoroça a novidade;
> Quisera o Rei sublime ser primeiro,
> Não lho sofre a régia Majestade.
> Qualquer dos cortesãos aventureiro
> Deseja ser, com férvida vontade
> E só fica por bem-aventurado
> Quem já vem pelo Duke nomeado.[55]

[The messenger has landed in Portugal. The whole court is excited with the news; the sublime king would have wanted to be the first [to join], but his royal kingship cannot allow it. All courtiers ardently wish to be one of the adventurers, but the only ones to think themselves lucky are those already named by the duke [in his letter].]

Also, in contrast to the adventure of *Sir Gawain and the Green Knight*, all Portuguese courtiers wish to accept the challenge without hesitation, but only twelve will be that fortunate.

The expectation to find champions amongst the Portuguese court is a high compliment when uttered by John of Gaunt. This is like a redress of Fernão Lopes's passage in his *Crónica de D. João I*, where João I and his knights at the siege of Coria compare themselves unfavorably to specific heroes of the Round Table. Ferreira de Vasconcelos also noticed the connection making it explicit in the *Memorial* when he refers to Fernão Lopes's passage in the paragraph immediately preceding the summary of The Twelve of England as told in the *Cavalarias*.

Magriço's departure by land in search of adventure, as opposed to the other knights who traveled by sea, increases the dramatic tension expected of a romance of chivalry. The reader intuitively expects a late arrival, perhaps even tragic death en route. The attention is then diverted to the whole group of eleven, who, symbolizing the Portuguese nation, are ready to meet any odds and thus gain greater glory. The appointed day for the combat is Pentecost, another deadline favored by Arthurian romances.[56] The combat finally takes place but its description is comparatively short in relation to the building up of dramatic tension. Camões exploits it further by making *Magriço* arrive in the very last minute. In the *Cavalarias*, *Magriço* arrives in London two days before the combat. For the duel in Paris, however, he arrives at the very last moment when his prospective French opponent is already about to leave and declare victory by default.[57]

The second and final part of the *Cavalarias* ends with a paragraph which closes the circle of the narrative by bringing it back to King João I in his quality of monarch displaying the royal virtues of justice and largesse. Álvaro Gonçalves's deeds on behalf of the counts of Flanders are duly rewarded. The foundation of his own house, together with the title of count, which has been left as a blank space in the text, give the reader the impression that the time for adventure has come to an end and all has returned to the peaceful normality of the opening lines.

W.R.J. Barron, the late Arthurian medievalist, aware of the difficult task of defining *romance* as a genre, settled for a combination of elements, which, as a rule, are present in most medieval romances. Above all, he noted a panegyric tone in the narrative line, the expression of "the specific idealism of a particular society," and a generally consistent set of values expressed through the depiction of the human experience of love, honor, valor, fear, and self-knowledge.[58] According to Barron, these experiences are often presented through conventional motifs typically consisting of "the mysterious challenge or summons to a single combat against overwhelming odds or a monstrous opponent."[59] Most of these elements are present in both parts of the text of the *Cavalarias*. The panegyric tone is set by the climate of peace after the turmoil of the Anglo-Portuguese campaign in 1386–87 and the respite enjoyed by the two earlier comrades in arms, Lancaster and João I. This was a won peace and not a moment of truce imposed by a third party. The *Cavalarias* as a whole can be read either as a panegyric of Álvaro Gonçalves or as a national romance of chivalry presided by King João I. By extension, it is also a romance of Anglo-Portuguese relations. The human experiences of love, honor, valor, fear, and self-knowledge are also present. There is the symbolic demonstration of love and gratitude by the ladies for the persons who defended their honor, which is accentuated in *Magriço*'s case. He is the sensitive, rugged warrior who, despite his tough appearance and unsightly hairy hands, possesses a gentle heart and unsuspected shyness.[60] The refusal to have his hands washed by his lady evokes the dilemmas often found in Arthurian romances. For the sake of his soul and out of respect for his host, Sir Gawain must reject the persistent advances of Lady Bertilack, though he cannot afford to appear uncourteous for the sake of chivalry, his renown, and that of his companions of the Round Table. In her first visit to his chamber, Lady Bertilack says: "Sir, if you are really Gawain, it seems very strange to me that a knight who is so well disposed in every respect to noble behaviour, cannot comprehend the usages of polite society."[61] *Mutatis mutandis*, the same words could be addressed to *Magriço*, though in this case it is not his morals or soul that are in question, but the dilemma between hiding his physical blemish from the gentle eyes of a woman and the expected chivalric good manners.

In the duality typical of medieval thought, fear is also a constant in a knight's life. It needs to be overcome in order to achieve great deeds. A clear insight is provided by King Duarte's *Livro da ensinança de bem cavalgar toda sela*, which contains a whole section dedicated to fear. He uses the more decorous word *receio* rather than the raw feeling of *medo*: "Acabase a primeira parte do seer forte e começase a ssegunda: de seer sem receio" [Here ends the first section on being strong and begins the second on being without fear], wrote King Duarte as transitional words between two sections.[62] This is a remarkable psychological study of fear as a partner in the life and skill of a knight, observes Richard Barber in his book on *Tournaments*.[63]

In The Twelve of England, fear is used as a strategy to heighten suspense: *Magriço*'s lady fears that he will not arrive to defend her honor, the Portuguese knights, though valiant seasoned warriors, fear their English opponents not because the latter are better combatants but because they want to kill them. It is the fear of an unlawful act of treason that leads them to complain to the duke of Lancaster and seek his protection. This is also their justification for a speedy departure after the combat.[64] In the second part of the narrative, treason is still the most feared enemy of the Portuguese knights. The German from Basle, who fights against Álvaro de Almada, is accused of treason when he suddenly pulls off a hidden weapon and tears a piece of flesh from Almada's shoulder: "E vendo o Imperador a traição do Alemão, e como usara de traidor em não cumprir os pontos com que entraram no Campo, houve Álvaro de Almada por bom Cavaleiro e ao Alemão por traidor" [And as the emperor saw the treachery of the German, and how he had acted treacherously disobeying the rules of combat, he declared Álvaro de Almada to be a good knight and the German a traitor].[65] Curiously, in such a relatively short passage, there are three references to treacherous behavior which may cause fear in others. This is the only fear acceptable to the Portuguese because it is not shameful and highlights courage in the face of danger.

In conclusion, The Twelve of England in the *Cavalarias de Alguns Fidalgos Portugueses* is a multifaceted and multipurpose narrative, an icon of the close Anglo-Portuguese relations at the end of the fourteenth century and, therefore, of the Treaty of Windsor. The text, as appended to Part II of a sixteenth-century copy of Fernão Lopes's *Crónica de D. João I*, is an example of pseudo-history derived from the combination of different oral traditions subjected to considerable literary treatment. The heightened sense of adventure and chivalry in the story shows the Portuguese as superior to their English allies, which is not surprising given the occasional frustration and acrimony of relations as illustrated by chapter 6 in this volume.

The fusion of these elements associated to the narrative tone of a romance of chivalry may explain why a remote and uncertain incident attributed to historical characters became a favorite legend to the point of overshadowing the foundation of the house of the Coutinhos it purports to celebrate. As a closing commentary, one final question comes to mind: Why "The Twelve of England" if the knights were Portuguese? "Deeds of twelve brave Portuguese" is a more accurate designation and closer to the original *Cavalarias de Alguns Fidalgos Portugueses*. Nevertheless, "Os Doze de Inglaterra" is more synthetic, the preposition *de* denotes connection, not necessarily origin, and holds England as a point of reference. Camões consecrated it, even at the cost of intimating to the uninitiated that the heroes were English and not Portuguese.

Notes

1. Luis Adão da Fonseca, *O Essencial sobre o Tratado de Windsor* (Lisbon: Imprensa Nacional-Casa da Moeda, 1986), p. 52.
2. Fernão Lopes, *Crónica de D. João I*, 2 vols., pt. 1 (Porto: Livraria Civilização, 1945), p. 21.
3. Dom Duarte, *Livro da ensinança de bem cavalgar toda sela que fez El-rey Dom Eduarte*, ed. Joseph M. Piel (Lisbon: Imprensa Nacional-Casa da Moeda, 1986), p. 16.
4. Fernão Lopes, *Crónica de D. Fernando* (Lisbon: Imprensa Nacional-Casa da Moeda, 1975), chap. 150, p. 524; Fernão Lopes, *D. João I*, Vol. 1, pt. 1, chap. 193, p. 424 and Vol. 2, pt. 2, chap. 31, p. 72.
5. Philippa "introduced the Salisbury missal to the chapter at Lisbon cathedral" and corrected the clerics when mistakes were made. See Peter E. Russell, *The English Intervention in Spain and Portugal in the Time of Edward III and Richard II* (Oxford: Clarendon Press, 1955), p. 544. In chapter 7 in this book Joyce Coleman analyzes other cultural and literary Anglo-Portuguese interactions promoted by Phillipa.
6. This crucial period of crisis for Portuguese national identity has been the object of many studies by Portuguese and foreign scholars. It is connected to the strife of other Western European nations equally afflicted by dynastic problems, which brought the Hundred Years' War to the battlefields of the Iberian Peninsula. See Russell, *The English Intervention*, pp. 357–99; Derek W. Lomax and R.J. Oakley, *The English in Portugal 1367–87* (Warminster: Aris & Phillips, 1988), pp. x–xxiv; A.H. de Oliveira Marques, *History of Portugal*, 2nd ed. (New York: Columbia University Press, 1976), pp. 124–28; A.H. de Oliveira Marques, *Portugal na Crise dos Séculos XIV e XV* (Lisbon: Editorial Presença, 1987), pp. 519–46; José Mattoso, *História de Portugal*, 2. *A Monarquia Feudal (1096–1480)* (Lisbon: Editorial Estampa, 1997), pp. 412–17; Humberto Baquero Moreno, "Contestação da nobreza portuguesa ao poder político nos finais da Idade Média," in *Ler História* 13 (1988): 3–14; Salvador Dias Arnaut, "A Crise Nacional dos fins do Século XIV (Contribuição

para o seu Estudo)," *Anais* 30, II series (1985): 51–79; António Borges Coelho, *A Revolução de 1385* (Lisbon: Portugália Editora, 1965); Damião Peres, *História de Portugal Monumental*, 2 (Portucalense Editora: Barcelos, 1929), chap. 24, pp. 365–91.

7. Luis de Camões, *Lusíadas* (Lisbon: Imprensa Nacional-Casa da Moeda, 1975). Cantos and stanzas are indicated for all quotations from *Os Lusíadas*, instead of page numbers, so that the reader can use any edition of the epic.

8. Published by Artur de Magalhães Basto, *Relação ou Crónica Breve das Cavalarias dos Doze de Inglaterra* (Porto: Imprensa Portuguesa, 1935); Basto, *O essencial sobre Os Doze de Inglaterra* (Lisbon: Imprensa Nacional-Casa da Moeda, 1986), pp. 21–46.

9. Jorge Ferreira de Vasconcelos, *Memorial das Proezas da Segunda Távola Redonda*, ed. João Palma-Ferreira (Porto: Lello Editores, 1998), chap. 46, p. 367.

10. Joaquim Costa, *"Os Doze de Inglaterra": o célebre episódio de "Os Lusíadas" na História e na Lenda* (Porto: Imprensa Portuguesa, 1935), p. 7.

11. Pedro Mariz, *Diálogos de Vária História* (Coimbra: António de Mariz, 1599), chap. 2, dialogue 4, pp. 139v.–140v., henceforth referred to as *Diálogos*. This is the second edition. The first edition does not contain this dialogue. Manuel Correia, *Lusiadas de Luiz de Camões. Comētados pelo licenciado Manuel Correia* (Lisbon: P. Crasbeek, 1613), fols. 175–77.

12. Francisco Soares Toscano, *Parallelos de Príncipes e Varões Illustres* (Évora: Manoel Carvalho, 1623), fol. 91; Manuel Soeiro, *Anales de Flandes* (Anvers: Pedro y Juan Bellero, 1624), 2, pp. 26–27; Manuel de Faria e Sousa's *Lusiadas de Luis de Camoens Comentados por Manuel Faria i Sousa*, 4 vols. (Madrid: Juan Sánchez, 1639), 3:99–101; Dom Fernando de Meneses, Count of Ericeira, *Vida e Acçoens d'El Rey Dom João o Primeyro* (Lisbon: João Galrão, 1677), p. 340; Duperron de Castera, *La Lusiade de Camoens* (Paris, 1768), Vol. 2, p. 252. For a detailed commentary on these and other references to the episode see Costa, *"Os Doze de Inglaterra,"* pp. 7–16.

13. All translations belong to the present author. Basto, *O essencial*, p. 46. All references to the text of the *Cavalarias* are based on this edition, because it is the most readily available. One of the objectives of the present essay is to make the chronicle of the *Cavalarias* better known outside a restricted circle of Portuguese academics.

14. *Lusíadas*, canto 6, stanza 42. See also *Luis Vaz de Camões, The Lusiads*, trans. William C. Atkinson (Harmondsworth: Penguin Books, 1952), p. 148.

15. António José Saraiva, *Fernão Lopes* (Lisbon: Europa-América, 1965), p. 21; Aubrey Bell, *Fernam Lopez*, Hispanic Society of America, Portuguese Series (Oxford: Oxford University Press, 1921), pp. 46–49.

16. Vasconcelos, *Memorial*, chap. 44, p. 366. For Fernão Lopes's reference to the siege of Coria where King João I chides his knights for not coming up to the standards of bravery of the Round Table, see Fernão Lopes, *D. João I*, Vol. 2, pt. 2, chap. 75, pp. 187–88.

17. Mariz, *Diálogos*, chap. 2, Dialogue 4, p. 39v.
18. Correia, *Lusiadas Comētados*, fol. 175.
19. There are several studies about the relationship between the *Cavalarias* and *Os Lusíadas*: Joaquim Costa and Magalhães Bastos's introduction to the volume *Relação ou Crónica Breve das Cavalarias dos Doze de Inglaterra*, partly reproduced in the volume *O essencial sobre Os Doze de Inglaterra*; António Salgado Júnior, "A Relação ou Crónica Breve das Cavalarias dos Doze de Inglaterra," *Labor*, II series (January 1937): 317–26; Joaquim Moreira dos Santos, "Medievalismo em Camões: os Doze de Inglaterra," *Revista da Universidade de Coimbra*, 33 (1986): 209–20.
20. Statement made at a University of Salford Middle Ages Seminar, UK, 1990; also Carlos Guilherme Riley, "Os Doze de Inglaterra: Ficção e Realidade," M.A. thesis (Ponta Delgada: Universidade dos Açores, 1988), pp. 304–05.
21. Basto, *O essencial*, pp. 45–46.
22. Riley, "Os Doze," p. 128.
23. Riley, "Os Doze," p. 299.
24. Russell, *English Intervention*, pp. 186–203.
25. The monarchs of Western Iberia were divided into two blocks by the mid-fourteenth century. Enrique of Trastámara was committed to provide naval aid to France, to attack the southern shores of Great Britain. In return, the French provided military support to the Castilian monarch in order to help him gain the Portuguese Crown, thus spreading French influence in the Peninsula and neutralizing British allies. From England's point of view, if Portugal could be helped to resist Castile and curb its military power, France would be denied the promised Castilian reinforcements, which were engaged on home shores. For England, the alliance with the Portuguese had the added attraction of the commitment of a squadron of Portuguese galleys to defend its coast from French incursions. Russell, *English Intervention*, pp. 365, 527, and 547.
26. T.W.E. Roche, *Philippa: Dona Filipa de Portugal* (Chichester, UK: Phillimore & Co., 1971), pp. 73–74.
27. F.G. Beltz (Lancaster Herald), *Memorials of the Most Noble Order of the Garter* (London: Pickering, 1841), p. 132.
28. Gomes Eanes de Zurara, *Crónica da Tomada de Ceuta* (Mem-Martins: Edições Europa-América, 1992), chap. 41, pp. 152–54.
29. Riley, "Os Doze," p. 261 and n39. For the ducal charter addressed to the Portuguese in Flanders in recognition of their deed, see *Monumenta Henricina*, Vol. 2, document 8, pp. 39–47. Also quoted by Riley, "Os Doze."
30. Basto, *O essencial*, pp. 21–33.
31. Basto, *O essencial*, pp. 34–45.
32. Basto, *O essencial*, pp. 21–22.
33. Russell, *English Intervention*, pp. 485–86.
34. Basto, *O essencial*, p. 22.
35. Basto, *O essencial*, p. 22.
36. Russell, *English Intervention*, p. 178.

37. Russell, *English Intervention*, pp. 178–79 and p. 179 n1.
38. *John of Gaunt's Register, 1379–1383*, ed. E.C. Lodge and R. Sommerville (London: Camden Society, 1937), p. 39.
39. Correia, *Lusiadas Comētados*, p. 175.
40. *Cavalarias*, p. 260r., transcribed by Carlos Riley, p. 29.
41. Vasconcelos, *Memorial*, p. 367.
42. Mariz, *Diálogos*, p. 139v.; Camões, *Lusíadas*, canto VI, stanza 44; Correia, *Lusiadas Comētados*, p. 175.
43. Meneses, *Vida e Acçoens d'El Rey Dom João o Primeyro*, p. 340; and Soeiro, *Anales*, II, p. 26.
44. *Chroniques d'Enguerrand de Monstrelet*, in "Collection des chroniques nationales françaises...," vols. 26–40, ed. J.A.C. Bouchon (Paris: Verdière, 1826–27), 28, chap. 141, pp. 288–89; *Mémoires de Jean Lefevre: dit Toison-d'or, seigneur de Saint-Remy*, in *Collection des Chroniques Nationales Françaises*, vols. 32–33, ed. J.A.C. Bouchon (Paris: Verdière, 1826), 32, chap. 52, pp. 470–75; both quoted by Riley, "Os Doze," pp. 352–57.
45. Soeiro, *Anales*, p. 272; Basto, *Relação*, p. lii.
46. Jean Froissart, *Chronicles of England, France, Spain and the Adjoining Countries*, 2 vols. (London: W. Smith, 1942), 2:164.
47. Froissart, *Chronicles of England*, pp. 477–79.
48. Dom Pedro Count of Barcelos, "Livro de Linhagens," in *Portugaliae Monumenta Historica*, 1. *Scriptores*, ed. Alexandre Herculano (1856; repr. Lisbon: Typis Academicis, 1967), p. 243.
49. Riley, "Os Doze," p. 177 and n22; Martín de Ríquer, *Caballeros Andantes Españoles* (Madrid: Espasa-Calpe, 1967), p. 37.
50. Amélia P. Hutchinson, "Anglo-Portuguese Relations and Arthurian Revival in Portugal," in *Actas do Colóquio Comemorativo do VI Centenário do Tratado de Windsor (de 15 a 18 de Outubro de 1986)*, ed. Manuel Gomes da Torre (Porto: Faculdade de Letras do Porto, 1988), pp. 288–89 [275–89]; Hutchinson, "European Relations of Portuguese Arthurian Literature," unpublished M.Phil. dissertation (United Kingdom: University of Manchester, 1984), p. 219.
51. Norris J. Lacy, *The Arthurian Encyclopedia* (Woodbridge: The Boydell Press, 1986), p. 430. For the contents of King Duarte's library see *Livro dos Conselhos de El-rei D. Duarte (livro da cartuxa)*, ed. João José Alves Dias (Lisbon: Editorial Estampa, 1982), pp. 206–08, esp. 207.
52. Basto, *O essencial*, p. 21.
53. Basto, *O essencial*, p. 21.
54. Basto, *O essencial*, pp. 21–22.
55. Camões, *Os Lusíadas*, canto 6, stanza 51. See another translation in *The Lusiads*, p. 150.
56. The same day the "Seeda Perigosa" [the perilous seat] at the Round Table will be occupied in the Quest of the Grail. See *A Demanda do Santo Graal*, ed. Irene Freire Nunes (Lisbon: Imprensa Nacional-Casa da Moeda, 1995), p. 24.
57. Basto, *O essencial*, pp. 26–27 and 44 respectively.

58. W.R.J. Barron, *English Medieval Romance* (London and New York: Longman, 1987), p. 7.
59. Barron, *English Medieval Romance*, p. 5.
60. Basto, *O essencial*, pp. 30–31.
61. *Sir Gawain and the Green Knight*, ed. and prose trans. W.R.J. Barron (Manchester: Manchester University Press, 1998), p. 111.
62. Duarte, *Ensinança*, pp. 42–65.
63. Richard W. Barber and Juliet R.V. Barker, *Tournaments: Jousts, Chivalry, and Pageants in the Middle Ages* (Woodbridge: Boydell, 1989), p. 202.
64. Basto, *O essencial*, pp. 27–28 and 32.
65. Basto, *O essencial*, p. 35.

CHAPTER 9

CHAUCER TRANSLATES THE MATTER OF SPAIN

R.F. Yeager

Although there is no concrete evidence of Spanish literary influence in Chaucer's work, it is likely that he learned Spanish and read at least the tale collections of Petrus Alfonsi and Don Juan Manuel—both works would have increased his receptivity to Boccaccian narrative on his subsequent travels to Italy.

Strictly speaking, in Jean Bodel's well-known tripartite classification of romance poetry—or poetry in general, since for Jean romance and poetry were nearly synonymous—there is of course no "Matter of Spain." Nor was there for George Ellis, who added the "Matter of England" to Bodel's "Matters" of France, Britain and Rome in 1805.[1] For readers of Chaucer, who is not after all very much given to writing romances, such associations have been of lesser critical importance than another triad, his supposed "Three Periods" when, it used to be said, the inspiration of France and Italy, and then contemporary English life, respectively shaped his poetry.[2] No nod toward Spain here, either—and it is this absence of recognized Spanish influences which for present purposes makes these blunt, outdated taxonomies of interest. They are testimony of a certain kind about the limits of our view of Chaucer, historically and presently, as a European citizen and writer.

Let me say very quickly that what follows will not conclude with a claim of parity of importance to Chaucer's readers of Iberia and the rest of the Continent, or England. I shall suggest, however, that there are abundant good reasons to consider more seriously than heretofore the "Matter of Spain," and Spain and Portugal themselves as significant loci, both for Chaucer and for Chaucer studies. Indeed, what I have to say would be unnecessary, were it not for the transformation wrought on English attitudes, toward Spain especially, first by the Reformation, which effectively cut Iberia loose from England as a place of extreme "otherness," and eventually by the Industrial Revolution, which rendered Spain unimportant—a view that, save for the occasional Olympics, Basque or al Qaeda bombing, lingers among us today.[3]

Yet such a view would be near-unrecognizable to Chaucer. For him the peninsula would have figured very differently, as a full participant in world—and particularly English—affairs. This is true beginning with its political geography. Though "Spain" was a generic term Chaucer used, Iberia would have been more familiar to him as a collection of kingdoms: Portugal, Castile, León (by 1230 essentially absorbed into Castile), Navarre, Aragon, Catalonia, and the territories in the south yet held by the Moors.[4] Of these states the largest and most powerful was Castile, but all were engaged in one or another form of aggression and/or alliance-seeking in order to expand their borders. This kept their strengths relative, and in flux, enough so that, from an English point of view, any or all could conceivably become a major force to be reckoned with. Primarily this activity was intra-peninsular, but not exclusively: on the one hand, both Navarrese and Aragonese ambitions affected various French, English, and Italian city-state claims in France and the Mediterranean and, on the other, Iberia, as the last European stronghold of Islam, was a continued focus of international crusading zeal, which could be (and was) harnessed from time to time by the Iberian kings for what were essentially purposes of individual territorial expansion.[5] Moreover, all the peninsular kingdoms had formidable sea strength, both merchant and martial.[6] The former helped make Portugal, Castile, and León important commercial partners for England beginning in the twelfth century, when English trading colonies first sprang up along the Bay of Biscay and in Lisbon, dealing English wool and finished cloth for Iberian raw materials such as hides, iron, cork, dried fruits and, later, wines when the Hundred Years' War cut off French supply from the preferred ports of Bordeaux and La Rochelle. (Chaucer's "wyn of Lepe" [*CT* VI.563] is a Castilian product, Lepe being proximate to the coast southwest of Seville.)[7] In England itself, important Iberian merchant colonies developed in Bristol and in London, where trade policies often favored them from the time of Edward I, whose first wife Eleanor was Castilian.[8] As for the latter: because neither England nor France was an accomplished naval power, the armed galleys of Castile, Navarre, and Portugal played major roles in the ongoing struggle, at once diplomatic—to secure their aid—and military, insofar as Castilian and Navarrese ships, in alliance with France, at various times plagued English merchant shipping, and pillaged England's south coast and the Thames estuary, on one occasion nearly reaching London.[9] Nor should it be forgotten that the shrine of Saint James at Compostela, in Galicia, was one of the most visited pilgrimage sites, especially by Englishmen, from the eleventh century forward; or that the great monastery for noble ladies of Las Huelgas in Burgos was founded in 1175 with Leonor Plantagenet, daughter of Henry II, as its first prioress.[10] Here Edward I married Eleanor of Castile and León in 1254, and here Edward Black Prince took up residence after the victory of Nájera in 1367.[11] Although Chaucer does not mention Queen Eleanor, she—and her Castilian origin—were nonetheless well known in England, and inarguably to Chaucer himself.[12] And certainly a number of knights who rode with the Black Prince in Spain were part of his acquaintance.[13]

Some of this territory, we now know, Chaucer visited first hand. It's a journey that can stand a closer look. According to a document discovered in the royal archives of Navarre, in 1366 Chaucer, along with three companions, their servants, horses, and baggage, was granted safe-conduct by Carlos II (the Bad) to travel between February 22 and Pentecost (May 24).[14] A variety of explanations has been offered for this trip, ranging from the absurd to the most likely, that is, that he went as a last-minute emissary from Edward III to find and dissuade a number of English and Gascon knights, including Hugh Calveley, Matthew Gournay, and Eustache d'Aubrichicourt, from joining the French-financed Free Companies in support of Enrique Trastámara against his legitimate half-brother and king of Castile, Pedro I, known as "the Cruel," of "Monk's Tale" fame.[15] If that were truly Chaucer's mission, he either failed, or failed to find them in time, since all three knights played significant parts in the overthrow of Pedro in March, 1366.[16] However, this might not have been Chaucer's mission: in truth, we do not know where Chaucer went once he traveled through Navarre, or how long he stayed overseas. The next life-record extant is dated June 20, 1367—so, although a much shorter visit seems most likely, Chaucer could have been in Iberia a year and more.

Certainly this is long enough to have picked up something of the "Matter of Spain," but even three months might have sufficed for a quick young man, as Chaucer doubtless was. Just how much occasion he would have had to absorb anything local—other than a first-hand sense of the topography and ambience—while on the peninsula depends of course on the conditions and urgency of his travel. Particularly if it were to intercept Calveley and the others, browsing Iberian libraries seems unlikely. But Chaucer would have been in his mid-twenties, and obviously thinking about poetry, with the *Book of the Duchess*—commemorating the death of Blanche of Lancaster in September 1368—but a year or two in the future.[17] It seems in character that, if there were an opportunity to sample and learn, he would have seized it. Although we know nothing about Chaucer's itinerary, it is nonetheless possible to speculate a little, to some useful purpose I shall get to later on, about what his opportunities, if they existed, might have been like.

Paramount is the question of language: Did Chaucer speak and/or read Spanish? The answer, in 1366 when he left, is probably not well, if at all. It would not have been a necessary consideration in his selection as messenger (if he were so selected), as his better knowledge of Italian probably was in 1372 and 1378 when he was sent to Genoa and Milan to conduct negotiations. In official Navarre his French would have served the turn (his safe-conduct document, for example, is written in French), and of course Calveley, Gournay, and d'Aubrichicourt spoke both French and English. Nonetheless, it is *possible*, thinly, that Chaucer had some Spanish, acquired in the same way we assume he got his early exposure to Italian— picked up amidst the mercantile world of his boyhood, where Spanish wine traders undoubtedly frequented his vintner parents' enterprise as often as did their Italian counterparts, and Spanish children, albeit rarer (one supposes) than Italians in young Chaucer's neighborhood, would have had their resident colony as well.[18] In fact, were the twenty-something Chaucer, as yet untested as a royal emissary, entrusted by Edward III in 1366 with an important maiden mission overseas, it is perhaps no *less* possible that a reputation for knowing some Spanish was a factor, than the opposite.

In any case, given what we surmise to be Chaucer's uncommon interest in, and capacity for, languages, it hardly seems likely that by the conclusion of his time on the peninsula he had not acquired, or added a bit to, his facility.[19] Obviously this likelihood increases (along with his potential capability) the longer his stay lasted. Equally obviously his opportunities vary depending upon where he went. In Navarre, if his party stayed for any length of time, either to acquire documents and supplies, or to rest before proceeding further, he would have encountered a society not unlike what applied in Gascony immediately to the north, but more bureaucratically and aesthetically literate.[20] Moreover, as a country where French and Spanish seem to have been spoken one as much as the other, and (apparently) somewhat macaronically, Navarre could have provided a Spanish-impaired but French-fluent (and presumably eager) Chaucer with the ideal beginning-point on a journey amongst Spanish speakers.[21] Yet for reasons to be noted below, Chaucer may have also traversed Aragon, to Barcelona, and perhaps to the monastery of Santa María de Montserrat to the northwest. If so, he would likely have observed the enlightened court of Pedro IV ("the Ceremonious"), whose interests in things intellectual reflected a long Catalan tradition of written and oral poetic culture, both rooted in, but by this time independent of, Provence.[22] Oral poetry would of course extend a different accessibility, at whatever level of appreciation Chaucer might have been capable.

So, Chaucer could have acquired "Matter of Spain" "on the ground," so to speak; but before tracing him further into Spain, to suggest more specifically what he absorbed, and how he used it, it may be helpful to locate two additional potential sources for Chaucer's Iberian associations at home in England. One is of course the customs house: although a great deal of the Iberian trade flowed through Bristol and southern ports, a substantial portion of the wool and cloth export to Spain and Portugal went out of London, and so would have involved Chaucer with peninsular merchants in his official rôle as customs chief. Of greater importance, however, is the household of John of Gaunt, who married Constanza, only legitimate child and heir of the murdered Pedro the Cruel in 1371. In her right, Gaunt claimed sovereignty over Castile and León (he was regularly addressed as "monseigneur d'Espaigne") and until 1387 actively sought means to oust the usurper Enrique Trastámara.[23] For most of this time, Gaunt and Constanza held an elegant court centered at the Savoy, which became a home-away-from-home for Castilian *emperogilados* and exiles of all stripes.[24] Gaunt's court was apparently a cultural melting-pot: he and Constanza self-consciously promoted Spanish styles in food, housewares, clothes, and jewelry design, and apparently encouraged a number of Castilian–English marriages as well as some formalized tutoring for native speakers of both languages.[25] As lady-in-waiting to Constanza, Philippa Chaucer was attendant there, and although Chaucer himself was variously employed at home and overseas by Edward III and Richard II, we must assume his acquaintance in London with a number of the peninsular knights and their companies.[26]

Gaunt's self-representation as king of Castile and León kept Iberian affairs highly visible in the English capital, particularly since he continuously sought monies for an invasion force from a succession of dubious, if not openly hostile, Parliaments.[27] In this he was helped somewhat by a mutual defense treaty signed in 1386 at Windsor between England and Portugal, which remains in force today and is the longest-standing such treaty in existence.[28] Portuguese sovereignty was challenged severely by Enrique Trastámara, and eventually this, plus the hope to neutralize the devastating effectiveness of the Castilian galleys in French service, won Gaunt the funding to gather ships and men for a Spanish campaign in 1386.[29] The army, when it left England at last, was sizeable—8,000 men—but with its attendant cohort the retinue was even larger. Anticipating victory, Gaunt took along with him all the necessary personnel to establish a royal court, including goldsmiths, jewelers, drapers, minstrels and jesters, an officer of a projected royal mint-to-be, and his intimate family—Constanza of course, and her ladies (one of whom, it has been proposed, was Philippa Chaucer) and also his two marriageable daughters Philippa and Catherine.[30] In the end, though the military adventure failed, Gaunt returned home with a vast pay-off from Enrique Trastámara to quit-claim his and Constanza's right in favor of the heir to the marriage of Catherine and the prince who later succeeded to the throne of Castile as Enrique III, and another alliance by marriage, too: elder daughter Philippa wed João I to become queen of Portugal.[31]

The effects of this activity on Chaucer, we can surmise, were several. Quite obviously it presented him with multiple opportunities to expand upon his first-hand peninsular experience. Not only would he very likely have been able to discuss Iberian affairs with the expatriates surrounding Gaunt and Constanza, perhaps improving his Spanish in the process, but here he might well have encountered Spanish texts, with time and unhurried access. Neither Gaunt nor Constanza are known to have shown great interest in reading (although Gaunt presumably absorbed and appreciated the *Book of the Duchess*), but both were literate, and saw to it that their daughters were educated.[32] Philippa especially seems to have had a tooth for literature. When she traveled, she is said to have taken books; certainly she bears the greatest measure of responsibility, directly or indirectly, for translations into Castilian and Portuguese of John Gower's *Confessio Amantis*, a poem she likely brought with her, in some form, to Iberia during the invasion in 1386.[33] Several of the *emperogilado* knights are known to have been literary after a fashion. Nothing would have prevented them from having books, and sharing them, particularly if the interests of Gaunt's daughters in such things were apparent, as undoubtedly was the case.

So Chaucer's Spanish connections "at home" are, on closer examination, more extensive than is often thought. What is important to recognize is that the realm of contact, and the context for his acquisition of the "Matter of Spain," like his contacts with and acquisition of the "Matters" of France and Italy, are not limited to time he spent there "on the ground," but rather had currency in England as well, where they could be encouraged and enlarged. Establishing this potential is the first necessary step toward rethinking Chaucer's work against an Iberian background, as has been accomplished so fruitfully for France and Italy. Let me suggest, then, several likely avenues such a pursuit might take.

The number and nature of the references made to Spain and things Spanish in the *Canterbury Tales* suggest both an interest and a familiarity on Chaucer's part that might derive from the sorts of geographical and cultural contacts he seems to have had abroad and at home: the Knight's service in campaigns against the Moors in Granada and Algeciras in 1344 (I.56–57); the Shipman's familiarity with Cartagena, Cape Finisterre, and "every cryke in Britaigne and in Spayne," which rings true to the rocky, stream-studded coast of Galicia where Cape Finisterre is located (I.404, 408–09); the Wife of Bath's pilgrimage to "Galicia at Seint-Jame" (I.466; and see also references to "Seint Jame" by the Wife [III.312], Reeve [I.4264], Friar [III.1443] and—as we might expect—the Shipman [VII.355]); the Pardoner's hailing from "Rouncivale," ultimately derived from the pass of Roncesvalles in Navarre, which Chaucer may have traversed in 1366 (I.670); the passage of Constance through the "Strayte of Marrok" and past "Jubaltare and Septe"—Gibraltar and the "Seven Brothers" ("septem fratres"), specifically a mountain range in Morocco (II.464–65, 947); the Franklin's "Toledan tables" ("tables Tolletanes" [V.1273]; the Pardoner's familiarity with the "wyn of Spaigne" especially from Lepe (V.562–72); Sir Thopas's shoes of "cordewane" (leather from Cordova [VII.732]); and of course the best known, the Monk's mournful account of the fall of "worthy Petro, glorie of Spayne" (VII.2375–90).

Like many of the "Spanish references" cited in past studies, however, these require careful winnowing.[34] The Knight's Iberian experiences at Algeciras and Granada were familiar to many Englishmen in the 1380s, since the real-life earls of Derby and Salisbury had seen service with Alfonso XI, presumably not unaccompanied by retainers.[35] Although he might have, certainly, Chaucer was hardly forced to learn of these campaigns in Spain. The Wife's journey to Compostela, and her asseverations by "St. Jame," like those of the Reeve, Friar, and Shipman, are none of them exceptional: indeed, to define an Englishwoman by her pilgrimage experience and *neglect* the popular Compostela would, rather, have been unusual; and, as one of the better-known saints in England, "St. Jame" was a commonplace oath. (Besides, in the *Canterbury Tales* in particular it affords a useful rhyme in each case, that is, with "game," I.4263; "dame," III.310; "name," III.1442; "dame," VII.354.) The Pardoner's connection with Roncesvalles, in so far as it also connects him to Navarre, is questionable too. It's real, but attenuated. By citing "of Rouncivale" as his home base, the Pardoner (and Chaucer) doubtless means the Augustinian Hospital of St. Mary Roncesvale near Charing Cross, a London offshoot of a Navarrese mother-house of similar name. Moreover, as a self-defining *locus vivendi* for a crooked *quaestor*, the Hospital of St. Mary Roncesvale in London was a perfect choice, since in 1382 and 1387 false pardons were sold over its name.[36] Similarly, the Franklin's "Toledan tables" and Sir Thopas's "cordewane" shoes require pause, in that both are unavoidable, being simply the names of things—familiar things, if one were interested, as Chaucer plainly was, in planetary motions, or in fashionable footwear.[37]

Of the "Spanish references" in the *Canterbury Tales*, then, we are left with the Pardoner's knowledge of wine from Lepe and its intoxicating effects, which could have been sampled—one can hardly say "enjoyed!"—in Spain or "in Chepe;" the Monk's thumbnail biography of Pedro the Cruel; and the geographical allusions of the Shipman and the Man of Law.

On the first, one is inclined to give Chaucer a pass. As a young man from the Vintry, he might have paid special attention to the wines he drank in Spain in 1366, noting their quality and provenance; but just so, as a young man from the Vintry, he might equally have grown up taking to heart the wine gossip of his professional family members, and his neighbors. The latter two instances, however, are more difficult to account for, save by turning to what we know of Chaucer's acquaintance and travels. As for the mini-history of "worthy Petro": Philippa Chaucer's tenure in service to Duchess Constanza in chambers, where assuredly talk (at very least for the sake of her claim) in the 1370s and 1380s would have lionized her father, and the convenient way Chaucer's sympathetic presentation of Pedro's "martyrdom" so featly glosses the Lancastrian cause, cannot fail to be both related and seminal to the inclusion of the narrative—all the more so, perhaps, if Chaucer's mission in 1366 were in any way formative, and had been to deter English soldiers of fortune from overthrowing the rule of the man who then in English eyes was Castile's rightful king.[38]

Nevertheless, from this perspective, of formative experience leading to literary outcomes, the most revealing references of all in the *Canterbury Tales* may be those of the Shipman and the Man of Law to Spain's northern and southern coasts. Significantly, in the places we find them Chaucer provides closer detail than seems strictly necessary to carry his narrative. Like "Hulle," "Cartage" (Cartagena, on the eastern coast and south of Murcia—I.404) is often passed over as a kind of geographical filler, just one of a pair of locales at opposite ends of the compass arbitrarily chosen to color up the otherwise-bland assertion that the Shipman is widely traveled. "Gootland to the cape of Fynystere" (I.408) does precisely the same thing—with almost precisely the same cartographical coordinates. It has of course been suggested that Chaucer intended these references, along with others (especially the name of the Shipman's boat, "the Maudelayne," which perfectly rhymes with "Spayne" in I.409–10), to be clues to the identity of a real-life sea captain known to a London readership, whom Chaucer wanted to implicate, for reasons of his own. No individual has clearly surfaced, but this might yet be so—in which case the striking "And every cryke in Britaigne and in Spayne" (I.409) might be primarily a topical, rather than a topographical, allusion.[39]

But it may be also that the "Maudelayne," instead of a clue, is in fact a red herring, its presence due not at all to biography but merely to placement, as a rhyme for "Spayne," in that case the potent half of the pair and what Chaucer was actually seeking rhymes to include, instead of viceversa. We have the Monk's lament for murdered king Pedro as evidence that Iberia sometimes occupied Chaucer's mind—and the Man of Law's seamanship offers a similar testament. For his story Chaucer relied upon two primary sources, Nicholas Trivet's *Chronicle* and the "Tale of Constance" from Book II of John Gower's *Confessio Amantis*.[40] Only in Chaucer's version, however, do we find Constance's boat trips so carefully particularized: he tells us that she floated "Thurghout the See of Grece unto the Strayte / Of Marrok" (II.464–65), and later through the strait of Gibraltar past Morocco again, this time identified, as noted above, by "Septe," its mountain range of seven peaks (II.947). Trivet merely says Constance passed along the Spanish coast ("en la mer despayne"), which Gower echoes ("Estward was into Spaigne drive").[41] That one must follow this route to traverse from Syria to Northumbria by boat is not in question, of course; what stands out is that Chaucer departed from his sources to identify the landmarks. In a time when detailed navigational maps weren't ready at hand, such specificity suggests familiarity born of remembrance.[42]

But *could* Chaucer somehow have seen Gibraltar in 1366, and sailed through its straits? They are a long way from Navarre, certainly. If, however, we decide to take seriously Chaucer's Canterbury references to Iberian geography, as evidence of first-hand knowledge—as perhaps we should, since they, unlike most of Chaucer's Spanish allusions, are least explained by other means—then we should look again at the *Hous of Fame*. Probably composed between 1374 and 1378, it therefore follows closely on the heels of Chaucer's Spanish mission, and may also draw upon its recollection.[43] Here Chaucer makes a curious, seemingly pointed reference to "alle that used clarion / In Cataloigne and Aragon, / That in her tyme famous were" (*HF* 1247–49)—curious, at least, unless it recalled something Chaucer had witnessed. (It is difficult to imagine a mere description of horn-playing somewhere in the then-southern hinterlands, offered while on one's maiden mission, passing through distant Navarre, making sufficient impression to prompt these lines years later.) And in fact, brass instruments, especially a version of trumpet, were from the thirteenth century a favored expertise throughout the Crown of Aragon, and figured largely in public celebrations and ceremonials in Catalonia.[44]

Actually, it makes some sense that Chaucer was there to hear them. If his supposed goal in 1366 were to intercept Calveley and the Gascon mercenaries, it's a reasonable supposition that to do so he would have gone to Aragon. Du Guesclin massed his forces in Barcelona in December 1365 before proceeding northward to attack Castile.[45] Calveley may have been in Barcelona already when, that same December, Edward III sent his firm forbiddance of participation by Calveley, Gournay, and d'Aubrichicourt in the planned assault on Pedro the Cruel.[46] In any case, the Black Prince must have informed his father of their destination after the royal message (dispatched first to Gascony) missed them. Hence it is likely that, were Chaucer sent to find them, he would have turned his horses toward

Aragon. (Indeed, if he heard in Navarre that Gournay and d'Aubrichicourt had passed but a little ahead of him—as apparently they did—he would without doubt have learned their direction and followed after.)[47]

If Chaucer did reach Aragon, his experience there might help make sense of another passage from the *Hous of Fame*—the description of Fame's dwelling, which, Chaucer says, "stood upon so hygh a roche, / Hier stant ther non in Spayne" (*HF* 1116–17). Perhaps the most striking landmark of Catalonia is the monastery of Santa María, some sixty kilometers northwest of Barcelona, built at Montserrat, atop unforgettably sheer, uniquely formed mountain peaks. That it was the inspiration for Fame's house has been proposed before, by Jesús L. Serrano Reyes, as part of an argument that Chaucer was present in Barcelona at New Year 1366 when Pedro the Ceremonious feasted his army, and that of du Guesclin, on the eve of the invasion.[48] The obvious catch with this suggestion, however, is that it won't accommodate the one hard fact we have about Chaucer's Spanish travels, his safe-conduct through Navarre in 1366. But Serrano does propose that Chaucer's use of "Reyes" in *HF* 1236, a *hapax legomenon* and apparently a kind of dance, derives in fact from "Bal des Reís," a popular Catalonian folkdance known from the fourteenth century.[49] Such sights, and such words, Chaucer might have seen and picked up equally well between February and May 1366 as in January—or even later.

"Or later" is probably a functional caveat here, however, because as was noted above, we have no better idea how long Chaucer actually spent in Spain than we do about his mission there or where he went. He was back in London on June 20, 1367, but the sixteen intervening months are a blank record. If he reached Barcelona and found Calveley and the others departed, did he stay to await further orders? Or, if he returned home immediately, might he have decided not to retrace his steps, since the Companies were taking the war in that direction, northward toward Navarre and Burgos? That he crossed into Spain through Navarre, and was legally able to exit that way, does not, after all, establish that he actually did so.

Indeed, there was another option. Barcelona in 1366 was one of the most active ports on the Mediterranean. Aragonese shipping frequented English waters. Could Chaucer have chosen to take a "safer" route back to England, by sail? The possibility is intriguing for several reasons. Selecting sea travel might have required waiting in Barcelona for a serviceable vessel, one going his way, and with appropriate accommodations for himself and his party, at (no doubt) an affordable price. Moreover, once under way, he would have rounded, as did the Shipman, "Cartage" (Cartagena) and maybe even put in for additional cargo, with consequent delay for unloading, loading, arrival of favorable winds—and hence more time on his hands, in yet another Iberian city. Finally, precisely like Custance's,

CHAUCER TRANSLATES THE MATTER OF SPAIN   199

his voyage would have brought him through the Straits of "Jubaltare" and "Marrok," tracing the shadow of the seven peaks of "Septe"—all the loci mentioned in the *Canterbury Tales* and awkward to account for otherwise.

In such circumstances, waiting in a foreign land with time to fill, how would Chaucer have occupied himself? Absorbing, undoubtedly, whatever there was to discover, from natural and man-made wonders to song and dance, and in conversation about such things with those he met—and doubtless, given what we know of Chaucer's habits, in books, if any he found there he could have read. His capacity for the last is of course difficult to assess. We do not know the quality of Chaucer's Spanish—any kind of Spanish—let alone his adaptability, if his previous experience were, say, with Castilian, a dialect markedly different from Aragonese and especially Catalan.[50] There is, moreover, the difference between everyday speaking comprehension and the sophistication required to understand and appreciate literary texts. (Even the scribal hands conventional in fourteenth-century Iberian manuscripts could have required getting used to.)

Nonetheless, some degree of speculation is possible, and potentially useful. We can assume that, if Spanish books made an impression on Chaucer, their influence would be observable in his writing produced soonest after 1366–67. Admitting the chance of lost and/or abandoned effort where such evidence might have been clear, the works we have to examine are the *Book of the Duchess* and the *Hous of Fame*. Of these, the first is quintessentially French and the second difficult to categorize as to influence of any single kind.[51] There are, however, in it the allusions to things Spanish discussed above. Significantly these, like the topographical references in the "Man of Law's Tale," are characteristic not of a bibliophile but of a sharp-eyed tourist with a wide range of interests: local brass bands, spectacular mountainous and coastal terrain, perhaps an unique form or two of indigenous folkdance ("reyes") and ritual.[52]

Still, it would probably be a mistake to conclude from this absence that Spanish literature affected Chaucer not at all. Doubtless constraints of language and travel precluded concentrated reading, but in Aragon and Catalonia, where as noted above a rich literary heritage existed, he was well positioned to absorb much on a variety of levels. Poetry combined with song in the Provençal manner was still in vogue both within and outside the court of Pedro IV. There were romances—the *Libro de Alexandre*, the *Libro de Apolonio*, the now-lost *Los votos del pavón*, and doubtless others— with the form and general content (if not the specific meaning) of which, like that of the *fin' amour* lyric, Chaucer would have felt at home.[53] There were also religious poems: if he got at all into Castile, the beauty and devotional intensity of Berceo's hymns to the Virgin (for example, *Milagros de Nuestra Señora, Loores de Nuestra Señora, Duelo que fizo la Virgen*) might have moved the author of "An ABC"; in Catalonia, he could have heard a celebrated pilgrims' paean to the Virgin of Montserrat.[54] And there were a few books by Spanish writers which he could read, because they were in Latin. Notable among the Iberians mentioned in the "Tale of Melibee" in the *Canterbury Tales* is "Piers Alfonce" (Petrus Alfonsi), a Sephardic Jew who became a Christian at age forty-four on June 29, 1106, and composed his best-known work, the *Disciplina clericalis*, sometime thereafter. Of course, Chaucer need not have gone to Spain to read it, as it is among the texts most frequently copied on the Continent and in England as well.[55] Moreover, all of the citations and several paraphrases of Petrus that appear in the "Melibee" are translated directly from Chaucer's French source.[56] But because the *Disciplina* was common, and in Latin, he might have picked it up in Spain.

If he did, he would have discovered a collection of moralized tales similar to those he probably knew—the *Legenda Aurea*, the *Gesta Romanorum*—but somewhat different, too, in several important ways. As a *converso* and not a cleric, Petrus's title is slightly misleading. He wrote for the private meditations of a secular, "educated" Christian audience, not for preaching friars or priests in search of a homily.[57] His sources, as he notes in his prologue, were eclectic, and (quite likely from Chaucer's point of view in 1366) exotic: "the parables and counsels of the philosophers...parables and counsels of the Arabs, from tales and poems, and finally from animal- and bird-fables."[58] For that matter, Petrus's prologue itself might have struck Chaucer as something new. Through it Petrus interjected himself into his collection, using a conversational voice to tie his tales together, explain his principles of tale-selection, and clarify his book's purpose, that is, to "soften and sweeten the pill" of wisdom with brief narratives of vigorous everyday life, which (if some could be mistaken by too-hasty perusal with "a human and exterior eyes") would nevertheless reveal their instructive meaning if thoughtfully reread.[59]

Notably, in these respects Petrus's *Disciplina clericalis* is representative of what might be considered an especially Iberian subgenre of collected exempla, in which the sources are openly Oriental, the moralizations address how best to live in this world instead of how to prepare one's way to the next, and literary style is self-consciously discussed. Similar works—albeit in Spanish—include *Calila e Digna* and the *Libro de los engaños*, both of which, judging from extant manuscripts, seem to have been popular enough for Chaucer to have run across them.[60] Such works offer a secularizing frame story (garrulous animals in *Calila*, a king's son who rejects his father's concubine and is charged by her with rape in *los engaños*), and include bawdy material as well as pious. The more influential *Libro de los enxiemplos del Conde Lucanor e de Patronio* is of this same variety: although lacking in bawdry, it too strings amusing, secularly moral tales upon a framing dialogue of two characters, Count Lucanor and his wise servant Patronio.[61] Completed ca. 1335, *El Conde Lucanor* (as it is generally abbreviated) was the most popular work of Don Juan Manuel, whose writings were in wide circulation throughout Iberia.[62] Chaucer was likely to have had it recommended him, if he asked after Spanish books at all.[63] Intriguingly—though probably altogether coincidentally—Don Juan Manuel's prologue voices concerns about careless scribes and miscopying shared by Chaucer in "To Adam Scriveyn" and at the end of *Troilus and Criseyde* (V.1795–99).[64]

And then there is the *Libro de Buen Amor*, by the Archpriest of Hita, Juan Ruiz, a text of radical style and scope, at one level far different from any thus mentioned, yet with affinities which, like the others, would have appealed to Chaucer. If he had access to it, as has been asserted, the difficulty of fixing its composition date complicates where and when.[65] The conventional claim of 1330, with revisions in 1343, would facilitate Chaucer's seeing it in Spain; but attractive arguments have been made for its writing in the 1380s.[66] In the latter case, it is possible that Chaucer's association with Gaunt's circle might have rendered it available in England. Duchess Constanza, immediately following the settlement of her claim to the Castilian crown, met with Juan I Trastamára (among other reasons, to present him with the crown given to John of Gaunt by Richard II, to wear as king of Castile) and traveled with her retinue in Castile in 1388–89. What we know of her itinerary has her spending time in Guadalajara, in the vicinity of Hita.[67] Perhaps when she and her entourage returned later that year, the *Libro* was stowed away on board.

In the end, however, it can only be admitted that Chaucer's involvement with Spanish literature—unlike his familiarity with the peninsula itself—must remain speculative. The kind of evidence of acquaintance with sources we find most persuasive—the clear allusions and borrowings either structural or specific, in the form of quotation—is lacking for Spanish literature as it so obviously is not for French or Italian. Yet that he knew *nothing* of it seems most unlikely: he had demonstrable opportunities to learn the language as a boy in the Vintry and later to polish his skills both in Spain and in London among merchants, and at Gaunt's court, where he could have gotten texts, perhaps, and found fellow-travelers with whom to discuss them. And he was there "on the ground" in 1366. He had eyes and ears, and a keen interest in poetry; details of the landscape and the music he seems to have carried with him for decades. What conclusions, if any, should be drawn from these things?

One clue, perhaps, lies in the directions both literary and geographical Chaucer pursued after leaving Iberia in 1366–67. That French poetic models remained foremost in his mind is evident from the writing he did then, the *Book of the Duchess*, and in great chunks of the *Hous of Fame*. In the latter, however, many have detected a reaching out to Dante, to classical literature, and other sources, some as yet unidentified. The overall tone is decidedly not French.[68] The Italian ventures of the 1370s are usually held to have changed all that—but in part, I think, by encouraging trends traceable to Spain. What is customarily credited to Italy, and to Boccaccio particularly, is Chaucer's discovery of a new kind of story and a fresh way to tell it: an expansive narrative, direct and unapologetically ribald as well as pious, cut loose from the coded allegories of the *Roman de la Rose* and its various Machauldian permutations, differently framed and ultimately populated with a rich panoply of characters no longer exclusively courtly, but embracing inhabitants as well of a wider world both urban and rural, one extending from Armenia to Spain, from England to Egypt.

But in fact Chaucer's first taste of all that—of what he would have found in the *Decameron* especially—may quite likely have occurred in Iberia.[69] Doubtless he was dazzled by Boccaccio, and challenged in ways he likely wasn't by Petrus Alfonsi and Don Juan Manuel; yet present in the *Disciplina clericalis* and *El Conde Lucanor* (as well as, to different degrees, in *Calila e Digna*, the *Libro de los engaños*, and certainly the *Libro de Buen Amor*) are the Orientalism, the basic proto-humanistic secularities, and the anterior literary dependencies of Boccaccio's narrative agenda. The easy weave of extraordinary learning, serio-comic material and unpretentious, conversational tale-telling characteristic of Boccaccio and the later Chaucer are signal features no less of the work of Petrus and Don Juan Manuel, albeit more sparely and (after the fashion of metafiction) *in parvo*.[70] Reading their work—if Chaucer did so—beginning in 1366–67 and thinking over the experience subsequently amidst the peninsular atmospherics of Gaunt's Savoy would have prepared the ground for his Italian discoveries in the 1370s, quickening his receptivity to Boccaccio's polyvalent originality by providing a kind of baseline from which to see it whole. Such is, I think, the preeminent contribution of the "Matter of Spain" to the evolution of Chaucer's work—predictive, salient undeniably, and, in the manner of much that influenced him (including Boccaccio, whose name he never names), visible in flashes, like a fish rolling bright beneath tarn water.

Notes

1. Jean Bodel, *Chanson des Saxons*, ed. Ann Brasseur (Geneva: Droz, 1989), ll. 6–7: "Ne sont que .iij maitieres à nul home atandant / De France, et de Bretaigne, et de Rome la grant" ["There are but three matters that anyone knows—those of France, of Britain, and of Rome the great"]. For Ellis, see *Specimens of Early English Metrical Romances: Chiefly Written during the Early*

Part of the Fourteenth Century, 3 vols. (London: Longman, Hurst, Rees, & Orme, 1805), p. 1.
2. See, for example, Larry D. Benson's introduction to *The Riverside Chaucer*, ed. Benson, 3rd ed. (Boston: Houghton Mifflin, 1987), p. xxix. All quotations from the works of Chaucer are taken from this edition.
3. Despite its unrivalled power in the sixteenth century, Spanish economic and religious isolation from the rest of Europe became nearly complete following the ascendancy of Charles V in 1516; see (on politics and economics) William C. Atkinson, *A History of Spain and Portugal* (Harmondsworth: Penguin, 1960), pp. 128–67, and further (on religion) Stanley G. Payne, *A History of Spain and Portugal*, 2 vols. (Madison: University of Wisconsin Press, 1973), 1:205–23. As for the Industrial Revolution: "Impoverished by internal wars, the selfishness of her ruling classes, and the backwardness of her masses," Spain only began to sustain industrialization near the end of the nineteenth century; see Jaime Vicens Vives, *An Economic History of Spain*, rev. Jorge Nadal Oller, trans. Frances M. López-Morillas (Princeton, NJ: Princeton University Press, 1969), pp. 524–39; 657–78; quotation, p. 7.
4. Chaucer refers to "Spaigne" or "Spayne" four times in the *Canterbury Tales* (I.409; VI.565; VI.570; VII.2375), once in the *Hous of Fame* (1117) and once in his translation of the *Romance of the Rose* (B 2573).
5. Navarre shed French rule in 1328 and thereafter struggled to maintain its independence through shifting alliances with, variously, France, England, and Castile. Despite being the smallest and weakest of the Iberian kingdoms, it was thus a perpetual player in the power struggles tied to the Hundred Years' War, in part because of its geographical position as the gateway to Iberia and in part because the ruling house of Evreux maintained an eye on the French throne itself. See Joseph F. O'Callaghan, *A History of Medieval Spain* (Ithaca, NY: Cornell University Press, 1975), pp. 408–09. Aragon, on the northeastern edge of the peninsula, looked toward the Mediterranean for expansion, and, through conquest, treaty, and marriage had, by the end of the thirteenth century, effectively absorbed the Balearic Islands, Sardinia, Corsica, and Sicily. In addition, through the durable fealty of the mercenary Catalan Company that overthrew the duke of Athens in 1311, Aragon claimed a foothold in Greece as well. All of these territories kept Aragon in contest for a century and a half against the Avignon papacy, France and Genoa, with more or less significant implications for English interests throughout. See J. Lee Shneidman, *The Rise of the Aragonese-Catalan Empire 1200–1350*, 2 vols. (New York: New York University Press, 1970), esp. 2.335–66; O'Callaghan, *Medieval Spain*, pp. 382–401; and further Angus MacKay, *Spain in the Middle Ages: From Frontier to Empire, 1000–1500* (London: Macmillan, 1977), pp. 127–28. In contrast, Castile in the first half of the fourteenth century was preoccupied with reducing the Moorish presence on the peninsula, and several times appealed to the papacy for crusade indulgences to attract knights from around Europe. (For Chaucerians, the most important of these campaigns is the successful siege of Algeciras—"Algezir"—in 1342–44 under Alfonso XI, which

attracted the king of Navarre, the count of Foix, the earls of Derby and Salisbury, and Chaucer's Knight [*CT* I.57].) In the latter half of the century, dynastic struggles culminating in the fratricidal murder of Pedro I "The Cruel" (Chaucer's "O noble, o worthy Petro, glorie of Spayne" [*CT* VII.2375]), the Trastámaran usurpation, and John of Gaunt's political ambitions against the larger backdrop of the English–French conflict dominated the country. See O'Callaghan, *Medieval Spain*, pp. 412–13, 419–27; 523–40.

6. Aragonese-Catalan naval power was significant in the Mediterranean beginning in the mid-thirteenth century, both for war and for trade—although by Chaucer's time the wearing conflict with Genoa had precipitated a decline; in the later fourteenth century, Castile, Portugal, and Navarre all maintained substantial shipping, often of dual use: see Shneidman, *Rise*, 2.315–18, and O'Callaghan, *Medieval Spain*, 602–03; Vives, *Economic History*, pp. 215–16.

7. See also *CT* VI.570–71: "He is in Spaigne, right at the toune of Lepe— / Nat at Rochele, ne at Burdeux toun." For the impact of the war on wine imports through Bordeaux, see especially Margery K. James, "The Fluctuations of the Anglo-Gascon Wine Trade during the Fourteenth Century," *Economic History Review*, 2nd series, 4 (1951): 170–96. On English–Iberian trade generally and in various commodities, see A.R. Bridbury, *England and the Salt Trade in the Later Middle Ages* (Oxford: Clarendon Press, 1955), 46, 54, 116, and esp. 124–26; Wendy R. Childs, *Anglo-Castilian Trade in the Later Middle Ages* (Manchester: Manchester University Press, 1978), especially chap. 1, "The Fortunes of the Trade, 1254–1369," pp. 11–39, chap. 2, "The Fortunes of the Trade, 1370–1485," pp. 40–70, and chap. 4, "Complimentary Markets II: England's Imports from Castile," pp. 103–48; and the important corrective of T.H. Lloyd, *Alien Merchants in England in the High Middle Ages* (Brighton, Sussex: Harvester Press, 1982), pp. 164–66. Shifting alliances during the Hundred Years' War, however, brought about significant breaks in English–Castilian trade, and consequent increases in commercial ties between England and Portugal. On the fluctuations, see Vives, *Economic History*, pp. 273–74; for Anglo-Portuguese trade, the fullest study remains V.M. Shillington and A.B. Wallis Chapman, *The Commercial Relations of England and Portugal* (London: Routledge, 1907); although see also Lloyd, *Alien Merchants*, pp. 162–64, and E.M. Carus-Wilson, *The Overseas Trade of Bristol in the Later Middle Ages* (1937; rpt. New York: Barnes and Noble, 1967), § 23–25, 34. On English trading presence in Castile, see Vives, *Economic History*, p. 275.

8. On Iberian trade colonies in England, see Childs, *Anglo-Castilian Trade*, chap. 6, "Mercantile Organization I: Techniques and Practices," pp. 170–201, and chap. 7, "Mercantile Organization II: The Men and Their Influence," p. 202. As Childs points out, however, as in the case of Southampton, such colonies were not always appreciated by the locals (*Anglo-Castilian Trade*, p. 14). The English crown under Edward I attempted to extend protection through legislation—the *Carta Mercatoria* of 1303— which covered all alien merchants, including Iberians; importantly, perhaps, among the first acts of the young Edward III was a protection in 1328 reaffirming and extending the *Carta Mercatoria* specifically for Aragonese,

Catalonian, and Majorcan merchants: see Lloyd, *Alien Merchants*, pp. 24–33. For the involvement of Edward I's queen Eleanor in the protection of Iberian merchants, see John Carmi Parsons, *Eleanor of Castile: Queen and Society in Thirteenth Century England* (New York: St. Martin's Press, 1995), pp. 113 and 306 n214.
9. On Franco-Castilian naval operations, see P.E. Russell, *The English Intervention in Spain and Portugal in the Time of Edward III and Richard II* (Oxford: Clarendon Press, 1955), pp. 227–47; for specific attacks on English coastal towns, see pp. 227, 239–40, 242; in 1380 Gravesend was sacked and London seemed vulnerable (p. 245).
10. On English pilgrims to Compostela, and English involvement with the Cistercian nunnery at Las Huelgas, see, respectively, Derek W. Lomax, "The First English Pilgrims to Santiago de Compostela," in *Studies in Medieval History Presented to R.H.C. Davis*, ed. Henry Mayr-Harting and R.I. Moore (London: Hambledon Press, 1985), pp. 165–75; Ana Echevarría Arsuaga, "The Shrine as Mediator: England, Castile and the Pilgrimage to Compostela," and Rose Walker, "Leonor of England and Eleanor of Castile: Anglo-Iberian Marriage and Cultural Exchange in the Twelfth and Thirteenth Centuries," chapters 3 and 4 in this volume.
11. For details of the marriage, see Parsons, *Eleanor of Castile*, pp. 16 and 262 n29. On the Black Prince's stay at Las Huelgas, see Russell, *English Intervention*, p. 109. Also in attendance at the discussions with Pedro I of Castile was John of Gaunt, and a number of knights subsequently of Chaucer's circle.
12. Parsons makes the point that Eleanor's Spanishness was never forgotten by her English subjects, sometimes to the detriment of her reputation (that is, as a rapacious "foreigner"; see *Eleanor of Castile*, pp. 61–67). More significant for Chaucer and his contemporaries than any residual memories of the queen pro or con, however, would have been her various monumental presences. Her tomb at Westminster, exhibiting her arms as a princess of Castile, is memorable for its full-length effigy, "the largest cast-metal work executed in England down to 1291," and she had similarly marked tombs at the Dominican church in London, and at Lincoln Cathedral as well, her viscera being buried in the latter, her heart in the former, and her body in Westminster (pp. 206–07 and figures 4.1 and 4.2; quote p. 207). In addition, Edward had twelve large sculptural crosses erected at the stopping points of her cortege between Lincoln, where she died, and London. Only three survive today (at Hardingstone, Geddington, and Waltham), and even at this distance, long stripped of their original polychrome and gilding, they are striking. Beneath each cross is a set of gothic arches forming a small "room," inhabited by multiple statues of Eleanor. Prominent on all the crosses were her Castilian arms (pp. 209–13 and figures 4.3–4.7). In the 1380s, Chaucer had occasion to pass those monuments often, we suppose, while commuting from London, since Duchess Constanza, to whom Philippa Chaucer was lady-in-waiting, had her primary residence not far from Lincoln.

13. The list could begin with John of Gaunt himself, and include Sir Lewis Clifford; on the latter's presence at Nájera, see Thomas A. Reisner and Mary E.Reisner, "Lewis Clifford and the Kingdom of Navarre," *Modern Philology* 75 (1978): 385–90. The Chandos Herald names Thomas Percy (in whose company Chaucer went to France and Flanders in 1377), William Beauchamp (who stood witness for Chaucer in the Cecily Chaumpaigne trial in 1380), John Devereaux (like Chaucer a justice of the peace in Kent), and Guichard d'Angle (who, according to Froissart, joined Chaucer in negotiations for the marriage of Richard II in 1377).
14. For the document, see *Chaucer Life-Records*, ed. Martin M. Crow and Claire C. Olson (Oxford: Oxford University Press, 1966), p. 64 and facing plate.
15. Various explanations for Chaucer's trip are offered by: Suzanne Honoré-Duvergé, "Chaucer en Espagne? (1366)," in *Recueil de Travaux offert à M. Clovis Brunel par ses amis, collègues et élèves* (Paris: Société de l'Ecole des Chartes, 1955), pt. 2, pp. 9–13 (Chaucer sought to join the Free Companies in the fight against Pedro); Thomas J. Garbáty, "Chaucer in Spain, 1366: Soldier of Fortune or Agent of the Crown?" *English Language Notes* 5 (1967): 81–87 (Chaucer, then a retainer of the Black Prince in Aquitaine, was dispatched to spy out conditions in Navarre before the Prince acted); Albert C. Baugh, "The Background to Chaucer's Mission to Spain," in *Chaucer und seine Zeit: Symposion für Walter F. Schirmer*, ed. Arno Esch (Tübingen: Max Niemeyer, 1968), pp. 55–69 (Chaucer was sent in "a last minute attempt to make contact with the Gascon knights and seek to detach them from the enterprise" [p. 69]); and Fernando Galván Reula, "Medieval English Literature: A Spanish Approach," in *Articles and Papers of the First International Conference of the Spanish Society for English Mediaeval Language and Literature* (Oviedo: Universidad de Oviedo, 1988), pp. 98–111. (Chaucer was sent to provide facts for Edward III, to guide his decision whether to commit military support to Pedro the Cruel.)
16. Calveley was in fact third in command of the Free Companies headed by Bertrand du Guesclin; Gournay and d'Aubrichicourt headed small companies of their own and became Calveley's chief lieutenants. Du Guesclin led a force of 10,000–12,000 men into Barcelona at the end of 1365, ostensibly on crusade against the Moors in Granada. Seeing through the ruse, Pedro I dispatched an envoy, Martín López de Córdoba, to Edward III, seeking English assistance under terms of a treaty signed between Edward and Pedro in 1362, and among other particulars requesting the disengagement of English and Gascon knights from the forces active on behalf of Enrique Trastámara. For the text of the treaty, see *Foedera, conventiones, litterae et acta publica*, ed. Thomas Rymer, Vol. 3, pt. 2 (London 1830), pp. 656–68. No copy of Pedro's letter exists, but his instructions to López are quoted by Francisco de Rades y Andrada; see *Chrónicas de las tres órdenes y cavallerías de Santiago, Calatrava y Alcántara* (Toledo, 1572), fol. 29v. A strong order was issued dated December 6, 1365, to Calveley, Gournay, and others, under threat of severe punishment, not to enter Castile (for the document,

see Rymer, *Foedera*, 3.2:779) but for some reason they were allowed to proceed, perhaps by different routes. Intriguingly enough, permission for Gournay and d'Aubrichcourt and their men to pass through Navarre was issued by Carlos II on February 22, 1366—the same time as Chaucer. Since Calveley is not mentioned, it must be assumed he traveled separately, and perhaps ahead of them. Russell takes the stand that Edward's message simply missed them; for the dates and sequence of events, see Russell, *English Intervention*, pp. 37–39. Clara Estow, however, argues that Edward's order reached the Black Prince in time to prevent Calveley and the others from going forward, but that the Prince exercised a "pocket veto" for his own purposes, until it was too late; see *Pedro the Cruel of Castile, 1350–1369* (Leiden: Brill, 1995), pp. 223–24, 236–37. On Calveley in general, whose troops indeed were the first to invade Castile, and the "important role" he played in putting Enrique Trastámara on the Castilian throne and in Iberia subsequently, see further Russell, *English Intervention*, pp. 40–50.

17. Larry Benson and others have pointed out that—obviously—Chaucer may not have begun the poem immediately upon Blanche's death: another possibility is 1374, when Gaunt ordered a tomb created for Blanche, and also granted Chaucer a life annuity of £10 " 'in consideration of the services rendered by Chaucer to the grantor' and 'by the grantee's wife Philippa to the grantor's late mother and to his consort' " (see *Riverside Chaucer*, pp. xxviii–xxix). Nonetheless, despite Gaunt's life-long devotion to his first wife (for example, he requested to be buried beside her in that same tomb), *BD* seems an unlikely poem to be written *too* long after the sad event.
18. On Italians in the Vintry where Chaucer grew up, and his opportunities there to pick up the language, see Derek Pearsall, *The Life of Geoffrey Chaucer: A Critical Biography* (Oxford: Blackwell, 1992), pp. 4, 18, 102. Childs, *Anglo-Castilian Trade*, pp. 26–33, makes a case for Spanish traders and agents in London and elsewhere ca. 1340–69, many of whom—especially after the outbreak of war with France in 1337—were engaged in the wine trade. The group, though not large, nonetheless was a persistent and effective commercial presence during what presumably were Chaucer's boyhood years, capable of entering into private treaty with the crown for protection and compensation; see particularly pp. 30–31.
19. Indeed, Chaucer's instruction could have begun on the boat across the channel: if Chaucer himself knew no Iberian language, it seems probable that one or more of the three others mentioned in his party by the Navarrese free conduct would.
20. Having been essentially under the control of France since 1234, the court of Navarre in 1366 was much influenced by French practices and preferences. Being directly athwart the main pilgrimage route to Compostela kept what might otherwise have been a mountain backwater abreast of current cultural trends, as well. Much there would have seemed socially familiar to a young English courtier. Noteworthy, perhaps, in this regard also is the comparatively unusual precision and clarity of the Navarrese accounting

records: see the assessment of Earl J. Hamilton, *Money, Prices, and Wages in Valencia, Aragon, and Navarre, 1351–1500* (Cambridge, MA: Harvard University Press, 1936; repr. Philadelphia, PA: Porcupine Press, 1975), pp. 145–46.

21. Evidence of such linguistic fluidity is apparent in the account books; see Hamilton, *Money, Prices and Wages*, p. 146, and nn1 and 2.

22. Pedro IV founded universities in Perpignan and Huesca in 1350 and 1354, respectively; a patron of scholars and the vernacular, he authorized important Catalan translations of classical and theological works, and represented himself as an autobiographer (although the chronicle bearing his name is not now thought to be the king's own work). See O'Callaghan, *History of Spain*, pp. 500, 516–17. As for poetry: Aragon like Navarre was linguistically fluid, with Latin and Hebrew in use alongside Aragonese, Catalan, and Provençal. The poetic traditions of the latter were influential in the thirteenth century, especially in the court of Alfonso II, a poet himself, and persisted into the fourteenth. See Irénée Cluzel, "Princes et troubadours de la Maison Royale de Barcelona-Aragon," *Boletín de la (Real) Academia de Buenas Letras de Barcelona* 27 (1957/1958): 330–70; Martin de Riquer, "La literature provençale à la cour d'Alphonse II d'Aragon," *Cahiers de Civilisation Medievale* 2 (1959): 180–87; and J.N. Hillgarth, *The Spanish Kingdoms, 1215–1516*, 2 vols. (Oxford: Clarendon Press, 1978), 1:12–13.

23. Gaunt received permission from Edward III to incorporate the royal arms of Castile and León into his own in 1372. Two weeks later Constanza, escorted by the prince of Wales, was given a formal entrance into London as queen of Castile; see *Anonimalle Chronicle:1333–1381, from a Manuscript Written at St. Mary's Abbey, York*, ed. V.H. Galbraith (Manchester: University of Manchester Press, 1927), p. 69. Three weeks thereafter Gaunt had appointed Juan Gutiérrez, the bishop of Dax, as royal chancellor, and was issuing letters patent (*carta abiérta*) for two royal ambassadors to the Portuguese court at Lisbon; see Russell, *English Intervention*, pp. 176–77 n4 and 177 n1. In November 1372 Gaunt and Constanza, as king and queen, signed a treaty of mutual alliance with Fernando I and Leonor of Portugal (printed by Russell, *English Intervention*, pp. 557–61); and see Rymer, *Foedera* (1709), 7:15–22 and 263. For this, both great and privy seals were cast; for discussion and reproduction see Sydney Armitage-Smith, *John of Gaunt: King of Castile and Leon, Duke of Aquitaine and Lancaster, Earl of Derby, Lincoln and Leicester, Seneschal of England* (London: Constable, 1904), pp. 456–58. An official coiner was named in 1380 to mint gold, silver, and copper coinage with Gaunt's name and image for use in Castile (although there now are no such coins known); see *John of Gaunt's Register 1379–83*, ed. Eleanor C. Lodge and Robert Somerville, 2 vols., Camden Society 3rd series, 56–57 (London: Camden Society, 1937), §1067. Attention to such things paid off: in March 1386 Richard II—who regularly addressed Gaunt as "nostre uncle d'Espaigne" and Constanza as "nostre treschere tante d'Espaigne" (see Russell, *English Intervention*, p. 175 n1)—seated Gaunt beside him at a

CHAUCER TRANSLATES THE MATTER OF SPAIN 209

Great Council as an equal, ahead of both archbishops; see *The Westminster Chronicle 1381–1394*, ed. L.C. Hector and Barbara F. Harvey (Oxford: Clarendon Press, 1982), pp. 164–65.

24. Russell, *English Intervention*, p. 178, noted that "though their number must not be exaggerated," Iberians in Gaunt's circle "were certainly enough...to give an appropriately exotic air to the Lancastrian household." Constanza came to England with a small but visible retinue: "demoisels d'Espaigne" required discipline in 1373 (*John of Gaunt's Register*, ed. Sydney Armitage-Smith, 2 vols., Camden Society 3rd series, 20–21 [London, 1911], §1597). Pedro I's most influential supporter Fernando de Castro, along with "quite a substantial retinue which included most of the other best-known *emperogilado* commanders who had evaded Enrique II's troops," joined Gaunt's court at the Savoy; see Russell, *English Intervention*, p. 180. Other noteworthy knights in attendance were Fernán Rodríguez de Aza, Fernán Alfonso de Zamora (from 1372 to 1381, both serving with the English army in France for part of that time), Juan Alfonso de Baeza, and García Fernández de Villodre; Russell, *English Intervention*, pp. 180–81. Russell (p. 181 n1) also points out Richard II's payments in 1379 that show Rodríguez de Aza and Zamora traveled with forty Castilian squires and six bowmen.

25. In addition to Castilians, Portuguese were common visitors at the Savoy, particularly after the treaty of 1372. Gaunt employed a number of them as emissaries, João Fernándes Andiero being the most (in)famous. It befit Gaunt's kingly status that foreign dignitaries stopped at the Savoy as well as Westminster, and Navarrese were particularly welcome. There such guests would have found retainers acquainted with Iberian protocols: Russell (*English Intervention*, p. 179) notes that "Both Doña Constanza and her husband included a number of Spaniards among their household staffs. A Castilian governess was appointed to look after the children of the marriage when these were born, and one...was attached to the personal suite of the princes Katherine. [Gaunt] himself also had several Castilian servants about him in the Savoy." Tutors were provided to teach the children Spanish (presumably Castilian, although other dialects were probably also heard at Savoy), and Constanza received instruction in English, making it available to her retinue as well. Doubtless some of this language-sharing facilitated such marriages as one Sancha García's, lady-in-waiting to Constanza, who wed Sir Walter Blount, among Gaunt's staunchest retainers, and Rodríguez de Aza's, who married Alice Clifford, an English counterpart of Sancha García; see Russell, *English Intervention*, p. 181. Important gifts of jewelry, to Richard II and others, at New Year and on feast days were set "in the style favoured by Spanish jewelers"; see Russell, *English Intervention*, p. 179 n3. It should be noted that there are dissenting views: Anthony Goodman remarks, without offering evidence, that "the personnel and culture of [Gaunt's] court remained Anglo-French: he apparently had little admiration for anything Spanish except the cult of Santiago, the crusading tradition (much decayed in English eyes) and

horse-harness"; see "Before the Armada: Iberia and England in the Middle Ages," in *England in Europe, 1066–1453*, ed. Nigel Saul (London: Collins and Brown, 1994), pp. 108–20, quote p. 114.

26. Philippa Chaucer attended Constanza at least from August 1372, when she received an annuity from Gaunt for her service (*Life-Records*, ed. Crow and Olson, pp. 85–87); when she ceased is unknown, although there are New Year's gifts to show she was in the duke's employ through 1382 (*Life-Records*, pp. 90–91; Gaunt's registers are missing from 1383). There is no record of her travel to Spain with the invasion force Gaunt mounted in 1386 (see below notes 29 and 30), which included Constanza. Thus Derek Pearsall's assessment is probably correct: "Philippa was not of the party. In 1386 she was probably residing more permanently with her sister in Lincolnshire" (*Life of Chaucer*, p. 142).
27. On Gaunt's various attempts to gain funding for an invasion of Castile in 1372, 1373–74, and 1377–83, see Russell, *English Intervention*, pp. 186–93, 205–17, 284–85, 315–43.
28. See Rymer, *Foedera*, iii (The Hague, 1740), pp. 200–03.
29. For an account of Gaunt's preparations and the invasion, see Russell, *English Intervention*, pp. 400–48.
30. Jesús L. Serrano Reyes has argued that—in addition to marrying Chaucer (whom she accompanied as one of his three unspecified companions noted in the Navarrese safe-conduct) in Spain in 1366—Philippa also died there, of plague, while in service to Constanza; see his "The Chaucers in Spain: From the Wedding to the Funeral," *Selim* [Journal of the Spanish Society for Medieval English Language and Literature] 8 (2001): 193–203.
31. On the marriages, see, Russell, *English Intervention*, pp. 495–525.
32. Some of Gaunt's letters survive, and are taken to be self-composed: see M. Dominica Legge, ed., *Anglo-Norman Letters and Petitions from All Souls MS 182*, Anglo-Norman Text Society 3 (Oxford: Blackwell, 1941), §74; for example, Gaunt to Richard II, August 25, 1397. At least one letter of Constanza's survives; see Mary Anne Everett Wood, ed., *Letters of Royal and Illustrious Ladies of Great Britain, from the Commencement of the Twelfth Century to the Close of the Reign of Queen Mary*, 3 vols. (London: Henry Colburn, 1846), 1:66.
33. On Philippa (and Catherine) and the *Confessio Amantis*, see R.F. Yeager, "Gower's Lancastrian Affinity: The Iberian Connection," *Viator* 35 (2004): 483–515, and further, Joyce Coleman, "Philippa of Lancaster, Queen of Portugal—and Patron of the Gower Translations?" chapter 7 in this volume.
34. For example, most recently by Patricia Shaw: see "The Presence of Spain in Middle English Literature," *Archiv für das Studium der neueren Sprachen und Literaturen* 229 (1992): 41–54. Antonio León Sendra and Jesús L. Serrano Reyes cover the same territory, while adding many additional references "explicitly to Spanish persons, subjects, topics or circumstances": see their "Spanish References in the *Canterbury Tales*," *Selim* [Journal of the Spanish Society for Medieval English Language and Literature]

2 (1992): 106–41; quotation, p. 106. A number of their sixty-four citations are shaky, however: not a few are to Seneca, who was perhaps more a classical "auctor" to Chaucer than a Spanish writer, as was Lucan, also born in Spain and whom Chaucer mentions as well; one might question similarly the "Spanishness" of Avicenna and Averroes, and Isidore of Seville.
35. On the notoriety in England of Algeciras and Granada, see Terry Jones, *Chaucer's Knight: The Portrait of a Medieval Mercenary*, rev. ed. (London: Methuen, 1994), pp. 60–64.
36. See the note of Christine Ryan Hilary on the Pardoner's portrait in the General Prologue, *Riverside Chaucer*, 824.
37. Chaucer explains the use of "tables Tolletanes" in the *Treatise on the Astrolabe*, II.§42–45. As for his interest in shoes: see for a few examples *CT* I.273, I.458, I.3267, I.3318.
38. If Froissart is to be believed, the notion of Pedro's legitimacy and Enrique's bastardy apparently weighed heavily with the Black Prince, enough to make it the deciding factor in his siding with Pedro, whom he knew to deserve his nickname; see *Chronicles*, chap. 231.
39. John Burrow and V.J. Scattergood list three very different candidates suggested over the years by various hands; see their note to the Shipman's General Prologue portrait in *Riverside Chaucer*, p. 815; and see further Pearsall, *Life of Chaucer*, p. 105, who connects Chaucer's references to shipmen of the west country and Dartmouth with a trip there on the king's business related to Genoese shipping in 1373.
40. On Chaucer's reliance on each, and in what ways, see Ernst Lücke, "Das Leben der Constanze bei Trivet, Gower und Chaucer," *Anglia* 14 (1892): 77–112 and 149–85; Margaret Schlauch, *Chaucer's Constance and Accused Queens* (New York: New York University Press, 1927), pp. 132–34; Peter Nicholson, " 'The Man of Law's Tale': What Chaucer Really Owed to Gower," *Chaucer Review* 26 (1991): 153–74; and R.F. Yeager, "John Gower's Images: 'The Tale of Constance' and 'The Man of Law's Tale,' " in *Speaking Images: Essays in Honor of V.A. Kolve*, ed. R.F. Yeager and Charlotte C. Morse (Asheville, NC: Pegasus Press, 2000), pp. 525–57.
41. For Trivet, see *Sources and Analogues of Chaucer's Canterbury Tales*, ed. W.F. Bryan and Germaine Dempster (New York: Humanities Press, 1941), p. 175; for Gower, see *Sources and Analogues of Chaucer's Canterbury Tales*, p. 193.
42. And smacks, perhaps, of competitive spirit: Chaucer may have been showing off an international experience that Gower, as far as we know, didn't have.
43. For the probable date of composition as 1379–80, see *Riverside Chaucer*, p. 347, and Pearsall, *Life of Chaucer*, pp. 109–10, who places it as I do, after 1374 and before 1378.
44. See Higini Anglès, *La Musica a Catalunya fins al segle* XIII (Barcelona: Biblioteca de Catalunya amb la collaboració de la Universitat Autònoma de Barcelona, 1988), p. 88.
45. See note 16, above.

46. Baugh, "Background of Chaucer's Mission," p. 63, claims that when du Guesclin arrived in Barcelona just before Christmas 1365 "Calveley was already there."
47. On the timetable of Gournay's and d'Aubrichicourt's march to Barcelona, see note 16, above.
48. Jesús L. Serrano Reyes, " 'Els Castells Humans': An Architectural Element in the *House of Fame*," *Proceedings of the 9th International Conference of the Spanish Society for Medieval English Language and Literature*, ed. Margarita Giménez Bon and Vickie Olsen (Vitoria-Gasteiz 1997), pp. 326–37; Shaw, "Presence of Spain," p. 44, suggests in contradiction that Chaucer's model was castles built on promontories in northern Spain.
49. Serrano, " 'Els Castells Humans,' " p. 329. Roland M. Smith, however, *Modern Language Notes* 65 (1950): 521–30, implies either a Spanish or Dutch origin, but encountered in England.
50. For a useful description of the differences, see William J. Entwistle, *The Spanish Language, together with Portuguese, Catalan and Basque*, 2nd ed. (London: Faber and Faber, 1962), pp. 82–150.
51. On the sources of the *Book of the Duchess* see especially James I. Wimsatt, *Chaucer and His French Contemporaries: Natural Music in the Fourteenth Century* (Toronto: University of Toronto Press, 1991); for the *Hous of Fame*, the summary by John M. Fyler, *Riverside Chaucer*, pp. 977–78 is a sufficient guide for my purposes here.
52. Serrano, "Els Castells Humans," pp. 30–35, in fact, argues in favor of Pedro IV of Aragon, "The Ceremonious," being the "man of gret auctorite" (*HF* 2158), based on a particular Aragonese tradition of building human pyramids ahead of an arriving dignitary's entrance into a city—a practice he believes Chaucer observed at close quarters.
53. See A.D. Deyermond, *A Literary History of Spain: The Middle Ages* (London: Benn, 1971), pp. 66–69.
54. On Berceo, see Deyermond, *Literary History*, pp. 59–66; on the pilgrims' hymn at Montserrat, see Jesús L. Serrano Reyes, "A Catalan 'Virolay' and the 'Femynyne Creature, Sitte in a See Imperiall,' " *Proceedings of the 10th International Conference of the Spanish Society for English Medieval Language and Literature*, ed. Ana María Hornero Corisco and María Pilar Navarro Errasti (Zaragoza: Institución "Fernando el Católico," 2000), pp. 235–43. Serrano argues for this as the source of Chaucer's portrait of Lady Fame in the *Hous of Fame*. I am grateful to Professor Serrano for an advance look at his work.
55. On the prominence of the *Disciplina clericalis*, see Deyermond, *Literary History*, p. 97, and further Joseph Ramon Jones and John Esten Keller, *The Scholar's Guide: A Translation of the Twelfth-Century Disciplina Clericalis of Pedro Alfonso* (Toronto: Pontifical Institute of Medieval Studies, 1969), p. 16; the text translates the edition of Alfons Hilka and Werner Söderhjelm, *Petri Alfonsi Disciplina Clericalis. I. Lateinische Texte*, Acta Societatis Scientiarum Fennicae, 38.4 (Helsingfors: Druckerei der Finnischen Literaturgesellschaft, 1911).

56. That is, *CT* VII.1053, 1189, 1218, 1309, 1566; for the French, see Bryan and Dempster, *Sources and Analogues*, 561–614.
57. For example, "The knowledgeable will remember what they have forgotten by means of the things which are contained here"; trans. Jones and Keller, *Scholar's Guide*, p. 34.
58. Jones and Keller, *Scholar's Guide*, p. 34.
59. Jones and Keller, *Scholar's Guide*, p. 34.
60. The *Libro de los engaños* has been edited by John Esten Keller, University of North Carolina Studies in Romance Languages and Literatures 20.1 (Chapel Hill: University of North Carolina Press, rev. ed. 1959). For discussion of it, *Calila e Digna*, and several other works of this type, see Keller's introduction, and further Deyermond, *Literary History*, pp. 96–99.
61. See the edition of Alfonso I. Sotelo (Madrid: Ediciones Cátedra, 1976); and also John Esten Keller and L. Clark Keating, ed., *The Book of Count Lucanor and Patronio: A Translation of Don Juan Manuel's El Conde Lucanor*, Studies in Romance Languages 16 (Louisville: University Press of Kentucky, 1977).
62. See Deyermond, *Literary History*, pp. 137–39.
63. That he did has been argued strenuously by Serrano; see his *Didactismo y moralismo en Geoffrey Chaucer y Don Manuel: Un estudio comparativo textual* (Córdoba: Servicio de Publicaciones de la Universidad de Córdoba, 1995).
64. *El Conde Lucanor*, ed. Sotelo, p. 68: "E porque don Johan vio e sabe que en los libros contesçen muchos yerros en los trasladar, porque las letras semejan unas a otras cuidando o la una letra que es otra, en escriviéndolo, múdase toda la razón e por aventura confóndesse, e los que después fallan aquello escripto, ponen la culpa al que fizo el libro; e porque don Johan se reçeló desto, ruega a los que leyeren qualquier libro que fuere trasladado del que él compuso, o de los libros que él fizo, que si fallaren alguna palabra mal puesta, que non pongan la culpa a él, fasta que bean el libro mismo que don johan fizo, que es emendado, en muchos logares, de su letra" ["And because Don Juan saw and knew that in copying books many errors occur, because letters resemble one another, and it is thought that one letter is another, and in writing the entire meaning is changed and by chance confused; and people who later on find it so written, blame the one who wrote the book; and because Don Juan was fearful of this he beseeches people who read any book whatever which was copied from what he composed or wrote, that if they read an ill-couched word, they place not the blame on him, until they read the very copy which Don Juan wrote, which has been corrected in many places in his own hand"]; trans. Keller and Clark, *The Book of Count Lucanor*, p. 39.
65. See Deyermond, *Literary History*, p. 115, and more recently Kathleen Bishop, "*El Libro de Buen Amor* and the *Canterbury Tales*," in *Satura: Studies in Medieval Literature in Honour of Robert R. Raymo*, ed. Nancy M. Reale and Ruth E. Sternglantz (Donington: Shaun Tyas, 2001), pp. 227–37; and Eugenio M. Olivares Merino, " 'Glorie of Spayne': Juan Ruiz through the Eyes of an Englishman," *Revista Canaria de Estudos Ingleses* 45 (2002): 233–44.

66. See Deyermond, *Literary History*, for 1330 and 1343; for the claim of the 1380s, see Henry Ansgar Kelly, *Canon Law and the Archpriest of Hita*, Medieval and Renaissance Studies 27 (Binghamton, NY: Center for Medieval and Early Renaissance Studies, 1984), p. 8; "Juan Ruiz and Archpriests: Novel Reports," *La Corónica* 16 (1987–88): 32–54; and "A Juan Ruiz Directory for 1380–82," *Mester* 7 (1988): 69–93.
67. For a description, see Russell, *English Intervention*, pp. 518–20.
68. As David Wallace puts it: "In the *House of Fame*...Machaut yields to Dante as the English poet's chief mentor. This is not to say that the discovery of Dante rendered Machaut and his French forebears obsolete for Chaucer, or even that it pushed them into the background." See "Chaucer and Boccaccio's Early Writings," in *Chaucer and the Italian Trecento*, ed. Piero Boitani (Cambridge: Cambridge University Press, 1983), p. 141 [141–62].
69. The (excessive) debate over Chaucer's familiarity with the *Decameron* was put to rest by Donald McGrady, "Chaucer and the *Decameron* Reconsidered," *Chaucer Review* 12 (1977): 1–26; see further Michael Leonard Koff and Brenda Deen, eds., *The "Decameron" and the "Canterbury Tales": New Essays on an Old Question* (Madison, NJ: Fairleigh Dickinson University Press, 2000), especially Koff's Introduction and Peter G. Beidler, "Just Say Yes, Chaucer Knew the *Decameron*: or, Bringing the *Shipman's Tale* Out of Limbo," pp. 25–46, in the same volume.
70. Per Nykrog makes a similar point on a more particularized level by triangulating the *Disciplina*'s relation to the fabliaux; see his *Les Fabliaux: Etude d'histoire litteraire et de stylistique medievale*, (1957; new ed. Geneva: Librarie Droz, 1973). The metafictional qualities of the *Decameron* are approached by Pier Massimo Forni (who does not himself use that term) in *Adventures in Speech: Rhetoric and Narration in Boccaccio's "Decameron"* (Philadelphia: University of Pennsylvania Press, 1996); see his distinction between the *Novellino* and the *Decameron* (pp. 1–2), and his discussion of the importance of the frame-tale, pp. 3–28. Both apply equally to the *Canterbury Tales*. Helpful as well is the sketch of the *Decameron* (again extendable to Chaucer) by Guido Almansi, as "a completely self-sufficient text" in his chapter "Narrative Screens"; see *The Writer as Liar: Narrative Technique in the Decameron* (London: Routledge and Kegan Paul, 1975), pp. 1–18.

CONTRIBUTORS

María Bullón-Fernández is Associate Professor of English at Seattle University. Her book *Fathers and Daughters in Gower's "Confessio Amantis"* was published by D.S. Brewer in 2000. She has also published essays and articles on Chaucer, Gower, medieval theater, and *Pearl*.

Lluís Cabré is Associate Professor of Medieval Catalan Literature at the Universitat Autònoma de Barcelona. From 1990 to 1995 he was Lecturer and Visiting Research Fellow at Queen Mary and Westfield College (University of London). His publications include a critical edition of Pere March's *Poesies* (Barcelona 1993) and a number of articles on medieval poetry, sermon writing, and the intellectual background of Ramon Llull, Bernat Metge, and Ausiàs March.

Cynthia L. Chamberlin is a Ph.D. candidate in the Department of History at UCLA and is a research historian for the Center for Latino Health and Culture at UCLA. Her dissertation, titled "*No m'a dejado*: A Social and Political History of Seville, 1265–1350," is in progress. She has published various articles on medieval Castilian history, including ones on the Castilian siege of Algeciras (1278–79) and on the proto-cult of Saint Fernando III.

Joyce Coleman is the Rudolph C. Bambas Professor of Medieval English Literature and Culture at the University of Oklahoma. Previously she taught at the University of North Dakota. Her research centers on literary performance and reception, with the goal of situating literary analysis within a wider awareness of cultural process. Her 1996 book, *Public Reading and the Reading Public in Late Medieval England and France* (Cambridge University Press), has been followed by articles in *Speculum*, *Studies in the Age of Chaucer*, *The British Library Journal*, and other journals and anthologies.

Ana Echevarría Arsuaga is Associate Professor of Medieval History at the Universidad Nacional de Educación a Distancia, Madrid (Spain). She is the author of *The Fortress of Faith: The Attitude towards Muslims in*

Fifteenth-Century Spain, Catalina de Lancaster (1372–1418), and a number of essays focusing on queenship in Medieval Castile.

Jennifer C. Geouge is a Ph.D. candidate in Late Medieval Iberian History at the University of Kentucky, Lexington. Her dissertation is titled "The Role of the Noble Family in Anglo-Portuguese Trade in the Fifteenth Century." She has given various papers on Anglo-Portuguese topics, including "Foreign Relations during the Reigns of João I of Portugal and Henry IV of England."

Amélia P. Hutchinson received her Ph.D. in Portuguese Studies from the University of London (UK) in 2002 and is currently a Lecturer and Supervisor for the Portuguese Language Program at the University of Georgia, GA. She has published numerous articles on Portuguese chronicle-writing and Portuguese Arthurian Literature and is a member of the International Arthurian Society. She is also Director of the Fernão Lopes Project, which will produce the first complete edition of Fernão Lopes's chronicles in English.

Rose Walker has a Ph.D. from the Courtauld Institute of Art, University of London. She is currently the Deputy Secretary and Academic Registrar at the Courtauld Institute of Art. She is author of *Views of Transition: Liturgy and Illumination in Medieval Spain*, as well as articles and essays on spanish medieval art.

Jennifer Goodman Wollock is Professor of English at Texas A&M University. She has numerous publications on medieval topics including, *Chivalry and Exploration, 1298–1630; British Drama to 1660; The Legend of Arthur in British and American Literature to 1985; Malory and Caxton's Prose Romances of 1485*.

R.F. Yeager teaches medieval literature at the University of West Florida. He is President of the John Gower Society and the author of *John Gower: The Search for a New Arion* and, most recently, *Who Murdered Chaucer?* with Terry Jones, Terry Dolan, Alan Fletcher, and Juliette Dor. He has edited books on Gower and Chaucer, including *Chaucer and Gower: Difference, Mutuality and Exchange* and *Re-Visioning Gower* and is the translator of *John Gower: The Minor Latin Poetry*. He has also authored numerous articles and essays.

BIBLIOGRAPHY

Primary Sources

Acta Aragonensia. Quellen zur deutschen, italienischen, französischen, spanischen, zur Kirchen- und Kulturgeschichte aus der diplomatischen Korrespondez Jaymes II (1291–1327). Ed. Heinrich Finke. 3 vols. Berlin and Leipzig: Walther Rothschild, 1908–22.

Adae Murimuth Continuatio chronicarum. Robertus de Avesbury De gestis mirabilibus Regis Edwardi Tertii. Ed. Edward Maunde Thompson. Rerum Britannicarum Medii Aevi Scriptores, 93. London: Longman, 1889. Repr., Wiesbaden, Germany: Kraus Reprints, 1965.

Age of Chivalry: Art in Plantagenet England, 1200–1400. Ed. Jonathan Alexander and Paul Binski. London: Royal Academy of Arts, Weidenfeld and Nicolson, 1987.

Almeida, Virginia De Castro e, ed. *Conquests and Discoveries of Henry the Navigator.* Trans. Bernard Miall. London: Allen & Unwin, 1936.

Anonimalle Chronicle: 1333–1381, from a Manuscript Written at St. Mary's Abbey, York. Ed. V.H. Galbraith. Manchester: University of Manchester Press, 1927.

Aramon, Ramon, ed. *Curial e Güelfa.* 3 vols. Barcelona: Barcino, 1930–33.

As Gavetas da Tore do Tombo. Lisbon: Centro de Estudos Ultramarinos, 1970.

Barbour, John. *The Bruce.* Ed. A.A.M. Duncan. Edinburgh: Canongate Books, 1997.

Barragán Domeño, María Dolores, ed. *Archivo General de Navarra (1322–1349), I. Documentación real.* Fuentes documentales medievales del País Vasco, 74. Donostia, Spain: Eusko Ikaskuntza-Sociedad de Estudios Vascos, 1997.

Basto, Artur de Magalhães. *O Essencial sobre Os Doze de Inglaterra.* Lisbon: Imprensa Nacional-Casa da Moeda, 1986.

———. *Relação ou Crónica Breve das Cavalarias dos Doze de Inglaterra.* Porto: Imprensa Portuguesa, 1935.

Beckington, Thomas, Bishop of Bath and Wells. *Memorials of the Reign of Henry VI.* London: Longman, 1872.

Bernáldez, *Don Fernando è Doña Isabel.* In *Crónicas de los reyes de Castilla.* Ed. Cayetano Rosell y López. Biblioteca de Autores Españoles 3. Madrid: Ediciones Atlas, 1953.

Bodel, Jean. *Chanson des Saxons.* Ed. Ann Brasseur. Geneva: Droz, 1989.

Bouchon, A.C., ed. *Chroniques d'Enguerrand de Monstrelet.* In *Collection des chroniques nationales françaises.* Vols. 26–40. 14 vols. Paris: Verdière, 1826–27.

Bouchon, A.C., ed. *Mémoires de Jean Lefevre: dit Toison-d'or, seigneur de Saint-Remy.* In *Collection des chroniques nationales françaises.* Vols. 32–33. Paris: [s.n.], 1826.

Brie, Friedrich W.D., ed. *The Brut, or the Chronicles of England.* 2 vols. Early English Text Society, 131, 136. London: Kegan Paul, Trench, Trübner, 1906–08.

The Bruce. Ed. Matthew P. McDiarmaid. 3 vols. Edinburgh: Scottish Text Society, 1985.

Cahn, Walter. *Romanesque Manuscripts. The Twelfth Century.* 2 vols. London: Harvey Miller, 1996.

Calendar of Chancery Warrants, A.D. 1244–1326. Preserved in the Public Record Office.

Calendar of Close Rolls. Nedeln: Kraus Reprint, 1971.

Calendar of Close Rolls. Preserved in the Public Record Office.

Calendar of Entries in the Papal Registers Relating to Great Britain and Ireland. Papal Letters. 16 vols. London, 1893–1986. Repr., Nedeln, Lichtenstein: Kraus Reprints, 1971.

Calendar of Fine Rolls. Preserved in the Public Record Office.

Calendar of Patent Rolls. Nedeln, Lichtenstein: Kraus Reprint, 1971.

Calendar of Patent Rolls. Preserved in the Public Record Office.

Calendar of Signet Letters of Henry IV and Henry V, 1399–1422. Ed. J.L. Kirby. London: His Majesty's Stationery Office, 1978.

Camões, Luis de. *Luiz Vaz de Camões: The Lusiads.* Trans. William C. Atkinson Harmondsworth: Penguin Books, 1952.

———. *Lusíadas.* Lisboa: Imprensa Nacional-Casa da Moeda, 1975.

———. *The Lusiads.* Trans. Leonard Bacon. New York: Hispanic Society of America, 1950. Repr., 1966.

Canals, Antoni, trans. *Scipió e Aníbal. De providència (de Sèneca). De arra de ànima (d'Hug de Sant Víctor).* Ed. Martí de Riquer. Els Nostres Clàssics, A49. Barcelona: Barcino, 1935.

Castera, Duperron de. *La Lusiade de Camoens.* 3 vols. Paris: Nion, 1768.

Chaucer, Geoffrey. *The Riverside Chaucer.* 3rd ed. Gen. ed. Larry D. Benson. Oxford: Oxford University Press, 1987; Boston: Houghton Mifflin, 1987.

Chaucer Life-Records. Ed. Martin M. Crow and Claire C. Olson. Oxford: Oxford University Press, 1966.

Clanvowe, Sir John. *The Works of Sir John Clanvowe.* Ed. V.J. Scattergood. Cambridge, UK: Brewer, 1975.

Cleriadus et Meliadice. Ed. Gaston Zink. Geneva: Droz, 1984.

Conlon, D.J., ed. *Le Rommant de Guy de Warwik et de Herolt d'Ardenne.* Chapel Hill: The University of North Carolina Press, 1969.

Correia, Manuel. *Lusiadas de Luiz de Camões. Comētados pelo licenciado Manuel Correia.* Lisboa: P. Crasbeek, 1613.

Costa, Joaquim. *"Os Doze de Inglaterra": o célebre episódio de "Os Lusíadas" na História e na Lenda.* Off-print. Porto: Imprensa Portuguesa, 1935.

Crécy, Marie-Claude de, ed. *Le Roman de Ponthus et Sidoine.* Geneva: Droz, 1997.

Crónica del muy alto et muy católico rey don Alfonso el Onceno deste nombre, que venció la batalla del Río Salado, et ganó a las Algeciras. Ed. Cayetano Rosell. Biblioteca de Autores Españoles, 66. Madrid: 1875, 1877. Repr., Madrid: Rivadeneyra, 1953.

Crow, Martin M. and Clair C. Olson, eds. *Chaucer Life-Records*. Austin: University of Texas Press, 1966.

Dante Alighieri. *La "Commedia" secondo l'antica Vulgata*. Ed. Giorgio Petrocchi. 4 vols. Milan: Mondadori, 1966–67.

Dauncey, John. *A Compendious Chronicle of the Kingdom of Portugal, from Alfonso, the First King, to Alfonso the Sixth, now Reigning: Together with a Cosmographical Description of the Dominions of Portugal*. London, 1661. Ann Arbor, University Microfilms, 1964.

Díez de Gámez, Gutierrez. *The Unconquered Knight: A Chronicle of the Deeds of Don Pero Niño, Count of Buelna*. Trans. Joan Evans (selection only). London: George Routledge and Sons, Ltd., 1928.

———. *El Victorial: Crónica de don Pero Niño*. Ed. Rafael Beltrán Llavador. Salamanca: Universidad de Salamanca, 1997.

Documentos de Clemente IV (1265–1268): referentes a España. Ed. S. Domínguez Sánchez. León: Universidad de León, 1996.

Duarte, Dom. *Livro dos Conselhos de El-rei D. Duarte livro da cartuxa*. Ed. João José Alves Dias. Lisboa: Editorial Estampa, 1982.

———. *Livro da ensinança de bem cavalgar toda sela que fez El-rey Dom Eduarte*. Ed. Joseph M. Piel. Lisboa: Imprensa Nacional-Casa da Moeda, 1986.

Eiximenis, Francesc. *Dotzè llibre del Crestià*. Ed. Curt Wittlin et al. 2 vols. Girona: Col·legi Universitari i Diputació, 1987.

———. *La societat catalana al segle XIV*. Ed. Jill Webster. Antologia Catalana, 30. Barcelona: Edicions 62, 1967.

Ewert, Alfred, ed. *Gui de Warevic: roman du XIIIe siècle*. Les Classiques Français du Moyen Age, 74 and 75. Paris: Champion, 1933.

Fernandes, Hirondino da Paixão. *Bibliografia do Distrito de Bragança*. Documentos (textos) Publicados. Bragança: Instituto Superior Politécnico de Bragança, 1996.

Férotin, Marius, ed. *Recueil des chartes de l'Abbaye de Silos*. Paris: Imprimerie Nationale, 1897.

Froissart, Jean. *Chronicles*. Trans. John Bourchier, Lord Berners. 6 vols. London: Tudor Translation Series, 1901–03.

———. *Chronicles*. Trans. and ed. Geoffrey Brereton. Harmondsworth: Penguin, 1968.

———. *Chronicles of England, France, Spain and the Adjoining Countries*. London: W. Smith, 1942.

———. *Oeuvres: Chroniques*. Ed. Kervyn de Lettenhove. 25 vols. Brussels: Victor Devaux, 1867–77.

Gal·les, Joan de. *Breviloqui*. Ed. Norbert d'Ordal. Els Nostres Clàssics, A28. Barcelona: Barcino, 1930.

García Arancón, M.R. *Colección diplomática de los reyes de Navarra de la dinastía de Champaña. Vol. II: Teobaldo II (1253–1270)*. San Sebastián: Sociedad de Estudios Vascos, 1985.

Gesta Edwardi Carnarvan auctore canonico Bridlingtoniensi. In Stubbs, *Chronicles*, Part 2.

González Crespo, Esther, ed. *Colección documental de Alfonso XI. Diplomas reales conservados en el Archivo Histórico Nacional, Sección de Clero. Pergaminos*. Madrid: Universidad Complutense, 1985.

Gower, John. *The English Works of John Gower*. Ed. G.C. Macaulay. 2 vols. EETS e.s. 81–82. London: Kegan Paul, Trench, Trübner, 1900–01.

Gras, Mossèn. *Tragèdia de Lançalot*. Ed. Martí de Riquer. Barcelona: Quaderns Crema, 1984.

The Great Roll of the Pipe for the Twenty-Sixth Year of the Reign of King Henry the Second: AD 1179–80. London: Wyman and Sons, 1930.

Hingeston, F.C., ed. and trans. *Royal and Historical Letters during the Reign of Henry the Fourth, King of England and France and Lord of Ireland*. 2 vols. Rolls Series 18. London, 1860 and 1965.

———. *Royal and Historical Letters during the Reign of Henry the Fourth, King of England and of France and Lord of Ireland*. New York: Kraus, 1964.

Hog, Thomas, ed. *Adami Murimuthensis Chronica sui temporis, nunc primum per decem annos aucta, M.CCC.III.–M.CCC.XLVI. cum eorundem continuatione ad M.CCC.LXXX. a quodam anonymo*. London: Sumptibus Societatis, 1846.

Huon de Bordeaux, roman en prose du XVème siècle. Ed. Michel J. Raby. Studies in the Humanities 27. New York: Peter Lang, 1998.

The Hystorye of Olyuer of Castylle. Ed. Gail Orgelfinger. Trans. Henry Watson. New York: Garland, 1988.

Irving, Washington. *A Chronicle of the Conquest of Granada by Fray Antonio Agapida*. Intro. Earl N. Harbert. Ed. Miriam J. Shillingsburg. Boston: Twayne, 1988.

———. *A History of New York*. Ed. Edwin T. Bowden. New Haven: College and University Press; Boston: Twayne, 1964.

Istore et croniques de Flandres, d'après les textes de divers manuscrits. Ed. Kervyn de Lettenhove. 2 vols. Brussels: Hayez, 1879–80.

Jiménez de Rada, Rodrigo. *Historia de rebus Hispaniae, sive Historia Gothica*. Ed. Juan Fernández Valverde. Corpus Chirstianorum. Continuatio Medievalis, 72 A. Turnholt, Belgium: Brepols, 1987.

João I. *Livro da montaria*. In *Obras dos príncipes de Avis*. Ed. M. Lopes de Almeida. Porto: Lello & Irmão, 1981.

John Gower: Confesión del Amante. Traducción de Juan de Cuenca (s. xv). Ed. Elena Alvar. Anejos del Boletín de la Real Academia Española 45. Madrid: Real Academia Española, 1990.

John of Gaunt's Register. Ed. Sydney Armitage-Smith. 2 vols. Camden 3rd ser., Vols. 20–21. London: Camden Society, 1911.

John of Gaunt's Register, 1379–1383. Ed. Eleanor C. Lodge and Robert Somerville. 2 vols. Camden 3rd ser., Vols. 56–57. London: Camden Society, 1937.

Johnstone, Hilda, ed. *Letters of Edward Prince of Wales, 1304–1305*. Cambridge: Cambridge University Press/Roxburghe Club, 1931.

Jones, Joseph Ramon and John Esten Keller. *The Scholar's Guide: A Translation of the Twelfth-Century Disciplina Clericalis of Pedro Alfonso*. Toronto: Pontifical Institute of Medieval Studies, 1969.

Juan Manuel. *Libro de los enxiemplos del Conde Lucanor e de Patronio*. Ed. Alfonso I. Sotelo. Madrid: Ediciones Cátedra, 1976.

Keller, John Esten and L. Clark Keating, eds. *"The Book of Count Lucanor and Patronio": A Translation of Don Juan Manuel's "El Conde Lucanor"*. Studies in Romance Languages 16. Louisville: University Press of Kentucky, 1977.

Legge, M. Dominica, ed. *Anglo-Norman Letters and Petitions from All Souls MS 182*. Anglo-Norman Text Society 3. Oxford: Blackwell, 1941.

Libro de los engaños. Ed. John Esten Keller. University of North Carolina Studies in Romance Languages and Literatures 20.1. Rev. ed. Chapel Hill: University of North Carolina Press, 1959.

Llull, Ramon. *Llibre de l'orde de cavalleria.* Ed. Albert Soler Llopart. Els Nostres Clàssics, A127. Barcelona: Barcino, 1988.

Lopes, Fernão. *Cronica do condestabre de Portugal, Dom Nunalvrez Pereyra, principiador da Casa de Bragança.* Lisbon: Antonio Alvarez Impressor, 1623.

———. *Crónica de D. Fernando.* Lisboa: Imprensa Nacional-Casa da Moeda, 1975.

———. *Crónica de D. João I.* 2 vols. Porto: Livraria Civilização, 1945. Repr., Porto: Livraria Civilização, 1983.

———. Extracts from the *Chronicles of Dom Fernando and Dom João de boa memoria.* In *The English in Portugal, 1367–87.* Ed. and trans. Derek W. Lomax and R.J. Oakley. Warminster, UK: Aris & Phillips, 1988. 155–356.

———. *Crónica del Rei Dom Joham I de boa memoria e dos reis de Portugal o decimo.* Part 2. Ed. William J. Entwistle. Lisbon: Imprensa Nacional-Casa da Moeda, 1968. Repr., Lisbon: Imprensa Nacional-Casa da Moeda, 1990.

López de Ayala, Pedro. *Crónica del rey D. Juan I.* In *Crónicas de los reyes de Castilla.* Ed. C. Rossell. 2 vols. Madrid: Real Academia Española, 1953.

Manuscritos e impresos del monasterio de Las Huelgas Reales de Burgos, Catálogo de la Real Biblioteca, Catálogo de los Reales Patronatos 14.2. Madrid: Patrimonio Nacional, 1999.

Mariz, Pedro. *Diálogos de Vária História.* Coimbra: António de Mariz, 1599.

Marques, João Martins da Silva. *Descobrimentos portugueses, documentos para a sua história.* Lisbon: Edição do Instituto de Alta Cultura, 1971.

Martí, Sadurní. "Les cartes autògrafes de Francesc Eiximenis." *Estudi General* 22 (2002): 235–49.

Martorell, Joanot, and Martí Joan de Galba? *Tirant lo Blanch.* Trans. David H. Rosenthal. New York: Warner, 1984.

———. *Tirant lo Blanch.* Ed. Albert G. Hauf and Vicent Josep Escartí. 2 vols. Valencia: Conselleria de Cultura de la Generalitat Valenciana, 1990.

Maxwell, Herbert, ed. and trans. *The Chronicle of Lanercost, 1272–1346.* Glasgow: James Maclehose and Sons, 1913.

Meneses, Dom Fernando de, Count of Ericeira. *Vida e Acçoens d'El Rey Dom João o Primeyro.* Lisboa: João Galrão, 1677.

Miquel y Planas, Ramon, ed. *Llegendes de l'altra vida.* Barcelona: Biblioteca Catalana, 1914.

Monachi cujusdam Malmesberiensis vita Edwardi II. In Stubbs, *Chronicles,* Part 2.

Monro, Cecil, ed. *Letters of Queen Margaret of Anjou and Bishop Beckington and Others.* New York: AMS Press, 1968.

Le Neve, John. *Fasti Ecclesiae Anglicanae, or A Calendar of the Principal Ecclesiastical Dignitaries in England and Wales. . . from the Earliest Time to the Year M.DCC.XV.* Continued by T. Duffus Hardy. 3 vols. Oxford, 1854.

Nunes, Irene Freire, ed. *A Demanda do Santo Graal.* Lisboa: Imprensa Nacional-Casa da Moeda, 1995.

Orto do esposo. Ed. Bertil Maler. 2 vols. Rio de Janeiro: Instituto Nacional do Livro, 1956.

Pacheco, Arseni, ed. *Viatges a l'altre món: dos relats dels segles XIV i XVI.* Antologia Catalana, 69. Barcelona: Edicions 62, 1973.
Paris, Matthew. *Matthaei Parisiensis, Monachi Sancti Albani Chronica Majora.* Ed. Henry Richard Luard. 7 vols. London: Longman, 1872–83.
Parsons, John Carmi. *The Court and Household of Eleanor of Castile in 1290. An Edition of British Library, Additional Manuscript 35294, with Introduction and Notes.* Toronto: Pontifical Institute of Mediaeval Studies, 1977.
Pedro, Dom, Count of Barcelos. "Livro de Linhagens." In *Portugaliae Monumenta Historica,* 1. *Scriptores.* Ed. Alexandre Herculano. 1856. Repr., Lisboa: Typis Academicis, 1967.
Peele, George. *The Battle of Alcazar.* Repr., in *Dramatic and Political Works of Robert Greene and George Peele.* Ed. Alexander Dyce. London: George Routledge, 1861.
———. *The Famous History of the Life and Death of Captain Thomas Stukeley.* London: Printed for Thomas Panyer, 1605. Repr., in R. Simpson, *The School of Shakespeare.* Vol. 1. New York: J.W. Bouton, 1878.
Perroy, Edouard, ed. *The Diplomatic Correspondence of Richard II.* Camden 3rd ser., Vol. 48. London: Camden Society, 1933.
Petri Alfonsi Disciplina Clericalis. I. Lateinische Texte. Ed. Alfons Hilka and Werner Söderhjelm. Acta Societatis Scientiarum Fennicae, Vol. 38.4. Helsingfors: Druckerei der Finnischen Literaturgesellschaft, 1911.
Pina, Rui de. *Chronica d'el rei dom Duarte.* Porto: Edição da Renascença Portuguesa, 1914.
Prestage, Edgar, ed. *Chronicles of Fernão Lopes and Gomes Eannes de Zurara.* Watford, UK: Voss & Michael, 1928.
Prior, Oliver H., ed. *Caxton's "Mirrour of the World."* EETS, Extra Series, 110. London: The Early English Text Society, 1913.
Rades y Andrada, Francisco de. *Chrónicas de las tres órdenes y cavallerías de Santiago, Calatrava y Alcántara.* Toledo, 1572.
Raine, James, ed. *Historical Papers and Letters from the Northern Registers.* Rerum Britannicarum Medii Aevi Scriptores, 61. London: Her Majesty's Stationery Office, 1873. Repr., Nedeln, Lichtenstein: Kraus Reprints, 1965.
The Registers of Bishop Henry Burghersh, 1320–1342. Ed. Nicholas Bennett. 2 vols. Lincoln Record Society, 87, 90. Woodbridge, England: Boydell Press, 1999, 2003.
The Registers of John de Sandale and Rigaud de Asserio, Bishops of Winchester A.D. 1316–1323, with an Appendix of Contemporaneous and Other Illustrative Documents. Ed. Francis Joseph Baigent. London: Simpkin, 1897.
The Registers of Walter Bromescombe (A.D. 1257–1280) and Peter Quivil (A.D. 1280–1291), Bishops of Exeter, with Some Records of the Episcopate of Bishop Thomas de Bytton (A.D. 1292–1307), also the Taxation of Pope Nicholas IV (A.D. 1291) Diocese of Exeter. Ed. F.C. Hingeston-Randolph. London: George Bell & Sons, 1889.
Les Registres de Benoît XI. Recueil des bulles de ce pape, publiées ou analysées d'après les manuscrits originaux des Archives du Vatican. Ed. Charles Grandjean. Paris: Ernest Thorin, 1883–1905.
Registrum Epistolarum Fratris Johannis Peckham, Archiepiscopi Cantuariensis. Ed. Charles Trice Martin. 3 vols. Rerum Britannicarum Medii Aevi Scriptores, 77,

Parts 1–3. London: Public Record Office. Repr., Wiesbaden, Germany: Kraus Reprints, 1965.

Registrum Henrici Woodlock, diocesis Wintoniensis, A.D. 1305–1316. Ed. A.W. Goodman. Canterbury and York Series, 43. Oxford: Oxford University Press, 1935–40.

Registrum Johannis de Pontissara, Episcopi Wyntoniensis. A.D. MCCLXXXII–MCCCIV. Ed. Cecil Deedes. Surrey Record Society, 1, 4, 6. London: Surrey Record Society and Canterbury & York Society, 1914–22.

Registrum Roberti Winchelsey, Archiepiscopi Cantuariensis. Ed. Rose Graham. 2 vols. Oxford: Oxford University Press, 1917–31.

Rôles gascons, transcrits et publiés par Francisque Michel. 4 vols. Collection de documents inédits sur l'histoire de France. 4th ser. Histoire politique. Paris, 1885–1962.

Rotuli Parliamentorum. London: 1832.

Royal and Historical Letters during the Reign of Henry IV, King of England and of France, and Lord of Ireland. Ed. F.C. Hingeston. 2 vols. New York: Kraus Reprint, 1964–66.

Rubió i Lluch, Antoni. *Documents per l'historia de la cultura catalana mig-eval.* 2 vols. Barcelona: Institut d'Estudis Catalans, 1908–21.

Rymer, Thomas, ed. *Foedera, conventiones, litterae, et cujuscunque generis acta publicae inter reges Angliae et alios quosvis imperatores, reges, pontifices, principes vel communitates (1101–1654).* The Hague: Neaulme, 1739–45.

———. *Foedera, conventiones, litterae, et cujuscunque generis acta publica, inter reges Angliae et alios quosvis imperatores, reges, pontifices, principes, vel communitates. . . (1069–1383). . .* London, 1816–69.

———. *Foedera, conventiones, litterae, et cujuscunque generis acta publica inter reges Angliae, et alios quosvis imperatores, reges, pontifices, principes, vel communitates.* 3rd ed. Rev. George Holmes, 1740. Repr., Farnborough, Hants.: Gregg Press, 1967.

Salgado Júnior, António. "A Relação ou Crónica Breve das Cavalarias dos Doze de Inglaterra." *Labor* 2nd ser. (January 1937): 317–26.

Santarém, Visconde de. *Quadro Elementar das relações politicas e diplomaticas de Portugal com as diversas potencias do mundo.* Paris: J.P. Aillaud, 1842.

Select Cases in the Court of King's Bench. Ed. G.O. Sayles. 7 vols. Publications of the Selden Society, 55, 57–58, 74, 76, 82, 88. London, 1936–71.

Shadwell, C.L., and H.E. Salter. *Oriel College Records.* Oxford Historical Society, 85. Oxford: Clarendon Press, 1926.

Soeiro, Manuel. *Anales de Flandes.* 2 vols. Anvers: Pedro y Juan Bellero, 1624.

Sources and Analogues of Chaucer's Canterbury Tales. Ed. W.F. Bryan and Germaine Dempster. New York: Humanities Press, 1941.

Sousa, Manuel de Faria e. *Lusiadas de Luis de Camoens Comentados por Manuel Faria i Sousa.* 4 vols. Madrid: Juan Sanchez, 1639.

Stubbs, William, ed. *Chronicles of the Reigns of Edward I and Edward II.* 2 vols. Rerum Britannicarum Medii Aevi Scriptores 76. Parts 1–2. London: Longman, 1883. Repr., Wiesbaden, Germany: Kraus Reprints, 1965.

Sutcliffe, Rosemary. *The Eagle of the Ninth.* London: Oxford University Press, 1954. Repr., 1973.

Toscano, Francisco Soares. *Parallelos de Príncipes e Varões Illustres.* Évora: Manoel Carvalho, 1623.

Veas Arteseros, Francisco de Asís, ed. *Documentos de Alfonso XI.* Colección de Documentos para la Historia del Reino de Murcia 6. Murcia: Real Academia Alfonso X el Sabio, 1997.

Vita et mors Edwardi II. Conscripta a Thoma de la Moore [sic]. In Stubbs, ed., *Chronicles,* Part 2.

Wavrin, Jean de. *Chroniques d'Angleterre.* British Library, Royal Ms. 14 E IV.

The Westminster Chronicle 1381–1394. Ed. L.C. Hector and Barbara F. Harvey. Oxford: Clarendon Press, 1982.

Wood, Mary Anne Everett, ed. *Letters of Royal and Illustrious Ladies of Great Britain, from the Commencement of the Twelfth Century to the Close of the Reign of Queen Mary.* 3 vols. London: Henry Colburn, 1846.

Zupitza, Julius, ed. *"The Romance of Guy of Warwick": The Second or 15th-century Version, Edited from the Paper Ms. Ff. 2.38. in the University Library, Cambridge.* EETS 25–26. London: Early English Text Society, 1875–76.

———. *"The Romance of Guy of Warwick": Edited from the Auchinleck Ms. in the Advocate's Library, Edinburgh, and from Ms. 107 in Caius College, Cambridge.* EETS 42 and 49. London: Early English Text Society, 1883–87.

Zurara, Gomes Eanes de. *Crónica da tomada de Ceuta por el rei D. João I.* Ed. Francisco Maria Esteves Pereira. Lisbon: Academia das Sciências de Lisboa, 1915.

———. *Crónica da Tomada de Ceuta.* Introduction and notes by Reis Brasil. Mem-Martins: Edições Europa-América, 1992.

Secondary Sources

Ainaud, Jordi. "Un traductor al Purgatori: a propòsit del *Viatge al Purgatori de sant Patrici* de Ramon de Perellós." In *Traducció i literatura: homenatge a Àngel Crespo.* Ed. G. González and F. Lafarga. Vic: EUMO, 1997. 133–41.

Allmand, C.T. *Henry V.* Berkeley: University of California Press, 1992.

Almansi, Guido. *The Writer as Liar: Narrative Technique in the "Decameron".* London: Routledge and Kegan Paul, 1975.

Alvar, Manuel. "Prólogo." In *John Gower: Confesión del Amante. Traducción de Juan de Cuenca (s. xv).* Ed. Elena Alvar. Anejos del Boletín de la Real Academia Española 45. Madrid, 1990.

Anglès, Higini. *La Música a Catalunya fins al segle XIII.* Barcelona: Biblioteca de Catalunya amb la collaboració de la Universitat Autònoma de Barcelona, 1988.

Anglo, Sydney. *Spectacle, Pageantry, and Early Tudor Policy.* 2nd ed. Oxford: Clarendon Press, 1997.

Armitage-Smith, Sydney. *John of Gaunt: King of Castile and Leon, Duke of Aquitaine and Lancaster, Earl of Derby, Lincoln, and Leicester, Seneschal of England.* London: Constable, 1904. Repr., New York: Barnes & Noble, 1964.

Arnaut, Salvador Dias. "A Crise Nacional dos fins do Século XIV (Contribuição para o seu Estudo)." *Anais* 30 ser. 2 (1985): 51–79.

Art of Medieval Spain A.D. 500–1200. New York: The Metropolitan Museum of Art, 1993.

Ashmole, Elias. *The Institution, Laws & Ceremonies of the Most Noble Order of the Garter*. London, 1672. Repr., Baltimore: Genealogical Publishing Co., 1971.

Atkinson, William C. *A History of Spain and Portugal*. Harmondsworth: Penguin, 1960.

D'Avray, David. "Another Friar and Antiquity." In *Religion and Humanism: Papers Read at the Eigtheenth Summer Meeting and the Nineteenth Winter Meeting of the Ecclesiastical History Society*. Ed. Keith Robbins. Oxford: Blackwell and The Ecclesiastical History Society, 1981. 49–58.

Badia, Lola. "Bernat Metge i els *auctores*: del material de construcció al producte elaborat." *Boletín de la Real Academia de Buenas Letras de Barcelona* 43 (1991–92): 25–40.

———. "Traduccions al català dels segles XIV i XV i innovació cultural i literària." *Estudi General* 11 (1991): 31–50.

———, ed. *Tres contes meravellosos del segle XIV*. Barcelona: Quaderns Crema, 2003.

Barber, Richard W. *The Knight and Chivalry*. Woodbridge: Boydell, 1995.

Barber, Richard W. and Juliet R.V. Barker. *Tournaments: Jousts, Chivalry and Pageants in the Middle Ages*. Woodbridge: Boydell, 1989.

Barcelona, Martí de, O.M. Cap. "La cultura catalana durant el regnat de Jaume II." *Estudios Franciscanos* 91 (1990): 215–95; 92 (1991): 383–492.

———. "Fra Francesc Eiximenis, O. F. M. 1340?–1409?: la seva vida, els seus escrits, la seva personalitat literària." *Estudis Franciscans* 40 (1928): 437–500. Repr., in Grahit, Emili, et al. *Studia bibliographica*: 185–239.

Barreiro Rivas, José Luis. *La función política de los caminos de peregrinación en la Europa medieval: estudio del Camino de Santiago*. Madrid: Tecnos, 1997.

Barron, W.R.J. *English Medieval Romance*. London and New York: Longman, 1987.

———, ed. and trans. *Sir Gawain and the Green Knight*. Manchester: Manchester University Press, 1998.

Barros, Henrique da Gama. *História da administração pública em Portugal nos séculos XII–XV*. Lisbon: Imprensa Nacional, 1885–1922.

Barrow, G.W.S. *Robert Bruce and the Community of the Realm of Scotland*. 3rd ed. Edinburgh: Edinburgh University Press, 1988.

Baugh, Albert C. "The Background of Chaucer's Mission to Spain." In *Chaucer und seine Zeit: Symposion für Walter F. Schirmer*. Ed. Arno Esch. Tübingen: Max Niemeyer, 1968. 55–69.

Beidler, Peter G. "Just Say Yes, Chaucer Knew the *Decameron*: or, Bringing the *Shipman's Tale* Out of Limbo." In *The "Decameron" and the "Canterbury Tales": New Essays on an Old Question*. Ed. Michael Leonard Koff and Brenda Deen. Madison, NJ: Fairleigh Dickinson University Press, 2000. 25–46.

Bell, Aubrey. *Fernam Lopez*. Hispanic Society of America, Portuguese Series. Oxford: Oxford University Press, 1921.

Bell, Susan Groag. "Medieval Women Book Owners: Arbiters of Lay Piety and Ambassadors of Culture." *Signs: Journal of Women in Culture and Society* 7 (1982): 742–68. Also in *Women and Power in the Middle Ages*. Ed. M. Erler and M. Kowaleski. Athens, GA: University of Georgia Press, 1988. 149–87.

Beltz, George Frederick. *Memorials of the Most Noble Order of the Garter, from Its Foundation to the Present Time*. London: Pickering, 1841.
Bennett, Michael. *Richard II and the Revolution of 1399*. Thrup: Sutton, 1999.
Berkeley, Alice and Susan Lowndes. *English Art in Portugal*. Lisbon: Edições Inapa, 1994.
Biddle, Martin, ed. *King Arthur's Round Table: An Archaelogical Investigation*. Woodbridge, UK: Boydell, 2000.
Billanovich, Giuseppe. *I primi umanisti e le tradizioni dei classici latini: prolusione al corso di letteratura italiana detta il 2 febbraio 1951*. Freiburg, Switzerland: Edizioni Universitarie, 1953.
Binski, Paul. "Reflections on *La estoire de Seint Aedward le rei*: Hagiography and Kingship in Thirteenth-Century England." *Journal of Medieval History* 16 (1990): 333–50.
———. *Westminster Abbey and the Plantagenets: Kingship and the Representation of Power, 1200–1400*. New Haven: Yale University Press, 1995.
Bishop, Kathleen. "*El Libro de Buen Amor* and the *Canterbury Tales*." In *Satura: Studies in Medieval Literature in Honour of Robert R. Raymo*. Ed. Nancy M. Reale and Ruth E. Sternglantz. Donington: Shaun Tyas, 2001. 227–37.
Bohigas, Pere. *Sobre manuscrits i biblioteques*. Barcelona: Curial & Publicacions de l'Abadia de Montserrat, 1985.
Botfield, Beriah, ed. *Manners and Household Expenses of England in the Thirteenth and Fifteenth Centuries, Illustrated by Original Records*. London: W. Nicol, 1841.
Boulton, D'Arcy J. *The Knights of the Crown: The Monarchical Orders of Knighthood in Later Medieval England, 1325–1520*. New York: St. Martin's Press, 1987.
Boxer, C.R. *The Portuguese Seaborne Empire, 1415–1825*. New York: A.A. Knopf, 1969.
Braddy, Haldeen. "Chaucer's Don Pedro and the Purpose of the 'Monk's Tale.'" *Modern Language Quarterly* 13 (1952): 3–5.
———. "The Two Petros in the 'Monkes Tale.'" *PMLA* 50 (1935): 69–80.
Bridbury, A.R. *England and the Salt Trade in the Later Middle Ages*. Oxford: Clarendon Press, 1955.
Brieger, Peter H. *The Trinity College Apocalypse: An Introduction and Description*. London: Eugrammia Press, 1967.
Brown, Jonathan and John Elliott, eds. *The Sale of the Century: Artistic Relations between Spain and Great Britain (1604–1655)*. New Haven: Yale University Press, 2002.
Burgo, Jaime del. *Historia de Navarra. La lucha por la libertad*. Madrid: Teba, 1978.
Burnam, Thomas E. "*Tafsīr* and Translation: Traditional Arabic Qur'āns Exegesis and the Latin Qur'āns of Robert of Ketto and Mark of Toledo." *Speculum* 73 (1998): 703–32.
Busqueta Riu, Joan Josep and Juan Pemán Gavín, eds. *Les universitats de la Corona d'Aragó, ahir i avui: estudis històrics*. Barcelona: Pòrtic, 2002.
Butinyà, Júlia. "Una nova font del *Tirant lo Blanc*." *Revista de Filología Románica* 7 (1990): 191–96.
El Camino de Santiago y la articulación del espacio hispánico. XX Semana de Estudios Medievales. Estella, 26 a 30 de julio de 1993. Pamplona: Gobierno de Navarra, 1994.

Carey, Frances. *The Apocalypse and the Shape of Things to Come.* London: The British Museum, 1999.

Carpenter, Dorothy M. "The Pilgrim from Catalonia/Aragon: Ramon de Perellós, 1397." In *The Medieval Pilgrimage to Saint Patrick's Purgatory: Lough Derg and the European Tradition.* Ed. Michael Haren and Yolande de Pontfarcy. Enniskillen: Clogher Historical Society, 1988. 190–201.

Carus-Wilson, E.M. *The Overseas Trade of Bristol in the Later Middle Ages.* 1937. Repr., New York: Barnes and Noble, 1967.

Chadd, David. "Liturgy and Liturgical Music: The Limits of Uniformity." In *Cistercian Art and Architecture in the British Isles.* Ed. Christopher Norton and David Park. Cambridge: Cambridge University Press, 1986. 299–314.

Chaplais, Pierre., ed. *English Medieval Diplomatic Practice, Part I, Documents and Interpretation.* 2 vols. London: Her Majesty's Stationery Office, 1982.

———— *English Diplomatic Practice in the Middle Ages.* London and New York: Cambridge University Press, 2003.

————, ed. *Treaty Rolls Preserved in the Public Record Office.* 2 vols. London: Her Majesty's Stationery Office, 1955.

————. *The War of Saint-Sardos (1323–1325). Gascon Correspondence and Documents.* Camden 3rd ser., Vol. 87. London: Offices of the Royal Historical Society, 1954.

Cheetham, Francis. *Alabaster Images of Medieval England.* Woodbridge: Boydell Press, 2004.

Cheyette, Fredric. "The Professional Papers of an English Ambassador on the Eve of the Hundred Years' War." In *Economies et Sociétés au Moyen Age. Mélanges offerts à Edouard Perroy.* Publications de la Sorbonne, Etudes, 5. Paris: Publications de la Sorbonne, 1973. 400–13.

Childs, Wendy R. *Anglo-Castilian Trade in the Later Middle Ages.* Manchester and Totowa, NJ: Manchester University Press, 1978.

————. "Anglo-Portuguese Relations in the Fourteenth Century." In *The Age of Richard II.* Ed. James L. Gillespie. Stroud: Sutton, 1997. 27–49.

———— "Anglo-Portuguese Trade in the Fifteenth Century." *Transactions of the Royal Historical Society* 6th ser., 2 (1992): 195–219.

Cingolani, Stefano M. *El somni d'una cultura: "Lo somni" de Bernat Metge.* Barcelona: Quaderns Crema, 2002.

Clanchy, Michael T. *From Memory to Written Record. England, 1066–1307.* 2nd ed. Oxford: Blackwell, 1993.

Clavería, Carlos. *Historia del Reino de Navarra.* Pamplona: Editorial Gómez, 1971.

Cluzel, Irénée. "Princes et troubadours de la Maison Royale de Barcelona-Aragon." *Boletín de la (Real) Academia de Buenas Letras de Barcelona* 27 (1957/1958): 330–70.

Cohen, Jeffrey Jerome, ed. *The Postcolonial Middle Ages.* New York: Palgrave, 2001 (first published 2000 by St. Martin's Press).

Cohen, Walter. *Drama of a Nation: Public Theater in Renaissance England and Spain.* Ithaca: Cornell University Press, 1985.

Coelho, António Borges. *A Revolução de 1385.* Lisboa: Portugália Editora, 1965.

Coleman, Joyce. " 'A bok for king Richardes sake': Royal Patronage, the *Confessio*, and the *Legend of Good Women*." In *John Gower: Essays at the Millennium*. Ed. R.F. Yeager. Kalamazoo: Medieval Institute Publications, in press.

———. "The Flower, the Leaf, and Philippa of Lancaster." In *Rethinking the "Legend of Good Women": Context and Reception*. Ed. Carolyn Collette. Cambridge, UK: Boydell & Brewer, 2006. 33–58.

Collins, Hugh E.L. *The Order of the Garter, 1348–1461: Chivalry and Politics in Late Medieval England*. Oxford: Clarendon Press, 2000.

Cook, E. Thornton and Catherine Moran. *Royal Daughters*. London: Heath Cranton, 1935.

Cortijo Ocaña, Antonio. "*O livro do Amante*: The Lost Portuguese Translation of John Gower's *Confessio Amantis* (Madrid, Biblioteca de Palacio, MS II-3088)." *Portuguese Studies* 13 (1997): 1–6.

———. "La traducción portuguesa de la *Confessio Amantis* de John Gower." *Euphrosyne* n.s. 23 (1995): 457–66.

Costa Lobo, Antonio de Sousa Silva. *História da sociedade em Portugal no século XV*. Lisboa: Rolim, 1984.

Crump, C.G. "The Arrest of Roger Mortimer and Queen Isabel." *English Historical Review* 26 (1911): 331–32.

Cunha, Mafalda Soares da. *Linhagem, parentesco e poder: a casa de Bragança*. Lisbon: Fundação da Casa de Bragança, 1990.

Cuttino, G.P. and Thomas W. Lyman, "Where Is Edward II?" *Speculum* 53 (1978): 522–44.

Davies, James Conway. *The Baronial Opposition to Edward II, Its Character and Policy. A Study in Administrative History*. Cambridge: Cambridge University Press, 1918.

Deknatel, Frederick B. "The Thirteenth Century Gothic Sculpture of the Cathedrals of Burgos and Leon." *Art Bulletin* 17 (1935): 243–389.

Deyermond, A.D. *A Literary History of Spain: The Middle Ages*. London: Benn, 1971.

Dias, Pedro. "Alabastros medievais ingleses em Portugal: Subsídios para a sua inventariação e estudo-região das Beiras." *Biblos* 55 (1979): 259–87.

Dias-Ferreira, Júlia. "Another Portuguese Analogue of Chaucer's Pardoner's Tale." *Chaucer Review* 11 (1977): 258–60.

Dicionário de história de Portugal. Ed. Joel Serrão. Vol. 2. Lisbon: Iniciativas Editoriais, 1975.

Dictionary of National Biography from the Earliest Times to 1900. Ed. Leslie Stephan and Sidney Lee. 32 vols. Repr. ed. London, Oxford University Press, 1937–90.

Dictionnaire d'histoire et de géographie Ecclésiastiques. Ed. Alfred Baudrillart, Albert Vogt, and Urban Rouziès. Paris: Letouzey et Ané, 1963.

Diffie, Bailey W. *Foundation of the Portuguese Empire: 1415–1580*. Minneapolis: University of Minnesota Press, 1977.

Doherty, Paul. *Isabella and the Strange Death of Edward II*. London: Constable & Robinson, 2003.

Duarte, Luis Miguel. "Aspectos menos conhecidos das relações entre Portugal e a Inglaterra na segunda metade do século XV." *Congresso Internacional: Bartolomeu Dias e sua Época. Actas.* Vol. 3. Porto: University of Porto, 1989. 551–61.

Dunn, M. and L. Davidson, eds. *The Pilgrimage to Compostela in the Middle Ages.* New York: Routledge, 1996.

——. *The Pilgrimage to Santiago de Compostela: A Comprehensive, Annotated Bibliography.* New York: Garland, 1994.

Earle, Peter. *The Life and Times of Henry V.* London: Weidenfeld & Nicolson, 1972.

Echevarría, Ana. "Catalina of Lancaster, the Castilian Monarchy and Coexistence." In *Medieval Spain: Culture, Conflict, and Coexistence: Studies in Honour of Angus MacKay.* Ed. Roger Collins and Anthony Goodman. Hound mills, UK: Palgrave, 2002. 79–122

——. *Catalina de Lancaster, reina regente de Castilla.* Hondarribia: Nerea, 2002.

Edwards, John. "The Cult of 'St.' Thomas of Lancaster and Its Iconography." *Yorkshire Archaeological Journal* 64 (1992): 103–22.

Ellis, George. *Specimens of Early English Metrical Romances: Chiefly Written during the Early Part of the Fourteenth Century.* 3 vols. London: Longman, Hurst, Rees, & Orme, 1805.

Emden, A.B. *Biographical Register of the University of Oxford to 1500.* 3 vols. Oxford: Clarendon Press, 1957–59.

Entwistle, William J. *The Arthurian Legend in the Literatures of the Spanish Peninsula.* London: J.M. Dent, 1925. Repr., New York: Phaeton Press, 1975.

——. "Observacions sobre la dedicatòria i la primera part del *Tirant lo Blanc.*" *Revista de Catalunya* 7 (1927): 381–98.

——. *The Spanish Language, Together with Portuguese, Catalan and Basque.* 2nd ed. London: Faber and Faber, 1962.

——. "*Tirant lo Blanch* and the Social Order of the End of the 15th Century." *Estudis Romànics* 2 (1949–50): 149–64.

Entwistle, William J. and P.E. Russell. "A Rainha D. Felipa e a sua côrte." In *Congresso do mundo português. Memórias e comunicações apresentadas ao Congresso de História Medieval (II Congresso).* Vol. 2. Lisbon: Comissão Executiva dos Centenários, 1940. 317–46.

Estow, Clara. *Pedro the Cruel of Castile, 1350–1369.* Leiden: Brill, 1995.

Fernández Alvarez, Manuel. *Tres embajadores de Felipe II en Inglaterra.* Madrid: Instituto Jerónimo Zurita, 1951.

Fernández Duro, Cesáreo. *La marina de Castilla desde su origen y pugna con la de Inglaterra hasta la refundición en la Armada Española.* Madrid: El Progreso Editorial, 1894.

Fitzmaurice-Kelly, James. "Some Correlations of Spanish Literature." *Revue Hispanique* 15 (1906): 58–85.

Fonseca, Luis Adão da. *O essencial sobre o Tratado de Windsor.* Lisbon: Imprensa Nacional/Casa da Moeda, 1986.

——. *O Tratado de Tordesilhas e a Diplomacia Luso-Castelhana no Século XV.* Lisbon: Edições Inapa, 1991.

Forni, Pier Massimo. *Adventures in Speech: Rhetoric and Narration in Boccaccio's "Decameron."* Philadelphia: University of Pennsylvania Press, 1996.

Fredell, Joel. "Reading the Dream Miniature in the *Confessio Amantis.*" *Medievalia et Humanistica* n.s. 22 (1995): 61–93.
Fryde, Natalie. "Antonio Pessagno of Genoa, King's Merchant of Edward II of England." In *Studi in Memoria di Federigo Melis*. Ed. Luigi da Rosa. 5 vols. Naples: Giannini, 1978. 2:159–78.
———. *The Tyranny and Fall of Edward II, 1321–1326*. Cambridge: Cambridge University Press, 1979.
Galbraith, V.H. "Extracts from the *Historia Aurea* and a French 'Brut' 1317–47." *English Historical Review* 43 (1928): 203–17.
Galván Reula, Fernando. "Medieval English Literature: A Spanish Approach." In *Articles and Papers of the First International Conference of the Spanish Society for English Mediaeval Language and Literature*. Oviedo: Universidad de Oviedo, 1988. 98–111.
Garbáty, Thomas Jay. "Chaucer in Spain, 1366: Soldier of Fortune or Agent of the Crown?" *English Language Notes* 5 (1967): 81–87.
García Fernández, Manuel. "Regesto documental andaluz de Alfonso XI." *Historia. Instituciones. Documentos* 15 (1988): 1–125.
García Mercadal, J. *Viajes de extranjeros por España y Portugal desde los tiempos más remotos hasta fines del siglo XVI*. Madrid: Aguilar, 1952.
Gauthier, M-M. "Le goût plantagenêt et les arts dans la France du Sud-Ouest." In *Stil und Überlieferung in der Kunst des Abendlandes I. Akten des 21. Internationalen Kongress für Kunstgeschichte, Bonn, 14–19 Sept. 1964*. Berlin: Mann, 1967. 139–55.
Gayoso, Andrea. "The Lady of Las Huelgas. A Royal Abbey and Its Patronage." *Cîteaux: commentarii cistercienses* 51 (2000): 1–2, 91–115.
Giménez Soler, Andrés. *Don Juan Manuel. Biografía y estudio crítico*. Saragossa: La Académica, 1932.
Gomes, Rita Costa. *The Making of a Court Society: Kings and Nobles in Late Medieval Portugal*. Trans. Alison Aiken. Cambridge, UK: Cambridge University Press, 2003.
Gómez Centurión, Carlos. *La Invencible y la empresa de Inglaterra*. Madrid: Nerea, 1988.
González González, Julio. *El reino de Castilla en la época de Alfonso VIII*. 3 vols. Madrid: Consejo Superior de Investigaciones Científicas, Escuela de Estudios Medievales, 1960.
Goodman, Anthony. "Before the Armada: Iberia and England in the Middle Ages." In *England in Europe, 1066–1453*. Ed. Nigel Saul. New York: St. Martin's Press, 1994. 108–20.
———. "England and Iberia in the Middle Ages." In *England and Her Neighbours, 1066–1453: Essays in Honour of Pierre Chaplais*. Ed. Michael Jones and Malcolm Vale. London: Hambledon Press, 1989. 73–96.
———. *John of Gaunt: The Exercise of Princely Power in Fourteenth-Century Europe*. New York: St. Martin's Press, 1992.
———. "Sentiment and Policy: English Attitudes toward Spain in the Later Middle Ages." In *Estudios sobre Málaga y el reino de Granada en el V Centenario de la Conquista*. Ed. J.E. López de Coca. Málaga: Diputación Provincial, 1987. 73–81.
Goodman, Jennifer R. *Chivalry and Exploration, 1298–1630*. Rochester, NY: Boydell, 1998.
———. *Malory and William Caxton's Prose Romances of 1485*. New York: Garland, 1985.

BIBLIOGRAPHY 231

Grahit, Emili, et al. *Studia bibliographica*. Girona: Collegi Universitari and Diputació de Girona, 1991.

Griffiths, R.A. *The Reign of King Henry VI*. Berkeley: University of California Press, 1981.

Guardiola Alcover, Conrado. "Juan de Gales, Cataluña y Eiximenis." *Antonianum* 64 (1989): 330–65.

Guedes, Armando Marques. *A aliança inglesa: notas de historia diplomatia, 1383–1943*. Lisboa: Editorial Enciclopedia, 1943.

Haines, Roy Martin. *King Edward II. Edward of Caernarfon, His Life, His Reign, and Its Aftermath, 1284–1330*. Montreal: McGill-Queen's University Press, 2003.

Hamilton, Earl J. *Money, Prices, and Wages in Valencia, Aragon, and Navarre, 1351–1500*. Cambridge, MA: Harvard University Press, 1936. Repr., Philadelphia, PA: Porcupine Press, 1975.

Hamm, Robert Warren. "An Analysis of the *Confisyon del Amante*, the Castilian Translation of Gower's *Confessio Amantis*." Ph.D. dissertation, University of Tennessee, 1975.

Hammerich, L.L. "Le Pélerinage du Louis d'Auxerre au Purgatoire de S. Patrice: correction du texte latin par une traduction catalane." *Romania* 55 (1929): 118–24.

Hartwell, J.G. "Celtic Britain and the Pilgrimage Movement." *Y Cymmrodor* 23 (1972): 255–65.

Harvey, John H. *Henry Yevele, c. 1320 to 1400: The Life of an English Architect*. 2nd ed. London: Batsford, 1946.

Harvey, John H. and Arthur Oswald. *English Medieval Architects: A Biographical Dictionary down to 1550*. Gloucester: Sutton, 1984.

Hauf, Albert G. "La dama de Rodes: tècnica i 'energia boccacciana' en un *novellino* del *Tirant lo Blanc*." In *Miscel·lània Joan Fuster*. Ed. Antoni Ferrando and Albert G. Hauf. 8 vols. Barcelona: Publicacions de l'Abadia de Montserrat, 1989–94. 8:79–118.

———. *D'Eiximenis a sor Isabel de Villena: aportació a l'estudi de la nostra cultura medieval*. Barcelona: Institut de Filologia Valenciana & Publicacions de l'Abadia de Montserrat, 1990.

Henderson, George. "Studies in English Manuscript Illumination, I-II." *Journal of the Warburg and Courtauld Institutes* 30 (1967): 71–104.

Hernando, Josep. *Llibres i lectors a la Barcelona del S. XIV*. 2 vols. Barcelona: Fundació Noguera, 1995.

Herrero González, Sonsoles. *Códices Miniados en el Real Monasterio de Las Huelgas*. Madrid and Barcelona: Patrimonio Nacional and Lunwerg Editores, 1988.

Hilgarth, J.N. *The Spanish Kingdoms, 1215–1516*. 2 vols. Oxford: Clarendon Press, 1976.

Hoffman, Louise M. "Irving's Use of Spanish Sources in the Conquest of Granada." *Hispania* 28.4 (1945): 483–98.

Honoré-Duverge, Suzanne. "Chaucer en Espagne? (1366)." In *Recueil de Travaux offert à M. Clovis Brunel par ses amis, collègues et élèves*. 2 vols. Paris: Société de l'Ecole des Chartes, 1955. 2:9–13.

Horst, Koert van der, William Noel, and Wilhelmina C.M. Wüstefeld, eds. *The Utrecht Psalter in Medieval Art. Picturing the Psalms of David*. Utrecht: HES Publishers, 1996.

Howell, Margaret. *Eleanor of Provence, Queenship in Thirteenth-Century England*. Oxford: Blackwell, 1998.

Hume, Martin A.S. *Spanish Influence on English Literature.* London: Nash, 1905. Repr., New York: Haskell House, 1964.

Hunter, Joseph. "On the Measures taken for the Apprehension of Sir Thomas de Gournay, one of the Murderers of King Edward the Second, and on Their Final Issue." *Archaeologia* 27 (1838): 274–97.

Hutchinson, Amélia P. "Anglo-Portuguese Relations and Arthurian Revival in Portugal." In *Actas do Colóquio Comemorativo do VI Centenário do Tratado de Windsor de 15 a 18 de Outubro de 1986.* Ed. Manuel Gomes da Torre. Porto: Faculdade de Letras do Porto, 1988. 275–89.

———. "European Relations of Portuguese Arthurian Literature." M.Phil. dissertation, University of Manchester, UK, 1984.

James, Margery K. "The Fluctuations of the Anglo-Gascon Wine Trade during the Fourteenth Century." *Economic History Review* 2nd ser., 4 (1951): 170–96.

Johnston, Mark D. *The Evangelical Rhetoric of Ramon Llull: Lay Learning and Piety in the Christian West around 1300.* New York: Oxford University Press, 1996.

Johnstone, Hilda. *Edward of Carnarvon, 1284–1307.* Publications of the University of Manchester, 295. Manchester: Manchester University Press, 1946.

Jones, Terry. *Chaucer's Knight: The Portrait of a Medieval Mercenary.* Rev. ed. London: Methuen, 1994.

Jordan, Weseley D. "Four Twelfth-Century Musico-Liturgical Manuscripts from the Cistercian Monastery of Las Huelgas, Burgos." *Manuscripta* 37 (1993): 21–70.

Kallendorf, Hillaire, ed. *Exorcism and Its Texts: Subjectivity in Early Modern Literature of England and Spain.* Toronto: University of Toronto Press, 2003.

Karge, Henrik. "Die königliche Zisterzienserinnenabtei Las Huelgas de Burgos und die Anfäge der gotischen Architektur in Spanien." In *Gotische Architektur in Spanien. Akten des Kolloquiums der Carl Justi-Vereinigung und des Kunstgeschichtlichen Seminars der Universität Göttingen, 4–6. Februar 1994.* Ed. Christian Freigang. Frankfurt am Main: Vervuert; Madrid: Iberoamericana, 1999. 13–40, 373–76.

Keen, Maurice H. *England in the Later Middle Ages.* London: Routledge, 1973.

Kelly, Henry Ansgar. *Canon Law and the Archpriest of Hita.* Medieval and Renaissance Studies 27. Binghamton, NY: Center for Medieval and Early Renaissance Studies, 1984.

———. "Juan Ruiz and Archpriests: Novel Reports." *La Corónica* 16 (1987–88): 32–54.

———. "A Juan Ruiz Directory for 1380–82," *Mester* 7 (1988): 69–93.

Kirby, J.L. *Henry IV.* London: Constable, 1970.

Koff, Michael Leonard, and Brenda Deen, eds. *The "Decameron" and the "Canterbury Tales": New Essays on an Old Question.* Madison, NJ: Fairleigh Dickinson University Press, 2000.

Labande, Edmond-René. "Les filles d'Aliénor de'Aquitaine: étude comparative." In *Cahiers de Civilisation Médiévale* 29 (1986): 105–11.

Labarge, Margaret W. *Viajeros medievales. Los ricos y los insatisfechos.* Hondarribia: Nerea, 2000.

Lacy, Norris J. *The Arthurian Encyclopedia.* Woodbridge: The Boydell Press, 1986.

Lambert, Elie. *L'art gothique en Espagne aux XIIe et XIIIe siècles*. Paris: Henri Laurens, 1931.
Lasater, Alice E. *Spain to England: A Comparative Study of Arabic, European, and English Literature of the Middle Ages*. Jackson: University Press of Mississippi, 1974.
León Sendra, Antonio and Jesús L. Serrano Reyes. "Spanish References in the *Canterbury Tales*," *Selim* [Journal of the Spanish Society for Medieval English Language and Literature] 2 (1992): 106–41.
Leslie, Ruth. "A Source for Juan Fernández de Heredia's *Rams de flores*." *Studia Neophilologica* 45 (1973): 159–60.
Lindley, Phillip. "The Sculptural Memorials of Queen Eleanor and Their Context." In *Eleanor of Castile 1290–1990: Essays to Commemorate the 700th Anniversary of her death: 28 November 1290*. Ed. David Parsons. Stamford: Paul Watkins, 1991. 69–92.
Linehan, Peter. "The English Mission of Cardinal Petrus Hispanus, the Chronicle of Walter of Guisborough, and News from Castile at Carlisle (1307)." *English Historical Review* 117 (2002): 605–21.
———. *History and the Historian of Medieval Spain*. Oxford: Clarendon Press, 1993.
Livermore, Harold V.A. *History of Portugal*. Cambridge: Cambridge University Press, 1947.
———. *Origens das relações luso-britânicas: o primeiro historiador inglês de Portugal*. Lisbon: Academia das Ciências de Lisboa, 1976.
Lizoaín Garrido, José Manuel. *Documentación del monasterio de las Huelgas de Burgos (1263–83)*. Fuentes medievales castellano-leonesas 32. Burgos: J.M. Garrido Garrido, 1990.
Lloyd, T.H. *Alien Merchants in England in the High Middle Ages*. Brighton, Sussex: Harvester Press, 1982.
Loftis, John. *Renaissance Drama in England and Spain: Topical Allusions and History Plays*. Princeton: Princeton University Press, 1987.
Lomax, Derek W. "Algunos peregrinos ingleses a Santiago en la Edad Media." *Príncipe de Viana* 31 (1970): 156–69.
———. "The First English Pilgrimages to Santiago de Compostela." *Studies in Medieval History Presented to R.H.C Davis*. Ed. Henry Mayr-Harting and R.I. Moore. London: Hambledon, 1985. 165–79.
———. "Los peregrinos ingleses a Santiago." In *Santiago. La Europa del peregrinaje*. Ed. Robert Plötz et al. Barcelona: Lunwerg, 1993. 373–84.
Lomax, Derek W., and R.J. Oakley. *The English in Portugal 1367–87*. Warminster: Aris & Phillips, 1988.
Loomis, Roger Sherman, ed. *Arthurian Literature in the Middle Ages: A Collaborative History*. Oxford: Clarendon, 1959.
Lowden, John. *The Making of the Bibles Moralisées, 1. The Manuscripts*. Philadelphia, PA: Pennsylvania State University Press, 2000.
Lücke, Ernst. "Das Leben der Constanze bei Trivet, Gower und Chaucer." *Anglia* 14 (1892): 77–112 and 149–85.
Macaulay, G.C. "Introduction." In *John Gower, The English Works of John Gower*. Ed. Macaulay. EETS e.s. 81, Vol. 1. London: Kegan Paul, Trench, Trübner, 1900. vii–clxxiv.
Macaulay, Rose. *They Went to Portugal*. London: Jonathan Cape, 1946.

MacKay, Angus. *Money, Prices, and Politics in Fifteenth-Century Castile.* London: Royal Historical Society, 1981.

———. *Society, Economy, and Religion in Late Medieval Castile.* London: Variorum Reprints, 1987.

———. *Spain in the Middle Ages: From Frontier to Empire, 1000–1500.* London: Macmillan, 1977.

Maltby, William S. *La leyenda negra en Inglaterra: Desarrollo del sentimiento antihispánico, 1558–1660.* México: Fondo de Cultura Económica, 1982.

Manly, John Matthews. "On the Question of the Portuguese Translation of Gower's *Confessio Amantis*." *Modern Philology* 27 (1930): 467–72.

March, Pere. *Obra completa.* Ed. Lluís Cabré. Els Nostres Clàssics, A132. Barcelona: Barcino, 1993.

Marcos Rodríguez, Florencio. *Catálogo de Documentos del Archivo Catedralicio de Salamanca Siglos XII–XV.* Salamanca: Universidad Pontificia de Salamanca, 1962.

Marques, A.H. de Oliveira. *Daily Life in Portugal in the Late Middle Ages.* Trans. S.S. Wyatt. Madison: University of Wisconsin Press, 1971.

———. *Guia do estudante de historia medieval portuguesa.* Lisbon: Edições Cosmos, 1964.

———. *História de Portugal, desde os tempos mais antigos até ao governo do Sr. Marcelo Caetano.* Lisboa: Ediçaoes Ágora, 1972.

———. *History of Portugal.* 2nd ed. New York: Columbia University Press, 1976.

———. *Portugal na Crise dos Séculos XIV e XV.* Lisbon: Editorial Presença, 1987.

Martínez Ferrando, J. Ernesto. *Jaime II de Aragón. Su vida familiar.* Consejo Superior de Investigaciones Científicas, Escuela de Estudios Medievales, Publicaciones de la Sección de Barcelona, 10. Barcelona: Consejo Superior de Investigaciones Científicas, 1948.

Martins, J.P. Oliveira. *A vida de Nun'Álvares: história do establecimento da dinastia de Avis.* Porto: Lello & Irmão, 1983.

Martins, Mário. "Dum poema inglês de John Gower e da sua tradução do português para o castelhano." *Didaskalia* 9 (1979): 413–31.

Martorell, Joanot, and Martí Joan de Galba. *Tirante el Blanco: versión castellana impresa en Valladolid en 1511.* Ed. Martín de Riquer. 5 vols. Madrid: Espasa-Calpe, 1974.

Mattoso, José. *História de Portugal, 2. A Monarquia Feudal 1096–1480.* Lisboa: Editorial Estampa, 1997.

McDermott, James. *A Necessary Quarrel: England and the Spanish Armada.* New Haven: Yale University Press, 2005.

McGrady, Donald. "Chaucer and the *Decameron* Reconsidered." *Chaucer Review* 12 (1977): 1–26.

McKitterick, David, Nigel Morgan, Ian Short, and Teresa Webber. *The Trinity Apocalypse (Trinity College Cambridge, MS R. 16.2).* London and Toronto: The British Library and University of Toronto Press, 2005.

McLamore, Richard V. "Postcolonial Columbus: Washington Irving and *The Conquest of Granada*." *Nineteenth-Century Literature* 48.1 (1993): 26–43.

McQuarrie, Alan. *Scotland and the Crusades, 1095–1560.* Edinburgh: John Donald, 1985.

Monfrin, Jacques. "La Bibliothèque de Francesc Eiximenis (1409)." *Bibliothèque d'Humanisme et Renaissance* 29 (1967): 447–87. Repr. with an appendix in Grahit et al., 241–87.

Morales Lezcano, Víctor. *Relaciones entre Inglaterra y los archipiélagos del Atlántico Ibérico*. La Laguna: Instituto de Estudios Canarios, 1970.

Moreno, Humberto Baquero. "Contestação da nobreza portuguesa ao poder político nos finais da Idade Média." *Ler História* 13 (1988): 3–14.

Morganstern, Anne McGee. *Gothic Tombs of Kinship in France, The Low Countries, and England*. Philadelphia, PA: The Pennsylvania State University Press, 2000.

Mortimer, Ian. *The Greatest Traitor. The Life of Sir Roger Mortimer, 1st Earl of March, Ruler of England, 1327–1330*. London: Jonathan Cape, 2003.

Moxó y de Montoliu, Francisco de. "La relación epistolar entre Alfonso XI y Alfonso IV en el Archivo de la Corona de Aragón." *En la España Medieval* 3 (1982): 173–95.

Munro, John. *Wool, Cloth and Gold: The Struggle for Bullion in Anglo-Burgundian Trade, ca. 1340–1478*. Toronto: University of Toronto Press, 1973.

Nicholson, Peter. " 'The Man of Law's Tale': What Chaucer Really Owed to Gower," *Chaucer Review* 26 (1991): 153–74.

Noppen, J.G. "Westminster Paintings and Master Peter." *The Burlington Magazine* 91 (1949): 305–09.

Nykrog, Per. *Les Fabliaux: Etude d'histoire litteraire et de stylistique medievale*. 1957. New ed. Geneva: Librarie Droz, 1973.

Oakeshott, Walter. *Sigena: Romanesque Paintings in Spain and the Winchester Bible Artists*. London: Harvey Miller and Medcalf, 1972.

———. *The Two Winchester Bibles*. Oxford: Clarendon Press, 1981.

O'Callaghan, Joseph. *A History of Medieval Spain*. Ithaca: Cornell University Press, 1975.

Olivar, Alexandre. "Sobre un manuscrit poc conegut de la versió catalana antiga del *Breviloquium de virtutibus* de Joan de Gal·les." In *Studia in honorem prof. M. de Riquer*. 3 vols. Barcelona: Quaderns Crema, 1988. 3:87–95.

Olivares Merino, Eugenio M. " 'Glorie of Spayne': Juan Ruiz through the Eyes of an Englishman." *Revista Canaria de Estudos Ingleses* 45 (2002): 233–44.

———. "Juan Ruiz's Influence on Chaucer Revisited: A Survey." *Neophilologus* 88 (2004): 145–61.

Ormrod, W.M. *The Reign of Edward III. Crown and Political Society in England 1327–1377*. New Haven and London: Yale University Press, 1990.

Owen, D.D.R. *The Vision of Hell: Infernal Journeys in Medieval French Literature*. Edinburgh: Scottish Academic Press, 1970.

Oxford English Dictionary. 2nd ed. Oxford: Clarendon Press, 1989.

Packe, Michael. *King Edward III*. Ed. L.C.B. Seaman. London: Routledge & Kegan Paul, 1983.

Pan Sánchez, María Rosa "Interrelaciones entre la literatura medieval inglesa y el Reino de Navarra." Ph.D. dissertation, Universidad de Deusto, 2001.

Parsons, John Carmi. *Eleanor of Castile. Queen and Society in Thirteenth-Century England*. Basingstoke, UK: Macmillan, 1994; New York: St. Martin's Press, 1995.

Paterson, Linda M. *The World of the Troubadours in Medieval Occitan Society c.1100–c.1300.* Cambridge: Cambridge University Press, 1993.

Paxeco, Fran. *The Intellectual Relations between Portugal and Great Britain.* Lisbon: Editorial Imperio, 1937.

Payne, G. *A History of Spain and Portugal.* 2 vols. Madison: University of Wisconsin Press, 1973.

Pearsall, Derek. *The Life of Geoffrey Chaucer: A Critical Biography.* Oxford: Blackwell, 1992.

Peres, Damião. *História de Portugal Monumental.* 7 vols. Barcelos: Portucalense Editora, 1929.

Phillips, William and Carla Phillips. *Spain's Golden Fleece: Wool Production and Wool Trade from the Middle Ages to the Nineteenth Century.* Baltimore: Johns Hopkins University Press, 1997.

Plötz, R.G. "Milites et nobilitates in itinere stellarum (saeculum XI ad saeculum XVI)." In *Viajes y viajeros en la España Medieval. Actas del V Curso de Cultura Medieval.* Aguilar de Campoo: Centro de Estudios del Románico; Madrid: Polifemo, 1997. 109–19.

Prescott, William H. *Ferdinand and Isabella.* New York: The Kelmscott Society, 1845.

———. "Irving's *Conquest of Granada.*" In *Biographical and Critical Miscellanies.* New York: The Kelmscott Society, 1845. 64–87.

Prestage, Edgar. *Chapters in Anglo-Portuguese Relations.* Watford: Voss and Michael, 1935. Repr., Westport, CT: Greenwood Press, 1971.

Prestwich, Michael. *The Three Edwards. War and State in England, 1272–1377.* Repr. ed. London: Routledge, 1993.

Pujol, Josep. *La memòria literària de Joanot Martorell: models i escriptura en el "Tirant lo Blanc."* Barcelona: Curial and Publicacions de l'Abadia de Montserrat, 2002.

Puyol, Julio. "El presunto cronista Fernán Sánchez de Valladolid." *Boletín de la Real Academia de la Historia* 77 (1920): 516–33.

Redworth, Glyn. *The Prince and the Infanta: The Cultural Politics of the Spanish Match.* New Haven: Yale University Press, 2003.

Reeves, A. Compton. "Richard II: A Case of Narcissistic Personality Disorder?" *Medieval Life* 12 (1999): 19–22.

Reilly, Bernard. *The Medieval Spains.* Cambridge: Cambridge University Press, 1993.

Reis, A. do Carmo Reis. *Introdução ao Pensamento Político de Nun'Álvares.* Vila do Conde: Edições Linear, 1982.

Reisner, Thomas A. and Mary E. Reisner. "Lewis Clifford and the Kingdom of Navarre." *Modern Philology* 75 (1978): 385–90.

Renedo, Xavier. "Una imatge de la memòria entre les *Moralitates* de Robert Holcot i el *Dotzè* d'Eiximenis." *Annals de l'Institut d'Estudis Gironins* 31 (1990–91): 53–61.

Ribera, Joan M. "Una altra lectura de Ramon de Perellós prèvia al seu viatge." *Revista de l'Alguer* 8 (1997): 233–51; 9 (1998): 273–89.

Rico, Francisco. "Antoni Canals y Petrarca: para la fecha y las fuentes de *Scipió e Aníbal.*" In *Estudios en memoria del professor Manuel Sanchis Guarner.* Ed. Emili Casanova. 2 vols. Valencia: Universidad de Valencia, 1984. 1:285–88.

———. "Nobiltà del Medioevo, nobiltà dell'Umanesimo." In *Gli Umanesimi medievali. Atti del II Congresso dell' Internationales Mittellateinerkomitee*

(Firenze, Certosa del Galluzzo, 11–15 settembre 1993). Ed. Claudio Leonardo. Florence: SISMEL & Edizioni del Galluzzo, 1998. 559–66.

Riley, Carlos Guilherme. "Os Doze de Inglaterra: Ficção e Realidade." M.A. thesis. Ponta Delgada, Universidade dos Açores, 1988.

Riquer, Martin de. *Aproximació al "Tirant lo Blanc."* Barcelona: Quaderns Crema, 1990.

———. *Caballeros Andantes Españoles.* Madrid: Espasa-Calpe, 1967.

———. *Història de la literatura catalana: part antiga.* 3 vols. Barcelona: Ariel, 1964.

———. "La literature provençale à la cour d'Alphonse II d'Aragon." *Cahiers de Civilisation Medievale* 2 (1959): 180–87.

———, ed. *Lletres de batalla.* Vol. 3. Els Nostres Clàssics, A99. Barcelona: Barcino, 1968.

———. *"Tirant lo Blanc," novela de historia y ficción.* Barcelona: Sirmio, 1992.

———. "El *Voyage* de sir John Mandeville en català." In *Miscel·lània d'homenatge a Enric Moreu Rey.* Ed. Albert Manent and Joan Veny. 3 vols. Barcelona: Publicacions de l'Abadia de Montserrat 1988. 3:151–62.

Roche, T.W.E. *Philippa: Dona Filipa of Portugal.* London: Phillimore, 1971.

Rodríguez García, José Manuel. "Los enfrentamientos bélicos con Inglaterra y sus gentes: la visión castellana (1250–1515)." *Revista de Historia Militar* 84 (1998): 11–44.

———. "Henry III, Alfonso X of Castile and the Crusading Plans of the Thirteenth Century (1245–1272)." In *England and Europe in the Reign of Henry III (1216–1272).* Ed. B.K.U. Weiler and Ifor W. Rowlands. Aldershot: Ashgate, 2002. 99–120.

Rodríguez Villasante y Prieto, Juan. "El camino marítimo de Santiago." *Revista General de Marina* 191 (1976): 21–28.

Rosenthal, Joel T. "The King's 'Wicked Advisers' and Medieval Baronial Rebellions." *Political Science Quarterly* 82 (1967): 595–618.

Roth, Cecil. "Perkin Warbeck and His Jewish Master." *Transactions of the Jewish Historical Society of England* 9 (1922): 143–62.

Ruiz, Teofilo F. "Burgos y el comercio castellano en la Baja Edad Media: economía y mentalidad." In Ruiz, *The City and the Realm.* Study 3.

———. "Castilian Merchants in England, 1248–1350." In Ruiz, *The City and the Realm,* Study 9.

———. *The City and the Realm: Burgos and Castile, 1080–1492.* Variorum Collected Studies. Aldershot, UK, 1992.

———. "The Transformation of the Castilian Municipalities: the Case of Burgos, 1248–1350." In Ruiz, *The City and the Realm,* Study 7.

———. "Two Patrician Families in Late Medieval Burgos: The Sarracín and the Bonifaz." In Ruiz, *The City and the Realm,* Study 6.

Ruiz Gómez, F. "El Camino de Santiago: circulación de hombres, mercancías e ideas." *IV Semana de Estudios Medievales: Nájera, 2 al 6 de agosto de 1993.* Logroño: Instituto de Estudios Riojanos, 1993. 167–88.

Ruiz Simon, Josep M. *L'Art de Ramon Llull i la teoria escolàstica de la ciència.* Barcelona: Quaderns Crema, 1999.

Russell, J.C. and E.W. Russell. "He Said that He Was the King's Father." In *Medieval Demography. Essays by Josiah C. Russell.* AMS Studies in the Middle Ages, 12. New York: AMS Press, 1987. 242–49.

Russell, Peter E. *The English Intervention in Spain and Portugal in the Time of Edward III and Richard II.* Oxford: Clarendon Press, 1955.

———. *Portugal, Spain and the African Atlantic, 1343—1490: Chivalry and Crusade from John of Gaunt to Henry the Navigator.* Aldershot: Variorum, 1995.

———. *Prince Henry "the Navigator": A Life.* New Haven: Yale University Press, 2000.

———. "Robert Payn and Juan de Cuenca, Translators of John Gower's *Confessio Amantis.*" *Medium Aevum* 30 (1961): 26–32.

———. "White Kings on Black Kings: Rui de Pina and the Problem of Black African Sovereignty." In *Medieval and Renaissance Studies in Honour of Robert Brian Tate.* Ed. Ian Michael and Richard A. Cardwell. Oxford: Dolphin Book, 1986. 151–64.

Sánchez Ameijeiras, Rocío. "La memoria de un rey victorioso: los sepulcros de Alfonso VIII y la fiesta del triunfo de la Santa Crus." In *Grabkunst und Sepulkralkultur in Spanien und Portugal.* Ed. Barbara Borngässer, Henrik Karge, and Bruno Klein. Frankfurt am Main: Vervuert, 2006. 289–315.

Santano Moreno, Bernardo. *Estudio sobre "Confessio Amantis" de John Gower y su versión castellana.* Cáceres: Universidad de Extremadura, 1990.

———. "The Fifteenth-Century Portuguese and Castilian Translations of John Gower, *Confessio Amantis.*" *Manuscripta* 35 (1991): 23–34.

Santos, Joaquim Moreira dos. "Medievalismo em Camões: os Doze de Inglaterra." *Revista da Universidade de Coimbra* 33 (1986): 209–20.

Saraiva, António José. *Fernão Lopes.* Lisboa: Europa-América, 1965.

Saul, Nigel. "England and Europe: Problems and Possibilities." In *England in Europe, 1066–1453.* Ed. Nigel Saul. London: Collins and Brown, 1994; New York: St. Martin's Press, 1994. 9–20.

———. *Richard II.* New Haven: Yale University Press, 1997.

Savage, Henry Lyttleton. "Chaucer and the 'Pitous Deeth' of 'Petro, Glorie of Spayne.'" *Speculum* 24 (1949): 357–75.

Scattergood, V.J. "Introduction." In *The Works of Sir John Clanvowe.* Ed. V.J. Scattergood. Cambridge, UK: Brewer, 1965. 9–31.

Schlauch, Margaret. *Chaucer's Constance and Accused Queens.* New York: New York University Press, 1927.

Sena, Jorge de. "O vitorianismo de Dona Filipa de Lancaster." In *Estudos de história e de Cultura.* Series 1a. Vol. 1. Lisbon: Edição da Revista "Ocidente," 1963. 93–100.

Sèneca, L.A. *Tragèdies: traducció catalana medieval amb comentaris del segle XIV de Nicolau Trevet.* Ed. Tomàs Martínez. Els Nostres Clàssics, B14–15. Barcelona: Barcino, 1995.

Serrano Reyes, Jesús. "A Catalan 'Virolay' and the 'Femynyne Creature, Sitte in a See Imperiall." In *Proceedings of the 10th International Conference of the Spanish Society for English Medieval Language and Literature.* Ed. Ana María Hornero Corisco and María Pilar Navarro Errasti. Zaragoza: Institución "Fernando el Católico," 2000. 235–43.

———. "The Chaucers in Spain: From the Wedding to the Funeral." *Selim* 8 (1998): 193–203.

———. *Didactismo y moralismo en Geoffrey Chaucer y Don Juan Manuel: un estudio comparativo textual.* Córdoba: Servicio de Publicaciones de la Universidad de Córdoba, 1995.

———. " 'Els Castells Humans': An Architectural Element in the *House of Fame*." *Proceedings of the 9th International Conference of the Spanish Society for Medieval English Language and Literature.* Ed. Margarita Giménez Bon and Vickie Olsen. Vitoria-Gasteiz, 1997. 326–37.

———. "Spanish Modesty in *The Canterbury Tales*: Chaucer and Don Juan Manuel." *Selim* 5 (1995): 29–45.

Serrão, Joel and A.H. de Oliveira Marques, eds., *Nova Histôra de Portugal. Portugal na Crise dos Séculos XIV e XV.* vol. 4 Lisboa: Editorial Presença, 1987.

Shaw, Patricia. "Pedro Alfonso y el primer fabliau inglés." *Archivum* 34 (1985): 329–42.

———. "The Presence of Spain in Middle English Literature." *Archiv für das Studium der neueren Sprachen und Literaturen* 229 (1992): 41–54.

Shillington, V.M., and A.B. Wallis Chapman. *The Commercial Relations of England and Portugal.* London: Routledge, 1907. Repr., New York: Burt Franklin, 1970.

Shneidman, J. Lee. *The Rise of the Aragonese–Catalan Empire 1200–1350.* 2 vols. New York: New York University Press, 1970.

Silva, Francisco Ribeiro da. "Portugal e o curso no Atlântico Norte na segunda metade do século XV. Alguns aspectos." *Congresso Internacional: Bartolomeu Dias e sua Época. Actas.* Vol. 3. Porto: University of Porto, 1989. 541–49.

Smalley, Beryl. *English Friars and Antiquity in the Early Fourteenth Century.* Oxford: Blackwell, 1960.

Soria y Puig, Arturo. "El Camino y los caminos de Santiago en España." In *Santiago. La Europa del peregrinaje.* Ed. Robert Plötz et al. Barcelona: Lunwerg, 1993. 195–232.

Southern, R.W. *The Heroic Age.* Vol. 2. With notes and additions by Lesley Smith & Benedicta Ward. In *Scholastic Humanism and the Unification of Europe.* 3 vols. Oxford: Blackwell, 2001.

———. *Western Society and the Church in the Middle Ages.* London: Penguin, 1970.

———. *Western Views of Islam in the Middle Ages.* Cambridge, MA: Harvard University Press, 1962.

Storrs, Constance C. *Jacobean Pilgrims from England from the Early Twelfth to the Late Fifteenth Century.* Santiago de Compostela: Xunta de Galicia, 1994.

Stubbings, Hilda Urén. *Renaissance Spain in Its Literary Relations with England: A Critical Bibliography.* Nashville: Vanderbilt University Press, 1969.

Sturcken, H.T. "The Unconsummated Marriage of Jaime of Aragon and Leonor of Castile October 1319." *Journal of Medieval History* 5 (1979): 185–201.

Suárez Fernández, Luis. *Navegación y comercio en el Golfo de Vizcaya.* Madrid: CSIC, 1959.

Taggie, Benjamin F. "John of Gaunt, Geoffrey Chaucer and 'O Noble, O Worthy Petro, Glorie of Spayne.' " *Fifteenth-Century Studies* 10 (1984): 195–228.

Tanquerey, Frédéric J. "The Conspiracy of Thomas Dunheved, 1327." *English Historical Review* 31 (1916): 119–24.

Tate, Robert B. "Joanot Martorell in England." *Estudis Romànics* 10 (1962): 277–79.
Taylor, Barry. "Los libros de viajes de la Edad Media hispánica: bibliografía y recepción." In *IV Congresso da Associação Hispânica de Literatura Medieval*. Ed. Aires A. Nascimiento and Cristina Almeida Ribeiro. Vol. 3. Lisbon: Cosmos, 1991. 57–70.
Taylor, John. "The French 'Brut' and the Reign of Edward II." *English Historical Review* 72 (1957): 423–37.
———. "The Judgment on Hugh Despenser, the Younger," *Medievalia et Humanistica* 22 (1958): 70–77.
Terlinden, C. "Les relations de famille entre les maisons souveraines de Belqique et de Portugal." In *Congresso do mundo português: Memórias e comunicações apresentadas ao Congresso de História Medieval (II Congresso)*. Lisbon: Comissão Executiva dos Centenários, 1940. 2:197–220.
Theilmann, John M. "Political Canonization and Political Symbolism in Medieval England," *Journal of British Studies* 29 (1990): 241–66.
Thomas, Jeffrey L. "Caerphilly Castle." http:// www.castlewales.com /caerphil.html.
Thomson, J.A.F. *The Transformation of Medieval England, 1370–1529*. New York: Longman, 1983.
Tolley, Thomas. "Eleanor of Castile and the 'Spanish' Style in England." In *England in the Thirteenth Century. Proceedings of the 1989 Harlaxton Symposium*. Ed. W.M. Ormrod. Stamford: Paul Watkins, 1991. 167–200.
Torres Balbás, L. "Las yeserías descubiertas recientemente en Las Huelgas de Burgos. Contribución al estudio de la decoración arquitectónica hispano-musulmana." *Al- Andalus* 3 (1943): 21–66.
Torres Fontes, Juan. *Estudio sobre la Crónica de Enrique IV del Dr. Galíndez de Carvajal*. Murcia: CSIC, 1946.
Tout, T.F. "The Captivity and Death of Edward of Carnarvon." In *The Collected Papers of Thomas Frederick Tout, with a Memoir and Bibliography*. Vol. 3. Manchester: Manchester University Press, 1934. 145–90.
———. *Chapters in the Administrative History of Mediaeval England. The Wardrobe, the Chamber and the Small Seals*. 6 vols. Manchester: Manchester University Press, 1928–37.
Trabut-Cussac, Jean-Paul. "Don Enrique de Castille en Angleterre." *Mélanges de la Casa de Velázquez* 2 (1966): 51–58.
Tyerman, Christopher. *England and the Crusades, 1095–1588*. Chicago: University of Chicago Press, 1988.
Vaeth, Joseph A. *"Tirant lo Blanch:" A Study of Its Authorship, Principal Sources and Historical Setting*. New York: Columbia University Press, 1918.
Valente, Claire. "The Deposition and Abdication of Edward II." *English Historical Review* 113 (1998): 852–81.
Vann, Theresa M. "The Theory and Practice of Medieval Castilian Queenship." In *Queens, Regents and Potentates*. Ed. Theresa M. Vann. Dallas: Academia Press, 1993. 125–47.

Varela, Consuelo. *Ingleses en España y Portugal (1450–1515): aristócratas, mercaderes e impostores*. Lisboa: Edições Colibri, 1998.

Vasconcelos, Jorge Ferreira de. *Memorial das Proezas da Segunda Távola Redonda*. Ed. João Palma-Ferreira Porto: Lello Editores, 1998.

Vázquez de Parga, Luis, José María Lacarra, and Juan Uría Ríu. *Las peregrinaciones a Santiago de Compostela*. 3 vols. Oviedo: Diputación Provincial, 1981.

Vercel, Roger. *Bertrand of Brittany. A Biography of Messire du Guesclin*. Trans. Marion Saunders. New Haven: Yale University Press, 1934.

Vicens Vives, Jaime. *An Economic History of Spain*. Rev. Jorge Nadal Oller. Trans. Frances M. López-Morillas. Princeton, NJ: Princeton University Press, 1969.

Villa Franca, Pedro da Costa de Sousa de Macedo, conde de. *D. João I a aliança inglesa, investigações histórico-sociais*. Lisbon: [Author's family], 1950.

Viñayo González, Antonio. *Caminos y peregrinos: huellas de la peregrinación jacobea*. León: Isidoriana, 1981.

Walker, Rose. "Leonor of England, Plantagenet Queen of King Alfonso VIII of Castile, and Her Foundation of the Cistercian abbey of Las Huelgas in Imitation of Fontevraud?" *Journal of Medieval History* 31 (2005): 36–68.

Walker, Simon. *The Lancastrian Affinity, 1361–1399*. Oxford: Clarendon Press, 1990.

Wallace, David. "Chaucer and Boccaccio's Early Writings." Ed. Piero Boitani. *Chaucer and the Italian Trecento*. Cambridge: Cambridge University Press, 1983. 141–62.

Watts, J.L. *Henry VI and the Politics of Kingship*. Cambridge: Cambridge University Press, 1996.

Wernham, R.B. *Expedition of Sir John Norris and Sir Francis Drake to Spain and Portugal, 1589*. Aldershot, Hants: Temple Smith, 1988.

———. *The Return of the Armadas: The Last Years of the Elizabethan War against Spain, 1595–1603*. Oxford: Oxford University Press, 1994.

Willard, Charity Cannon. "Isabel of Portugal and the French Translation of the *Triunfo de las donas*." *Revue belge de philologie et d'histoire* 43 (1965): 961–69.

———. "The Patronage of Isabel of Portugal." In *The Cultural Patronage of Medieval Women*. Ed. June Hall McCash. Athens: University of Georgia Press, 1996. 306–20.

———. "A Portuguese Translation of Christine de Pisan's *Livre des trois vertus*." *PMLA* 78 (1963): 459–64.

Williams, Frederick J. "Chaucer's 'The Pardoner's Tale' and 'The Tale of the Four Thieves' from Portugal's *Orto do Esposo* Compared." *Bulletin des études portugaises et bresiliennes* 44–45 (1983–85): 93–109.

Williams, John. *The Twelfth and Thirteenth Centuries*. Vol. 5. In *The Illustrated Beatus*. 5 vols. London: Harvey Miller, 2003.

Williams, Stanley T. "The First Version of the Writings of Washington Irving in Spanish." *Modern Philology* 28.2 (1930): 185–201.

Williamson, Paul. *Gothic Sculpture, 1140–1300*. New Haven: Yale University Press, 1995.

———. "Sculpture." In Alexander and Binski, *Age of Chivalry: Art in Plantagenet England*, 98–106.

Wimsatt, James I. *Chaucer and His French Contemporaries: Natural Music in the Fourteenth Century.* Toronto: University of Toronto Press, 1991.

Winius, George, ed. *Portugal: The Pathfinder.* Madison: Hispanic Seminary of Medieval Studies, 1995.

Winston, Graham. *The Spanish Armadas.* New York: Doubleday, 1972.

Wittlin, Curt J. "La *Suma de colaciones* de Juan de Gales en Cataluña." *Estudios Franciscanos* 72 (1971): 189–203.

———. "La traducció catalana anònima de les *Històries romanes* I–VIII de Titus Livi." *Estudis Romànics* 13 (1963–68): 277–315.

———. "Traductions et commentaires médiévaux de la *Cité de Dieu* de saint Augustin." *Travaux de Linguistique et de Littérature* 16 (1978): 531–55.

Wixom, William D. and Margaret Lawson. *Painting the Apocalypse: Illustrated Leaves from a Medieval Spanish Manuscript.* New York: The Metropolitan Museum of Art, 2002.

Wroe, Anne. *The Perfect Prince.* New York: Random House, 2003.

Wylie, James Hamilton. *History of England under Henry the Fourth.* 4 vols. 1894–98; Repr. New York: AMS Press, 1969.

Yarza Luaces, Joaquín. "Las miniaturas de la Biblia de Burgos." *Archivo español de arte* 42 (1969): 185–203.

———. "La miniatura en Galicia, León, y Castilla en tiempos de Maestro Mateo." In *Actas do Simposio Internacional sobre "O Portico da la Gloria e a Arte do seu Tiempo" (Santiago de Compostela, 3–8 de outubro de 1988).* Santiago de Compostela: Dirección Xeral de Cultura, 1991. 319–40.

Yeager, R.F. "Gower's Lancastrian Affinity: The Iberian Connection." *Viator* 35 (2004): 483–515.

———. "John Gower's Images: 'The Tale of Constance' and 'The Man of Law's Tale.'" In *Speaking Images: Essays in Honor of V.A. Kolve.* Ed. R.F. Yeager and Charlotte C. Morse. Asheville, NC: Pegasus Press, 2000. 525–57.

Zaluska, Yolanta. *L'enluminure et le scriptorium de Cîteaux au XIIe siècle.* Cîteaux: Centre National de la Recherche Scientifique du Centre National des Lettres, 1989.

Zarnecki, George, Janet Holt, and Tristram Holland, eds. *English Romanesque Art 1066–1200.* London: Arts Council of Great Britain with Weidenfeld and Nicolson, 1984.

INDEX

Note: Page numbers in *italics* indicate an endnote. The words "king" and "queen" are abbreviated as k. and q. respectively.

Agapida, Antonio, 14
Age of Exploration, 119, 131
Alfonso VIII (k. of Castile)
  Henry II and, 5, 50
  Las Huelgas and, 72, 76–79, 82–83
  Leonor of England and, 5, 67–68, 71, 73
  Poema de Mio Cid and, 71
  Sancho VI and, 50
  tomb, 77–79, 82–83
Alfonso X (k. of Castile)
  books and, 69
  Henry III and, 51, 59
  Historia regum Britanniae and, 71
  Las Huelgas and, 78, 79, 83
  Treaty of Toledo and, 5
Alfonso XI (k. of Castile)
  alliance with English, 12–13
  Chaucer and, 195, *203*
  Edward II and, 99–104
  Edward III and, 20, 54
  Eleanor of England and, 103
  finances, 103
  Gascony crisis and, 106
  Giles Despagne and, 101
  knighting of, 79
  Las Huelgas and, 79–80, 83
  as *rex Ispanniae*, 113
  Santiago, Apostle, and, 56
  Sir James Douglas and, 12
  trade and, 100
Alvar, Manuel, 155
Alvarez, Nun, 121
Anglo-Castilian Trade in the Middle Ages (Childs), 2
Antiphoners, 72, 73–75
Aragon, 5–6, 40, *203, 204, 208, 212*

Alfonso III and, 20
Castile and, 68, 73, 76
Chaucer and, 190, 192, 197–99
chivalric exchanges and, 20–21
Edward II and, 99–102, 104–5
libraries, 30–32
literature and, 23–24
safe-conducts, 53, 60
See also under individual kings of Aragon
Archpriest of Hita. *See* Ruiz, Juan
Armitage-Smith, Sydney, 149
Arnold, William, 151
Arthurian Legend in the Literatures of the Spanish Peninsula, The (Entwistle), 2
Astley, John, 21
Avignon papacy, 17, 32, 35, 37, 48, 57, 105, 121, *203*

Barber, Richard, 13, 16, 182
Barbour, John, 12–13
Basto, Magalhães, 169
Battel of Alcazar...with the Death of Captain Stukely, The (Peele), 12
battles
  Alcazar-Quivir, 12
  Aljubarrota, 14, 19, *30*, 56, 140, 147, 172, 173, 177
  Lepanto, 12
  Montiel, 55
  Nájera, 18, 191
Bayonne, Treaty of, 57, 143
Beatus manuscripts, 70–75
Becket, St. Thomas, 50, 69
Berenguela, 78–79, 83
Bernaldez, Andres, 14–15
Bible of Burgos, 71–72

INDEX

Black Prince. *See* Edward IV (k. of England)
Blanche of Castile, 76
Blanche of Lancaster, 19, 122, 137, 145, 151, 167, 191, *207*
Bodel, Jean, 189
Boïl, Felip, 21
Bolingbroke, Henry of. *See* Henry IV (k. of England)
Boniface, Pope, IX, 57
Botewelle, Lewis, 126
Breviloquium de virtutibus (John of Wales), 31, 35
Bruce, Robert, 12–13, 95
Bruce, The (Barbour), 12–13
Burgos Cathedral, 79–82
Bury Bible, 74

Camões, Luis de, 20, 169–71, 176, 179–80, 183
Canals, Antoni, 32, 34, 35
Canterbury Tales (Chaucer), 14, 18, 54, 150, 194–200
See also Chaucer
Castile, 2, 5–6, 99–106, *113, 114, 115*, 190
    Chaucer and, 7, 196, 199, *203, 204, 205, 206–7, 208, 210*
    chivalric fiction and, 23
    Confessio Amantis and, 6, 135, 151–52, 154, 156, 157
    Crusades and, 12–13, 15
    dynastic warfare and, 6, 17–18, 55–56, 139, 191, 193–94, *206, 207, 209*
    Edward II and, 90–93, 99–106
    Giles Despagne and, 100–2, 109–10
    John of Gaunt and, 55–57, 139–43, 193–94
    Las Huelgas tombs and, 77–80, 82–83
    literature, Castilian, 70, 71–74, 76, 189, 202
    Philippa of Lancaster and, 135, 139–44, 149, 156
    pilgrimages and, 50–62
    Rodrigo de España and, 90, 93
    Twelve of England and, 175, 177–78
    See also under individual kings and queens of Castile and England
Catalina of Lancaster (q. of Castile), 19, 56–60, 156, 177
Catalonia, 29–46, 73, *114*, 190, 197–200

Caxton, William, 14, 21, 24, 38, 40
Chapters in Anglo-Portuguese Relations (Prestage), 2
Charles IV (k. of France), 98, 99, 104–5
Charles V (Holy Roman Emperor), 16, 20–21, 37, *203*
Charles VI (k. of France), 14
Charles VII (k. of France), 61, 139
Chaucer, Geoffrey
    Aragon and, 197–98
    Elmham and, 149
    Gibraltar and, 197–99
    influence of Spanish literature, 199–202
    John of Gaunt and, 14, 193–94
    Legend of Good Women, 139
    Man of Law's Tale, 142, 196–97
    Monk's Tale, 18, 195–96
    Payn and, 153
    Philippa of Lancaster and, 135, 139, 142, 151
    references to Spain in *Canterbury Tales*, 194–98
    Ruiz, Juan, and, 3, 201
    Shipman and *Shipman's Tale*, 194–96, 198
    Spain and, 3, 7, 189–90
    Spanish language and, 192–93
    See also Canterbury Tales; Castile
    Wife of Bath, 54, 194
Chaucer, Philippa, 193, 196
Cheetham, Francis, 151
Childs, Wendy, 2, 120, 148, *204*
Chivalry and Exploration, 1298–1630 (Goodman), 11
Cistercian Order, 68, 72, 74–76, 150
    See also Las Huelgas
Clanvowe, John, 139, 148
Confessio Amantis (Gower), 6, 135, 139, 150, 151–57, 194, 197
    See also Gower
Conquest of Granada (Irving), 14
Constance of Castile. *See* Constanza of Castile
Constanza of Castile, 6, 19, 20, 56, 107, 137, 139–40, 142, 156, 167, 173, 175–77, 193–94, 196, 201
Correia, Manuel, 169, 171, 176
Cortijo Ocaña, Antonio, 152
Costa, Joaquim, 169

INDEX 245

Crusades, 11–17
  Alfonso XI and, 13
  Anglo-Iberian military contact and,
    11–12, 15–16
  De expugnatione Lynxbonensi and, 12
  Edward III and, 13
  Henry VIII and, 16
  João I and, 14
  Lord Scales and, 15
  Sir James Douglas and, 12–13

d'Anjou, Charles, 34, 39
Davenport, Adam, 147
de Bury, Richard, 32
De expugnatione Lynxbonensi, 11–12
Despagne, Giles, 5, 89–117
  Castile and, 104
  Edward II and, 104–8, 110
  Isabelle and, 104–5
Despenser, Henry (Bishop), 148, 151, 155
Despenser, Hugh, 97, 100
Despenser family, 97–98, 100, 101
Dicts and Sayengs of the Philosophres, The (Rivers), 14
Disciplina clericalis (Petrus Alfonso), 7, 200, 202, *214*
Dotzè del Crestià (Eiximenis), 34–35
Douce Apocalypse, The, 69–70
Douglas, James, 12–13, *25*, 95
du Guesclin, Bertrand, 17–18, 197–98, *206*
Duarte, Luis Miguel, 120, 130
Duarte I (k. of Portugal), 22, 136, 145–50, 153–55, 168, 182
Dunhead, Stephen, 109

Edward I (k. of England)
  Cardinal Petrus Hispanus and, 91
  Dinus of Portugal and, 168
  Eleanor of Castile and, 5, 19–20, 67–69, 76, 83, 91, 191
  Las Huelgas and, 79–80, 191
  marriage, 83
  trade with Iberia and, 190
Edward II (k. of England), 90–97, 99–110
  Despenser family and, 104–8, 110
  diplomacy, 99–101
  Giles Despagne and, 89–117
  hospitals and, 52
  Iberia and, 5

Edward III (k. of England)
  Alfonso XI and, 103
  Carta Mercatoria and, *204*
  Castile and, 13, 54–55
  Chaucer and, 191–93, 197, *206*
  coronation, 108
  family, 17, 19–20, 145
  Giles Despagne and, 92, 109
  John of Gaunt and, *208*
  Order of the Garter and, 13, 30, 173
  overview, 5–7
  St. James's Shrine, 54
Edward IV (k. of England), 14, 16, 21, 130
Edward the Confessor, Saint, 69, 77, 100
Eiximenis, Francesc, 33–35
Eleanor, daughter of Edward I, 20
Eleanor, daughter of Edward II, 100, 103, 106
Eleanor of Aquitaine, 67, 91
Eleanor of Castile (q. of England, wife of
  Edward I), 5, *10*, 19–20, 67–71, 90,
  91, *111*, 100, 103, 106, 190–91
  books and ownership, 69–71, 73
  tomb, 76–79, 82–83
Elizabeth I (q. of England), 12, 16, 22
Ellis, George, 189
Elmham, Elizabeth, 148–49
Elmham, Roger, 148, 151
Elmham, William, 155
Elys, Thomas, 153
English in Portugal 1367–87, The (Lomax
  and Oakley), 2
*English Intervention in Spain and Portugal in
  the Time of Edward III and Richard II,
  The* (Russell), 2
Enrique II (k. of Castile). *See* Enrique de
  Trastámara
Enrique III (k. of Castile), 6, 19, 23, 57–58,
  154, 194
Enrique IV (k. of Castile), 55, 61
Enrique de Trastámara (Enrique II,
  k. of Castile)
  Black Prince and, 6, 17–18
  Calveley and, *207*
  foreign support, 56
  France and, *185*, 191
  John of Gaunt and, 193–94
  overthrow of Pedro, 55, 139, *204*
  Portugal and, 193
Entwistle, William J., 2, *46*, 71, 153, *159*

Famous History of the Life and Death of Captain Thomas Stukeley, The (Panyer), 12
Fauconer, Thomas, 129
Felipe (Prince), 99, 102
Ferdinand II (k. of Castile), 50
Ferdinand III (k. of Castile), 19, 67–68, 79, 91
Ferdinand the Catholic (k. of Castile), 15, 20, 21
Fernando I (k. of Portugal), 140, 145, *208*
Fernando III. *See* Ferdinand III
Fernando IV (k. of Castile), 90–91
Fernando de Castro the Younger, 152–53
Fitzmaurice-Kelly, James, 2
Flower and Leaf motif, 139, 157
Fonseca, Luis Adão da, 120
Froissart, Jean
  on Black Prince, *211*
  Cronica de Juan I and, 56
  on earl of Pembroke, 16
  on Guillaume de l'Île, 38
  on Henry of Trastamara, 18
  on João, 141
  Philippa of Lancaster and, 156
  translation of work, 23
  Twelve of England and, 177

Galicia
  La Coruña, 48, 52, 56–57, 59–61, 140
  Santiago, St. James of Compostela, 47–52
Galicien, Pers, 100–2, 105–6
Gallensis, Johannes, 35
Geoffrey of Monmouth, 29, 31, 71, 178
Gerald of Wales, 37, 38
Gonsalyn, Lewis, 125
Goodman, Anthony, 2, 4, 5, 147, 209
Gourney, Thomas, 92, 109–10
Gower, John
  Philippa of Lancaster and, 6, 135–36, 149, 194
  translations of work, 150–57
  See also Confessio Amantis
Gui de Warewic, 30, 40
Guillem de Torroella, 36
Guillem de Vàroic (Martorell), 30, 39
Guy of Warwick, 23, 39

Hamm, Robert Warren, 154

Hauf, Albert, 34, 39
Henderson, George, 70
Henry II (k. of England)
  Alfonso VIII and, 50
  Castile and, 5
  Eleanor Plantagenet and, 191
  Ferdinand II and, 50
  Leonor (daughter) and, 68, 73
  marriage of Leonor (daughter) to Alfonso VIII and, 5, 67
  Sancho VI and, 50
Henry III (k. of England)
  Alfonso VIII's tomb and, 83
  Alfonso X and, 5, 51, 59
  Eleanor of Castile and, 67
  Master Peter and, 71
  Theobald II and, 51
  tomb, 76–77, 78
  Treaty of Toledo and, 5
  Vita of Saint Edward and, 71
Henry IV (k. of England)
  Confessio and, 155
  diplomacy with Castile, 58–59
  diplomacy with Portugal, 125–26
  João I of Portugal and, 20, 121, 144
  Payn and, 153
  Philippa of Lancaster and, 6, 137
Henry VI (k. of England), 21, 30, 60, 129–30, 148, 150
Henry VII (k. of England), 14, 16, 20, 21
Henry VIII (k. of England), 19, 20, 21
Henry of Blois, 50
Henry of Grossmont, 13
Henry of Lancaster, 13
Henry of Trastámara. *See* Enrique de Trastamara
Herrero González, Sonsoles, 73
Hervey of Glanvill, 12
Historia regum Britanniae (Geoffrey of Monmouth), 29, 71, 178
History of New York, The (Knickerbocker), 14
Holkot, Robert, 33
Holy Roman Empire, 2, 25
Hume, Martin, 2
Hundred Years' War
  literature and, 38–39
  pilgrimage and, 52, 57, 61–62
  Portugal and, 127, 172–73, 177, 190
  Spanish-English relations and, 17, 19

INDEX 247

Irving, Washington, 14–15
Isabella II (q. of Castile), 16, 20, 21
Isabelle (q. of France), 91, 104–8, 110

Jacobean pilgrimages from England, 52–62
Jaume II (k. of Aragon), 31–32, 99–100
Jeanne of Ponthieu, 67
Jiménez de Rada, Rodrigo, 91
Joan I (k. of Aragon), 31, 37
João I (k. of Portugal)
    Aljubarrota and, 19, 56, 140, 147, 179
    Ceuta and, 14
    Confessio and, 156
    John of Gaunt and, 140–41
    Order of the Garter and, 19, 20
    Philippa of Lancaster and, 19, 135–36, 139–49: children, 145; contact with England, 147–49; intellectual connection, 144; invasion of Castile and, 142–44; marriage arrangements, 141–42; myths surrounding, 145–47; Valentine's Day marriage, 142, 145
    rise to power, 140
    trade relations with England, 119–31, 167–71, 173–82: beginnings, 121–22; Henry IV and, 125–29; Henry V and, 129; Henry VI and, 129–30; overview, 119–21; preferential treatment of English in Portugal, 124; Richard II and, 122–25; seizure of goods, 123; Treaty of Windsor, 120, 122–23, 125, 130
John I (k. of England), 50, 155
John of Gaunt, 21, 23, 54, 122, 152–54
    Camões and, 20
    Castile and, 55–57, 139–43, 193–94
    Cavalarias and, 173–75, 178, 179–80
    Chaucer and, 14, 201–2
    Constance of Castile and, 19
    Froissart and, 177–78
    Juan I and, 156
    La Coruña and, 56–57
    Philippa of Lancaster and, 135–37, 139, 167
    Treaty of Windsor and, 172
    See also Portugal, John of Gaunt and
John of Wales, 31, 34–35, 40
Jordan, Weseley, 73–74

Juan I (k. of Castile), 6, 56–57, 140, 156, 201
Juan II (k. of Castile), 60, 154
Juan Manuel, 7, 100, 102, 189, 201, 202, *213*
Juan of Austria, 12
Juan of Biscay, 99–100, 102

King Arthur, 21, 36, 71, 170, 178–79
Knickerbocker, Diedrich, 14

La Coruña, 48, 52, 56–57, 59–61, 140
Labarge, Margaret W., 55
Lambeth Bible, 72, 75
Las Huelgas, 5, 19, 68, 72–83, 191
Lasater, Alice E., 2
Le Livre de Seyntz Medicines (Henry of Lancaster), 14
Leonor, Princess, sister of Alfonso XI (k. of Castile), 100, 103, 106
Leonor of England (q. of Castile, wife of Alfonso VIII), 5, *10*, 67–73, 76, 168
    books and ownership, 69–73
    tomb, 77–83
Leonor Teles (q. of Portugal, wife of Fernando I), 140, 145, 168, *208*
Leulingham, Truce of, 55, 58
Libro de Buen Amor. See Ruiz, Juan
Livermore, Harold V., 145
Llull, Ramon, 24, 30–31
Lomax, Derek W., 2
Lopes, Fernão
    Camões and, 170
    Crónica de D. João I, 180, 182
    Leonor and, 168
    Philippa and, 136, 137, 140–45, 150, 156
    Twelve of England and, 170, 180
Louis VIII (k. of France), 76
Louis XI (k. of France), 61
Louis d'Auxerre, 37
Loutfut, Adam, 24

MacKay, Angus, 120
Manly, John Matthews, 152, 154
Mariz, Pedro, 169, 171, 176
marriages, dynastic, 7, 11, 136, 157
    between Aragon and England, 20, 99–100, 105

marriages, dynastic—*continued*
  between Castile and England, 5–7,
      19–20, 21–22, 23, 54, 56, 67–83,
      91, 99–100, 102–3, 105–6, 136,
      139, 167, 175, 176, 193–94
  between Portugal and England, 6, 19,
      56, 122, 124, 125, 135, 136,
      139–45, 173, 175, 179
Martí I (k. of Aragon), 31–32
Martorell, Joanot
  influences, 23–24, 35–36
  Joan de Montpalau and, 20
  writing style, 29–30, 38–40
Martyr, Peter, 14
Master James of Spain, 90, 111
Metge, Bernat, 35, 37
Mohammed IV of Granada, 12
Montague, William, 13
Montserrat, 192, 198, 200
Morgan, Nigel, 70
Mortimer, Roger, 105–10
Muntaner, Ramon, 38

Navarre, 5–6, 40
  Chaucer and, 190–92, 195, 197–98, *206*
  Edward III and, *207*
  France and, *203, 207*
  Henry II and, 50
  Henry III and, 51
  literature and, *208*
  safe-conducts and, *207, 210*
  Savoy and, *209*

Oakley, R.J., 2
O'Callaghan, Joseph, 120
Order of Aviz, 140, 141
Order of the Band, 13
Order of the Garter
  Charles V and, 21
  Edward III and, 13, 30, 173
  establishment of, 13, 36, 173
  foreign kings and, 20
  João I and, 19, 125
  Philip II and, 22
  Tirant lo Blanc and, 23
Order of the Golden Fleece, 20–21
Orto do esposo, 150

Panyer, Thomas, 12
Paris Psalter, 73–75
Parsons, John Carmi, 67, *205*

Pedro I (k. of Castile), 17–18, 19, 167
  Chaucer and, 191, 193, 195–96,
    197
  death, 55, *204*
  Edward III and, 6, 55, *206*
  emperogilados and, 177, *209*
  João I and, 139–40, *205*
  John of Gaunt and, 56
Pedro IV (k. of Aragon), 192, 199, *208*,
    212
  See also Pere III
Pedro the Ceremonious
  See Pedro IV
Pedro the Cruel
  See Pedro I
Peele, George, 12
Pelegrín, Bernal, 98, 100, 101–2, 108
Pere III (k. of Aragon), 31, 32
  See also Pedro IV
Pereira, Nuno Alvarez, 140
Perellós, Ramon de, 37–38
Pero Niño, 15–16, 18
Pessagno, Antonio, 101
Peter of Blois, 30
Petrus Alfonsi (Pedro Alfonso), 7, 189, 200,
    202
Philip II (k. of Spain), 12, 16, 20, 22
Philippa of Lancaster (q. of Portugal)
  adaptation to Iberia, 139–45
  Anglophilia, 149–51, 168
  contact with England, 147–49
  cultural patronage, 150–51
  family, 19, 139, 173
  family stories, 149–50
  Gower translations and, 151–57
  Henry IV and, 129
  historical accounts of, 135–39
  marriage, 6, 122, 124, 167, 173, 194
  relationship with father, 139
Philippe IV (k. of France), 91
Philippe V (k. of France), 98
Phillip the Good of Burgundy, 130, 146, 173
Pilgrim's Guide, 52–53
pilgrimages
  Enrique IV and, 61
  Henry IV and, 59
  Henry VI and, 60
  Jacobean, 14th and 15th centuries, 52–62
  national sanctuaries, 48
  Santiago, 47–52
  shrine of Saint James, 52–54, 61–62, 191

INDEX

piracy, 52, 54–55, 59, 119, 130
Pontigny Bible, 75
Portugal, 2–3, 25, 40, *113*
   Anglo-Portuguese trade, 119–31
   Chaucer and, 189–90, 193–94
   chivalric fiction and, 22–24
   Crusades and, 11–12, 14, 16
   Edward III and, 6
   England and, 6–7
   Enrique de Trastámara and, 193
   Giles Despagne and, 92, 101–2
   John of Gaunt and, 19, 20, 56–57, 122, 125, 135–36, 139–43, 167, 172, 178, 193–94
   Philippa of Lancaster and, 135–36, 139–40, 142–43, 145–51, 155–56
   Twelve of England and, 167–83
   See also under individual kings and queens of Portugal
Prestage, Edgar, 2

Reconquest, 11, 16, 49, 121
   See also Reconquista
Reconquista, 5, 11, 119
   See also Reconquest
Richard I (k. of England), 121
Richard II (k. of England)
   Chaucer and, 7, 193
   coastal raids during reign, 55–56
   Confessio and, 154–55
   Edward III and, 5–6
   Flower and Leaf poems and, 139
   Guttierez and, 177
   João I of Portugal and, 122, 128
   John of Gaunt and, 201, *208*
   licenses granted to pilgrims, 58
   Payn and, 153, 154
   Perellós and, 37
   Philippa and, 139, 147–48, 155
   Schism and, 57
   suspension of travel to Spain, 57
Richard III (k. of England), 16
Riquer, Martí de, 30, 37–38
Rivers, Earl, 14
Rodrigo de España, 90–93
Roncesvalles, 49, 52, 195
Ros, Ramon, 31
Ruiz, Juan, 3, 7, 201, 202
Ruiz Simon, Josep M., 31
Russell, John, 59

Russell, Peter, 2, *157*, 175, *207, 209*
   on Anglophilia of Portuguese royalty, 149
   on Anglo-Portuguese court, 145
   on invasion of Castile, 142, 143
   on Payn, 152–53, 154
   on Richard II, 155

safe-conducts
   Chaucer and, 191–92, 198
   Edward II and, 93, 100
   Jacobean (Santiago) pilgrimages and, 50–55, 58–59, 61
   Saltrey, H of, 31, 37–38
Saint Godric of Finchale, 49
Saint James, shrine of, 52–54, 61–62, 191
   See also Santiago de Compostela
Saint William of Norwich, 49
Sancho VI (k. of Navarre), 50
Santiago de Compostela
   English pilgrimage to, 47–52
   documentation, 49–50
   miracle accounts, 50
   travel to, 48–49
   See also Saint James
Saul, Nigel, 1, *10*
Scales, Lord, 14–15
Schism, 48, 52, 57
Scotland, 11–13, 49, *164*
Sebastian (k. of Portugal), 12
Shillington, Violet, 120
Silva, Francisco Ribeiro da, 120
Sinclair, William, 13
Smalley, Beryl, 33
Southern, Richard, 33
Spain to England (Lasater), 2
Spanish Influence on English Literature (Hume), 2
Stonor, John, 100–2
Storrs, Constance C., 48, 54–55
studium generale, 31–32
Stukeley, Thomas, 12, 16
Sturmey, John, 96

Theobald II (k. of Navarre), 51
Thomas of Ireland, 33
Thomas of Lancaster, 96, 107
Tirant lo Blanc (Martorell)
   dedication, 29–30
   English bias in, 20, 23–24
   influences, 35, 38–40
   King Arthur in, 36